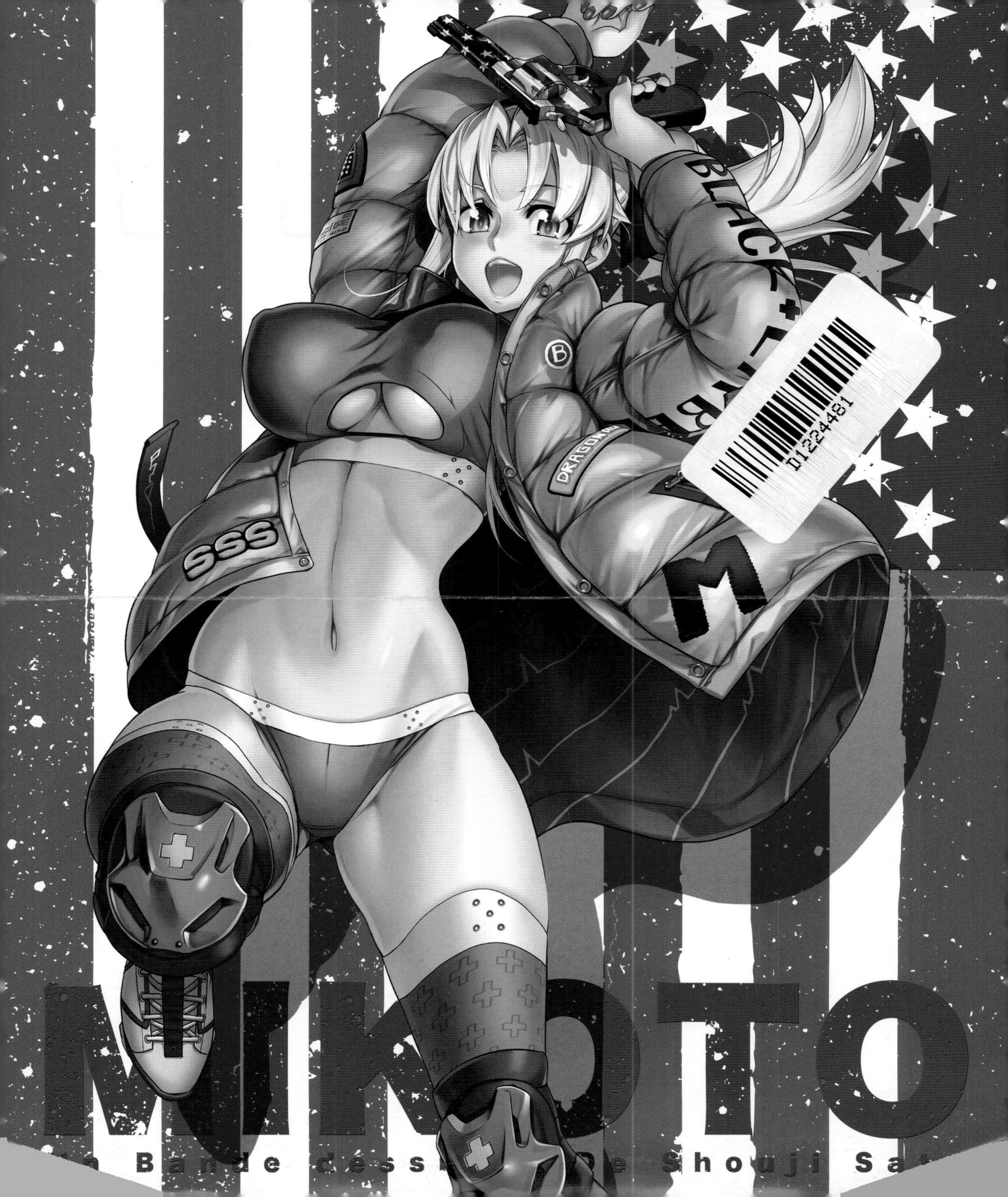
MIKOTO
SSS
DRAGON

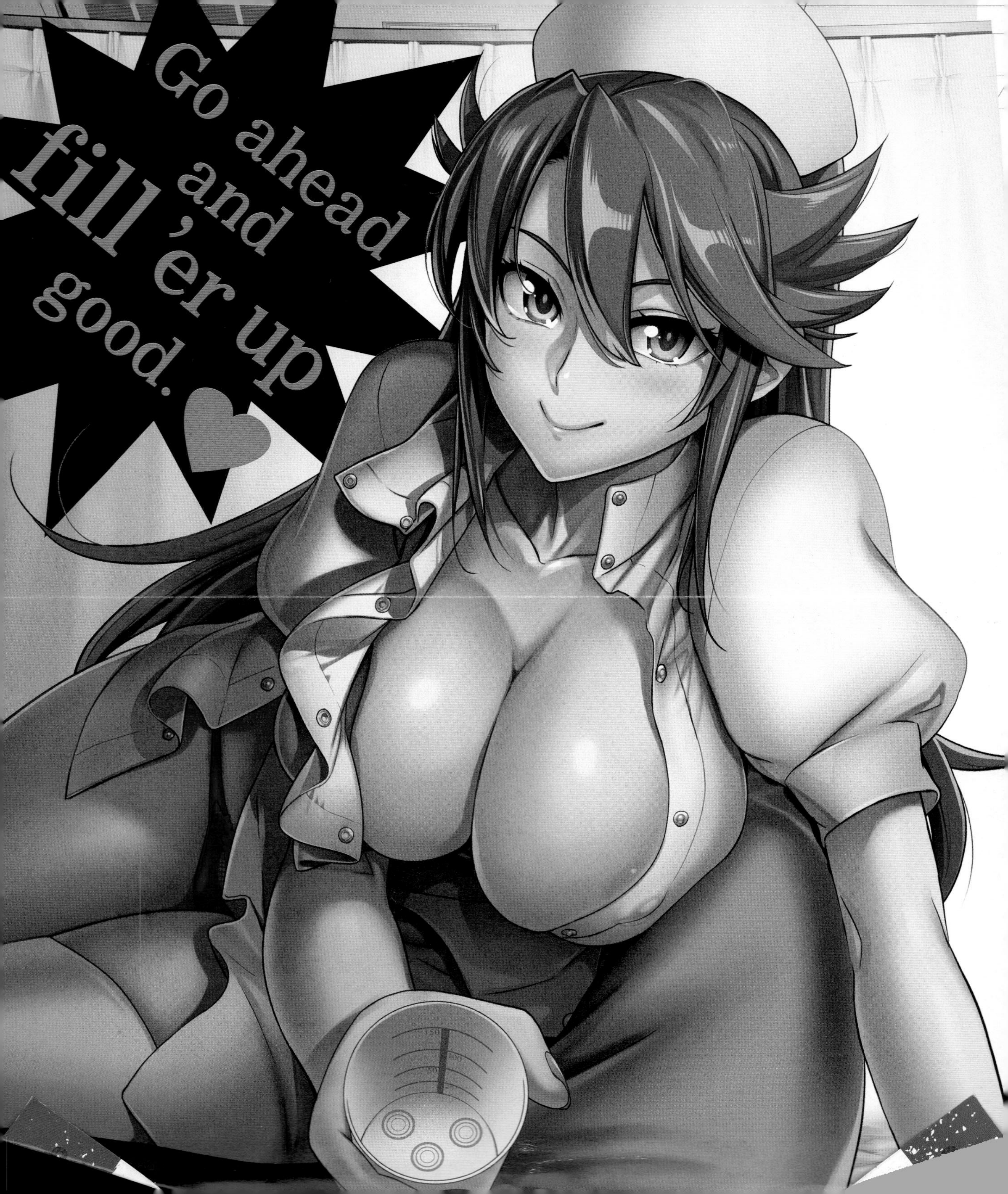
Go ahead and fill 'er up good. ♥

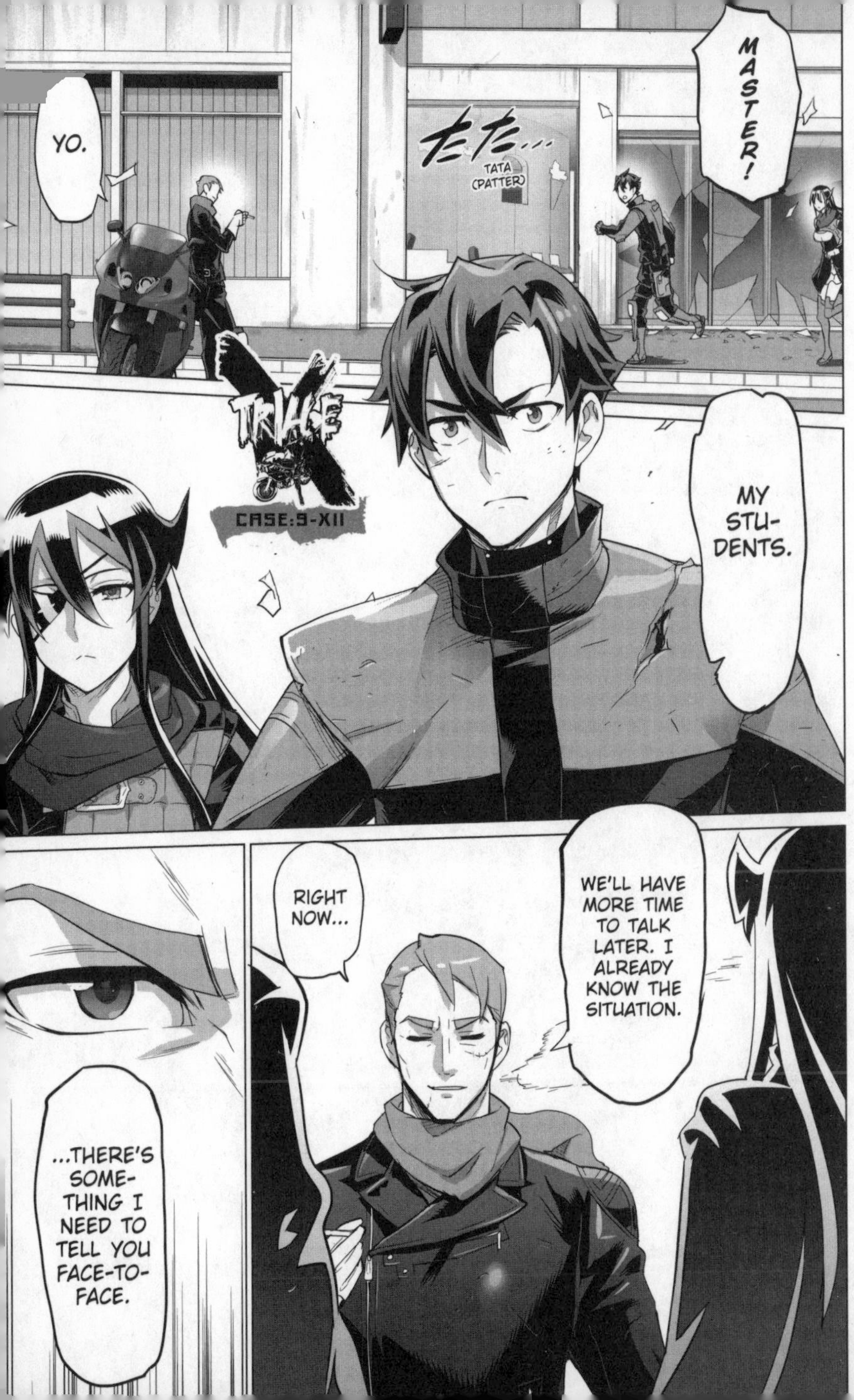
MASTER!
たた...
TATA (PATTER)
YO.
MY STU-DENTS.
TRIAGE X
CASE:9-XII
WE'LL HAVE MORE TIME TO TALK LATER. I ALREADY KNOW THE SITUATION.
RIGHT NOW...
...THERE'S SOME-THING I NEED TO TELL YOU FACE-TO-FACE.

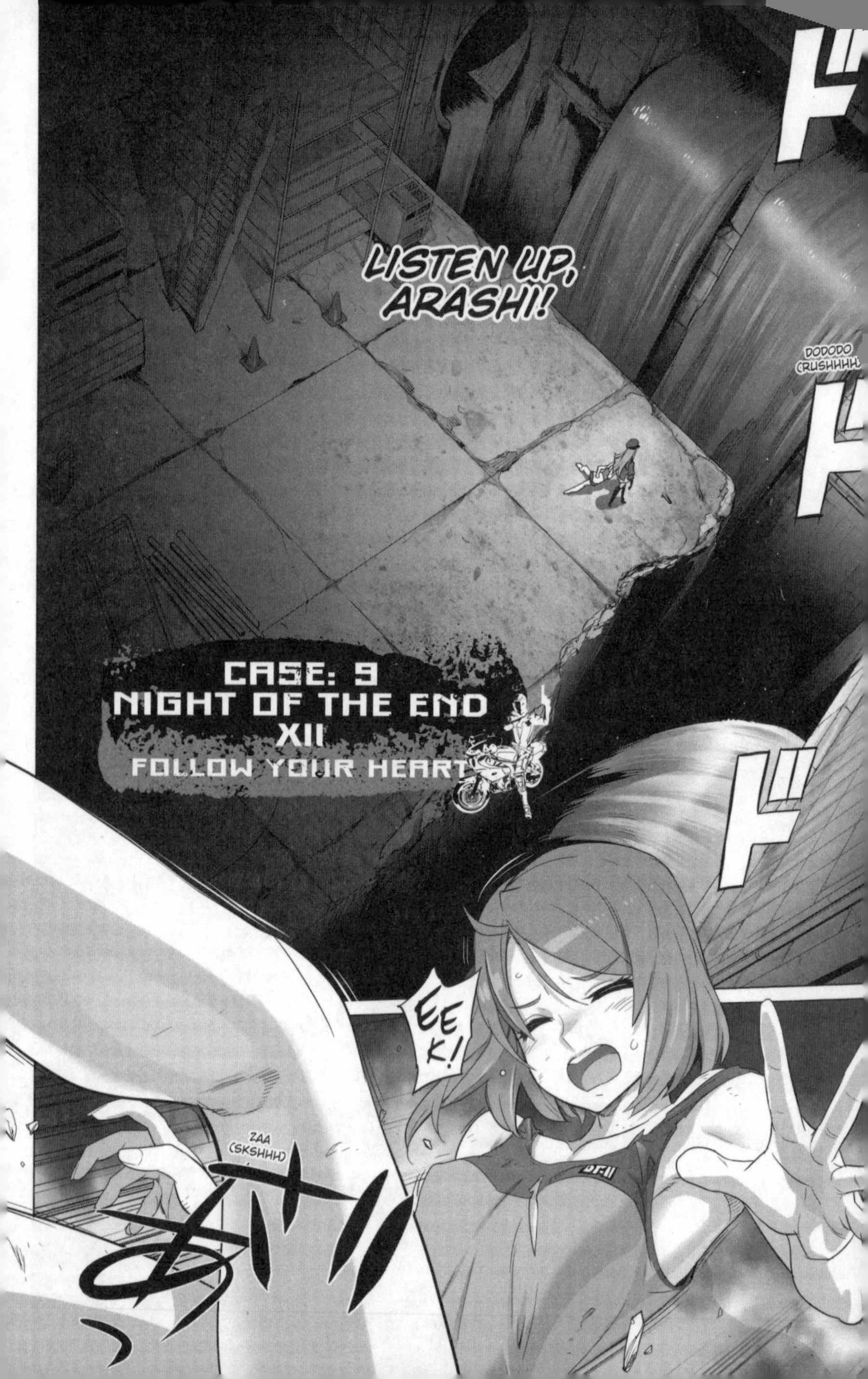

DODODO (RUSHHHH)
LISTEN UP, ARASHI!
CASE: 9
NIGHT OF THE END
XII
FOLLOW YOUR HEART
EEEK!
ZAA (SKSHHH)

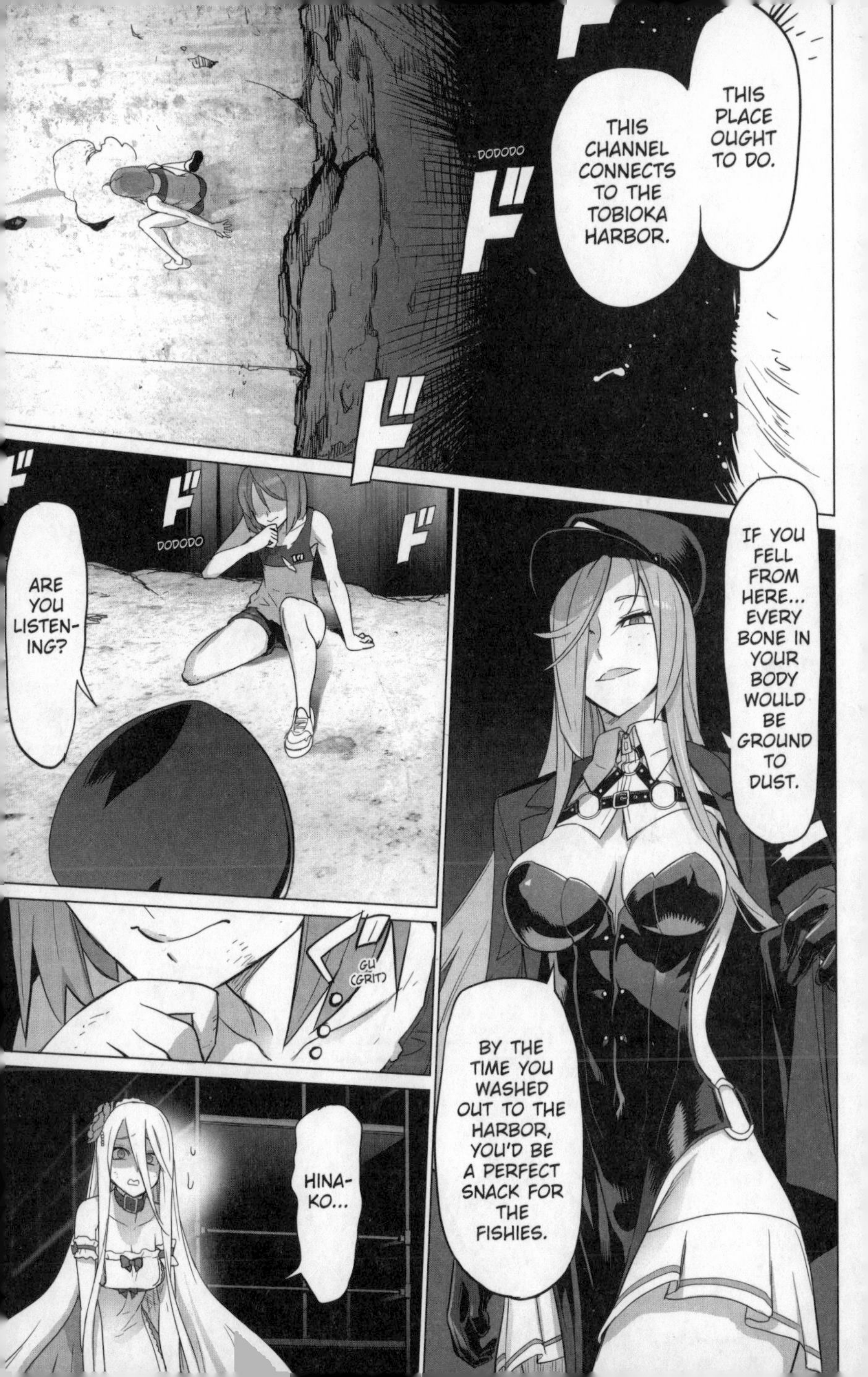
THIS PLACE OUGHT TO DO.
THIS CHANNEL CONNECTS TO THE TOBIOKA HARBOR.
DODODO
IF YOU FELL FROM HERE... EVERY BONE IN YOUR BODY WOULD BE GROUND TO DUST.
BY THE TIME YOU WASHED OUT TO THE HARBOR, YOU'D BE A PERFECT SNACK FOR THE FISHIES.
DODODO
ARE YOU LISTEN-ING?
GU (GRIT)
HINA-KO...

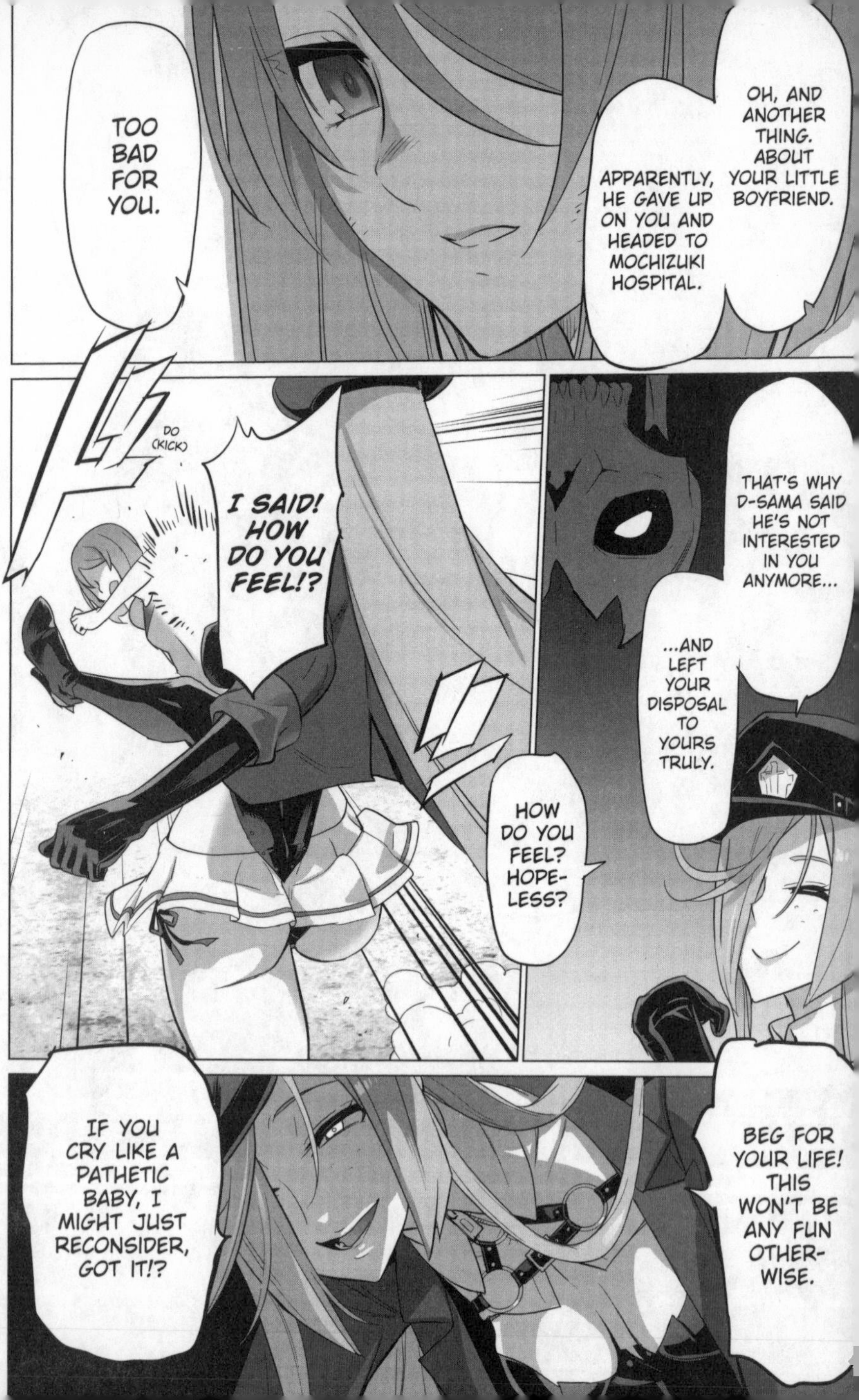
OH, AND ANOTHER THING. ABOUT YOUR LITTLE BOYFRIEND.
APPARENTLY, HE GAVE UP ON YOU AND HEADED TO MOCHIZUKI HOSPITAL.
TOO BAD FOR YOU.
THAT'S WHY D-SAMA SAID HE'S NOT INTERESTED IN YOU ANYMORE...
...AND LEFT YOUR DISPOSAL TO YOURS TRULY.
HOW DO YOU FEEL? HOPE-LESS?
I SAID! HOW DO YOU FEEL!?
DO (KICK)
BEG FOR YOUR LIFE! THIS WON'T BE ANY FUN OTHER-WISE.
IF YOU CRY LIKE A PATHETIC BABY, I MIGHT JUST RECONSIDER, GOT IT!?

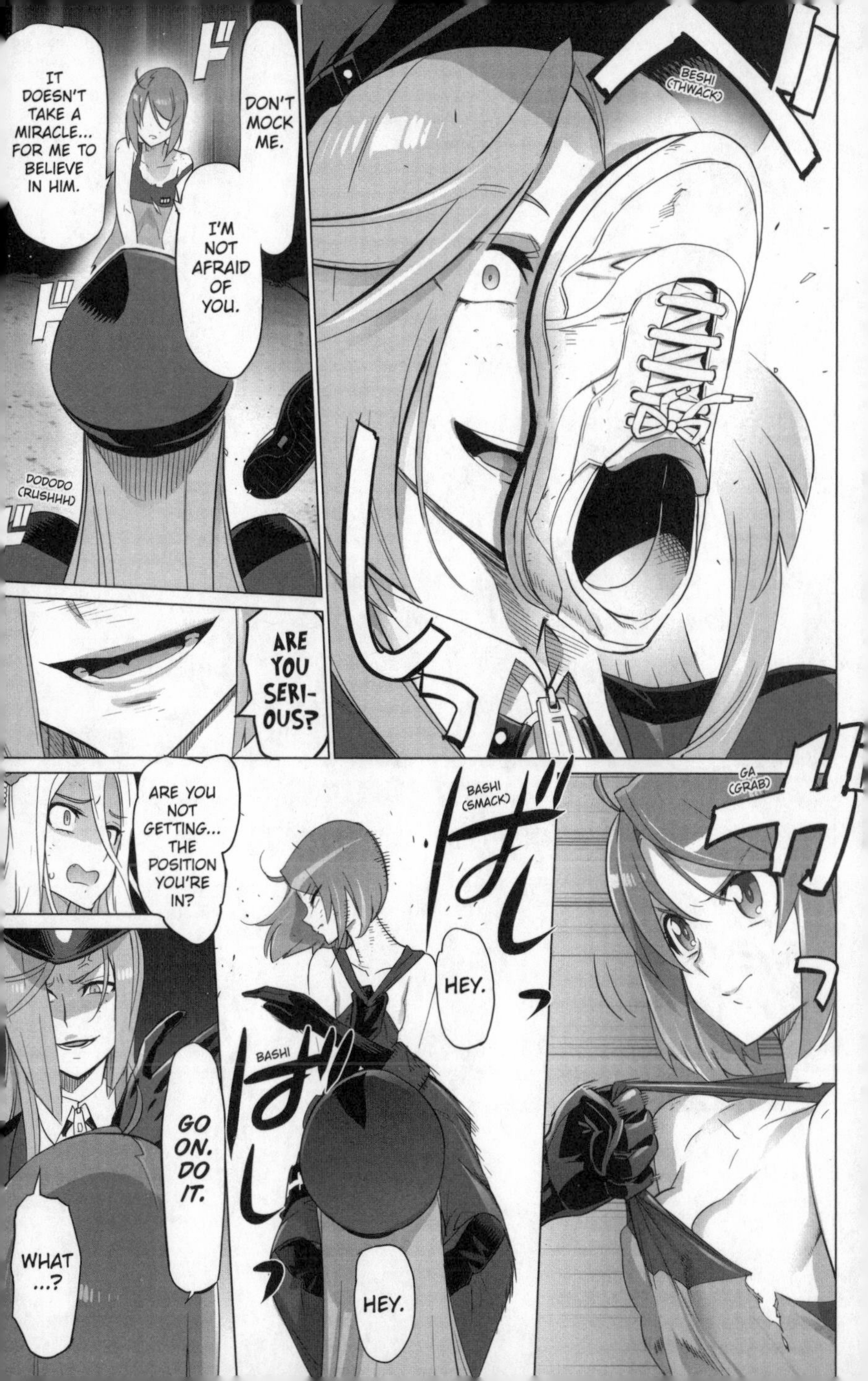
BESHI (THWACK)
DON'T MOCK ME.
I'M NOT AFRAID OF YOU.
IT DOESN'T TAKE A MIRACLE... FOR ME TO BELIEVE IN HIM.
DODODO (RUSHHH)
ARE YOU SERIOUS?
GA (GRAB)
BASHI (SMACK)
HEY.
BASHI
HEY.
GO ON. DO IT.
ARE YOU NOT GETTING... THE POSITION YOU'RE IN?
WHAT ...?

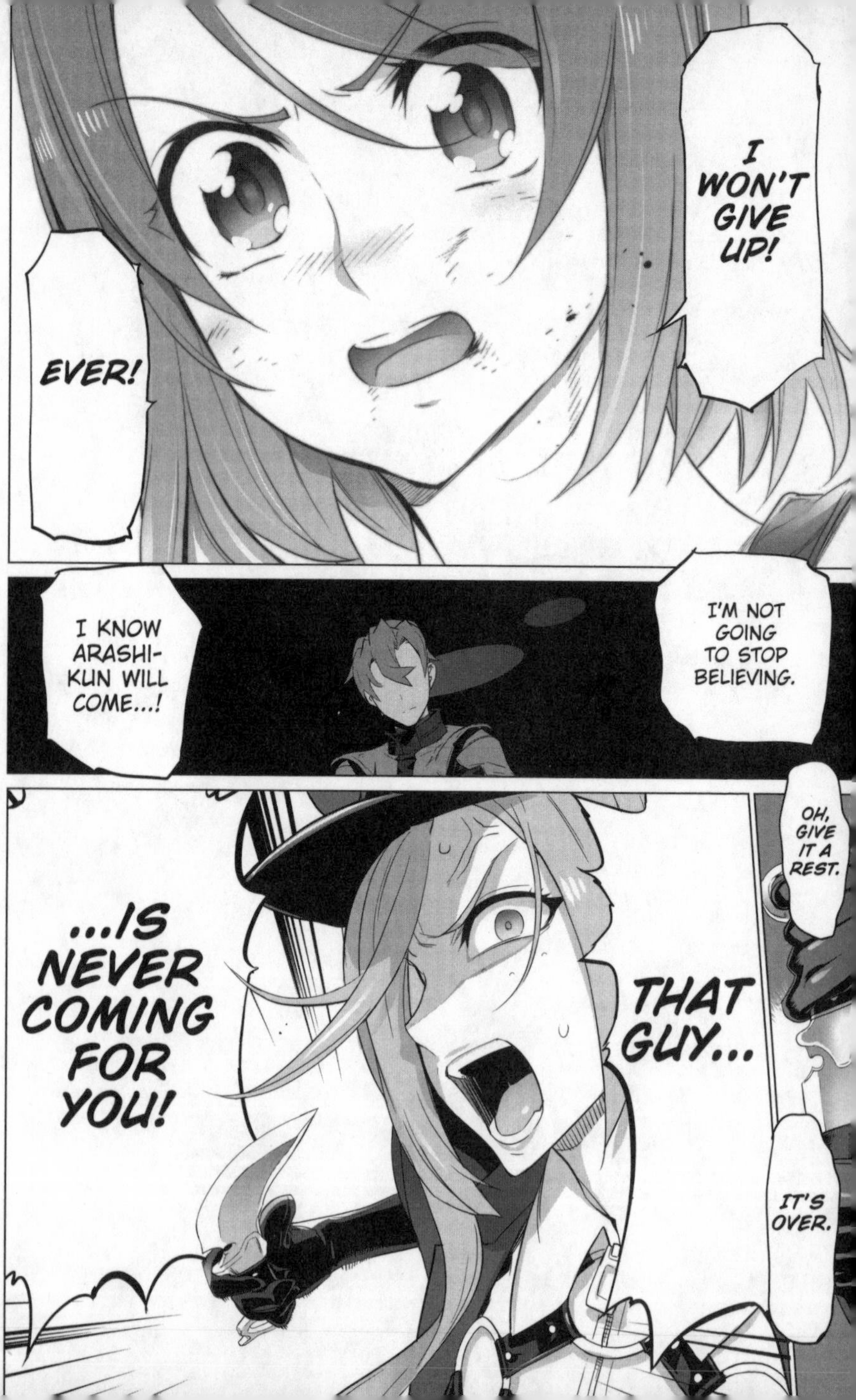
I WON'T GIVE UP!
EVER!
I'M NOT GOING TO STOP BELIEVING.
I KNOW ARASHI-KUN WILL COME...!
OH, GIVE IT A REST.
IT'S OVER.
THAT GUY...
...IS NEVER COMING FOR YOU!

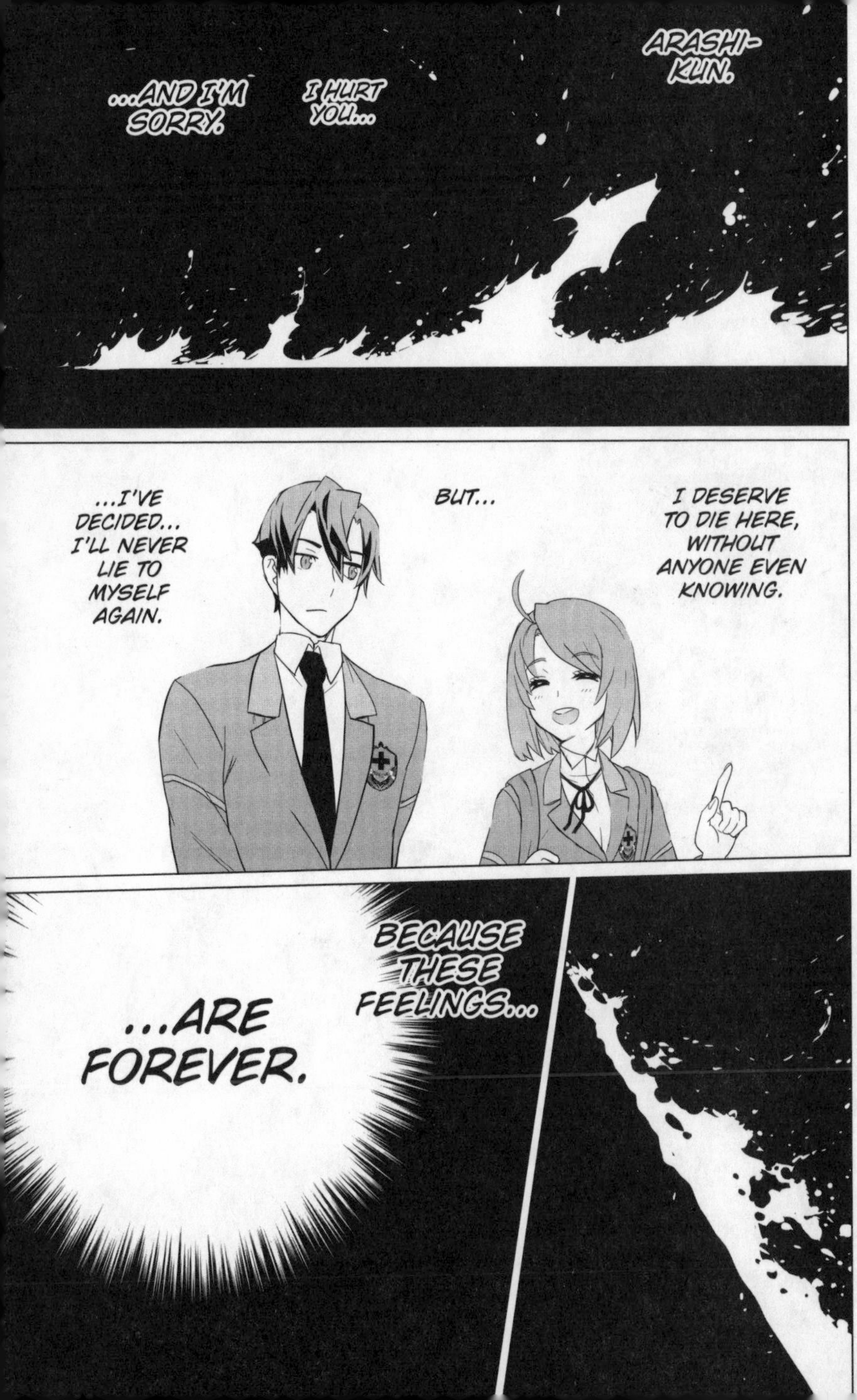
ARASHI-KUN.
I HURT YOU...
...AND I'M SORRY.
I DESERVE TO DIE HERE, WITHOUT ANYONE EVEN KNOWING.
BUT...
...I'VE DECIDED... I'LL NEVER LIE TO MYSELF AGAIN.
BECAUSE THESE FEELINGS...
...ARE FOREVER.

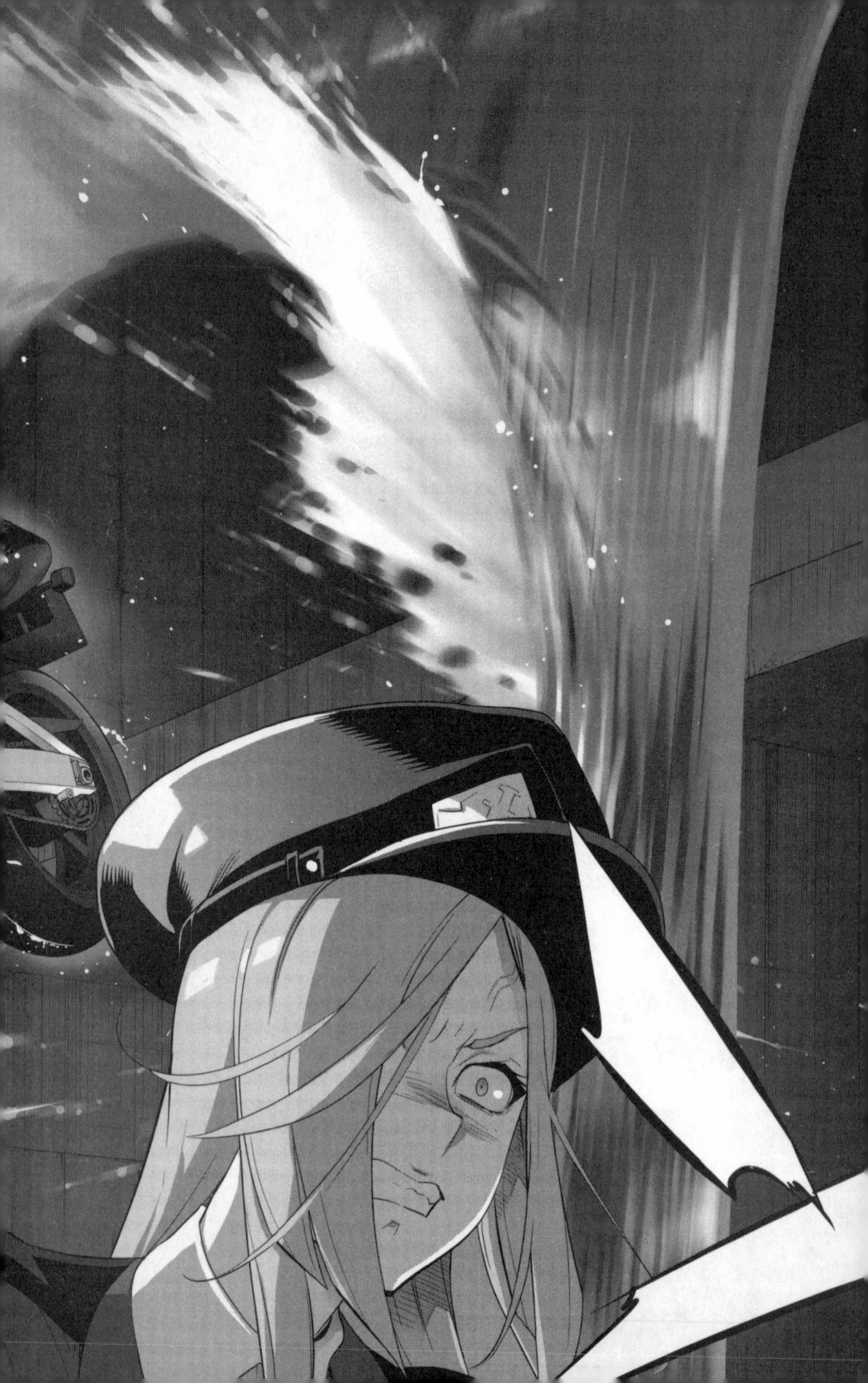

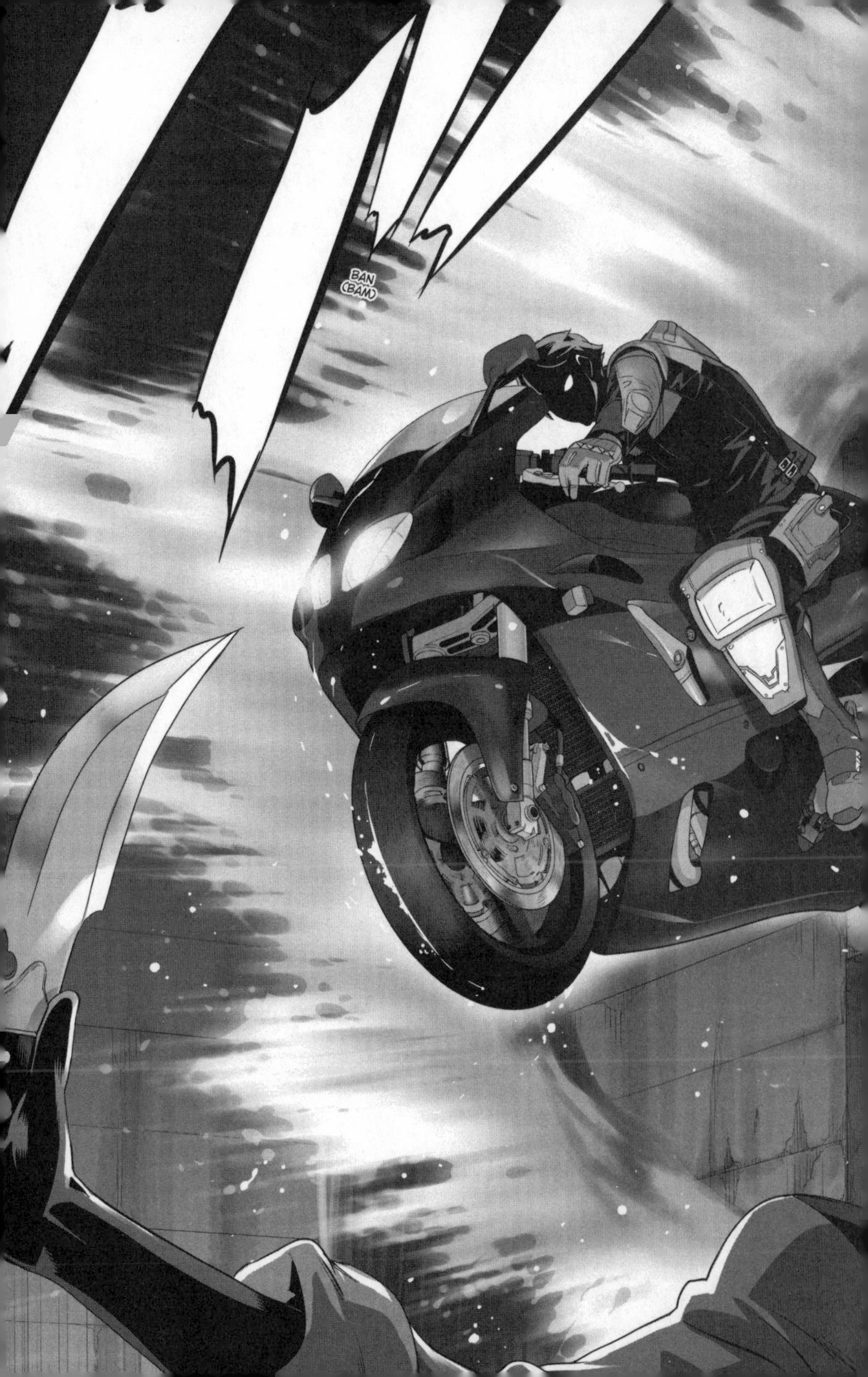
BAN
(BAM)

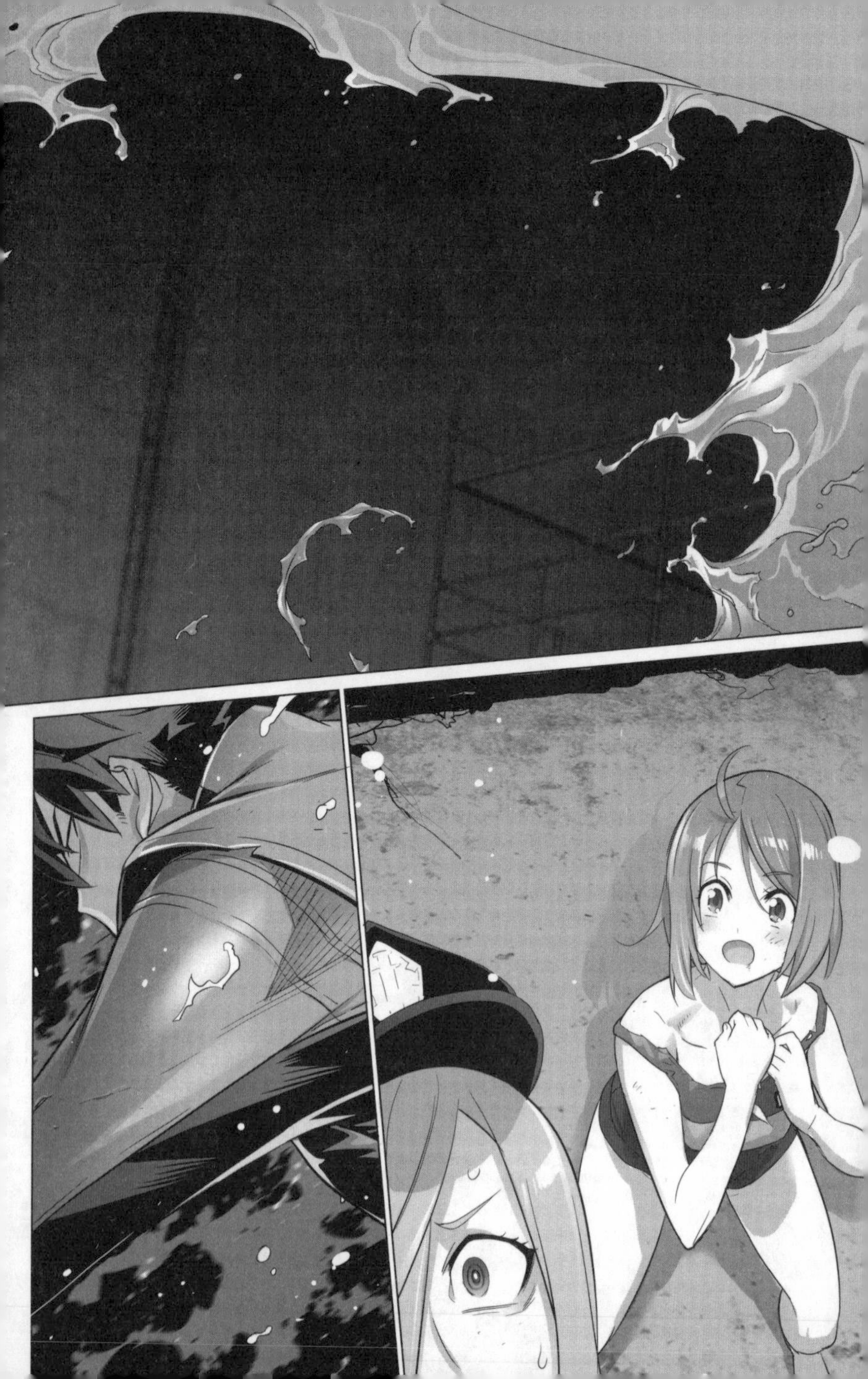

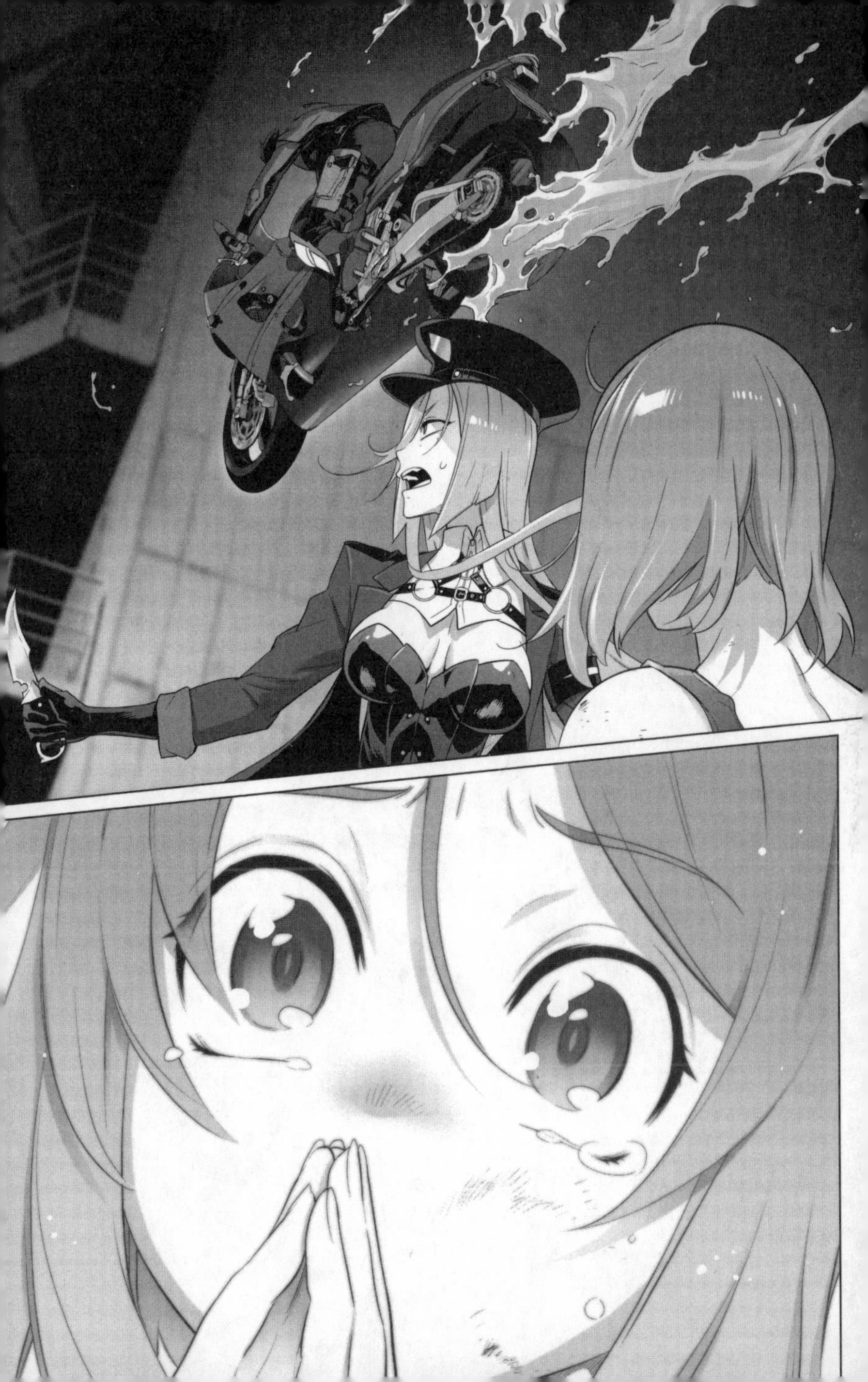

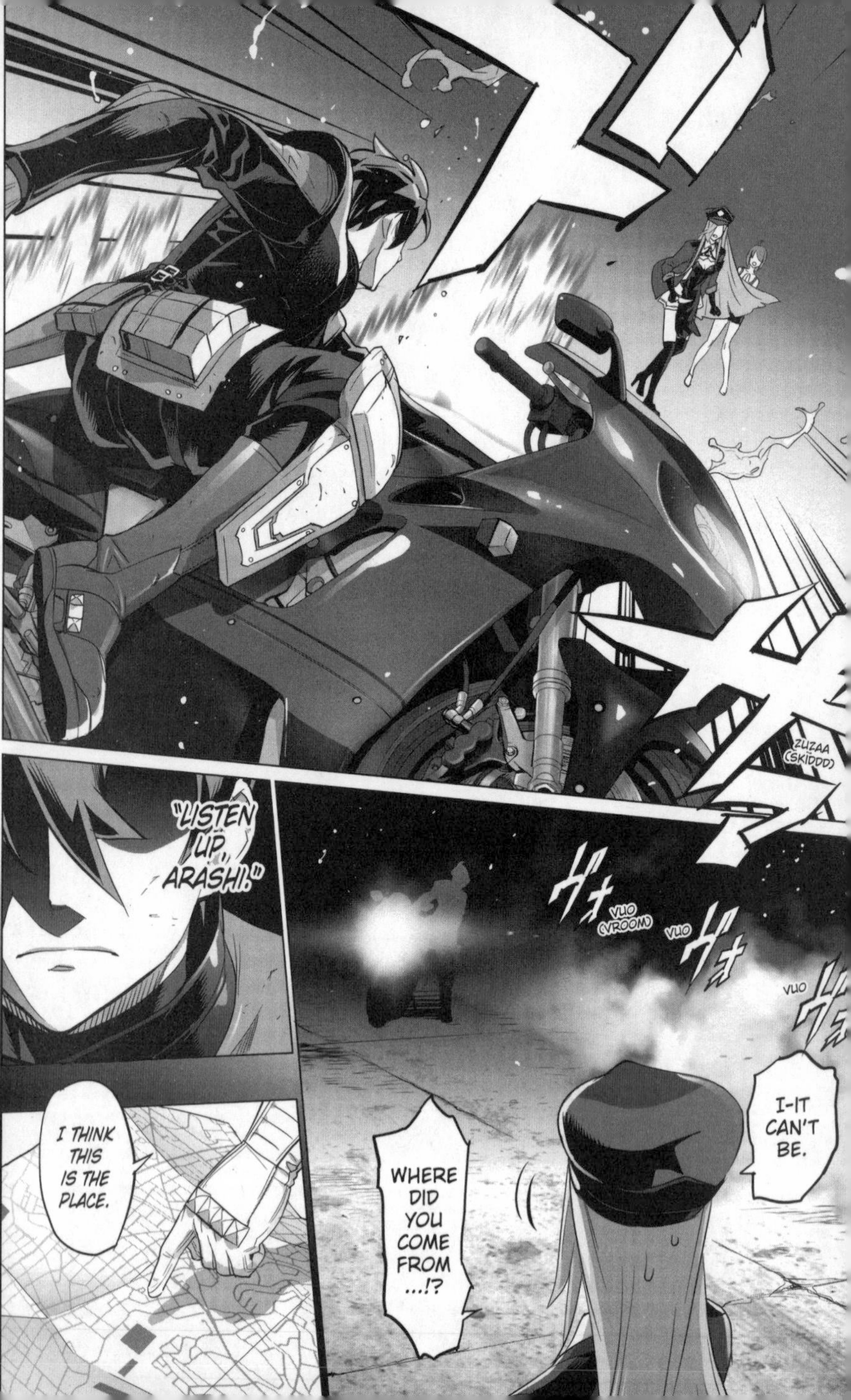
ZUZAA (SKIDDD)
VUO
VUO
VUO (VROOM)
I-IT CAN'T BE.
WHERE DID YOU COME FROM ...!?
"LISTEN UP, ARASHI."
I THINK THIS IS THE PLACE.

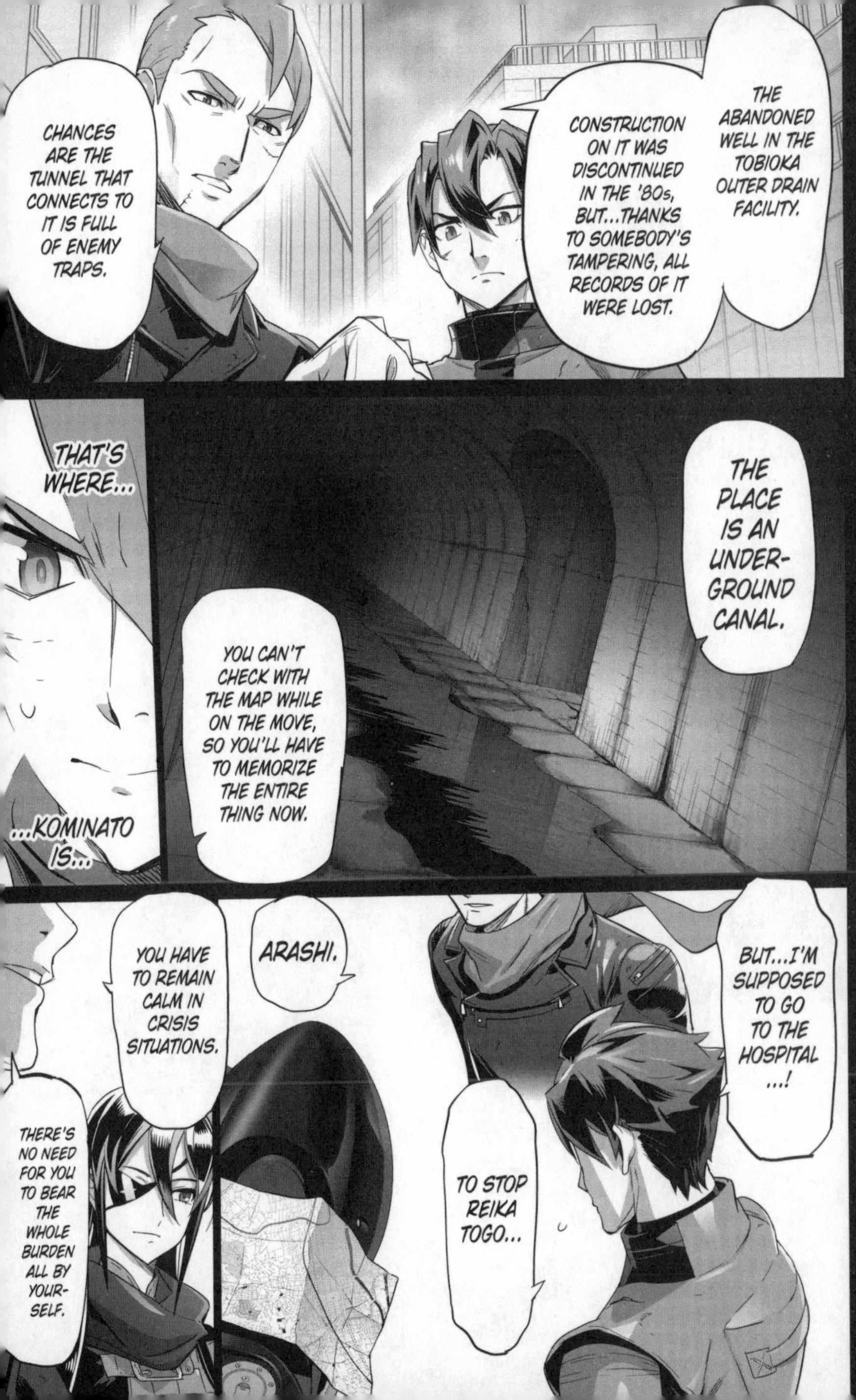
THE ABANDONED WELL IN THE TOBIOKA OUTER DRAIN FACILITY.
CONSTRUCTION ON IT WAS DISCONTINUED IN THE '80s, BUT...THANKS TO SOMEBODY'S TAMPERING, ALL RECORDS OF IT WERE LOST.
CHANCES ARE THE TUNNEL THAT CONNECTS TO IT IS FULL OF ENEMY TRAPS.
THE PLACE IS AN UNDER-GROUND CANAL.
YOU CAN'T CHECK WITH THE MAP WHILE ON THE MOVE, SO YOU'LL HAVE TO MEMORIZE THE ENTIRE THING NOW.
THAT'S WHERE...
...KOMINATO IS...
BUT...I'M SUPPOSED TO GO TO THE HOSPITAL ...!
TO STOP REIKA TOGO...
ARASHI.
YOU HAVE TO REMAIN CALM IN CRISIS SITUATIONS.
THERE'S NO NEED FOR YOU TO BEAR THE WHOLE BURDEN ALL BY YOUR-SELF.

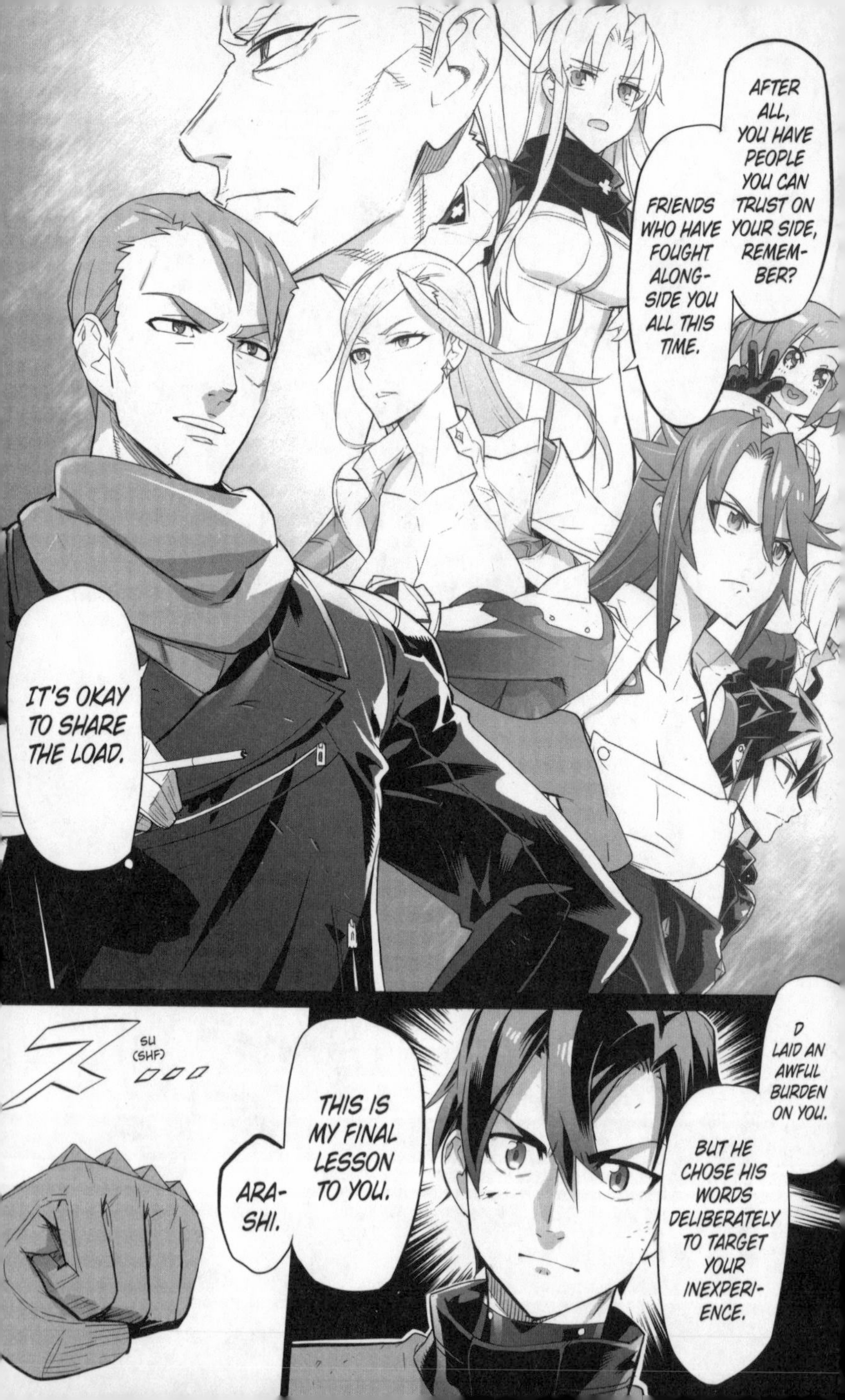
AFTER ALL, YOU HAVE PEOPLE YOU CAN TRUST ON YOUR SIDE, REMEMBER?
FRIENDS WHO HAVE FOUGHT ALONGSIDE YOU ALL THIS TIME.
IT'S OKAY TO SHARE THE LOAD.
D LAID AN AWFUL BURDEN ON YOU.
BUT HE CHOSE HIS WORDS DELIBERATELY TO TARGET YOUR INEXPERIENCE.
THIS IS MY FINAL LESSON TO YOU.
ARASHI.
SU (SHF)

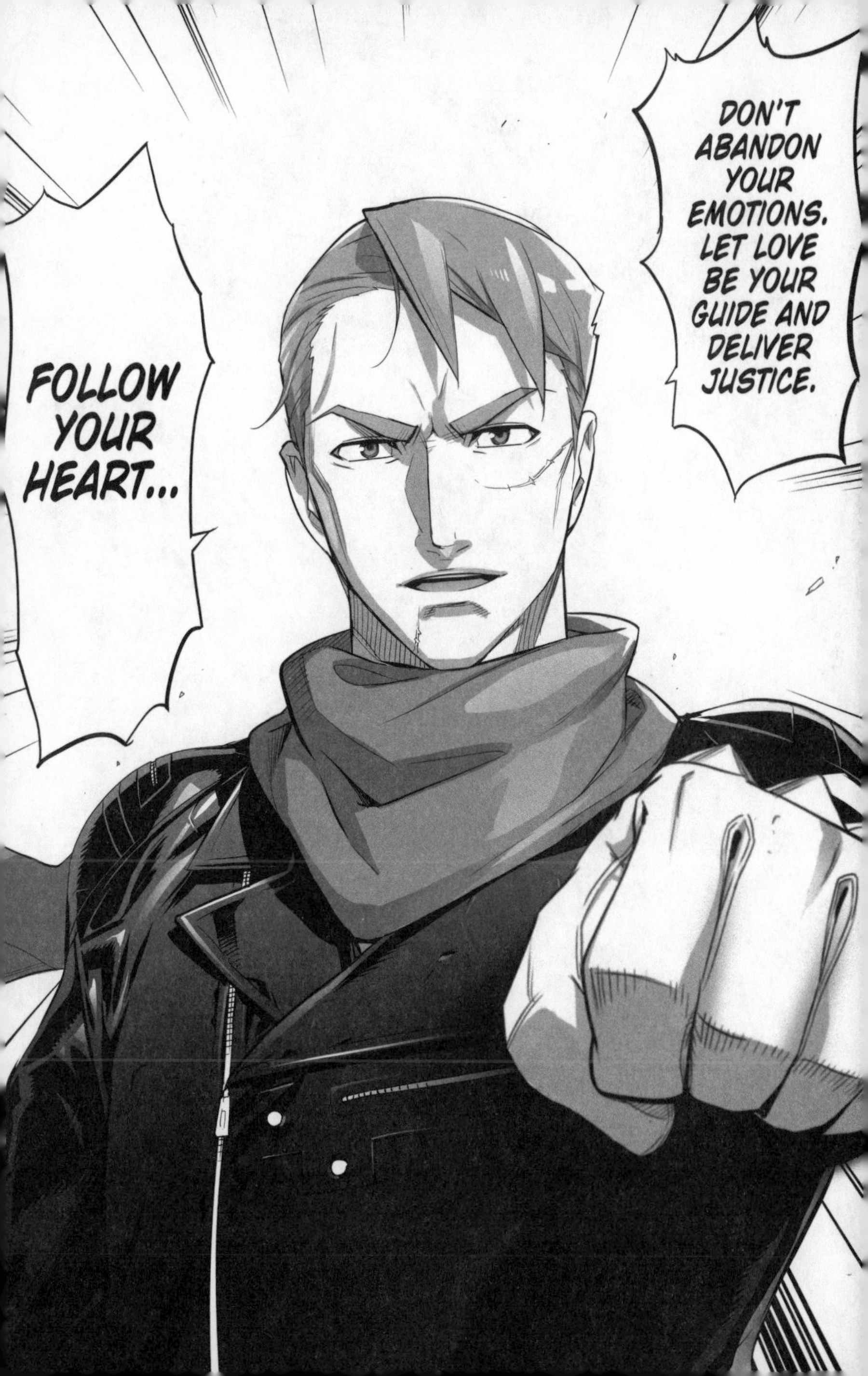
DON'T ABANDON YOUR EMOTIONS. LET LOVE BE YOUR GUIDE AND DELIVER JUSTICE.
FOLLOW YOUR HEART...

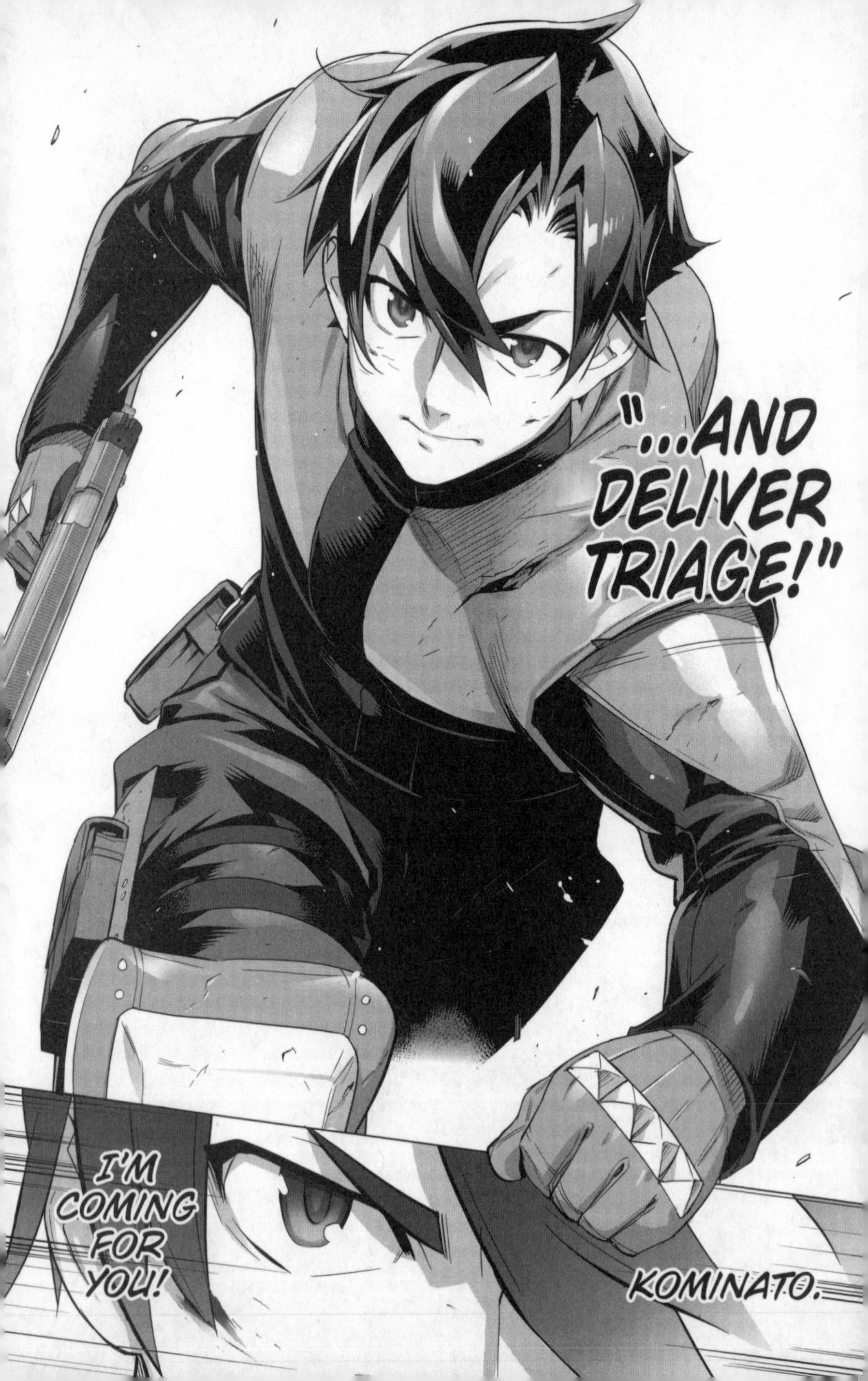
"...AND DELIVER TRIAGE!"
KOMINATO.
I'M COMING FOR YOU!

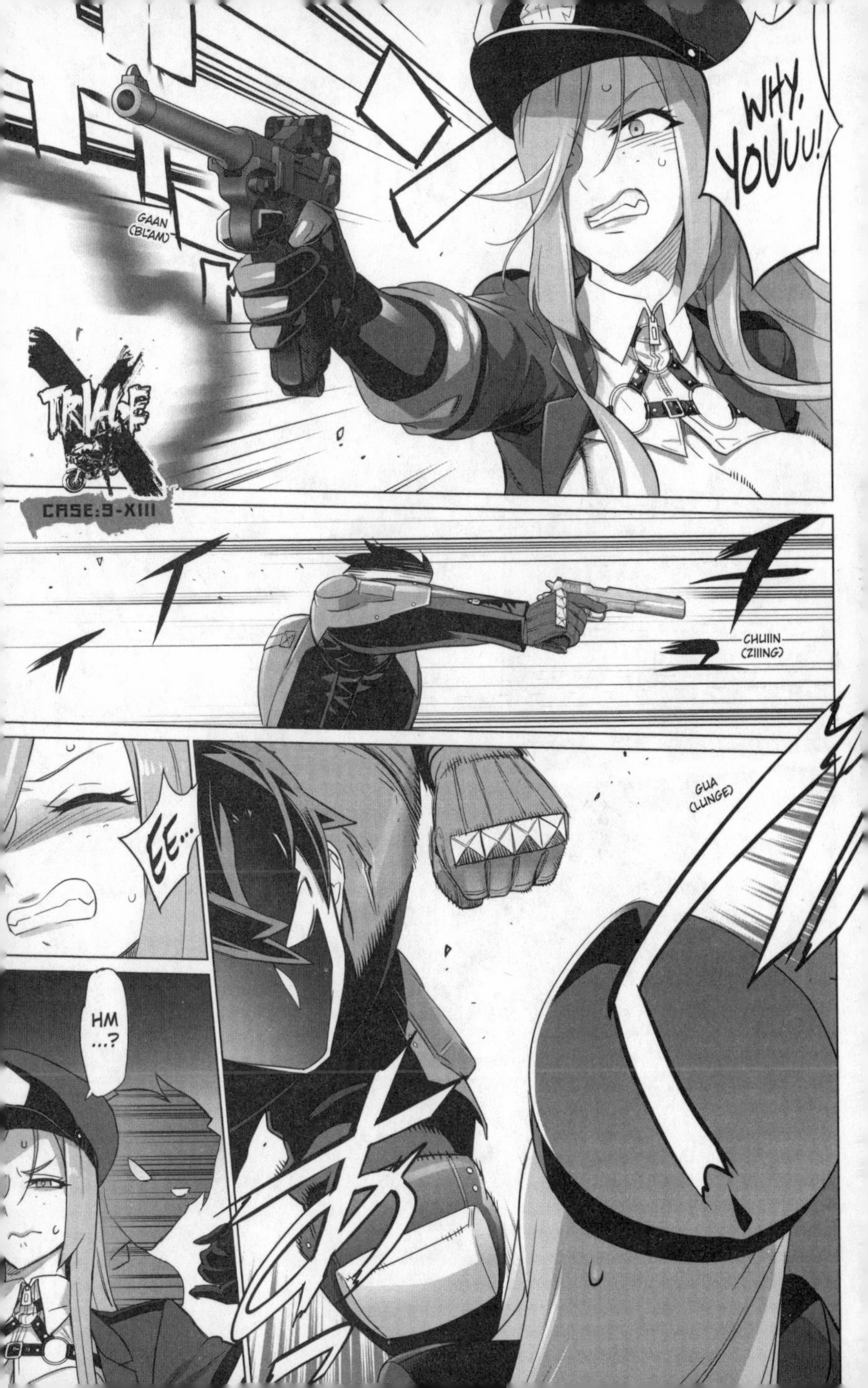
WHY, YOUUU!
GAAN (BL'AM)
TRIAGE X
CASE:9-XIII
CHUIIN (ZIIING)
GUA (LUNGE)
EE...
HM ...?

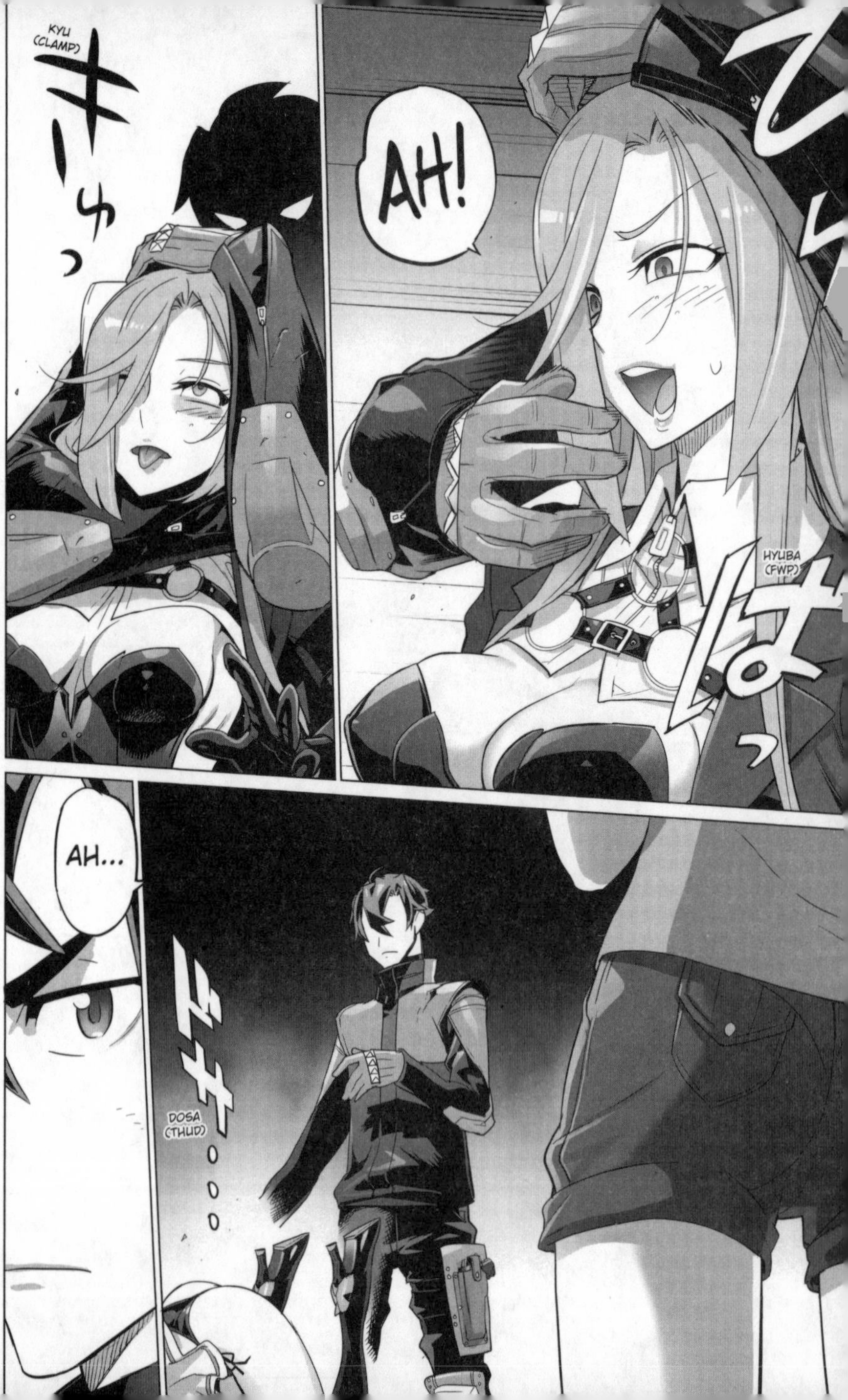
AH!
HYUBA (FWP)
ぱっ
KYU (CLAMP)
きゅっ
DOSA (THUD)
AH...

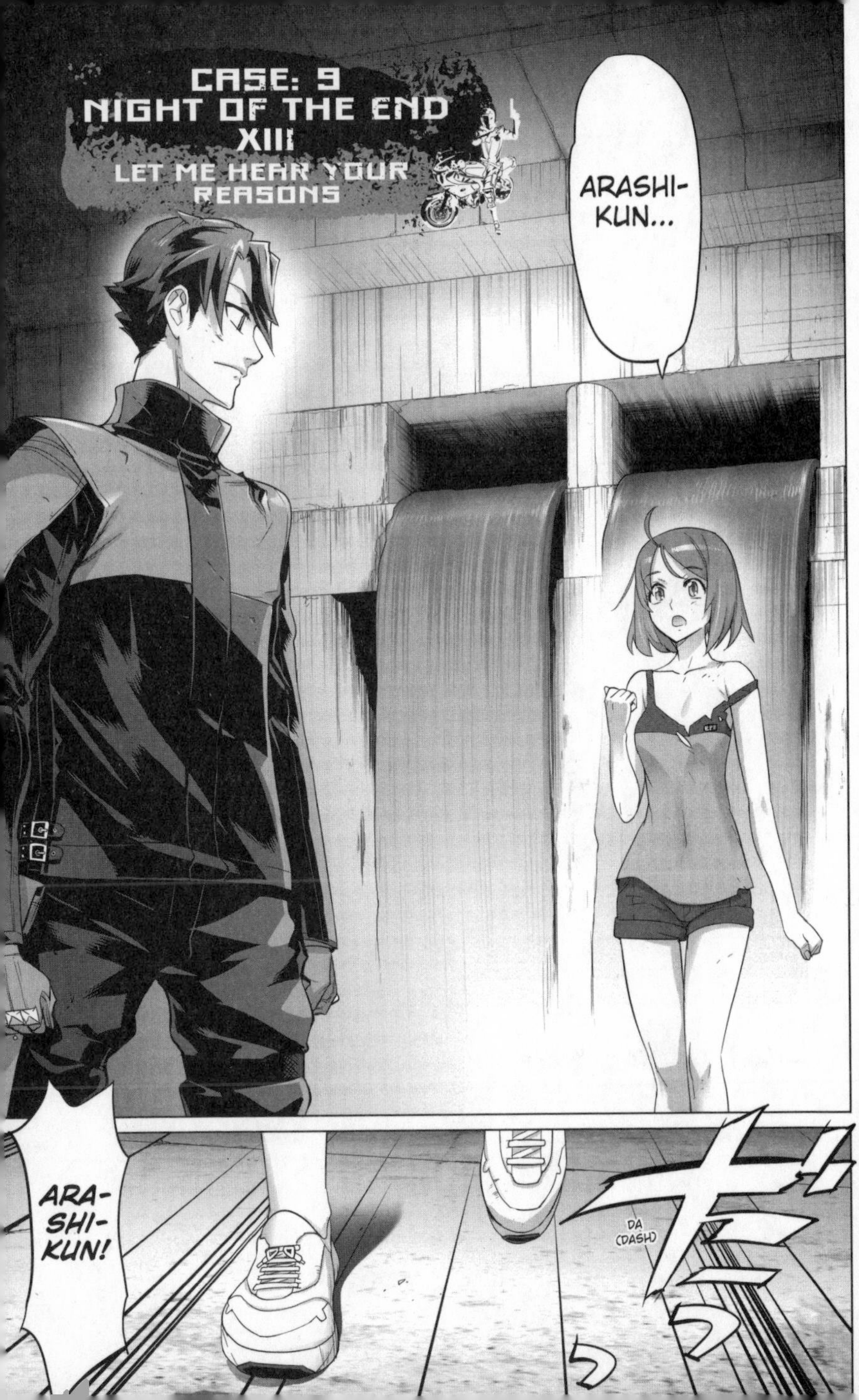
ARASHI-KUN...
CASE: 9
NIGHT OF THE END
XIII
LET ME HEAR YOUR REASONS
DA (DASH)
ARA-SHI-KUN!

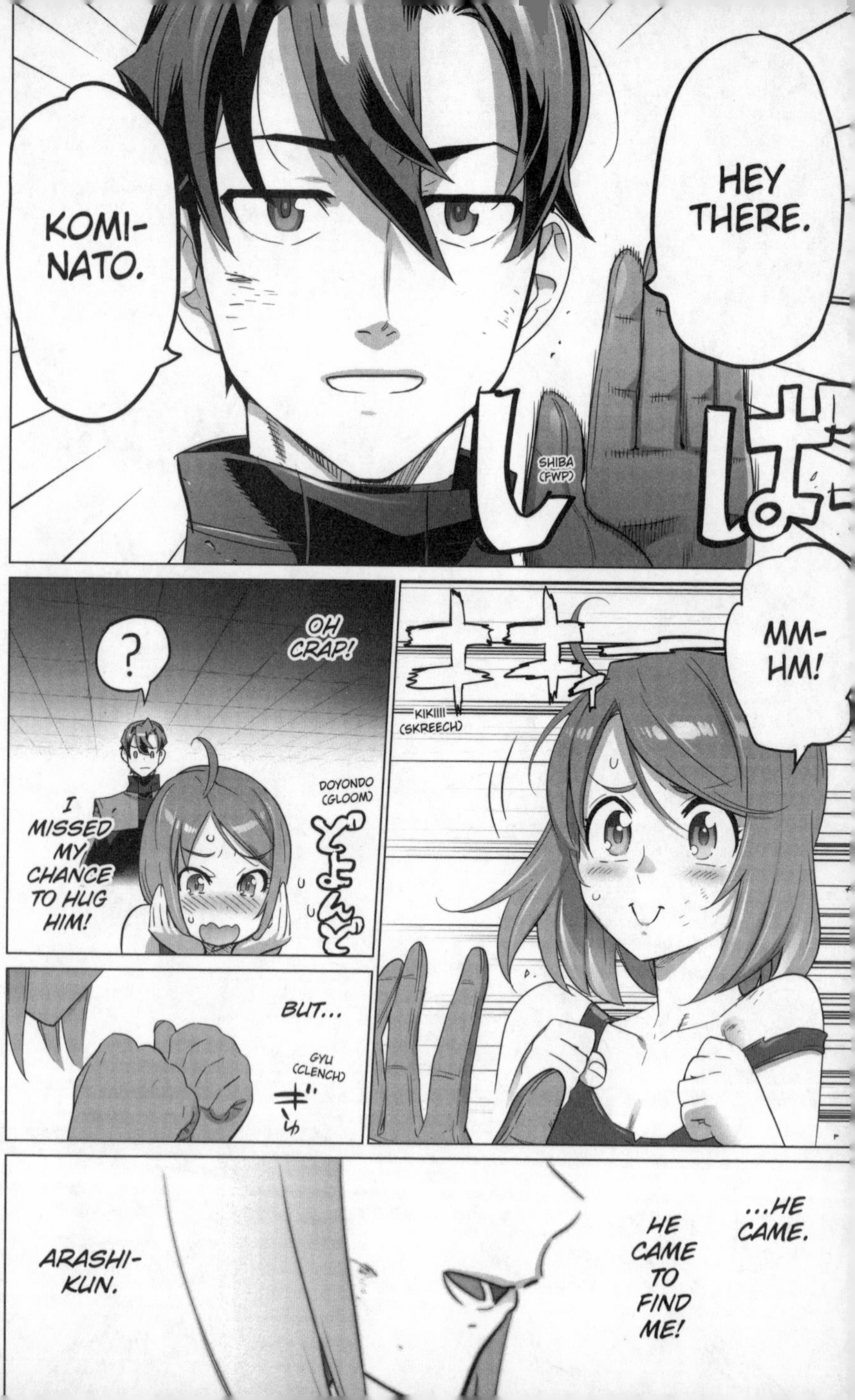
HEY THERE.
KOMI-NATO.
SHIBA (FWP)
しぱ
MM-HM!
キキー
KIKIIII (SKREECH)
OH CRAP!
?
DOYONDO (GLOOM)
どよんど
I MISSED MY CHANCE TO HUG HIM!
BUT...
GYU (CLENCH)
ぎゅ
...HE CAME.
HE CAME TO FIND ME!
ARASHI-KUN.

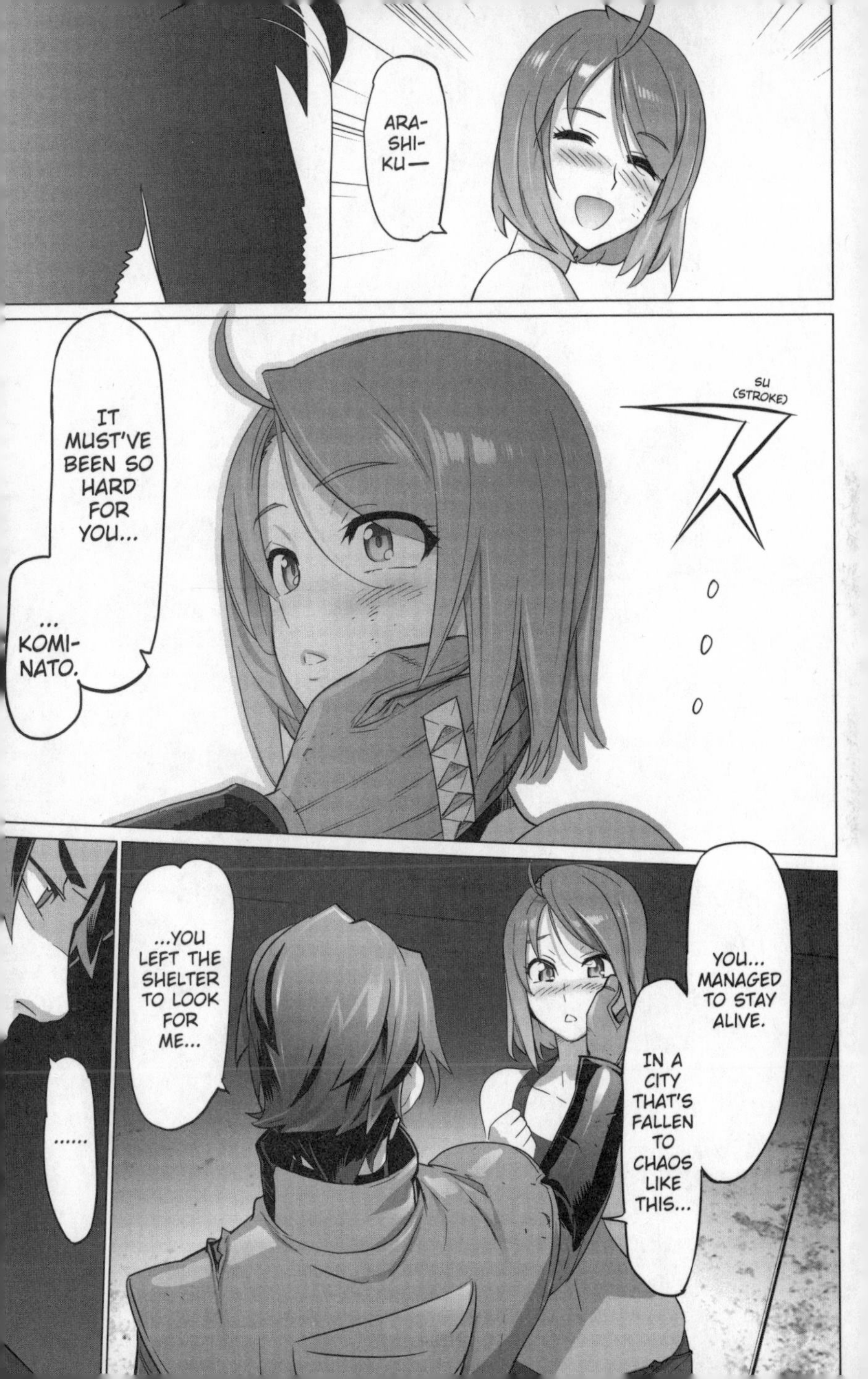
ARA-SHIKU—
SU (STROKE)
IT MUST'VE BEEN SO HARD FOR YOU...
... KOMINATO.
YOU... MANAGED TO STAY ALIVE.
IN A CITY THAT'S FALLEN TO CHAOS LIKE THIS...
...YOU LEFT THE SHELTER TO LOOK FOR ME...
......

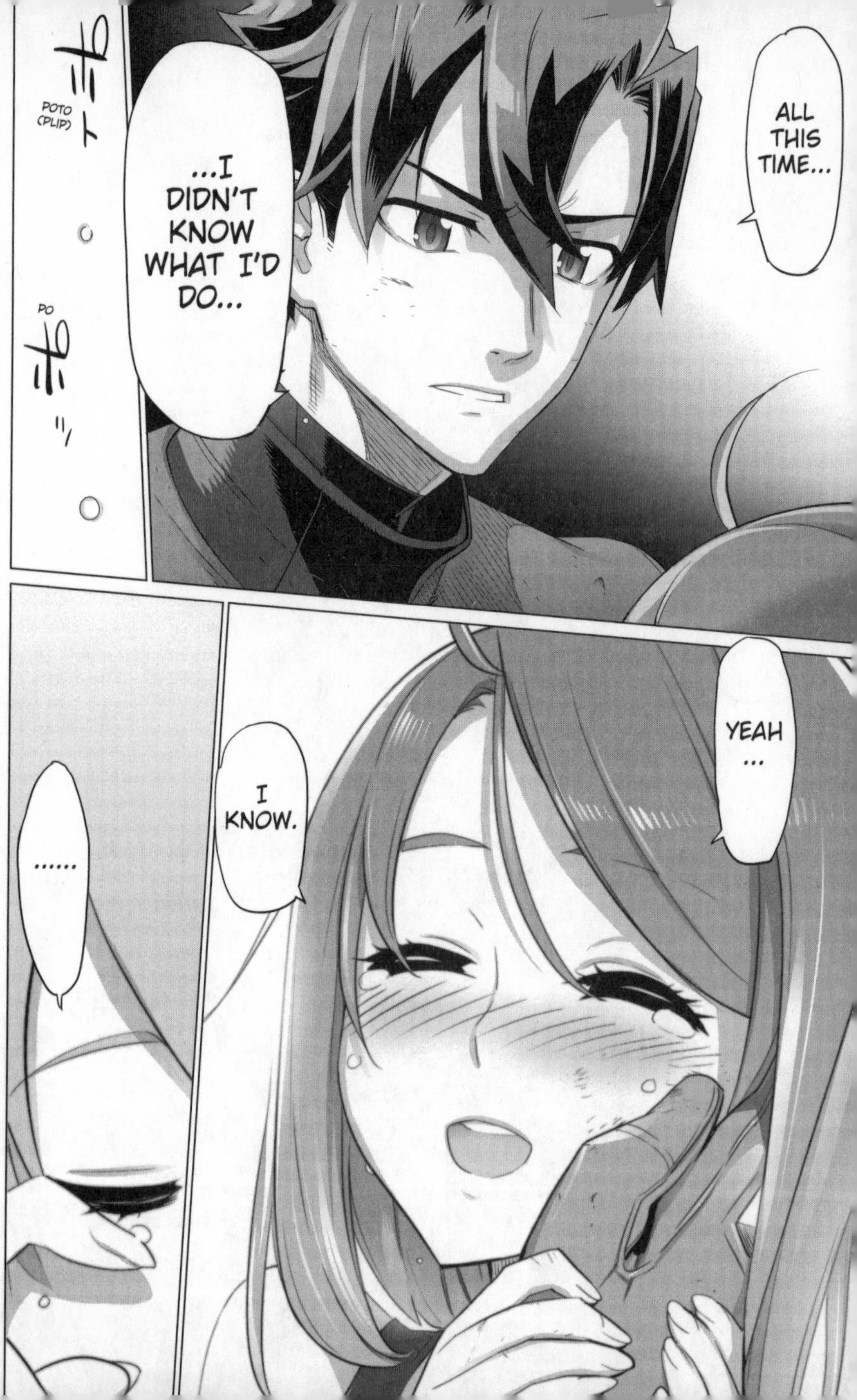
ALL THIS TIME...
...I DIDN'T KNOW WHAT I'D DO...
POTO (PLIP)
PO
YEAH ...
I KNOW.
......

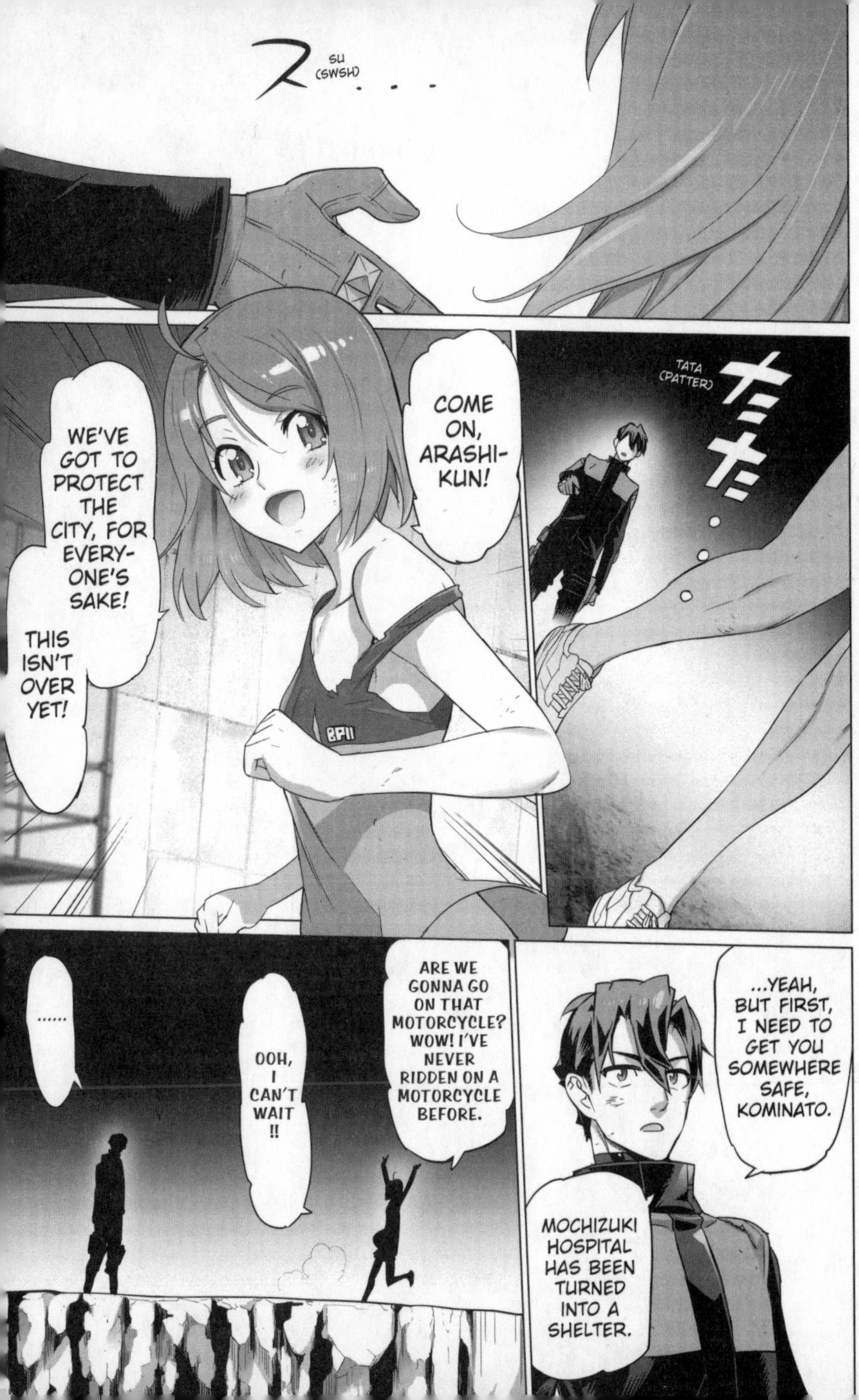
SU (SWSH)
...
TATA (PATTER)
COME ON, ARASHI-KUN!
WE'VE GOT TO PROTECT THE CITY, FOR EVERYONE'S SAKE!
THIS ISN'T OVER YET!
BPII
...YEAH, BUT FIRST, I NEED TO GET YOU SOMEWHERE SAFE, KOMINATO.
MOCHIZUKI HOSPITAL HAS BEEN TURNED INTO A SHELTER.
ARE WE GONNA GO ON THAT MOTORCYCLE? WOW! I'VE NEVER RIDDEN ON A MOTORCYCLE BEFORE.
OOH, I CAN'T WAIT!!
......

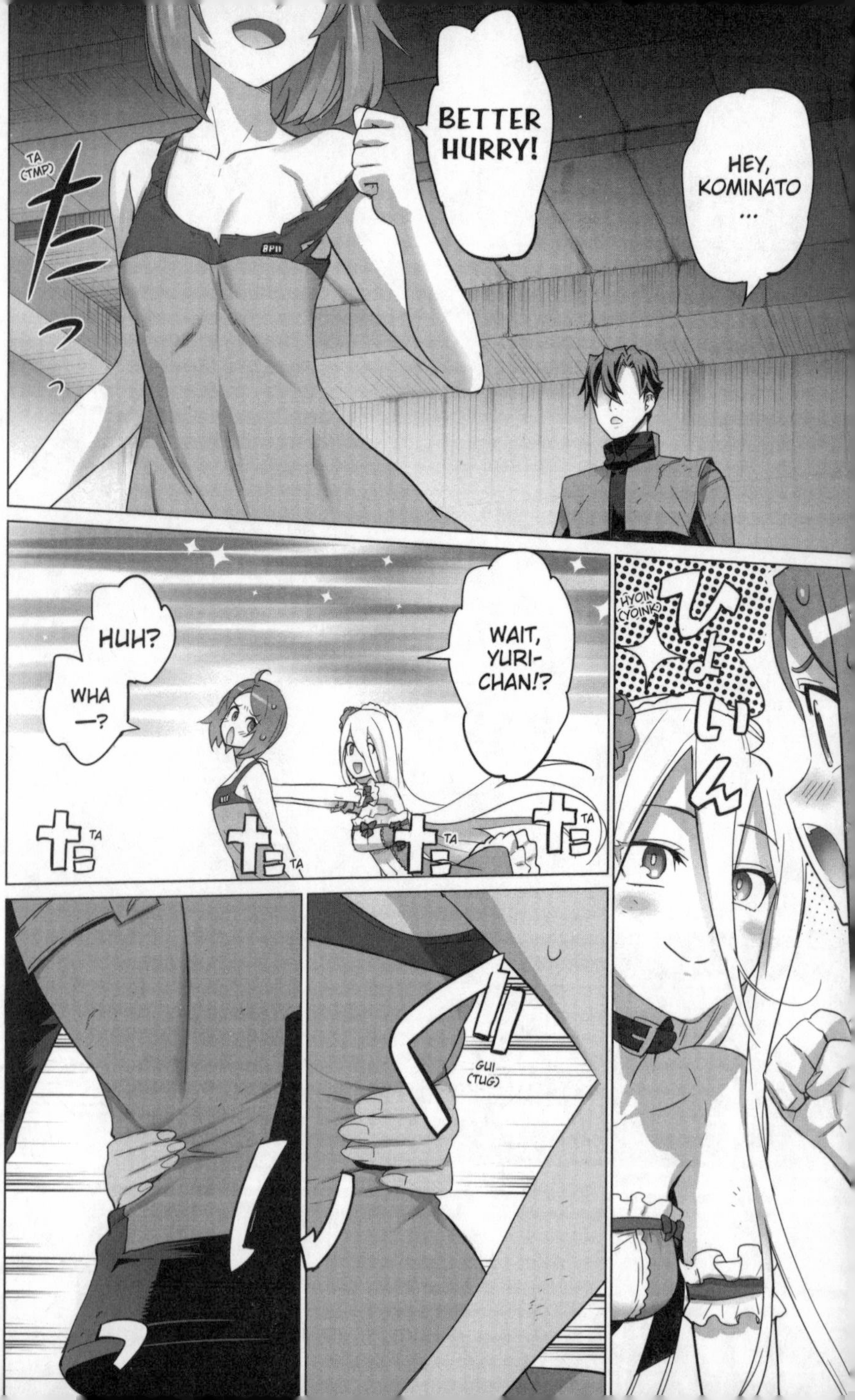
HEY, KOMINATO ...
BETTER HURRY!
TA (TMP)
HYOIN (YOINK)
WAIT, YURI-CHAN!?
HUH?
WHA—?
TA
TA
TA
TA
GUI (TUG)

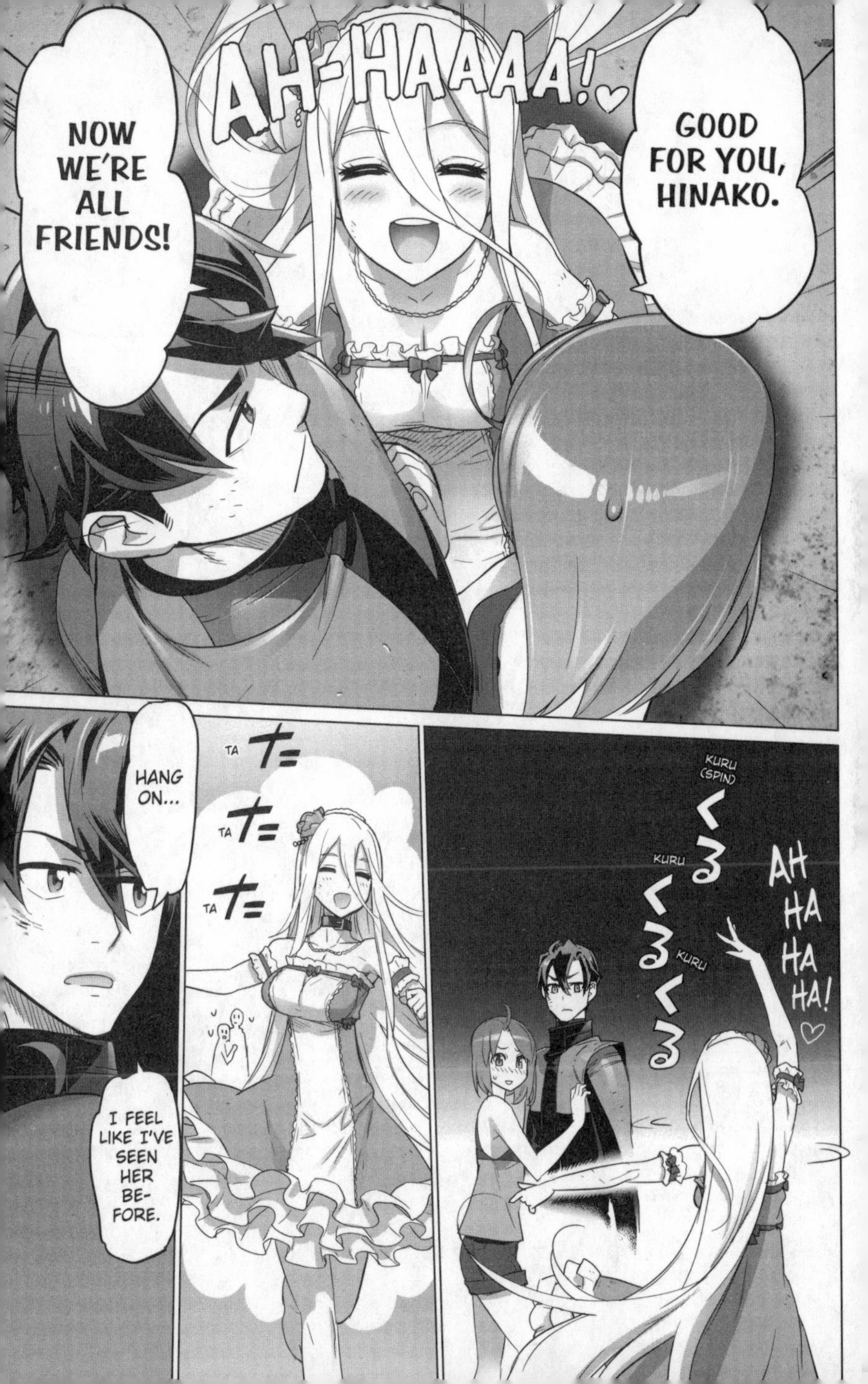
GOOD FOR YOU, HINAKO.
AH-HAAAA!♡
NOW WE'RE ALL FRIENDS!
KURU (SPIN) くる
KURU くる
KURU くる
AH HA HA HA!♡
TA た
TA た
TA た
HANG ON...
I FEEL LIKE I'VE SEEN HER BE-FORE.

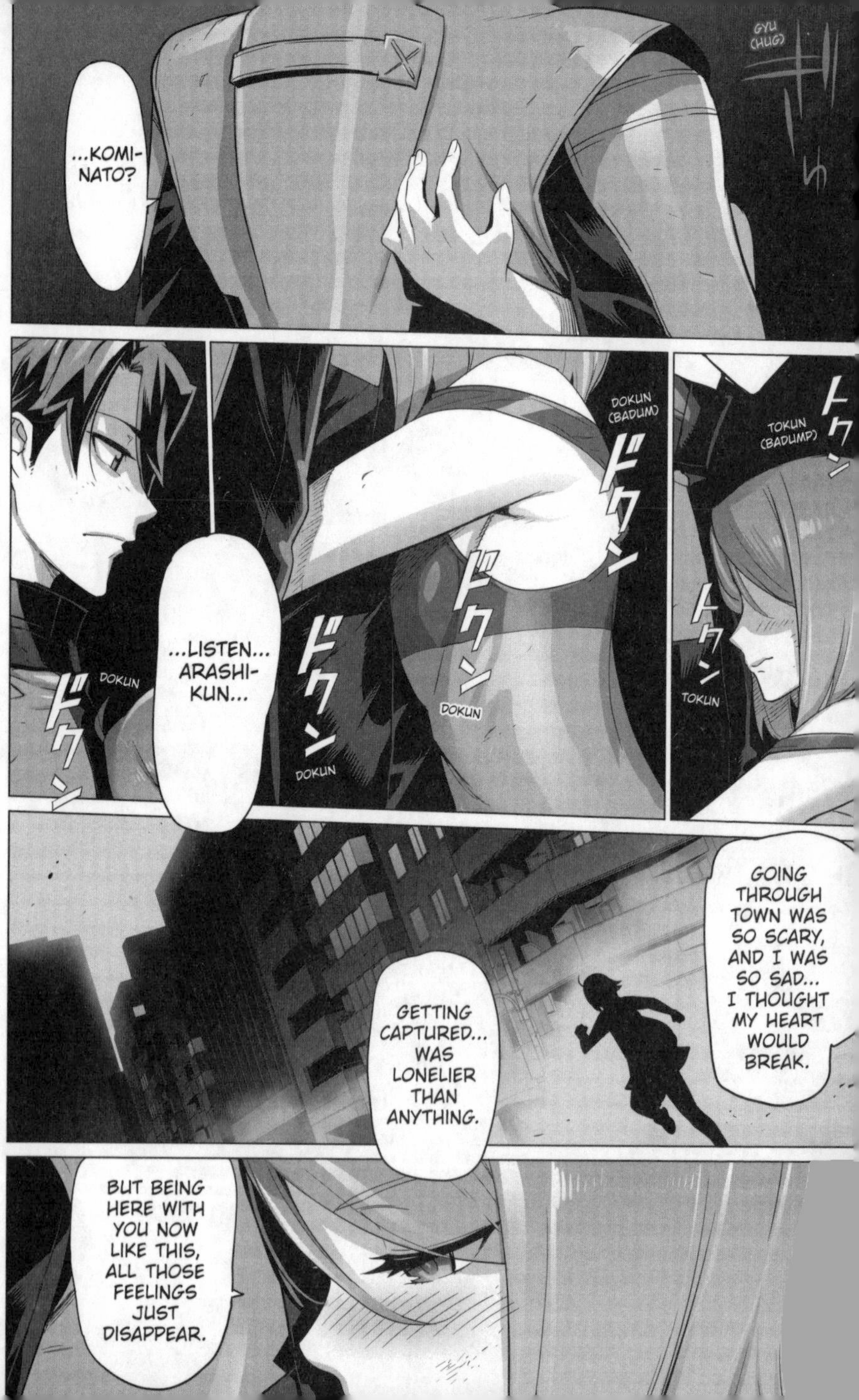

GYU (HUG)
...KOMI-NATO?
トクン
TOKUN (BADUMP)
トクン
TOKUN
ドクン
DOKUN (BADUM)
ドクン
DOKUN
ドクン
DOKUN
...LISTEN... ARASHI-KUN...
ドクン
DOKUN
GOING THROUGH TOWN WAS SO SCARY, AND I WAS SO SAD... I THOUGHT MY HEART WOULD BREAK.
GETTING CAPTURED... WAS LONELIER THAN ANYTHING.
BUT BEING HERE WITH YOU NOW LIKE THIS, ALL THOSE FEELINGS JUST DISAPPEAR.

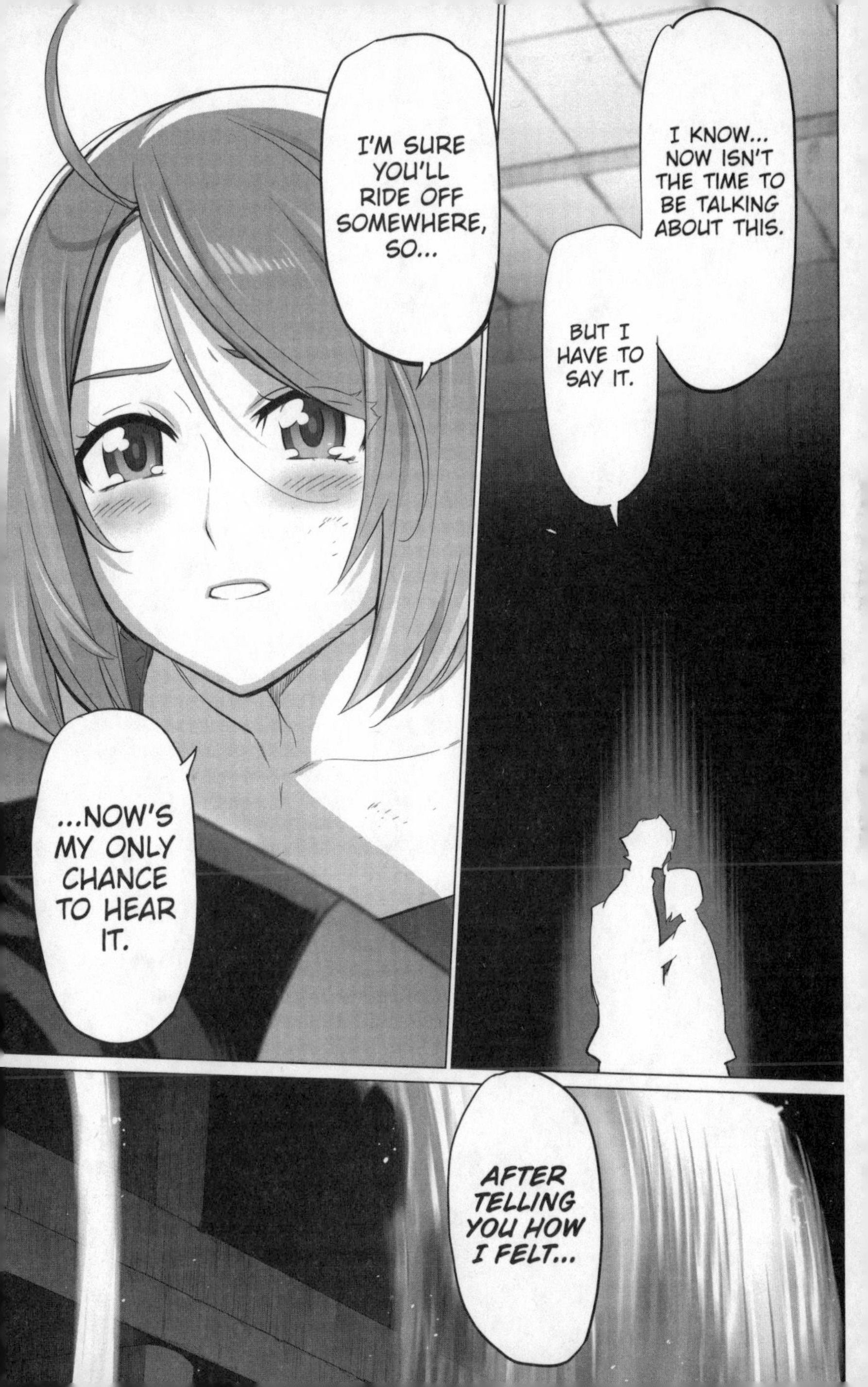
I KNOW... NOW ISN'T THE TIME TO BE TALKING ABOUT THIS.
BUT I HAVE TO SAY IT.
I'M SURE YOU'LL RIDE OFF SOMEWHERE, SO...
...NOW'S MY ONLY CHANCE TO HEAR IT.
AFTER TELLING YOU HOW I FELT...

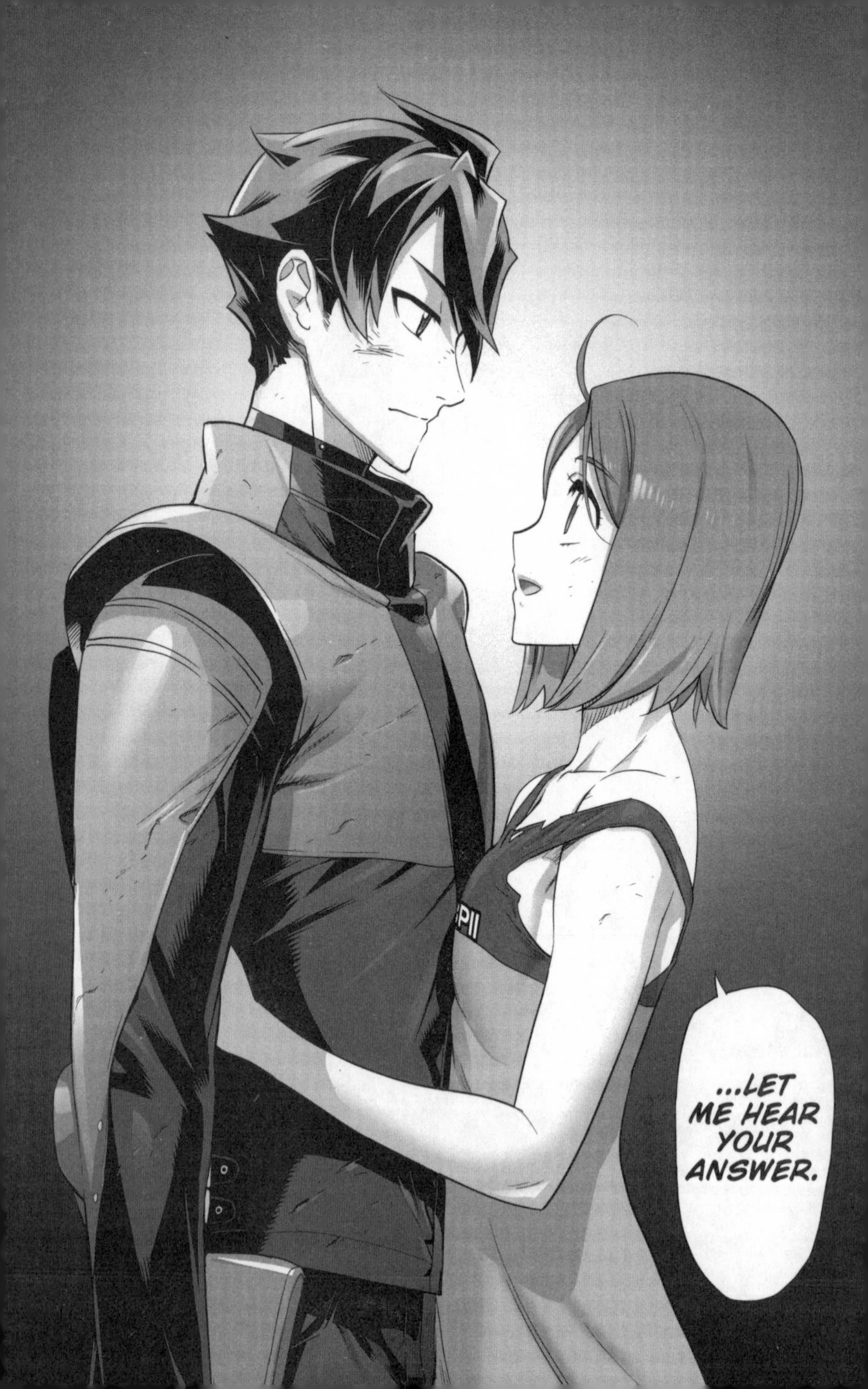
...LET ME HEAR YOUR ANSWER.

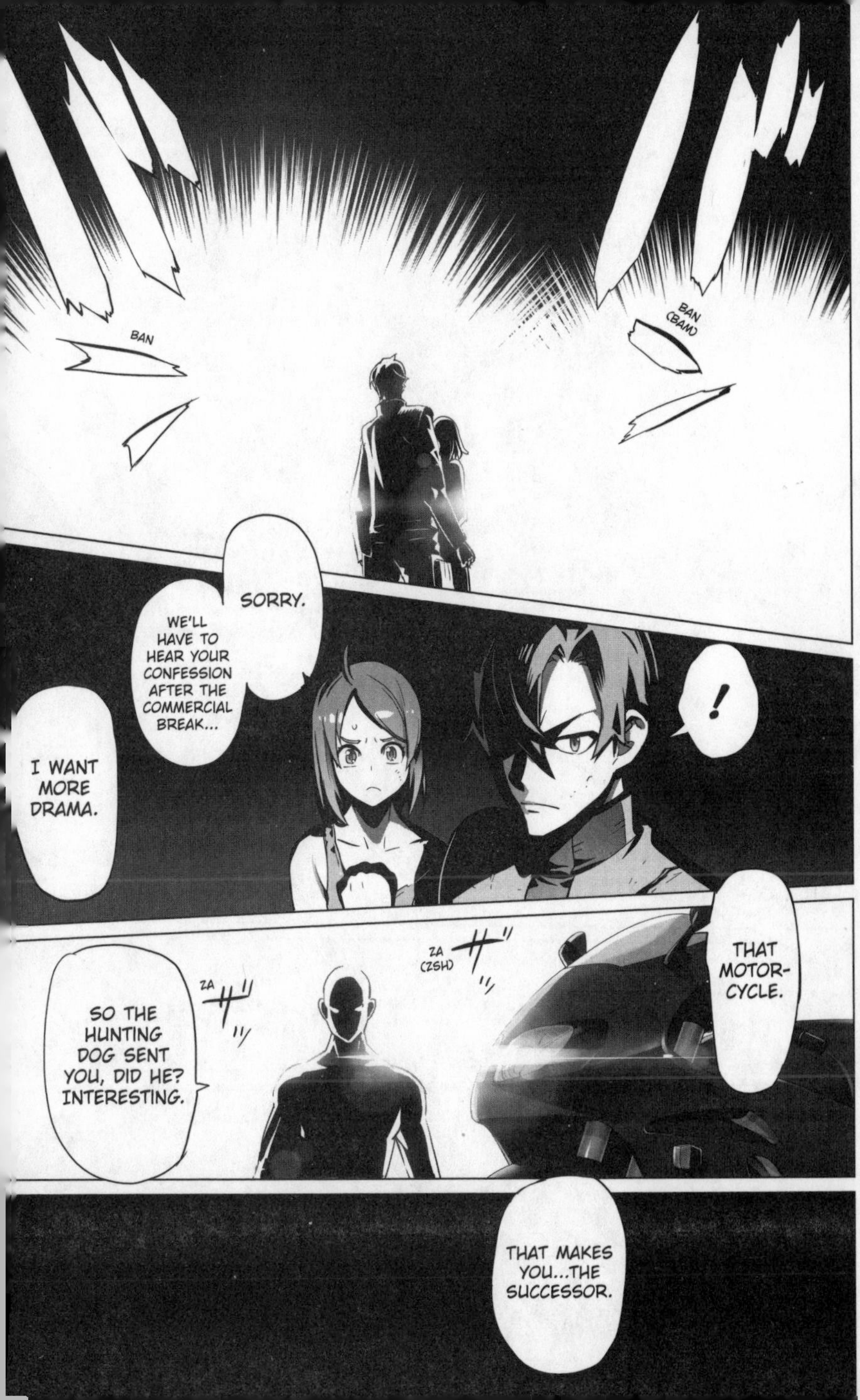
BAN (BAM)
BAN
!
SORRY.
WE'LL HAVE TO HEAR YOUR CONFESSION AFTER THE COMMERCIAL BREAK...
I WANT MORE DRAMA.
THAT MOTOR-CYCLE.
ZA (ZSH)
ZA
SO THE HUNTING DOG SENT YOU, DID HE? INTERESTING.
THAT MAKES YOU...THE SUCCESSOR.

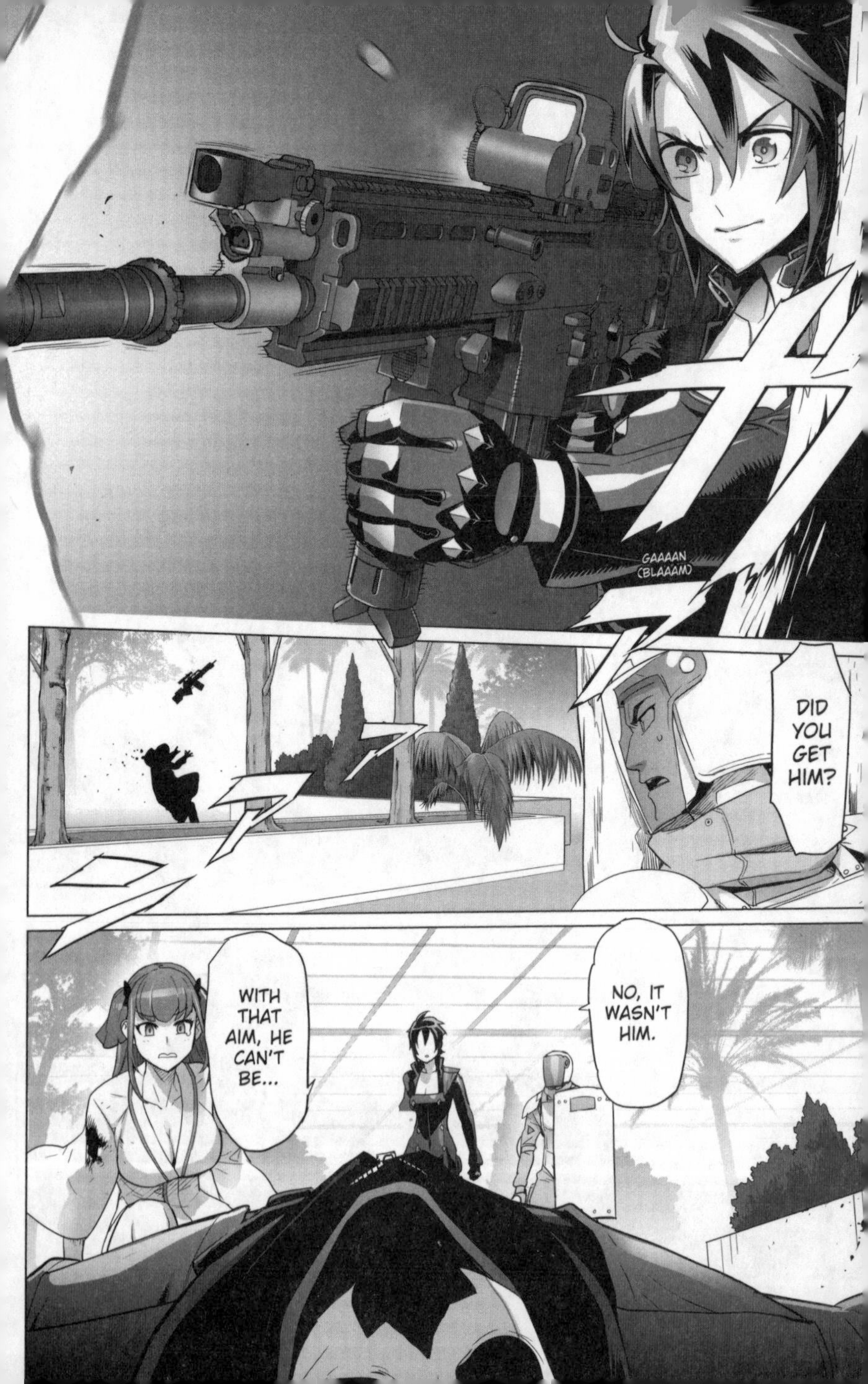
GAAAAN (BLAAAM)
DID YOU GET HIM?
NO, IT WASN'T HIM.
WITH THAT AIM, HE CAN'T BE...

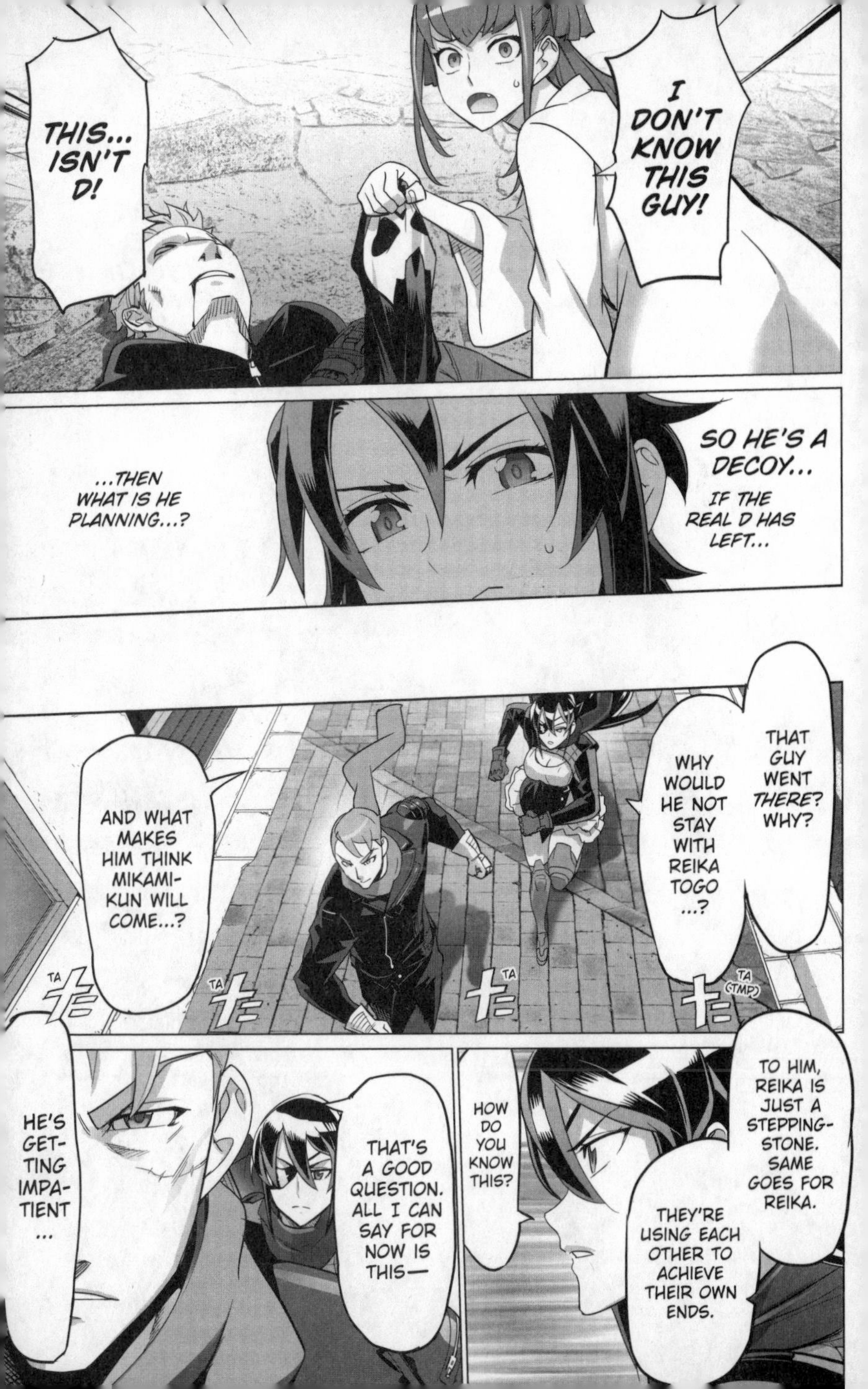
I DON'T KNOW THIS GUY!
THIS... ISN'T D!
SO HE'S A DECOY...
IF THE REAL D HAS LEFT...
...THEN WHAT IS HE PLANNING...?
THAT GUY WENT THERE? WHY?
WHY WOULD HE NOT STAY WITH REIKA TOGO ...?
AND WHAT MAKES HIM THINK MIKAMI-KUN WILL COME...?
TA (TMP)
TA
TA
TA
TO HIM, REIKA IS JUST A STEPPING-STONE. SAME GOES FOR REIKA.
THEY'RE USING EACH OTHER TO ACHIEVE THEIR OWN ENDS.
HOW DO YOU KNOW THIS?
THAT'S A GOOD QUESTION. ALL I CAN SAY FOR NOW IS THIS—
HE'S GET-TING IMPA-TIENT ...

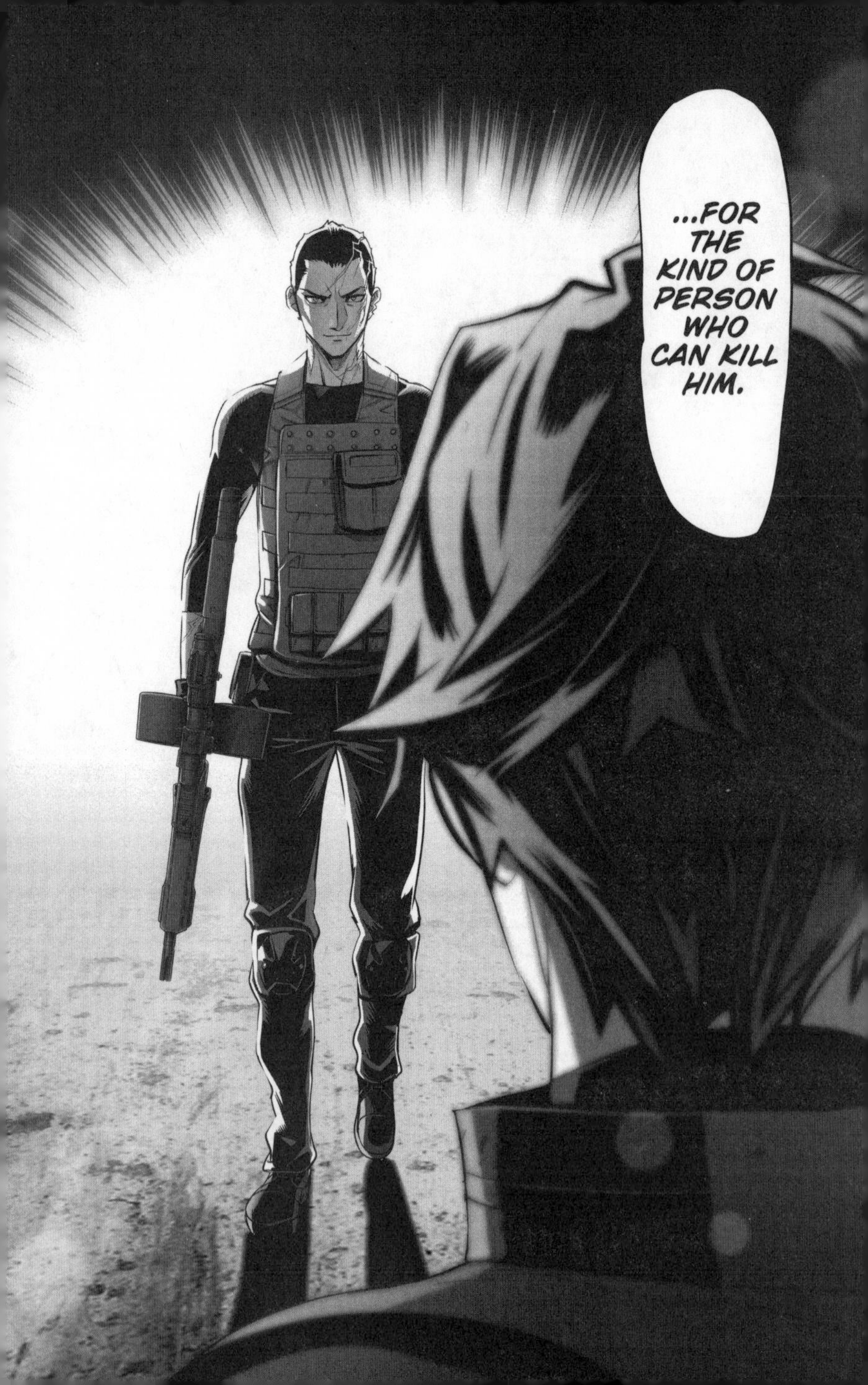
...FOR THE KIND OF PERSON WHO CAN KILL HIM.

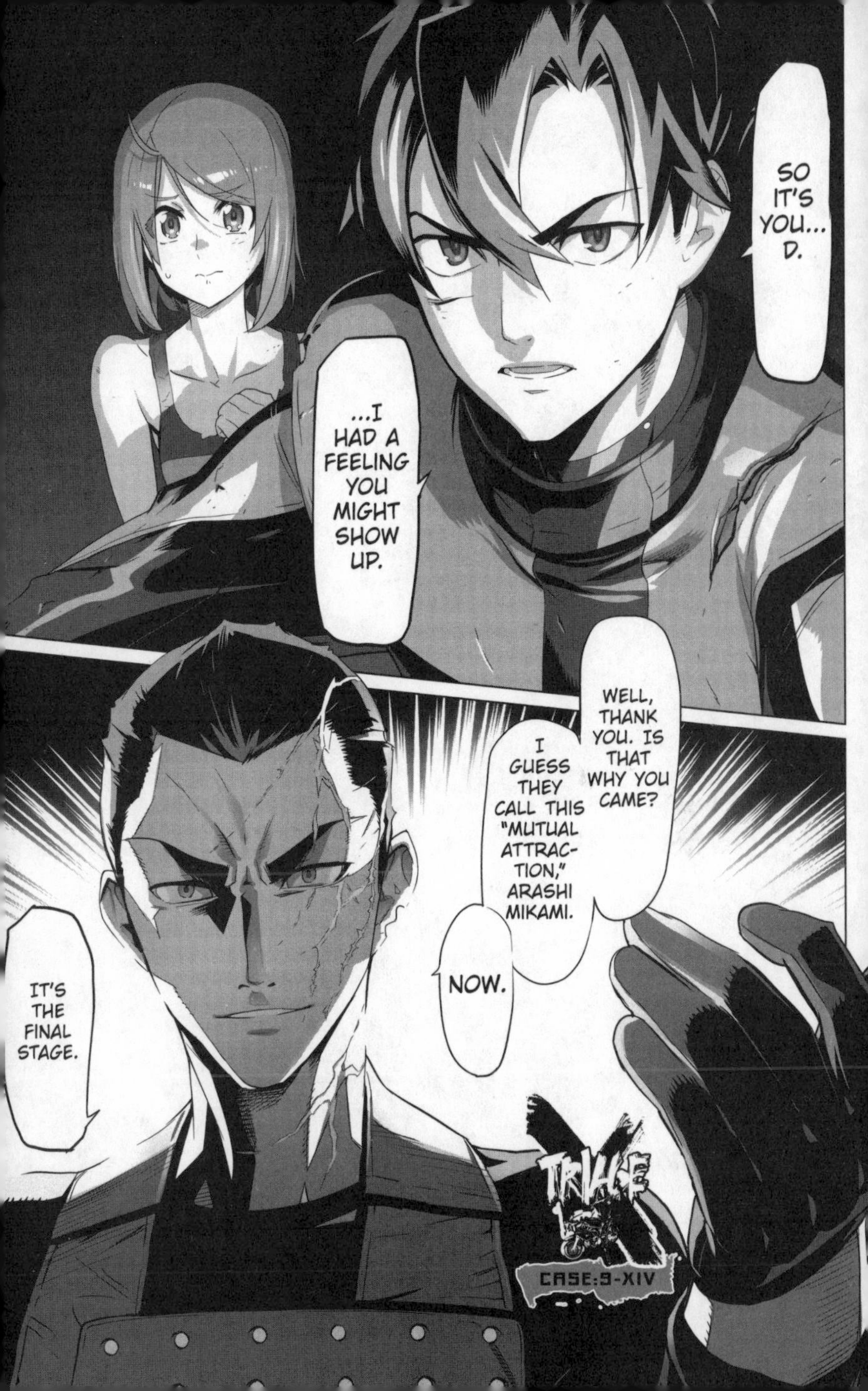
SO IT'S YOU... D.
...I HAD A FEELING YOU MIGHT SHOW UP.
WELL, THANK YOU. IS THAT WHY YOU CAME?
I GUESS THEY CALL THIS "MUTUAL ATTRACTION," ARASHI MIKAMI.
NOW.
IT'S THE FINAL STAGE.
CASE:9-XIV

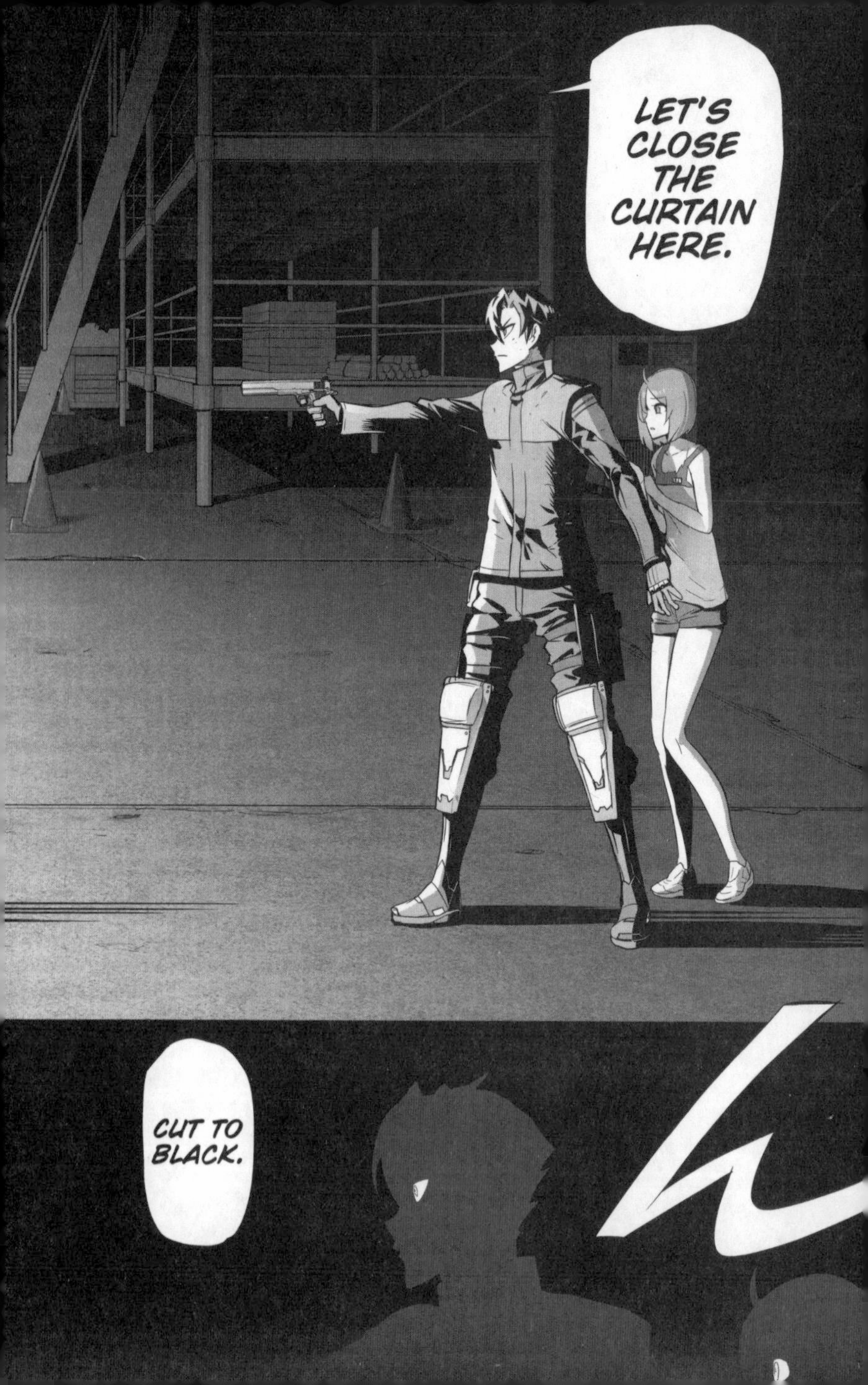
LET'S CLOSE THE CURTAIN HERE.
CUT TO BLACK.

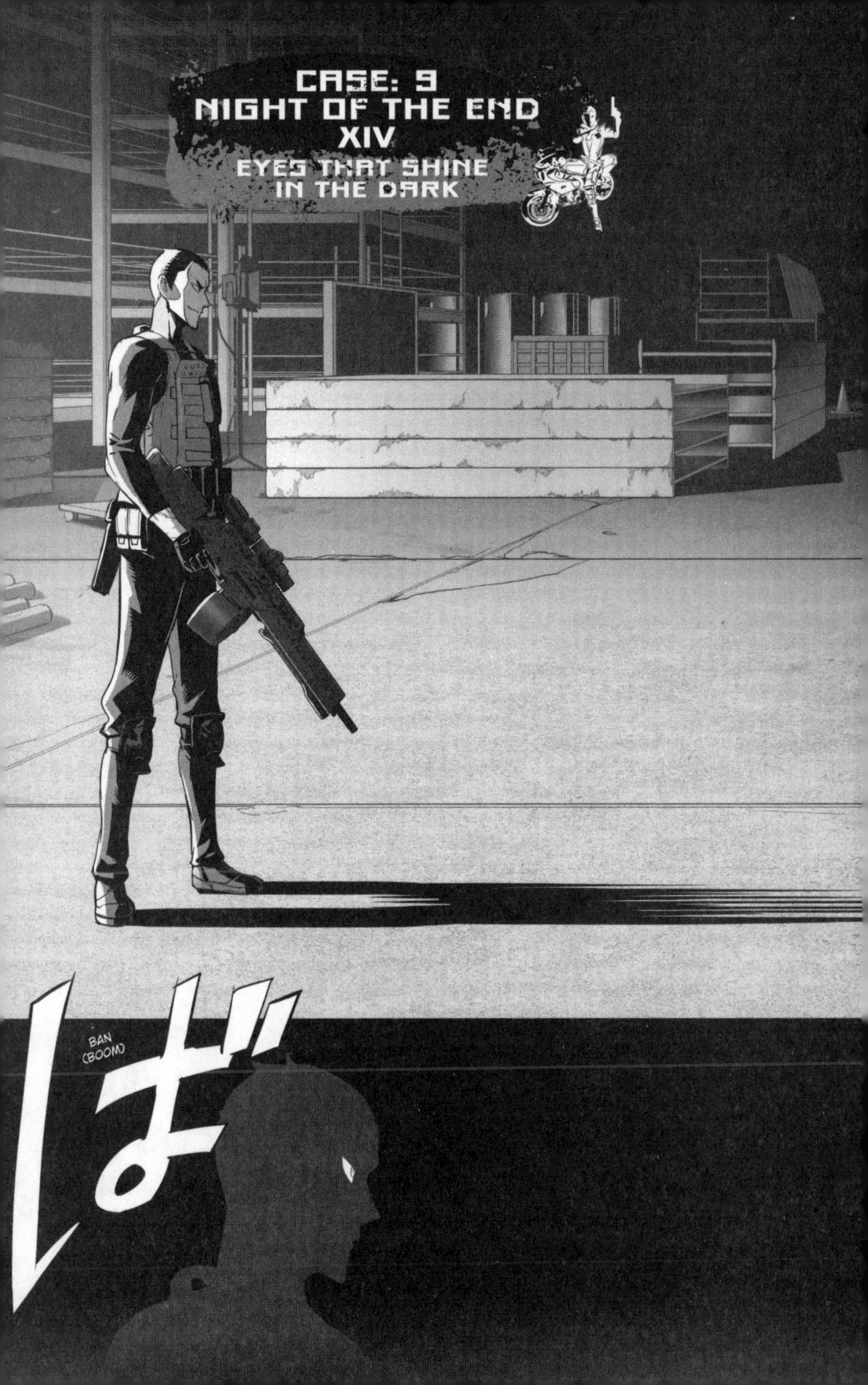
CASE: 9
NIGHT OF THE END
XIV
EYES THAT SHINE
IN THE DARK
ばっ
BAN
(BOOM)

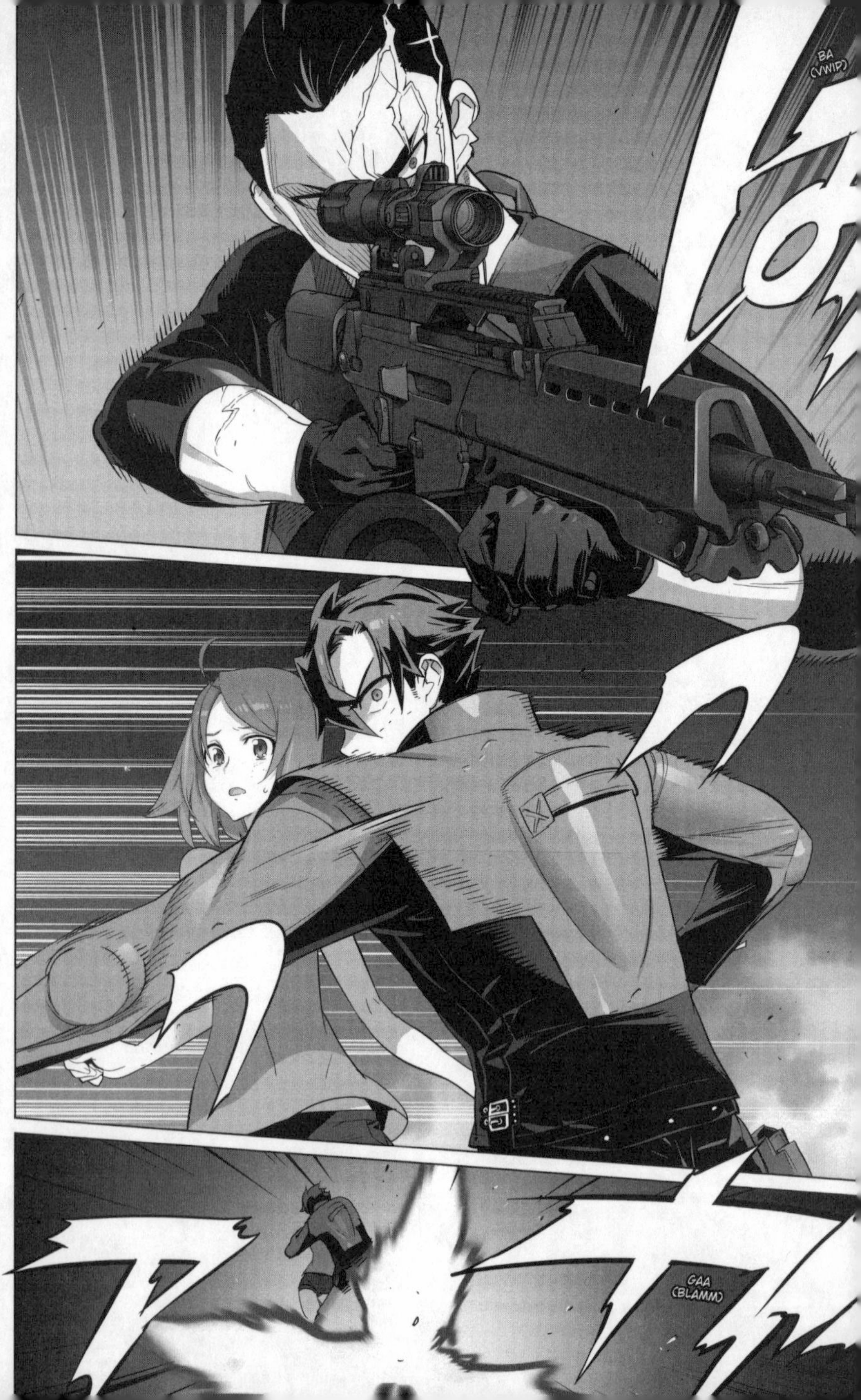
BA
(VWIP)
GAA
(BLAMM)

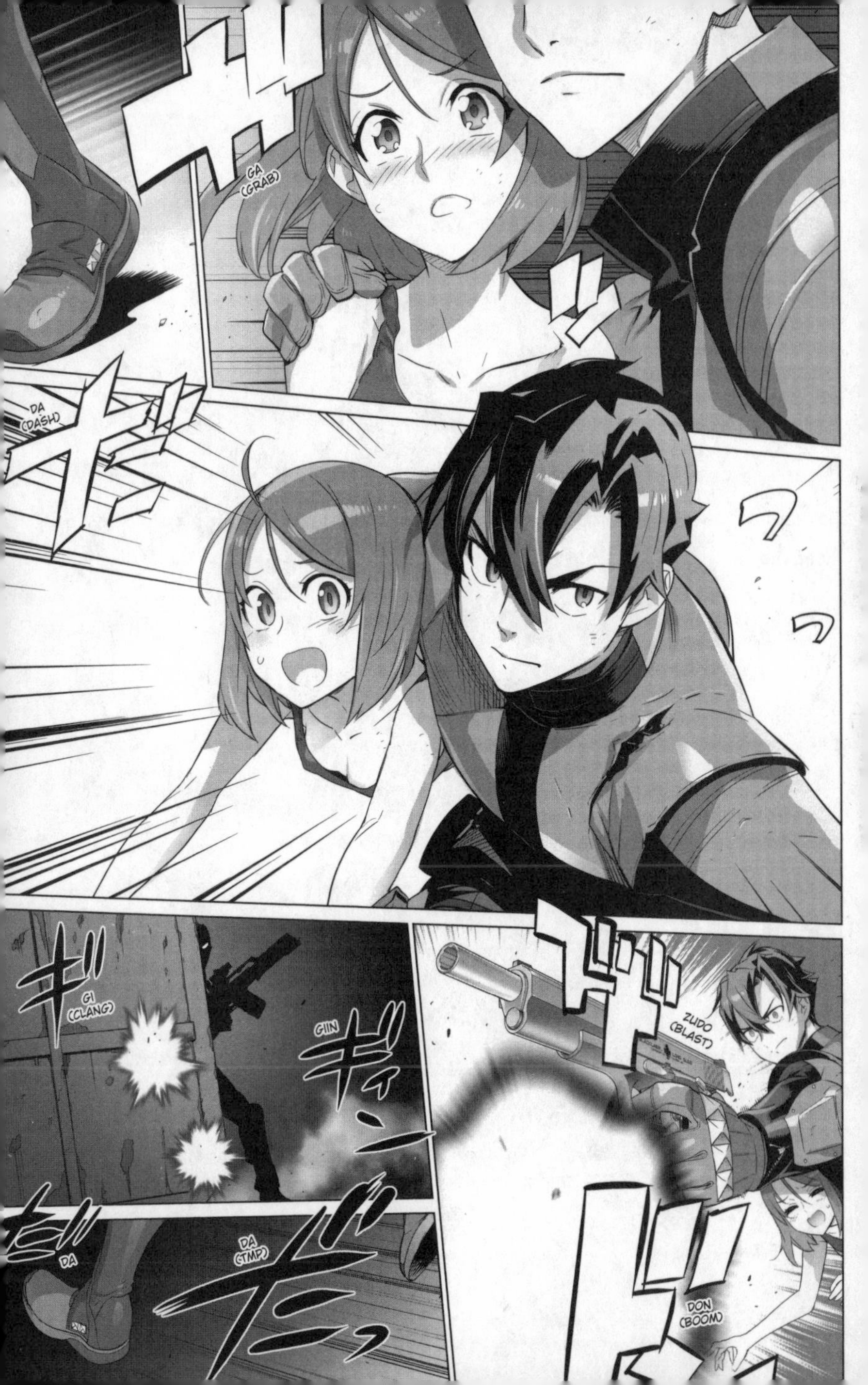
GA
(GRAB)
DA
(DASH)
ZUDO
(BLAST)
DON
(BOOM)
GI
(CLANG)
GIIN
DA
(TMP)
DA

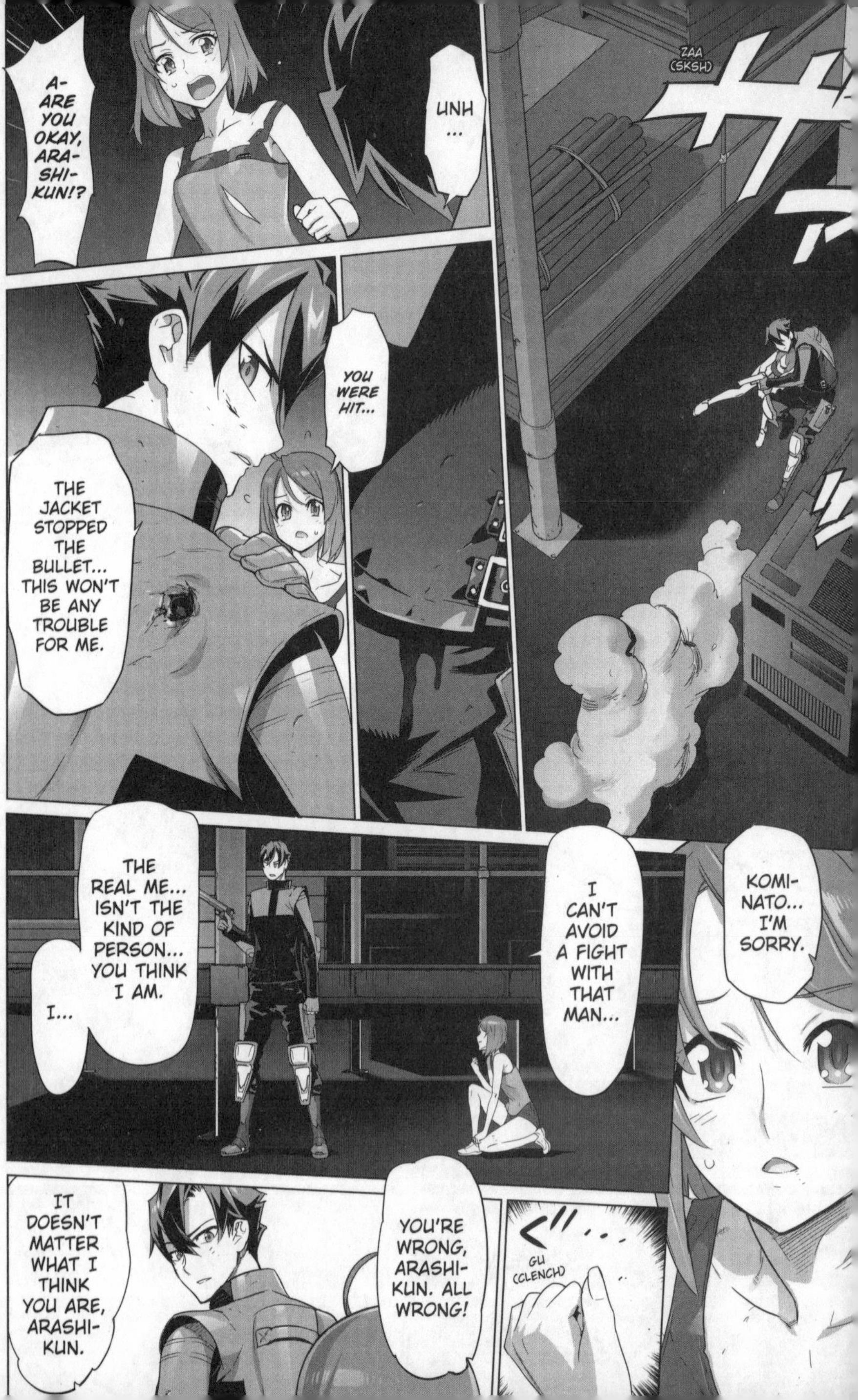
ZAA
(SKSH)
UNH...
A-ARE YOU OKAY, ARASHI-KUN!?
YOU WERE HIT...
THE JACKET STOPPED THE BULLET... THIS WON'T BE ANY TROUBLE FOR ME.
KOMINATO... I'M SORRY.
I CAN'T AVOID A FIGHT WITH THAT MAN...
THE REAL ME... ISN'T THE KIND OF PERSON... YOU THINK I AM.
I...
GU
(CLENCH)
YOU'RE WRONG, ARASHI-KUN. ALL WRONG!
IT DOESN'T MATTER WHAT I THINK YOU ARE, ARASHI-KUN.

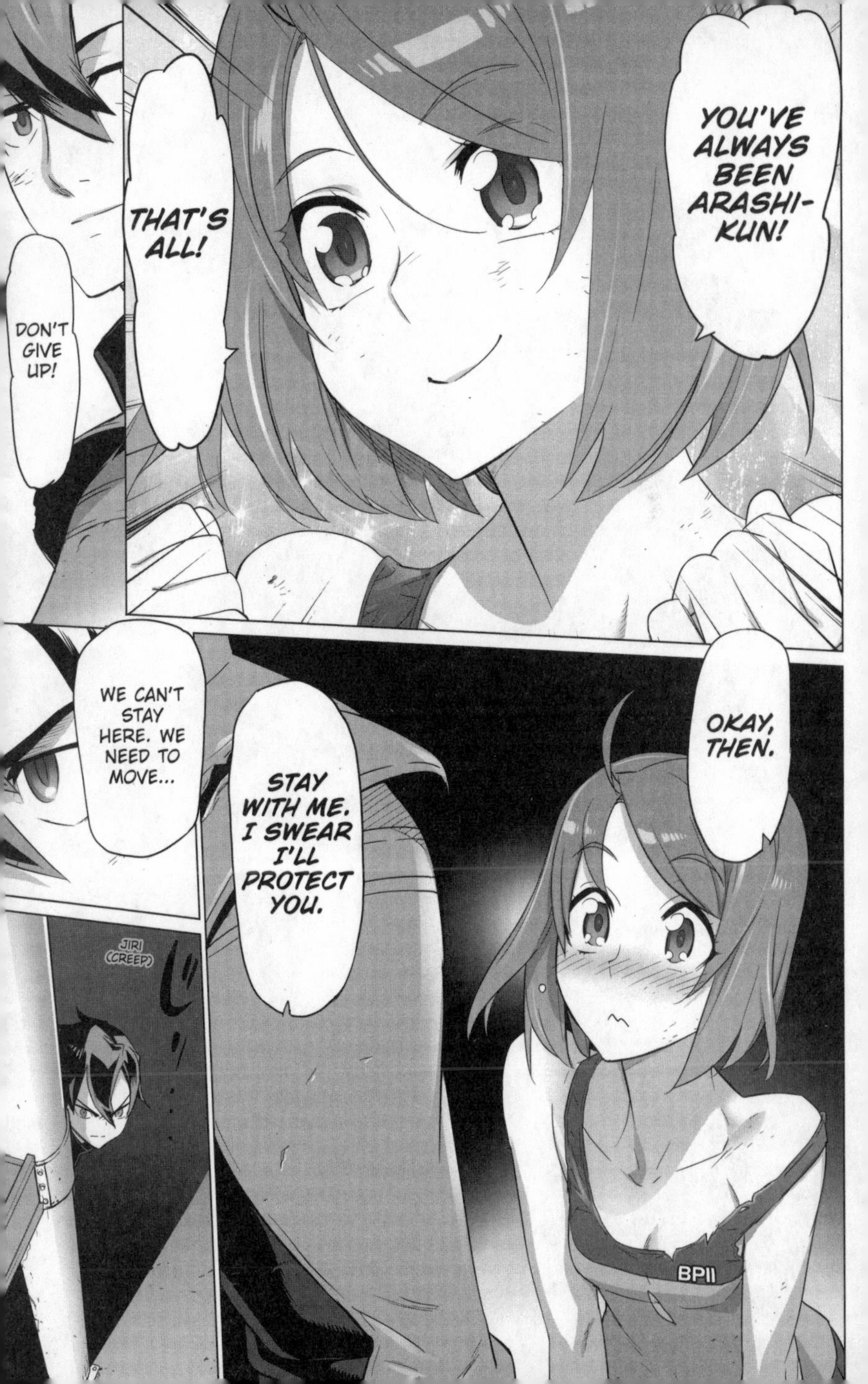
YOU'VE ALWAYS BEEN ARASHI-KUN!
THAT'S ALL!
DON'T GIVE UP!
OKAY, THEN.
STAY WITH ME. I SWEAR I'LL PROTECT YOU.
WE CAN'T STAY HERE. WE NEED TO MOVE...
JIRI (CREEP)
BPII

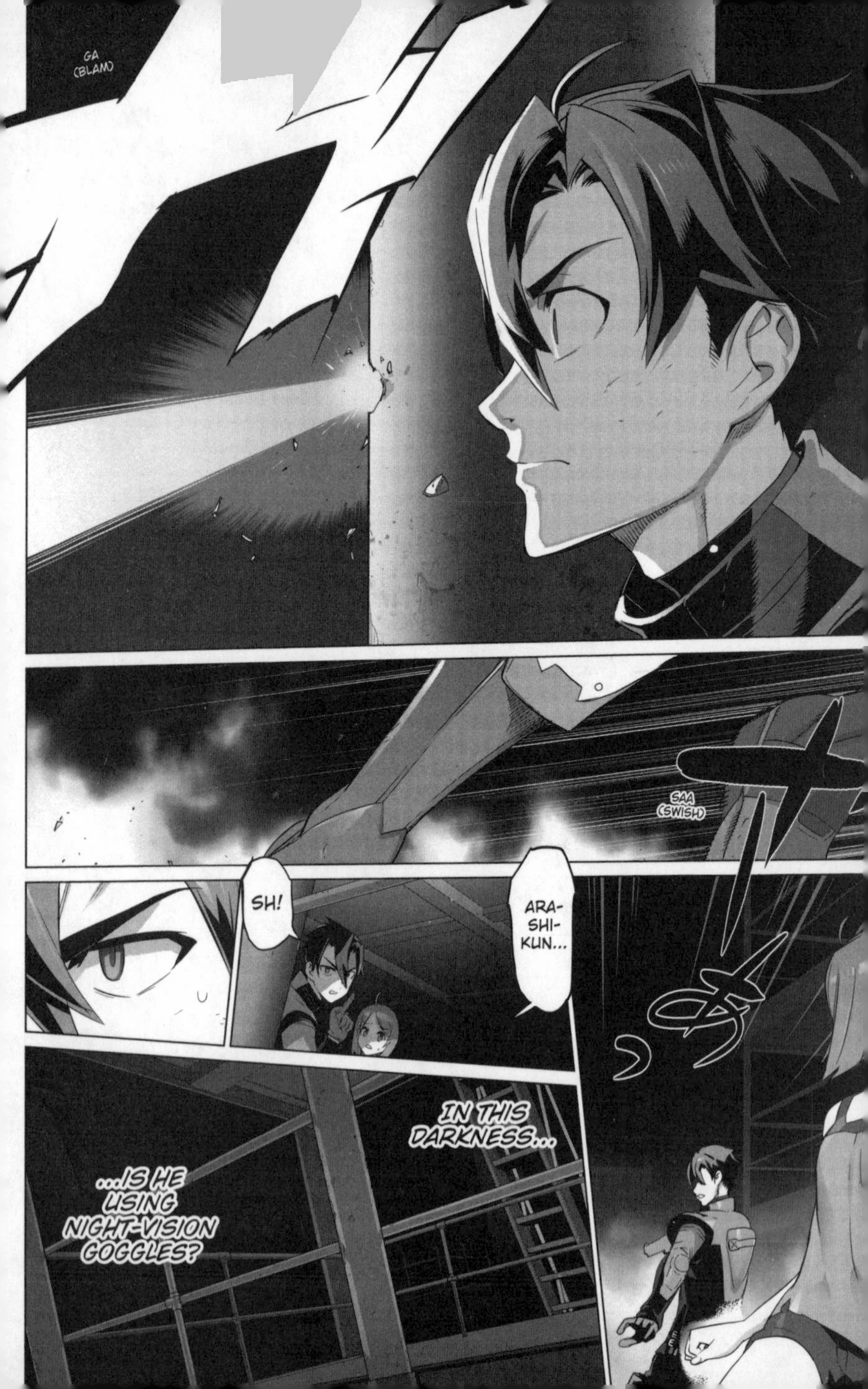
GA
(BLAM)
SAA
(SWISH)
ARA-SHI-KUN...
SH!
IN THIS DARKNESS...
...IS HE USING NIGHT-VISION GOGGLES?

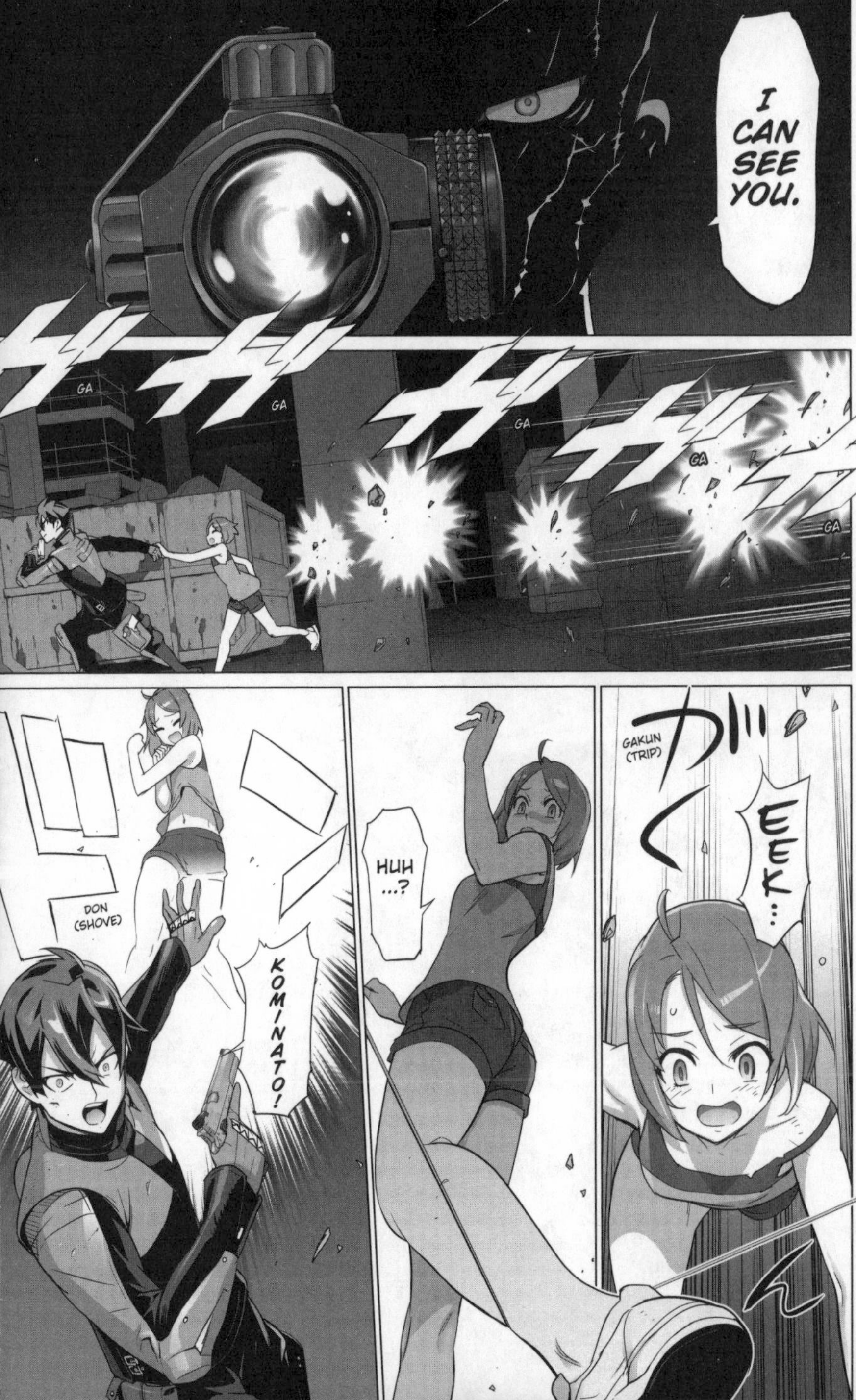
I CAN SEE YOU.
GA
GA
GA
GA
GA
GAKUN (TRIP)
EEK...
HUH ...?
KOMINATO!
DON (SHOVE)

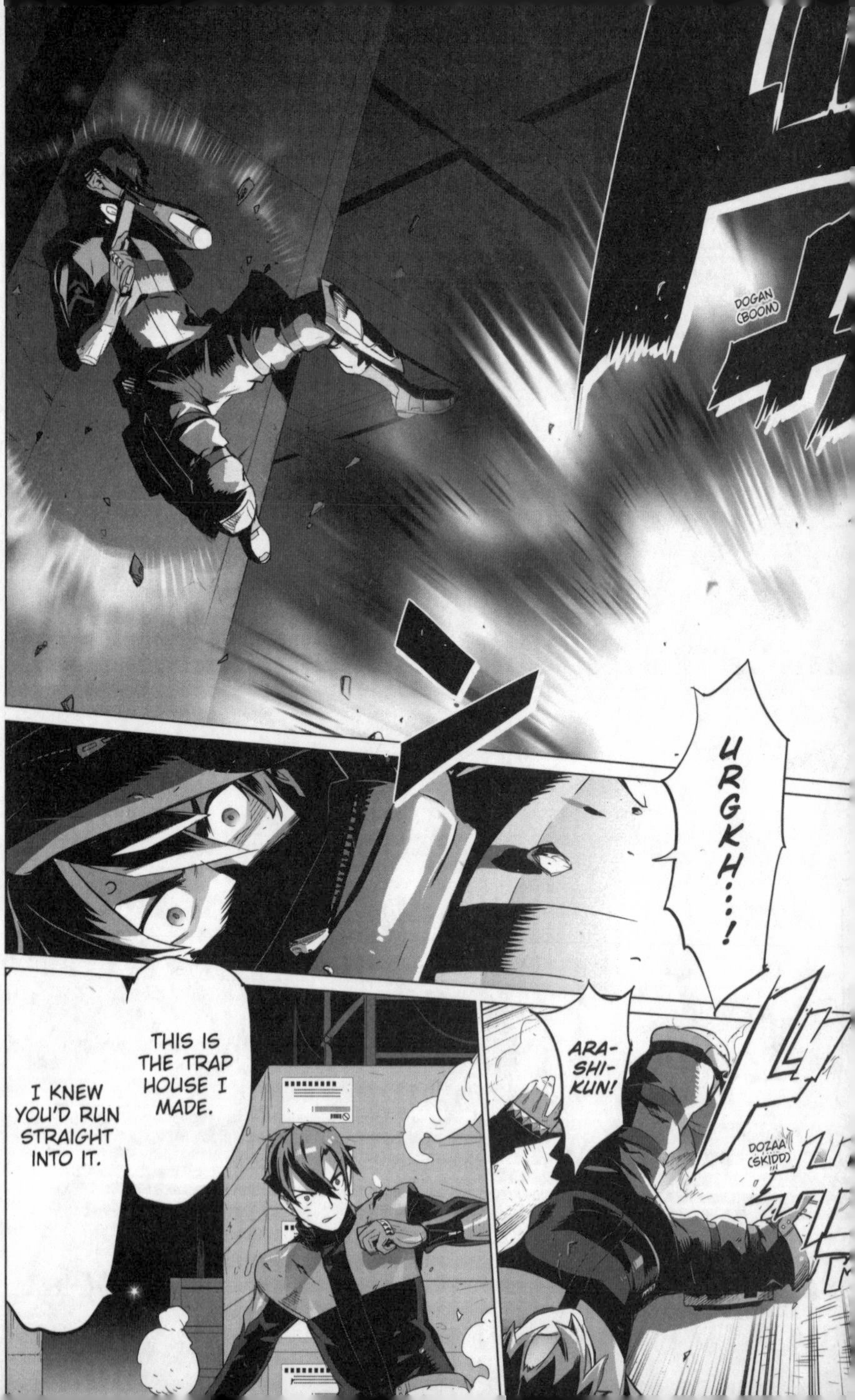
DOGAN (BOOM)
URGKH...!
ARA-SHI-KUN!
DOZAA (SKIDD)
THIS IS THE TRAP HOUSE I MADE.
I KNEW YOU'D RUN STRAIGHT INTO IT.

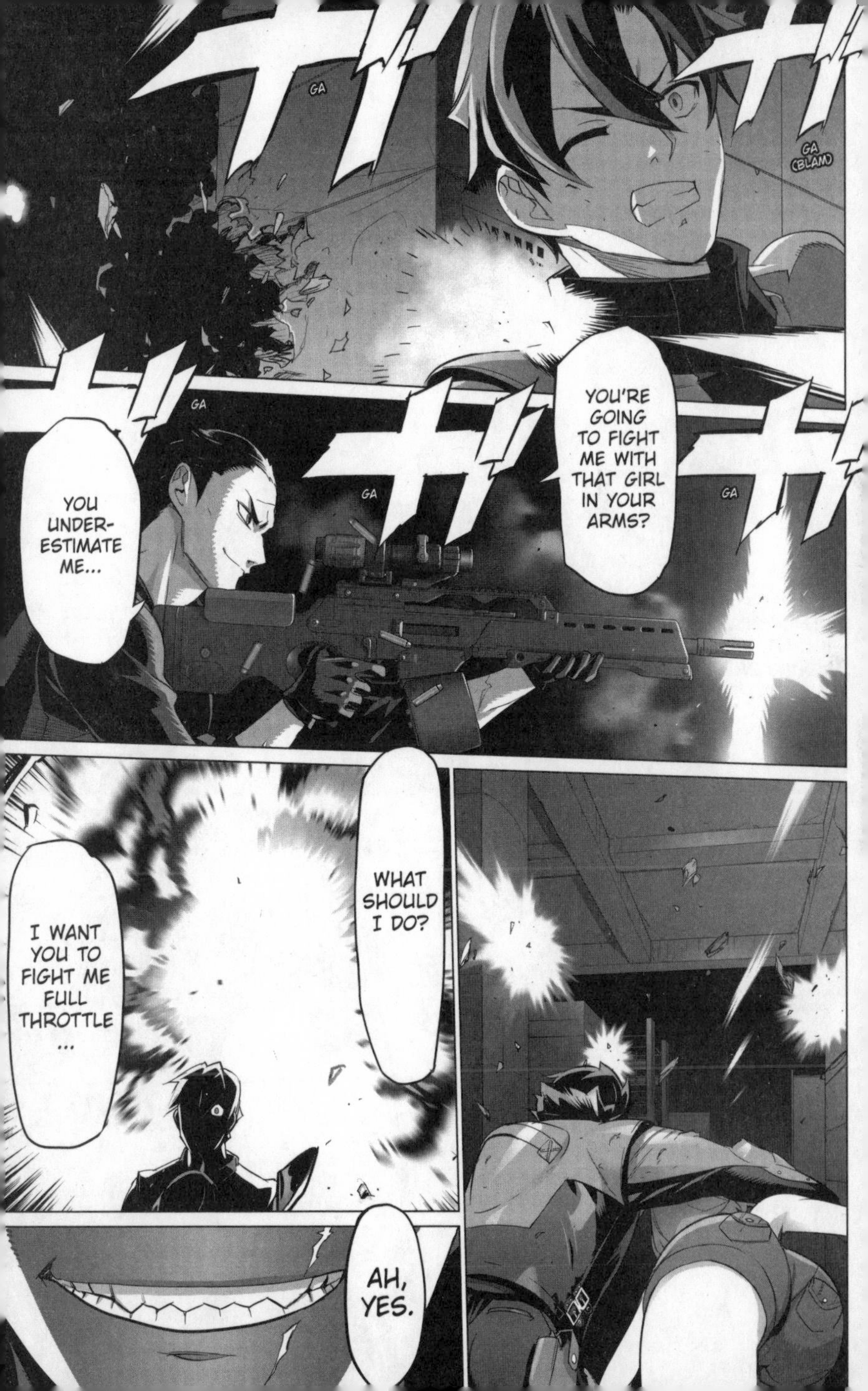
GA (BLAM)
GA
GA
YOU'RE GOING TO FIGHT ME WITH THAT GIRL IN YOUR ARMS?
GA
GA
YOU UNDER-ESTIMATE ME...
WHAT SHOULD I DO?
I WANT YOU TO FIGHT ME FULL THROTTLE ...
AH, YES.

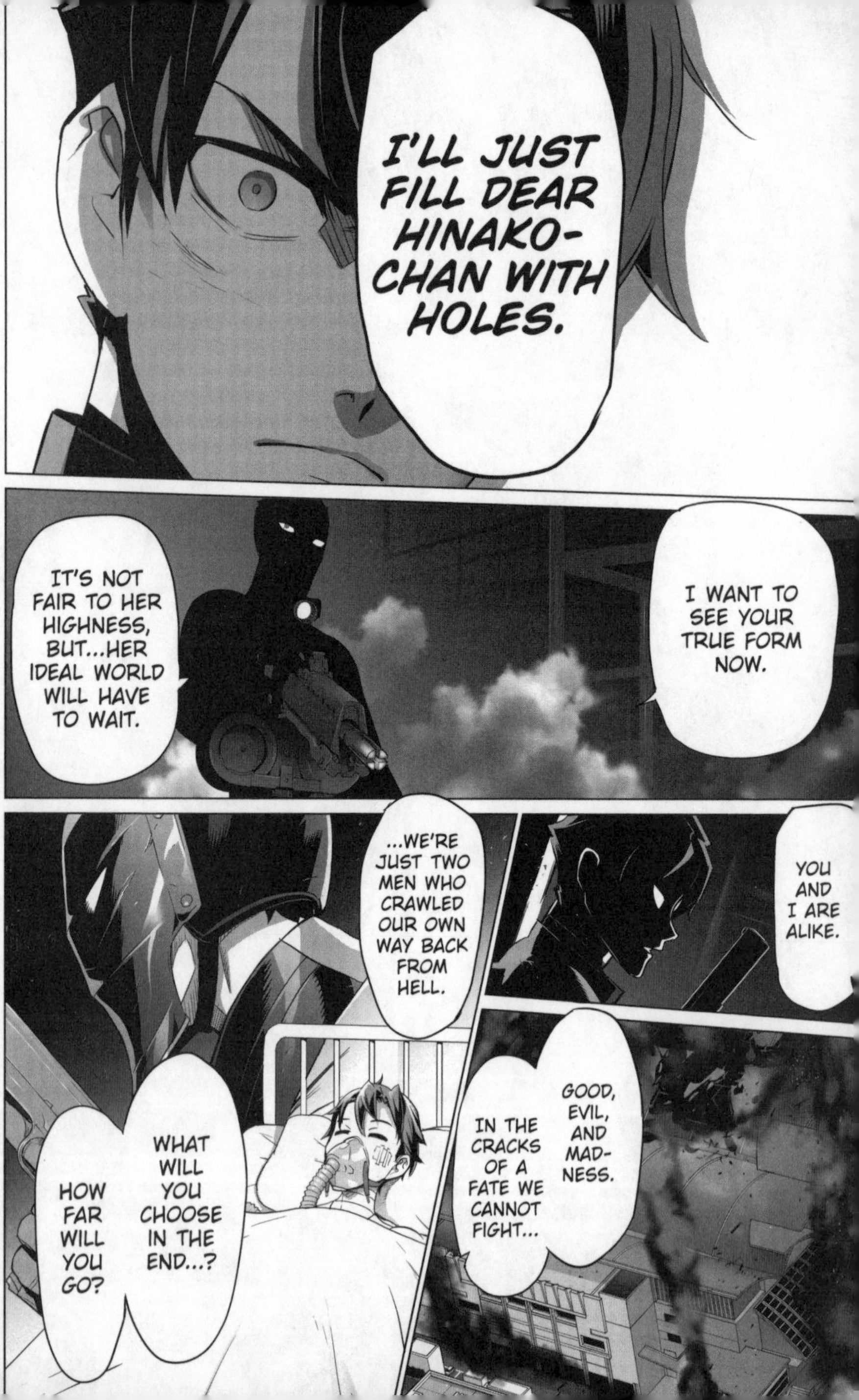
I'LL JUST FILL DEAR HINAKO-CHAN WITH HOLES.
I WANT TO SEE YOUR TRUE FORM NOW.
IT'S NOT FAIR TO HER HIGHNESS, BUT...HER IDEAL WORLD WILL HAVE TO WAIT.
YOU AND I ARE ALIKE.
...WE'RE JUST TWO MEN WHO CRAWLED OUR OWN WAY BACK FROM HELL.
GOOD, EVIL, AND MADNESS.
IN THE CRACKS OF A FATE WE CANNOT FIGHT...
WHAT WILL YOU CHOOSE IN THE END...?
HOW FAR WILL YOU GO?

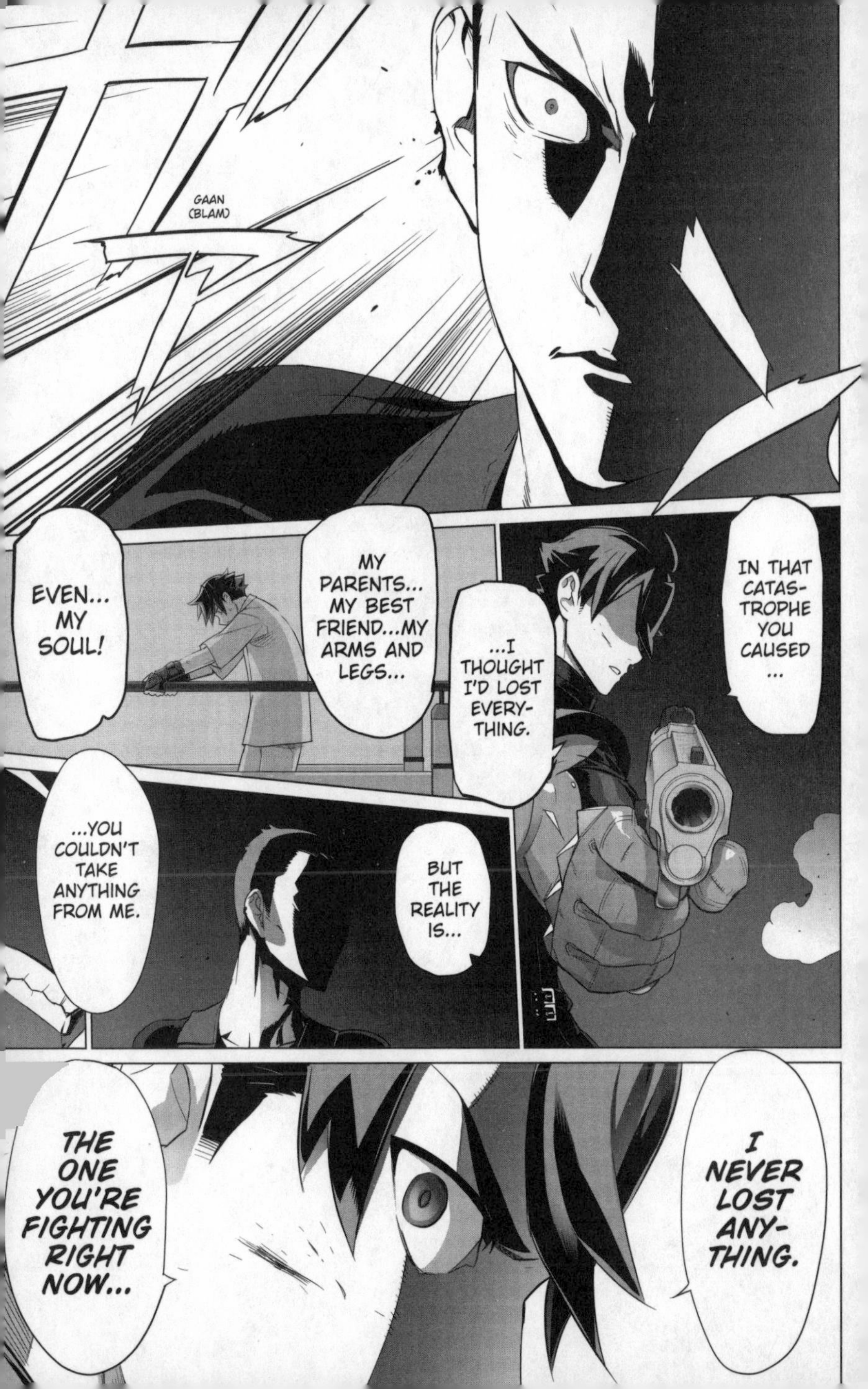
GAAN (BLAM)
IN THAT CATASTROPHE YOU CAUSED...
...I THOUGHT I'D LOST EVERYTHING.
MY PARENTS... MY BEST FRIEND...MY ARMS AND LEGS...
EVEN... MY SOUL!
BUT THE REALITY IS...
...YOU COULDN'T TAKE ANYTHING FROM ME.
I NEVER LOST ANYTHING.
THE ONE YOU'RE FIGHTING RIGHT NOW...

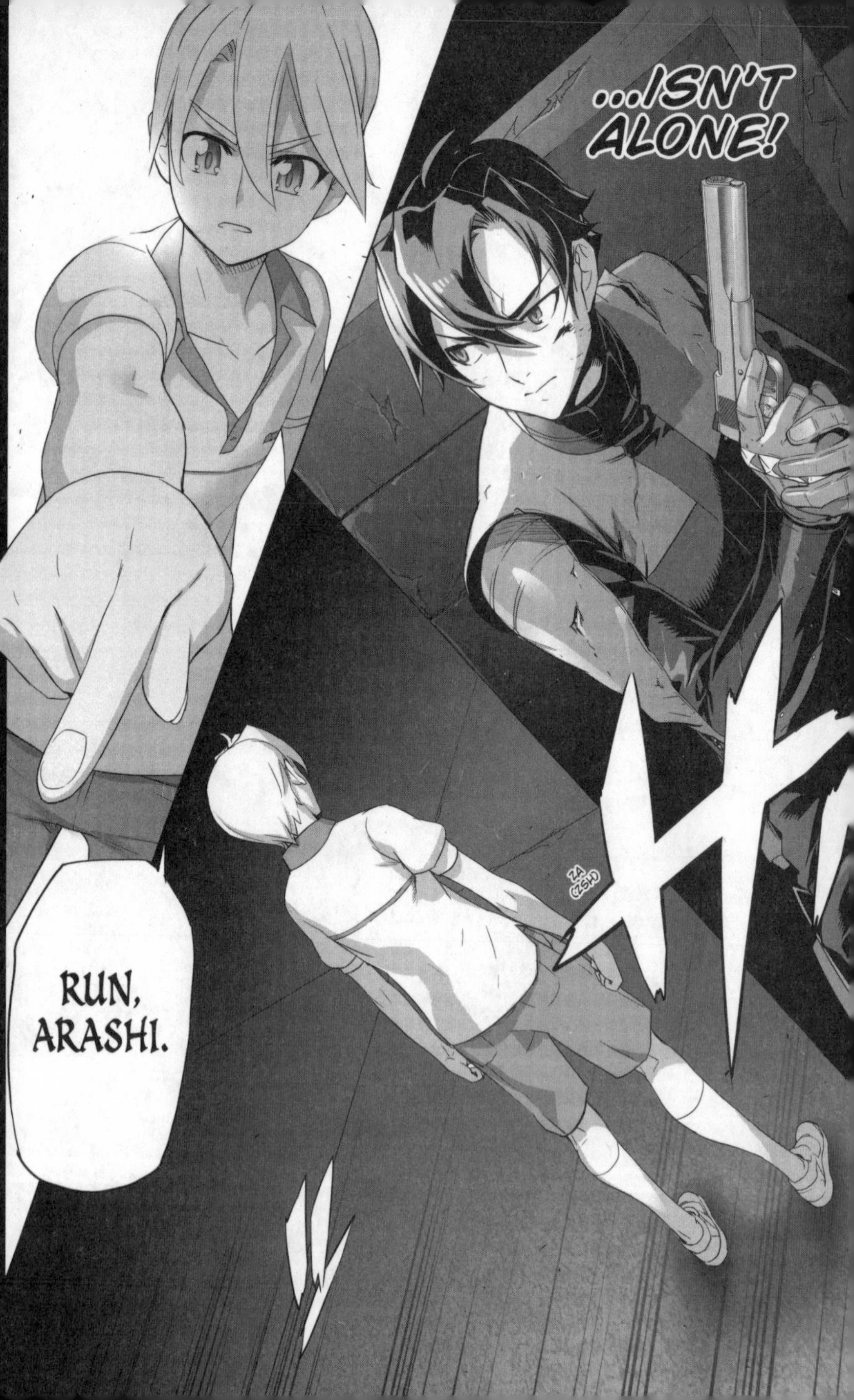
...ISN'T ALONE!
ZA (ZSH)
RUN, ARASHI.

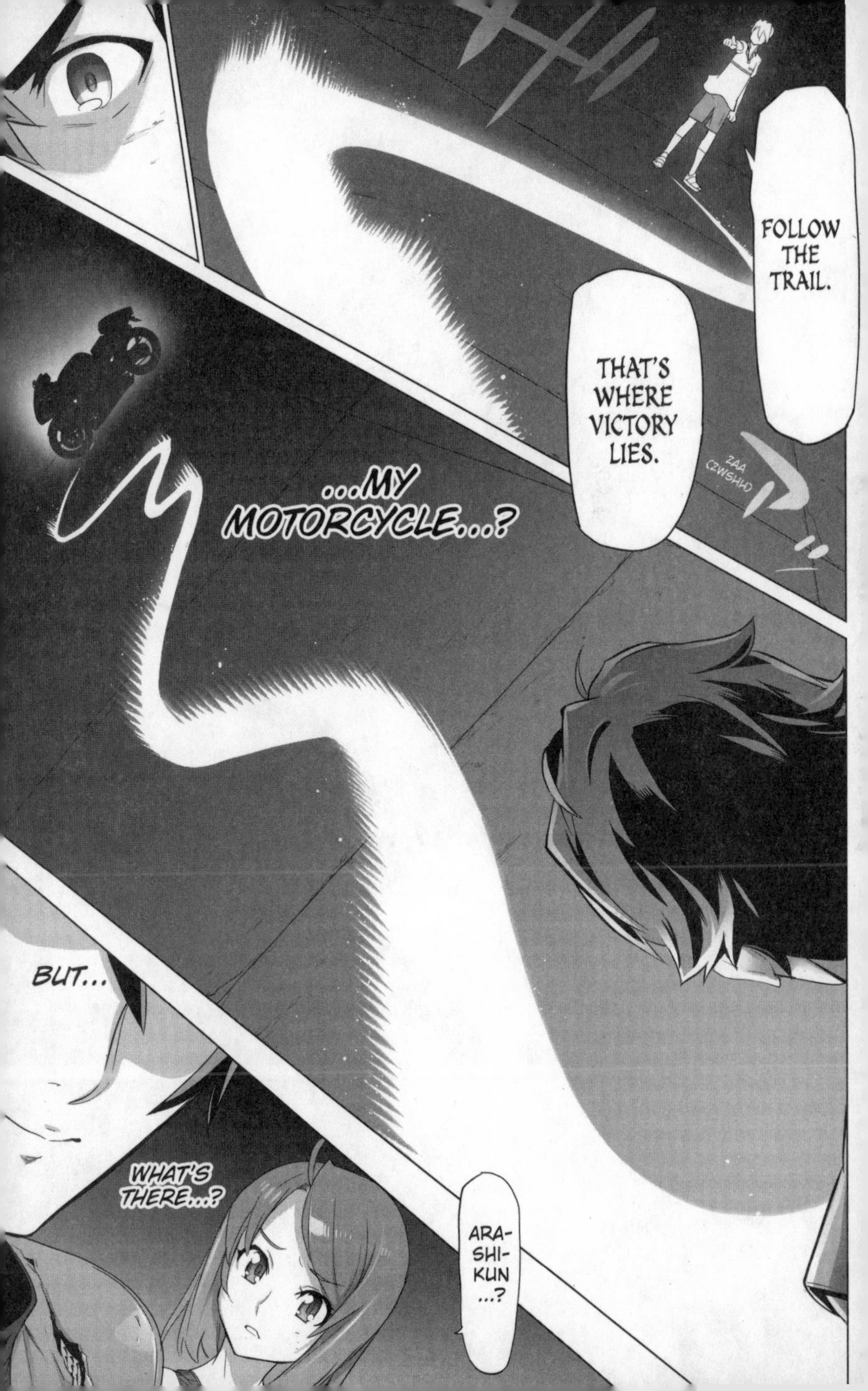
FOLLOW THE TRAIL.
THAT'S WHERE VICTORY LIES.
ZAA (ZWSHH)
...MY MOTORCYCLE...?
ARA-SHI-KUN...?
WHAT'S THERE...?
BUT...

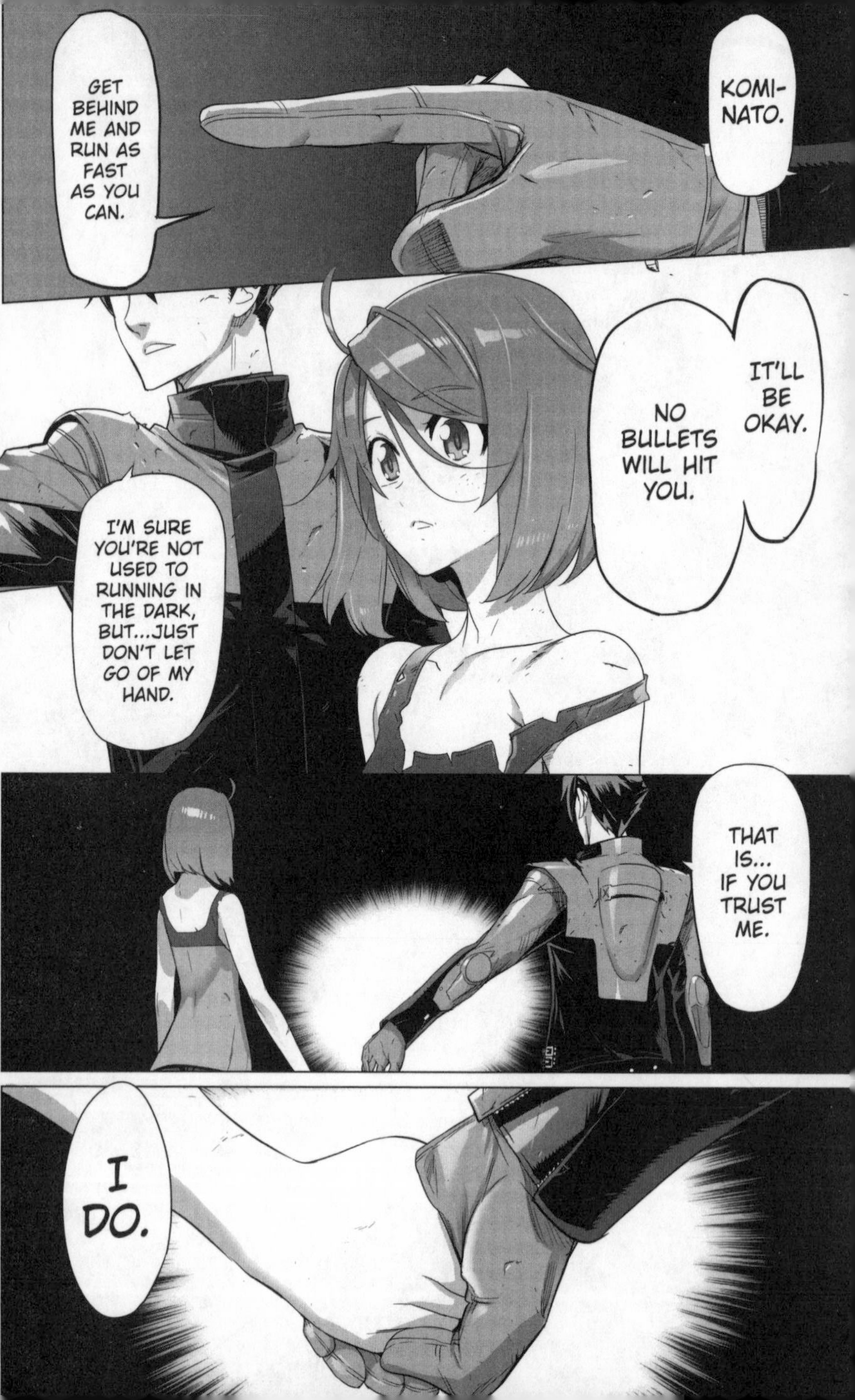
KOMI-NATO.
GET BEHIND ME AND RUN AS FAST AS YOU CAN.
IT'LL BE OKAY.
NO BULLETS WILL HIT YOU.
I'M SURE YOU'RE NOT USED TO RUNNING IN THE DARK, BUT...JUST DON'T LET GO OF MY HAND.
THAT IS... IF YOU TRUST ME.
I DO.

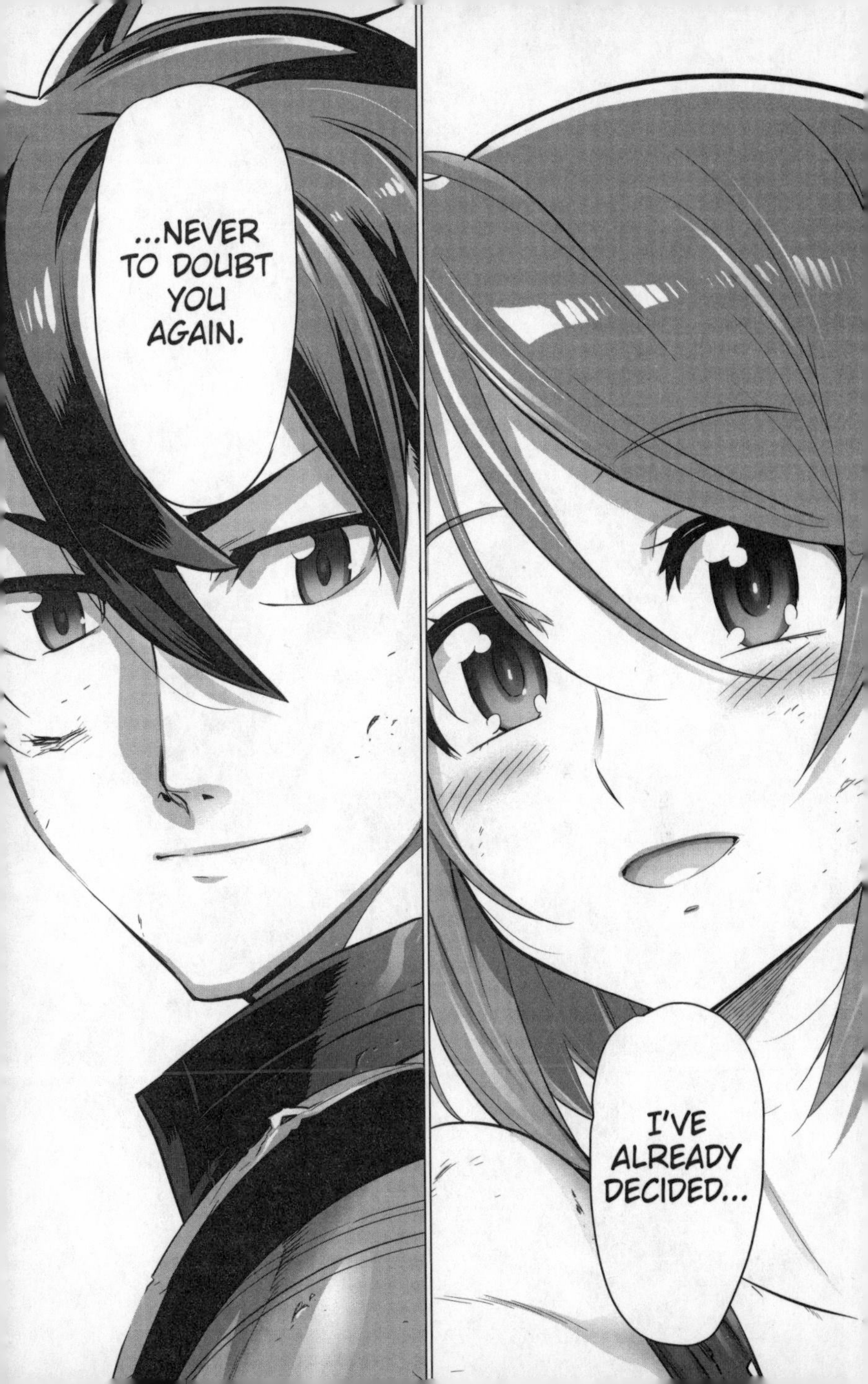
I'VE ALREADY DECIDED...
...NEVER TO DOUBT YOU AGAIN.

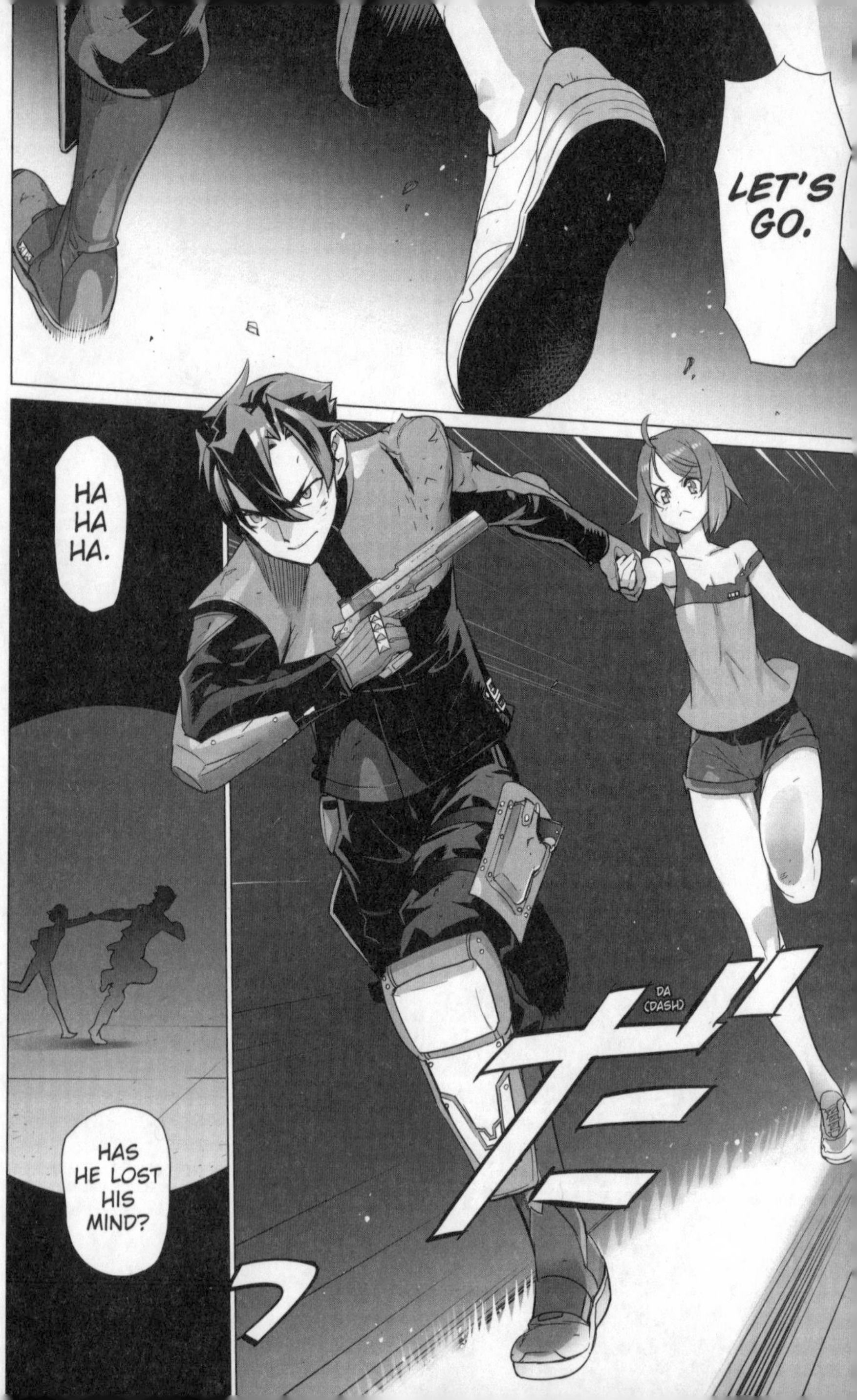
LET'S GO.
HA HA HA.
DA (DASH)
HAS HE LOST HIS MIND?

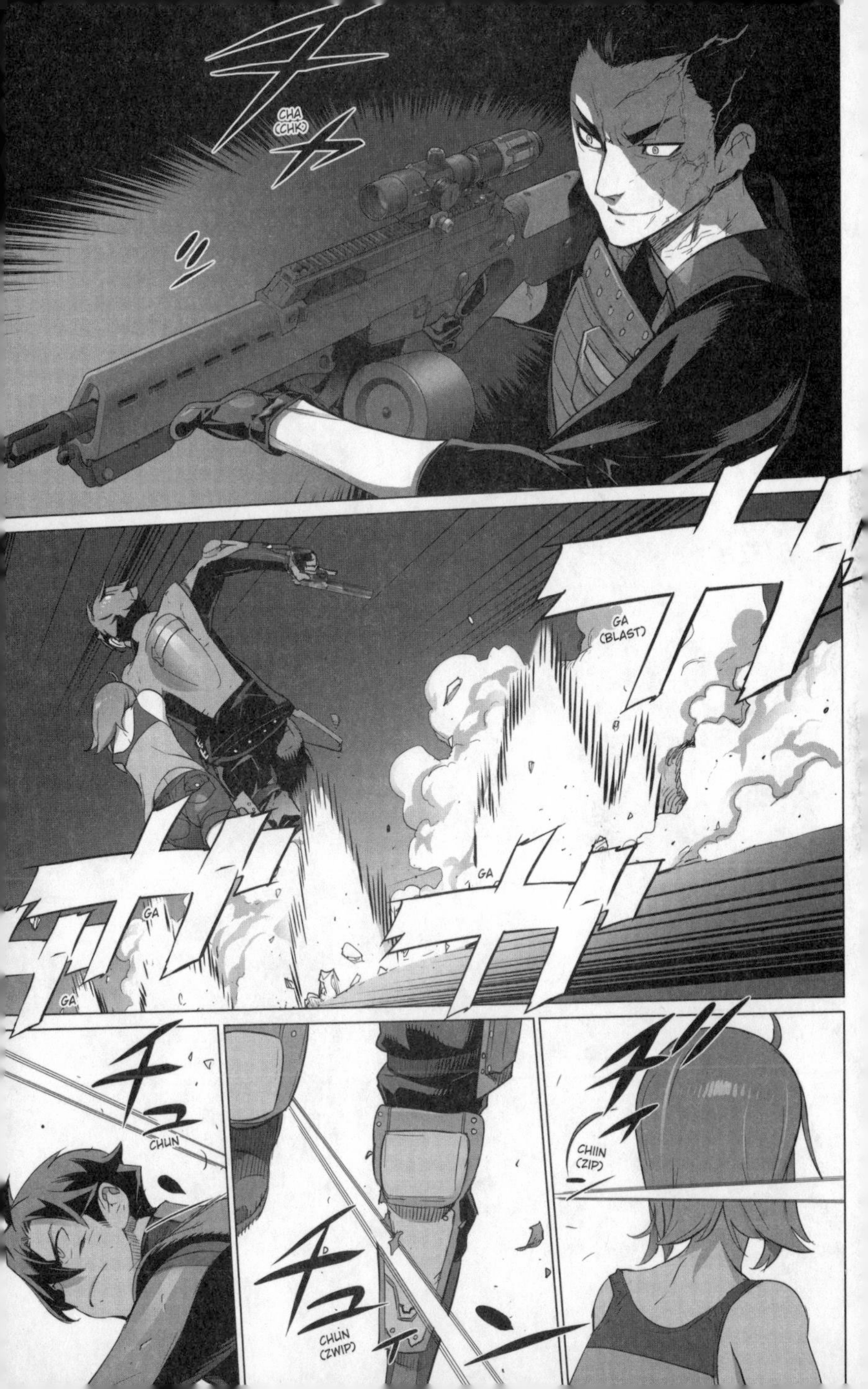
CHA (CHK)
GA (BLAST)
GA
GA
GA
CHIIN (ZIP)
CHUN
CHUN (ZWIP)

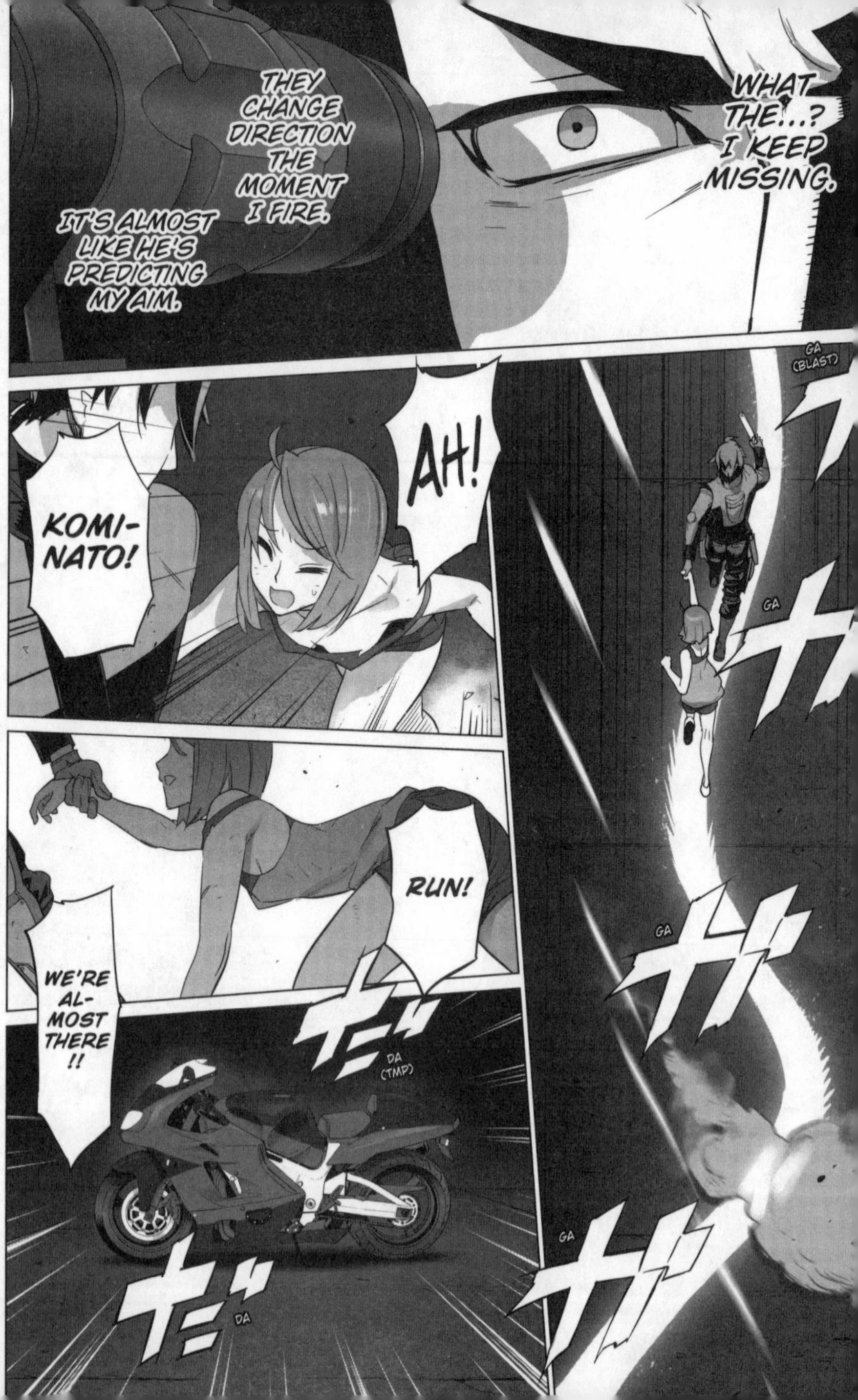
WHAT THE...? I KEEP MISSING.
THEY CHANGE DIRECTION THE MOMENT I FIRE.
IT'S ALMOST LIKE HE'S PREDICTING MY AIM.
GA (BLAST)
GA
GA
GA
AH!
KOMI-NATO!
RUN!
WE'RE AL-MOST THERE !!
DA (TMP)
DA

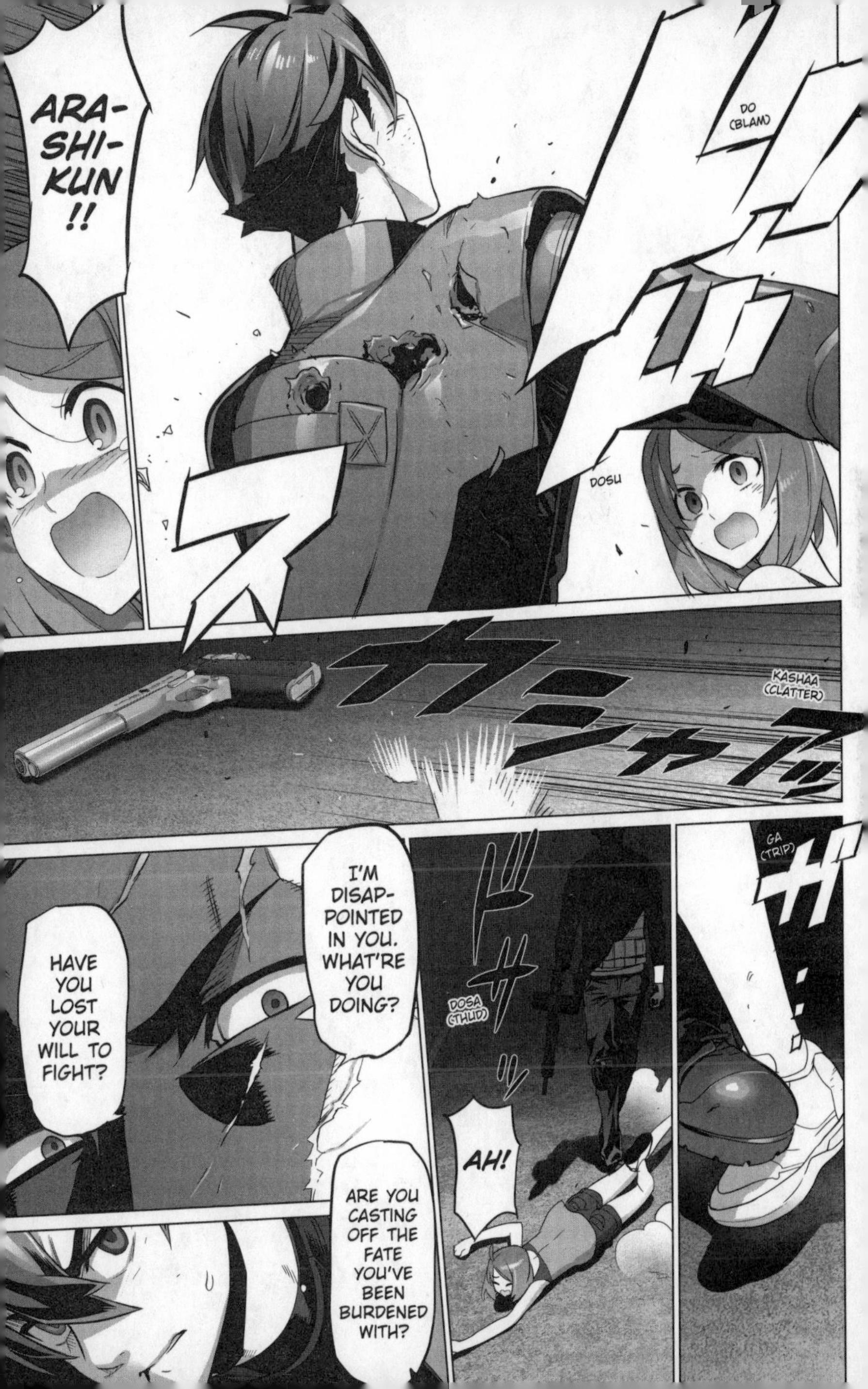
DO (BLAM)
DOSU
ARA-SHI-KUN!!
KASHAA (CLATTER)
GA (TRIP)
DOSA (THUD)
AH!
I'M DISAP-POINTED IN YOU. WHAT'RE YOU DOING?
HAVE YOU LOST YOUR WILL TO FIGHT?
ARE YOU CASTING OFF THE FATE YOU'VE BEEN BURDENED WITH?

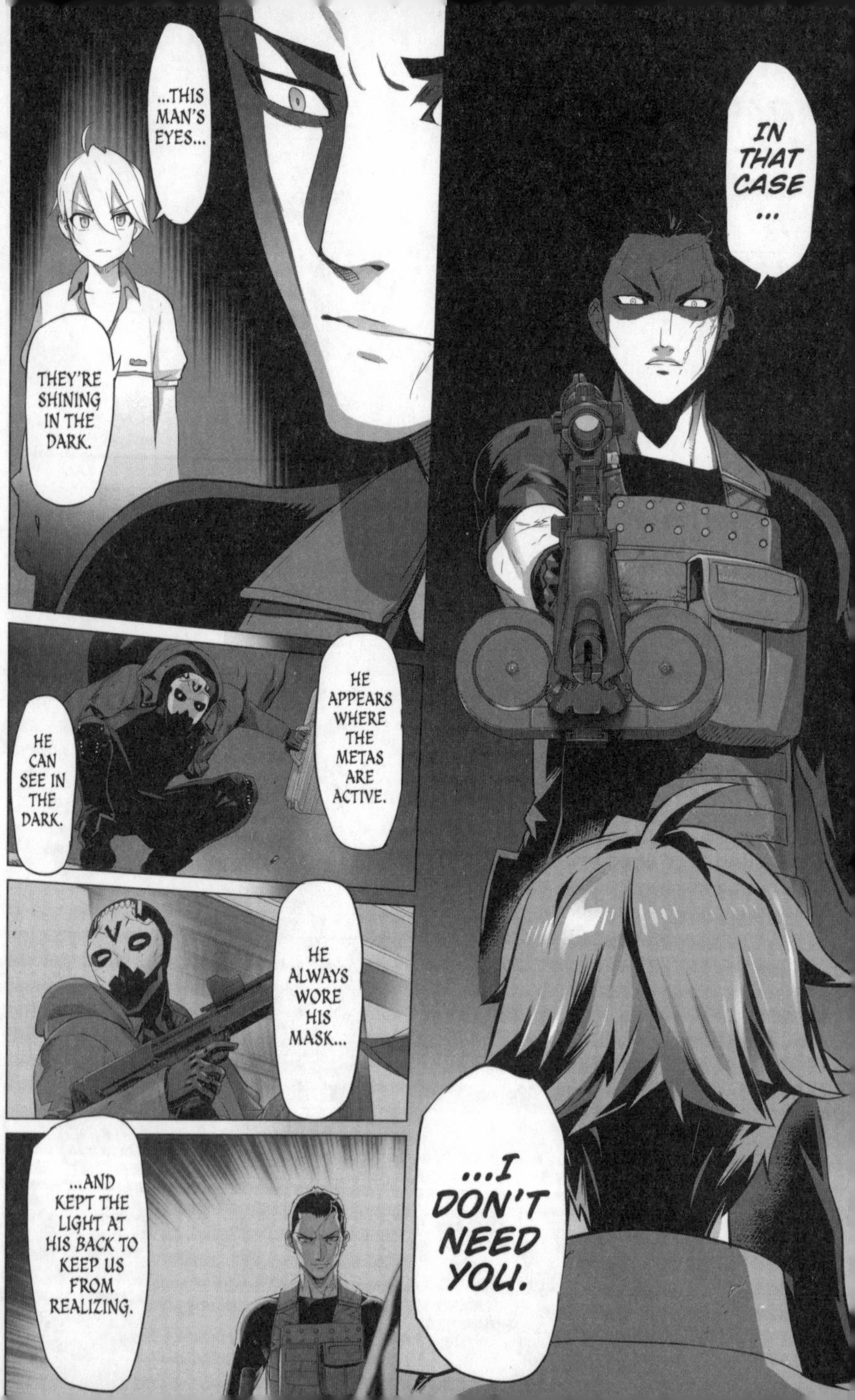
IN THAT CASE...
...I DON'T NEED YOU.
...THIS MAN'S EYES...
THEY'RE SHINING IN THE DARK.
HE APPEARS WHERE THE METAS ARE ACTIVE.
HE CAN SEE IN THE DARK.
HE ALWAYS WORE HIS MASK...
...AND KEPT THE LIGHT AT HIS BACK TO KEEP US FROM REALIZING.

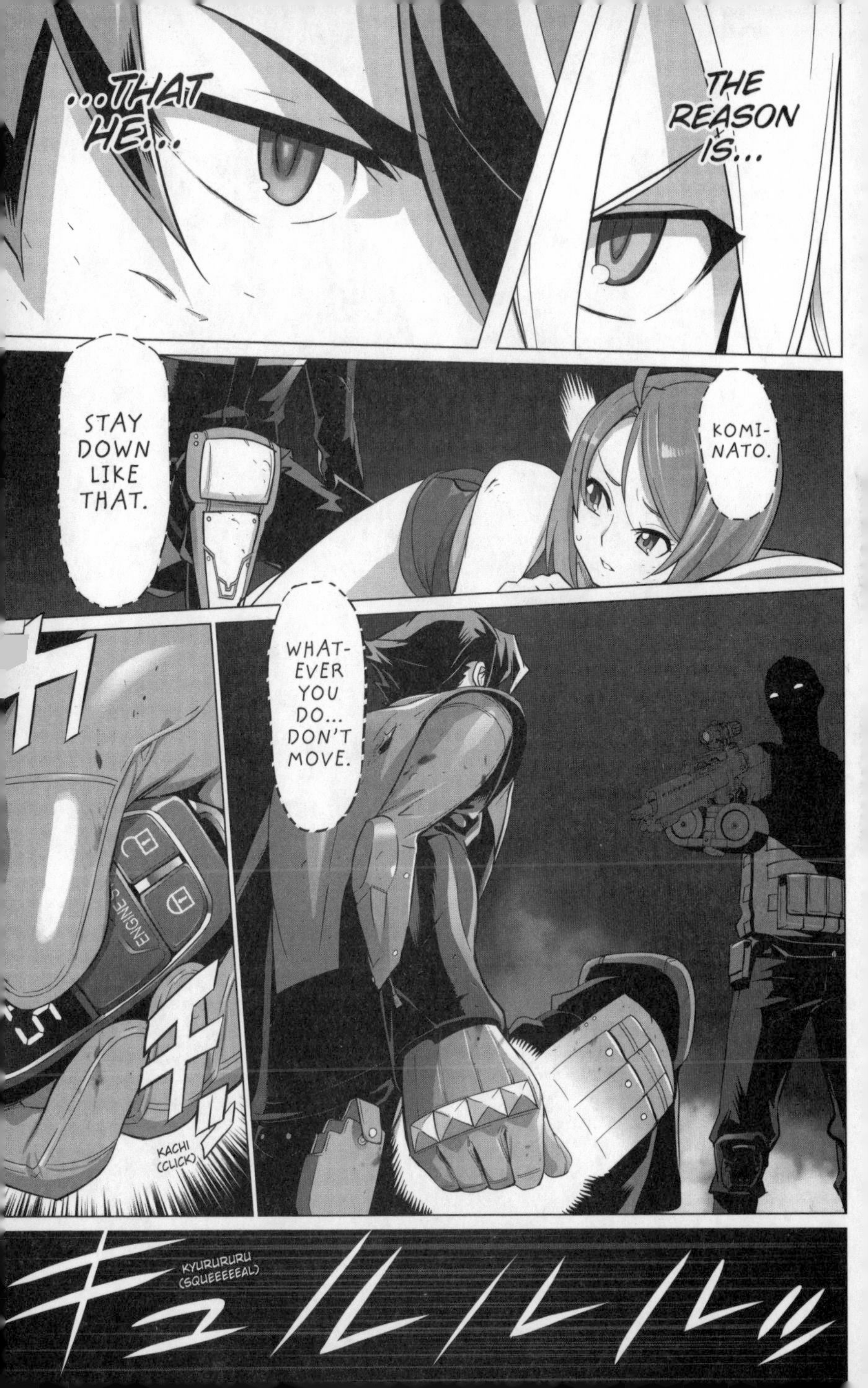
THE REASON IS...
...THAT HE...
KOMI-NATO.
STAY DOWN LIKE THAT.
WHAT-EVER YOU DO... DON'T MOVE.
ENGINE S
KACHI (CLICK)
KYURURURU (SQUEEEEEAL)

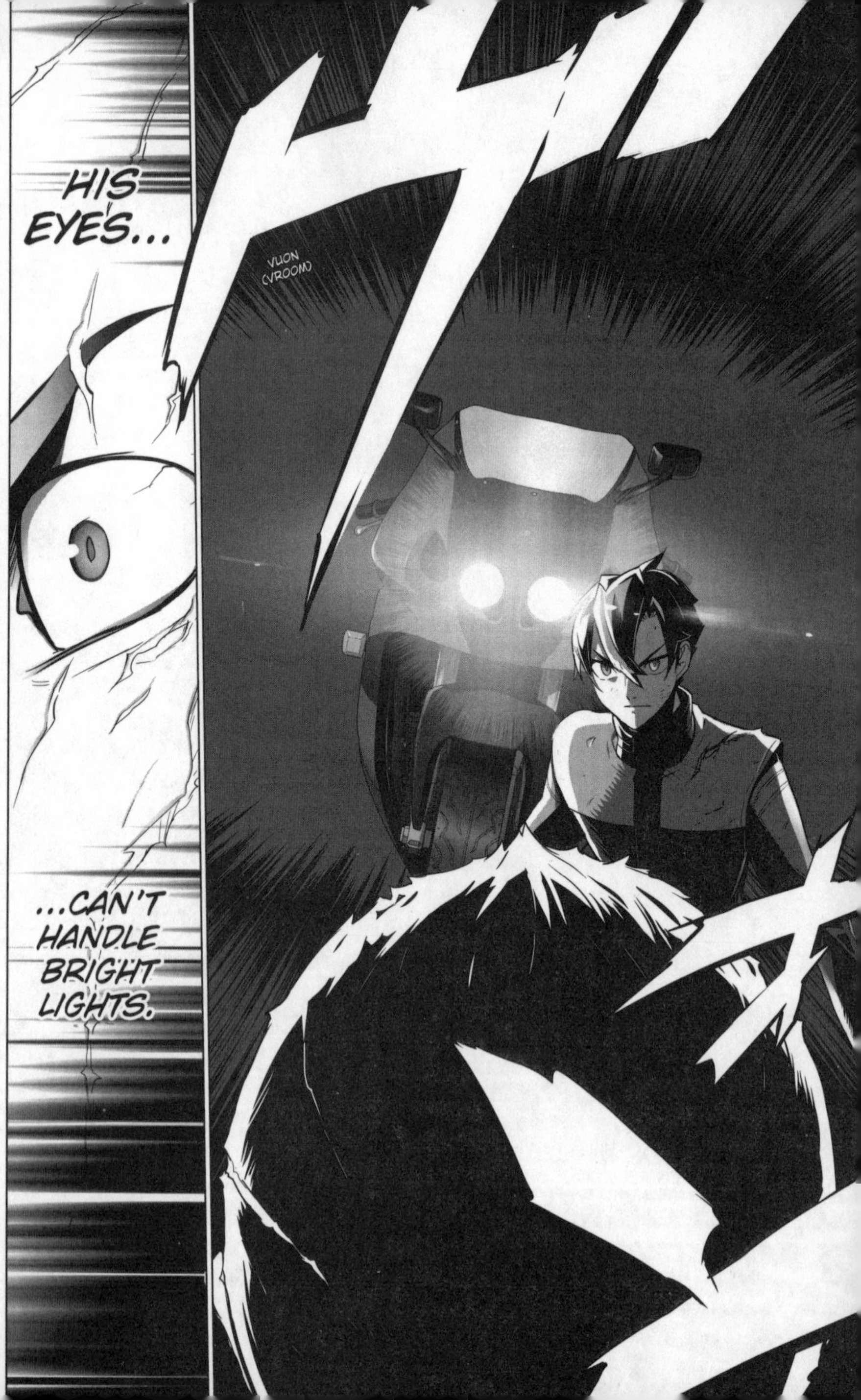
VUON
(VROOM)
HIS EYES...
...CAN'T HANDLE BRIGHT LIGHTS.

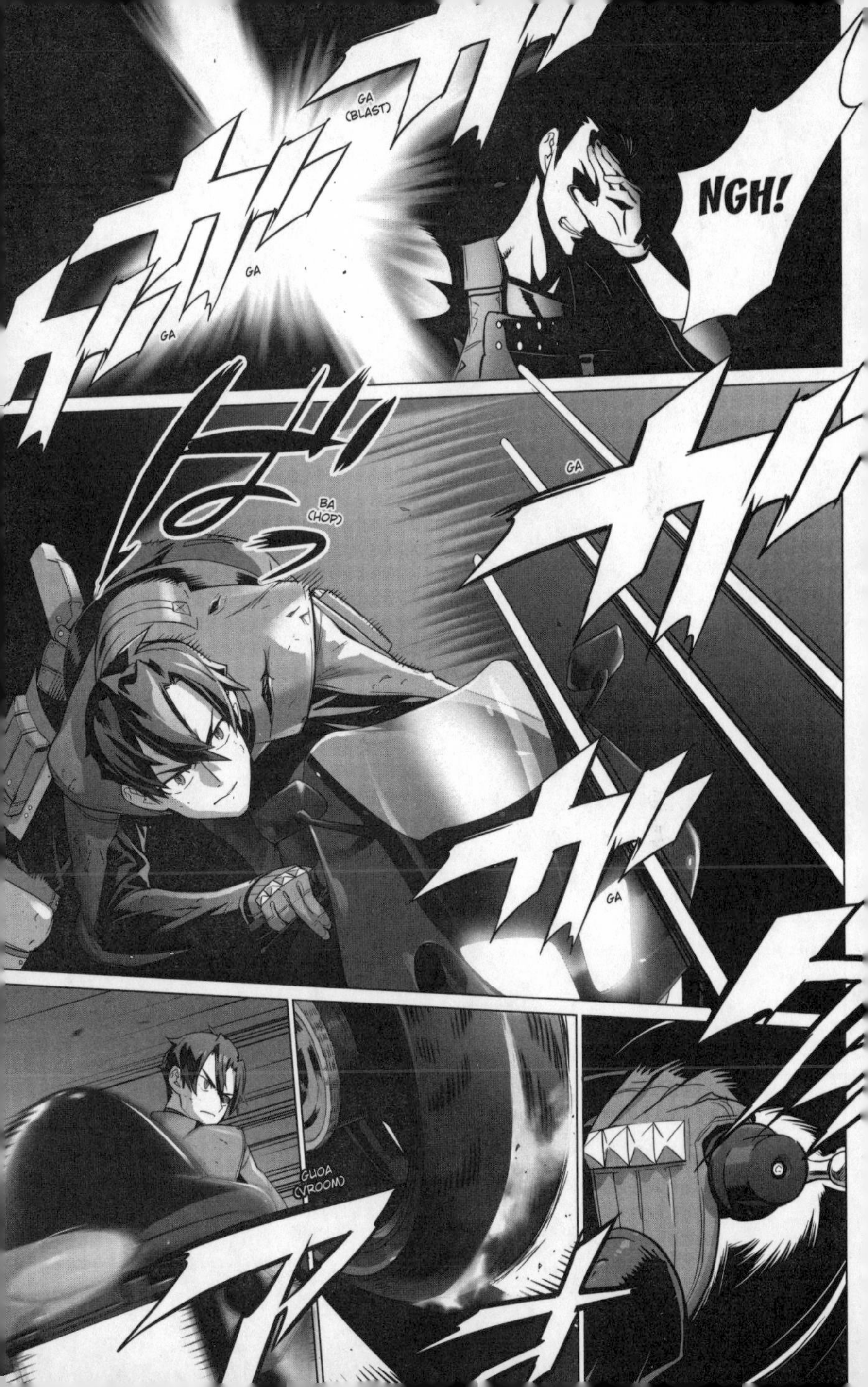
NGH!
GA
(BLAST)
GA
GA
GA
BA
(HOP)
GA
GUOA
(VROOM)

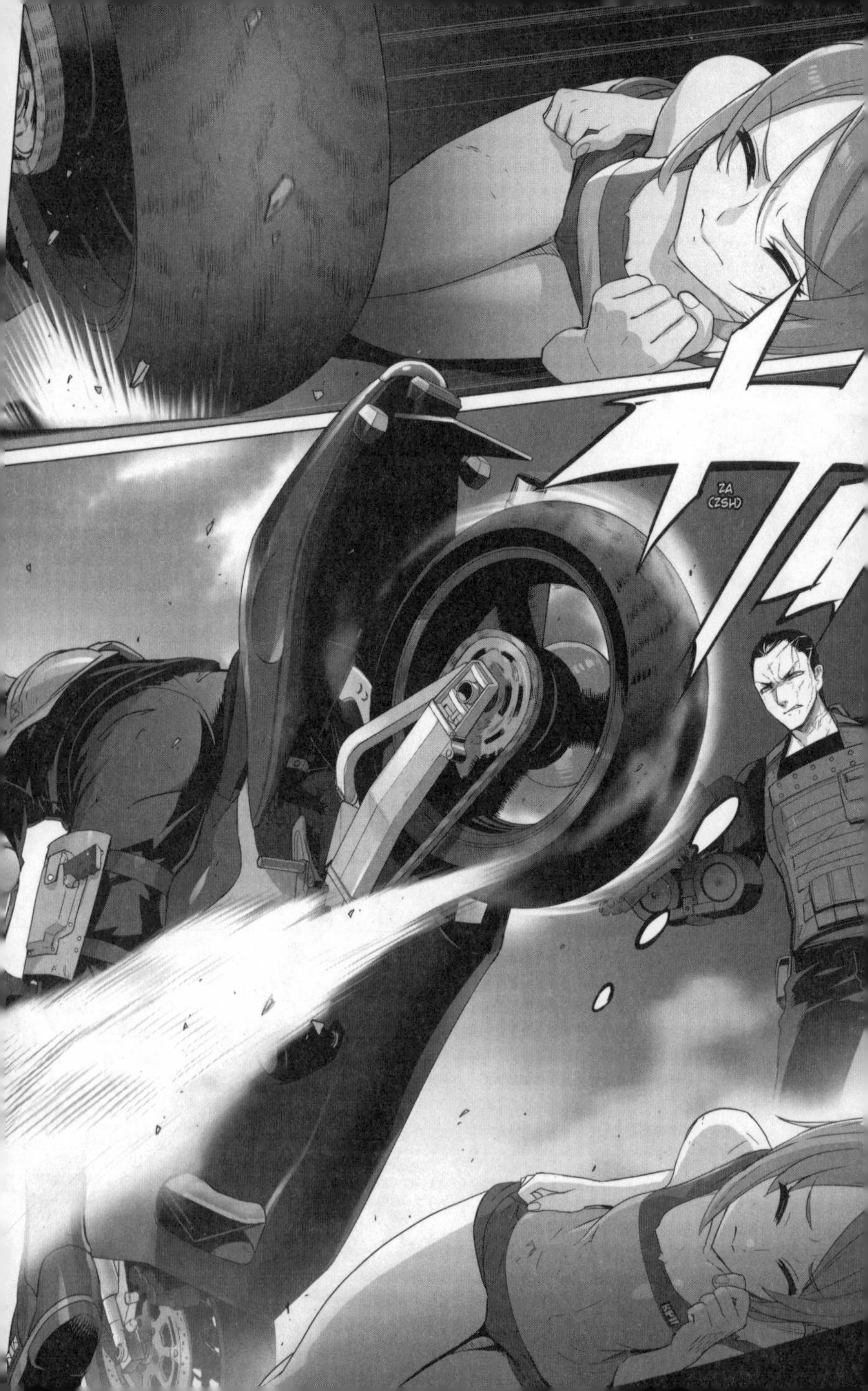
ZA
(ZSH)

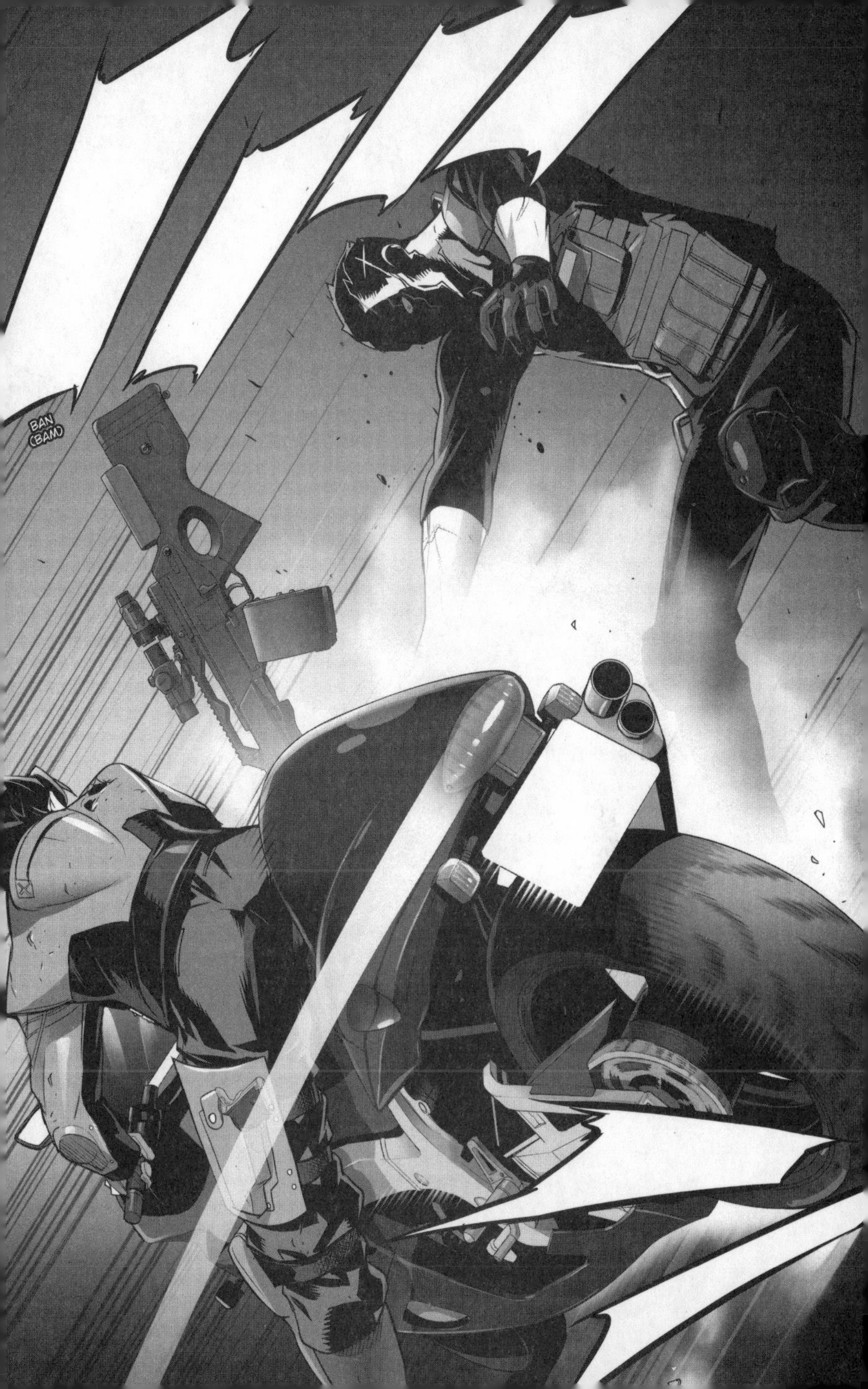
BAN
(BAM)

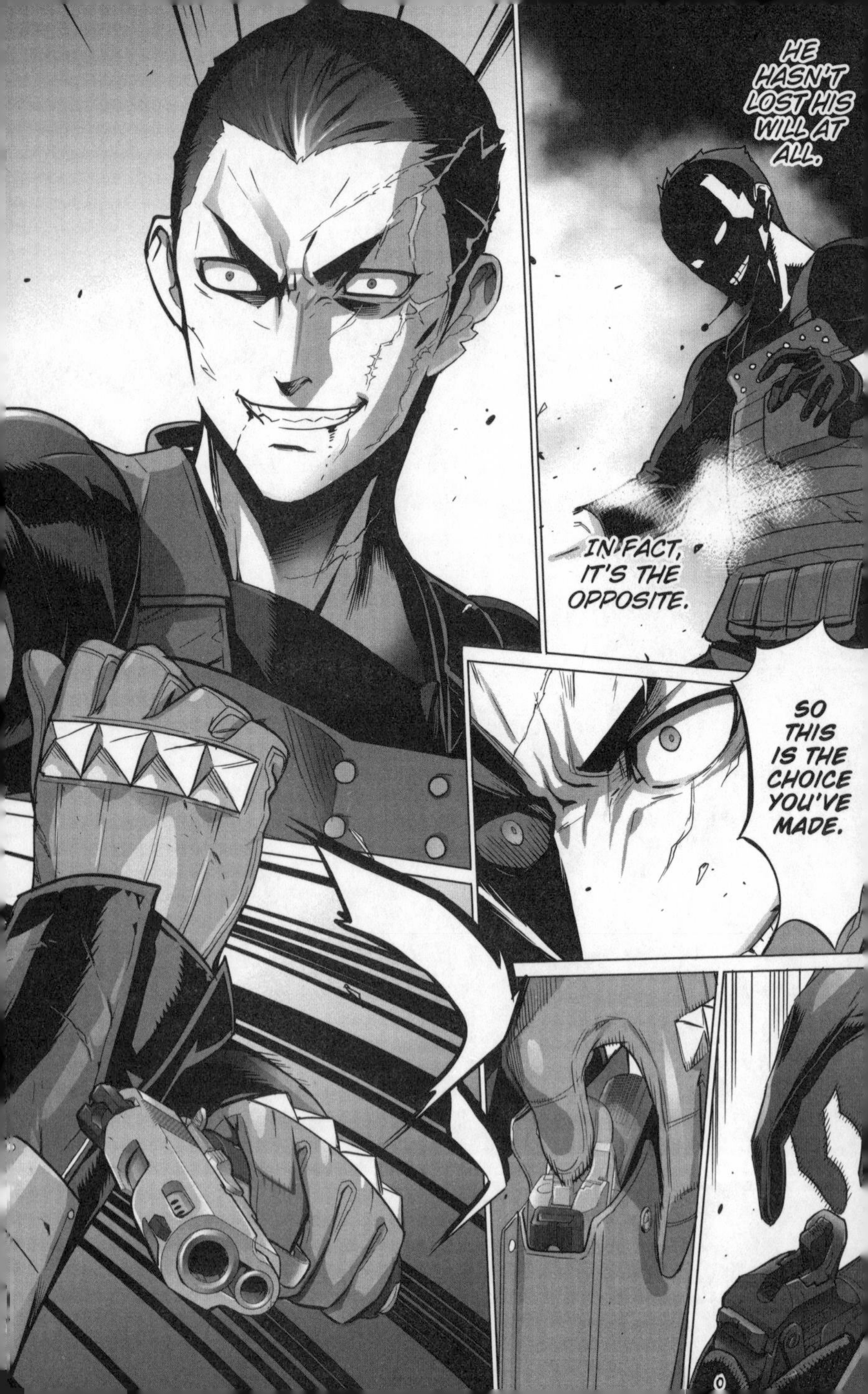
HE HASN'T LOST HIS WILL AT ALL.
IN FACT, IT'S THE OPPOSITE.
SO THIS IS THE CHOICE YOU'VE MADE.

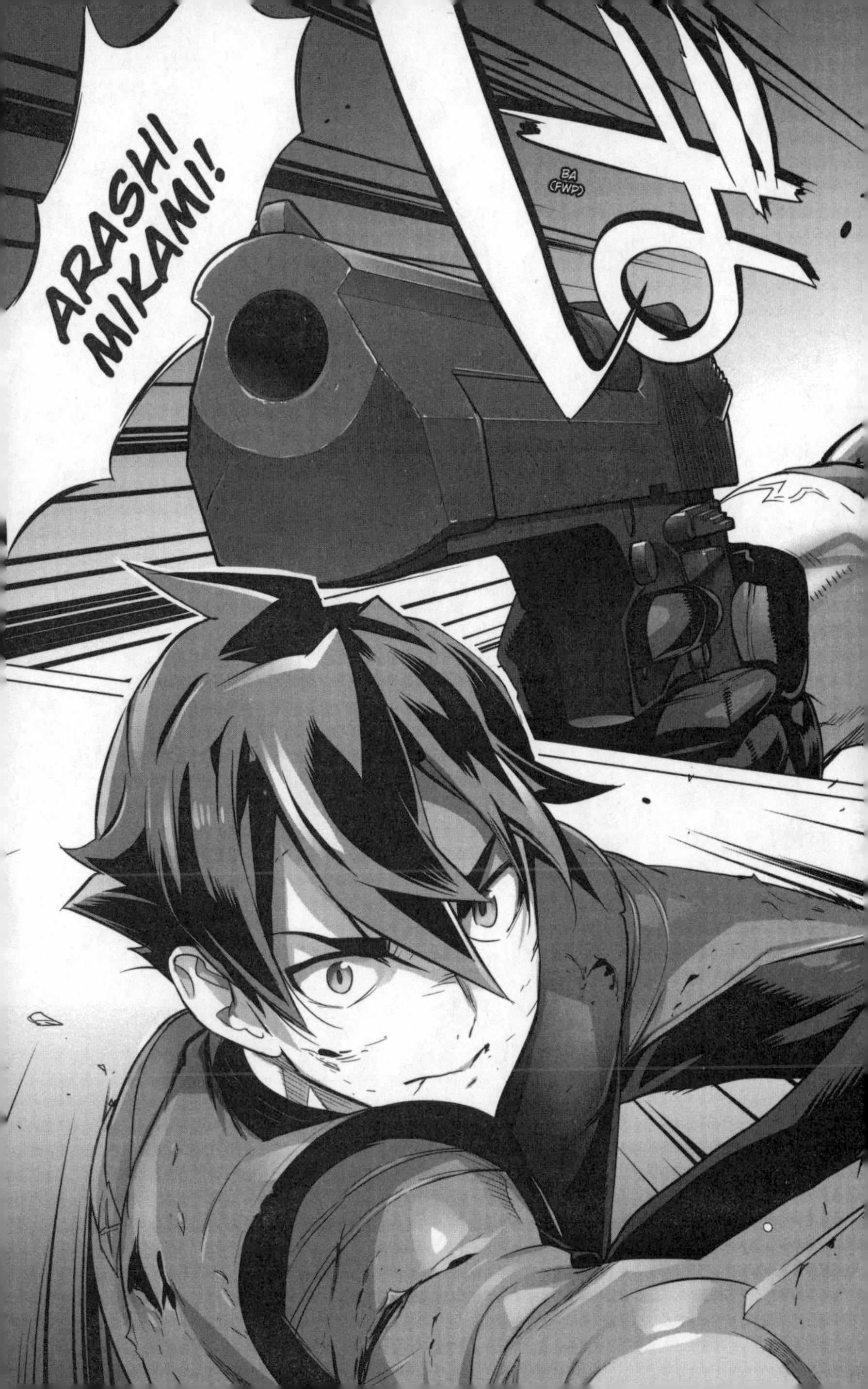
ARASHI MIKAMI!
BA (FWP)

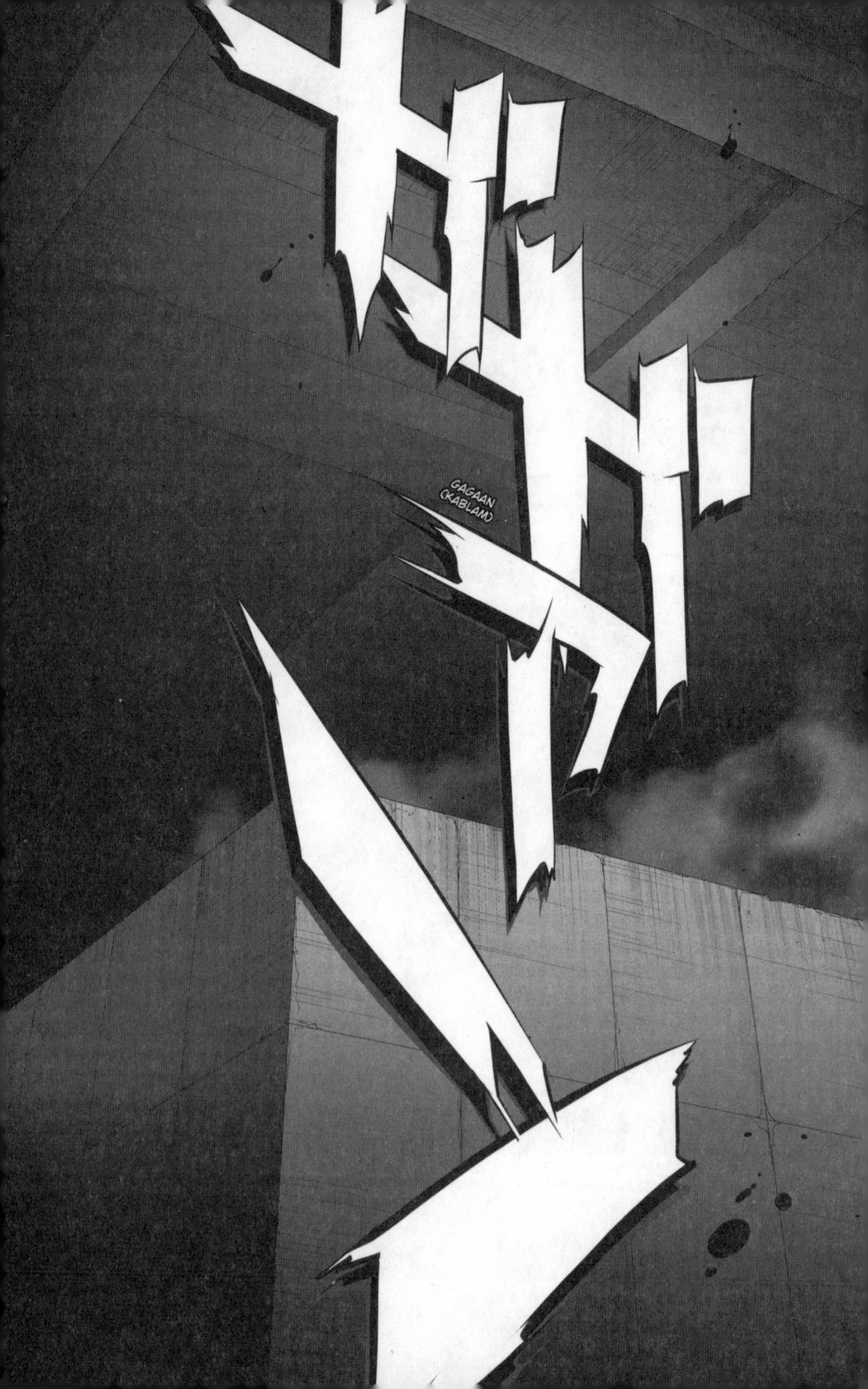
ガガーン
GAGAAN (KABLAM)

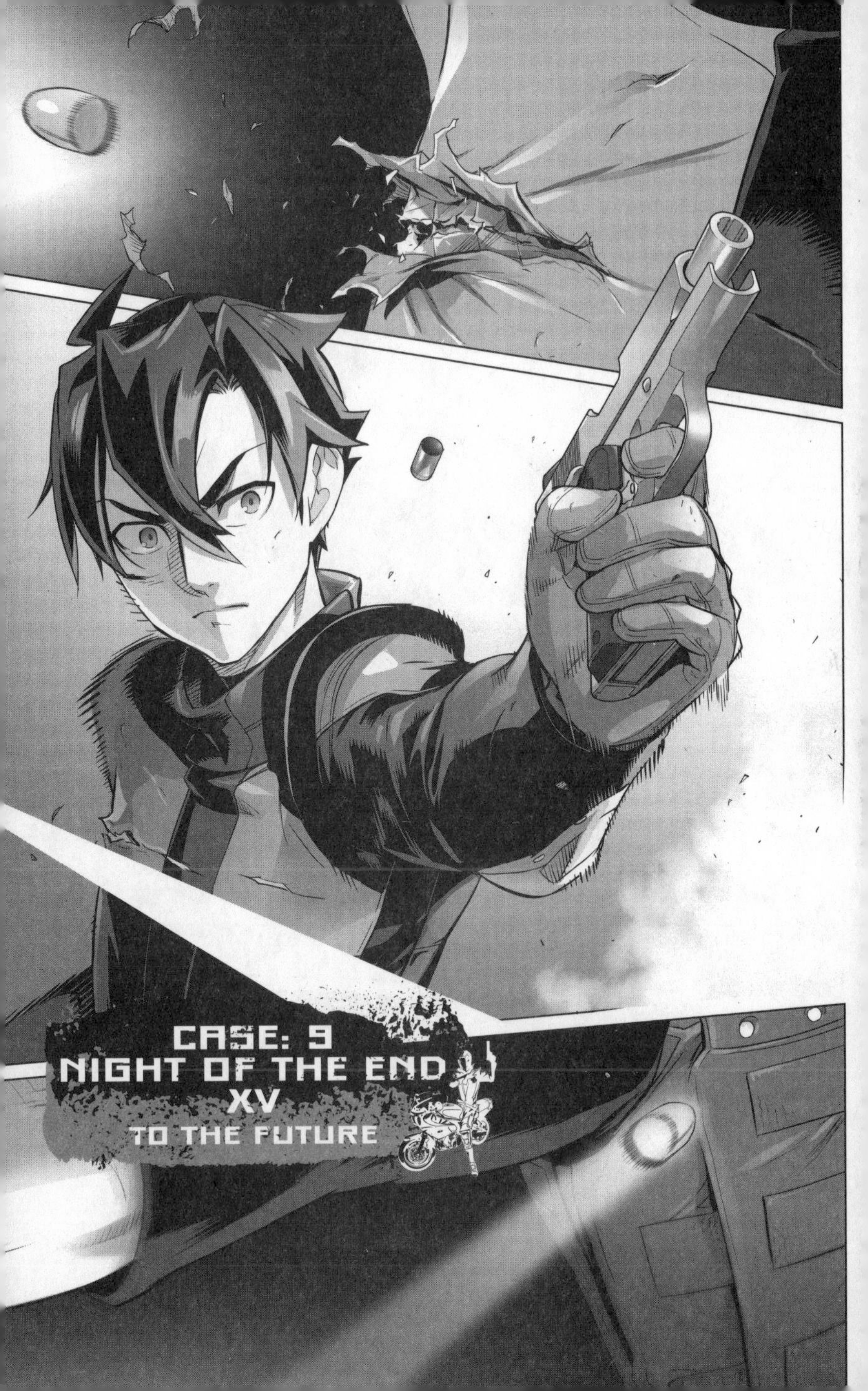
CASE: 9
NIGHT OF THE END
XV
TO THE FUTURE

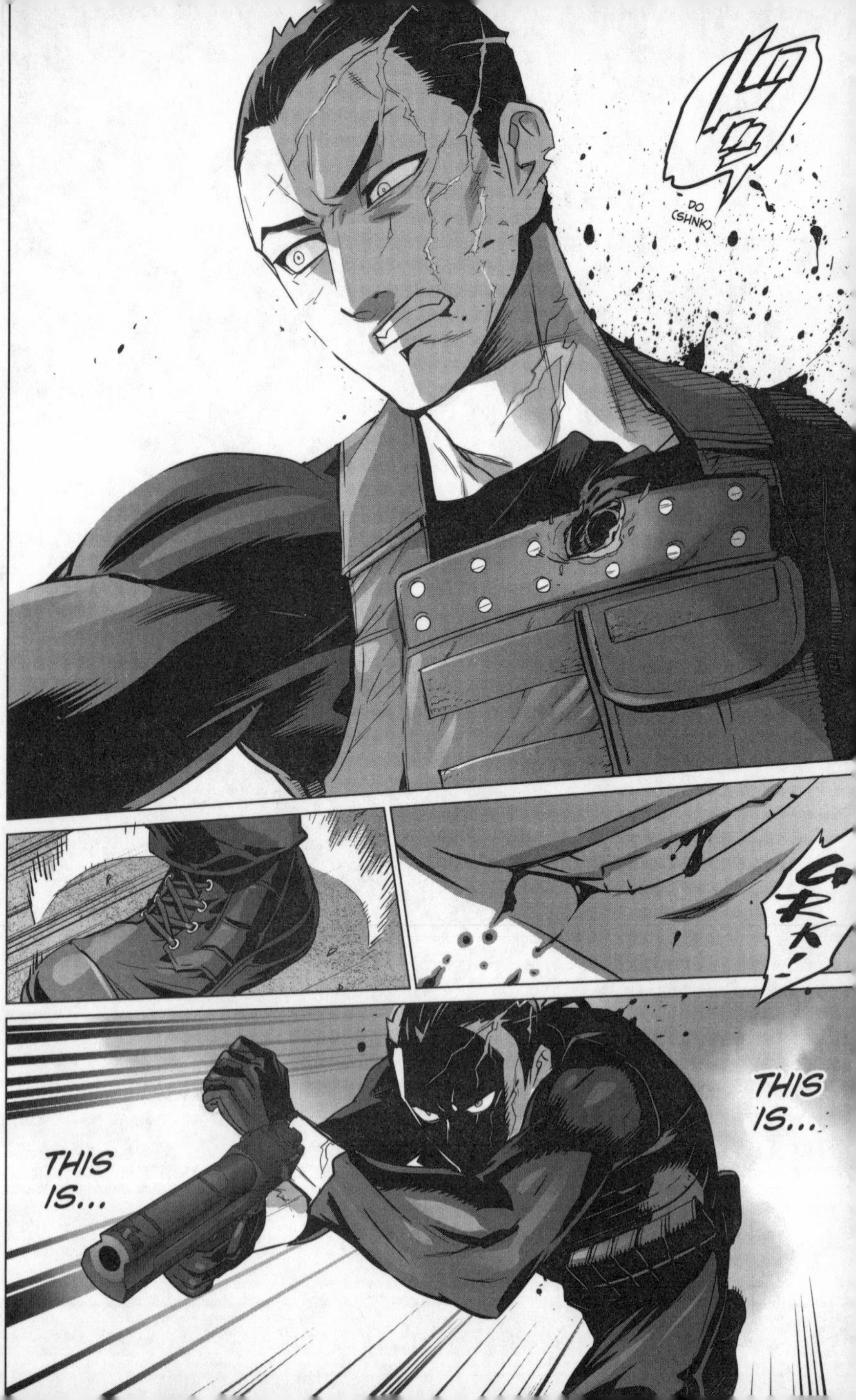
DO (SHNK)
GRK!
THIS IS...
THIS IS...

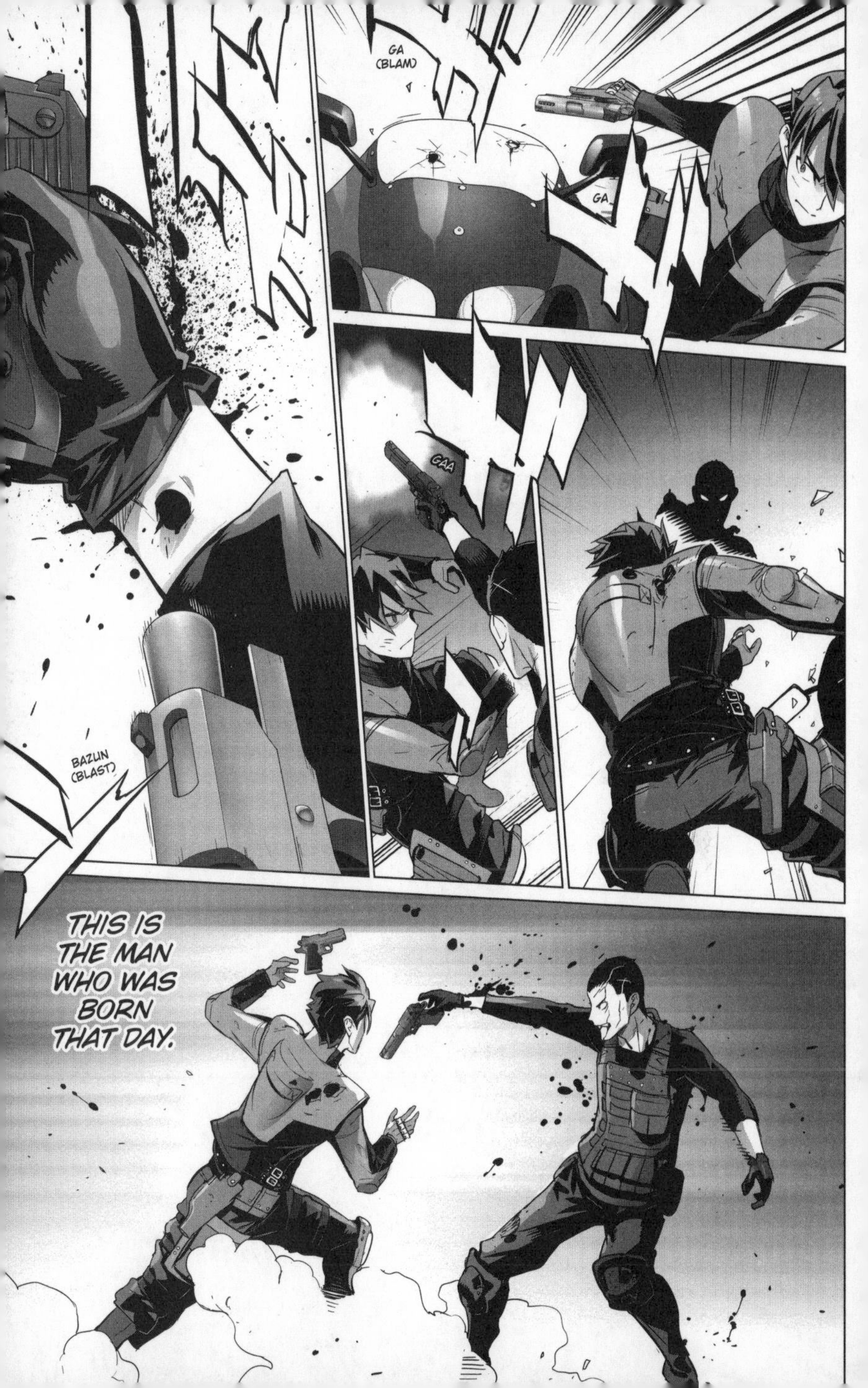
GA
(BLAM)
GA
GAA
BAZUN
(BLAST)
THIS IS THE MAN WHO WAS BORN THAT DAY.

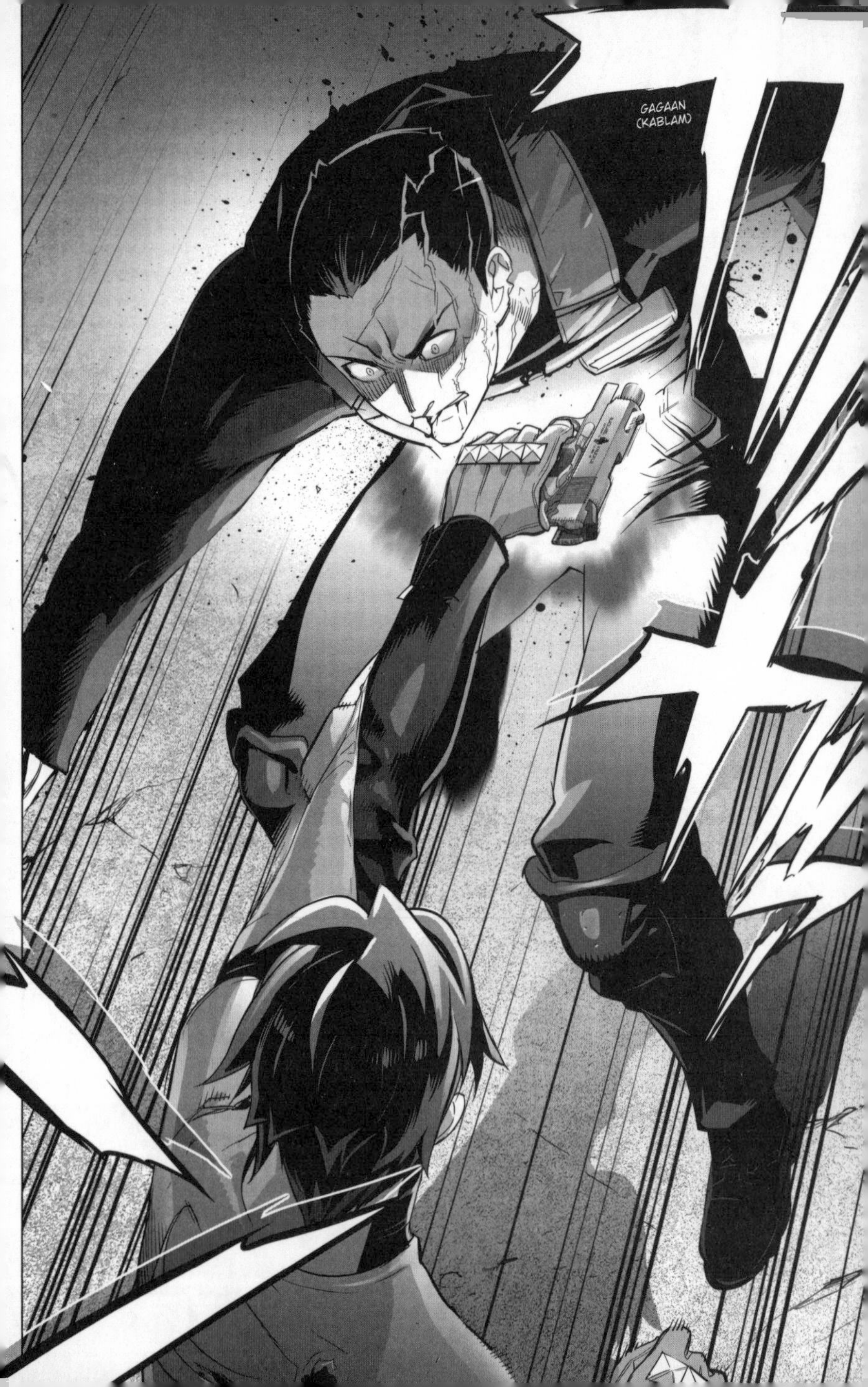
GAGAAN
(KABLAM)

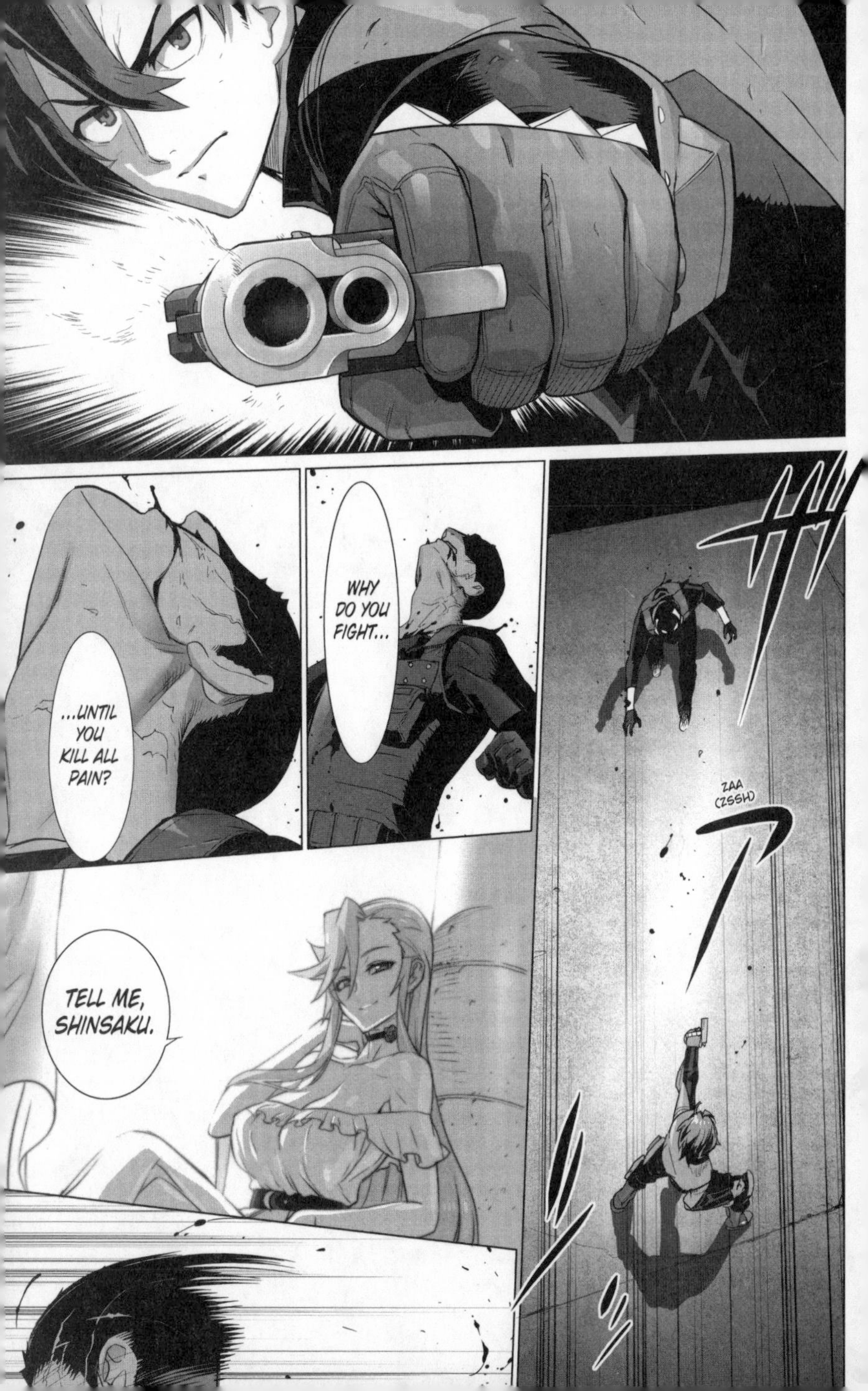
ZAA (ZSSH)
WHY DO YOU FIGHT...
...UNTIL YOU KILL ALL PAIN?
TELL ME, SHINSAKU.

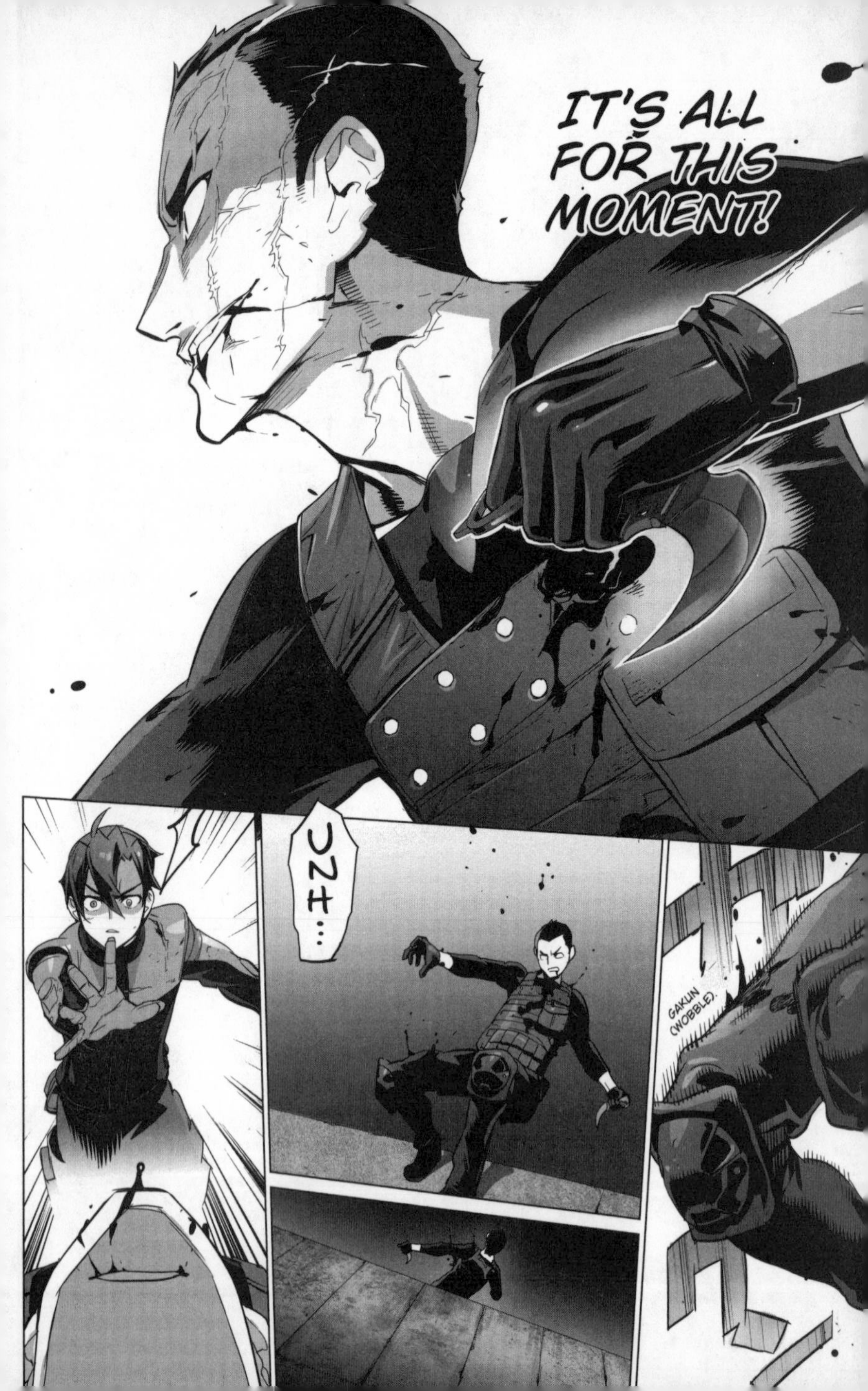
IT'S ALL FOR THIS MOMENT!
GAKUN (WOBBLE)
UNH...

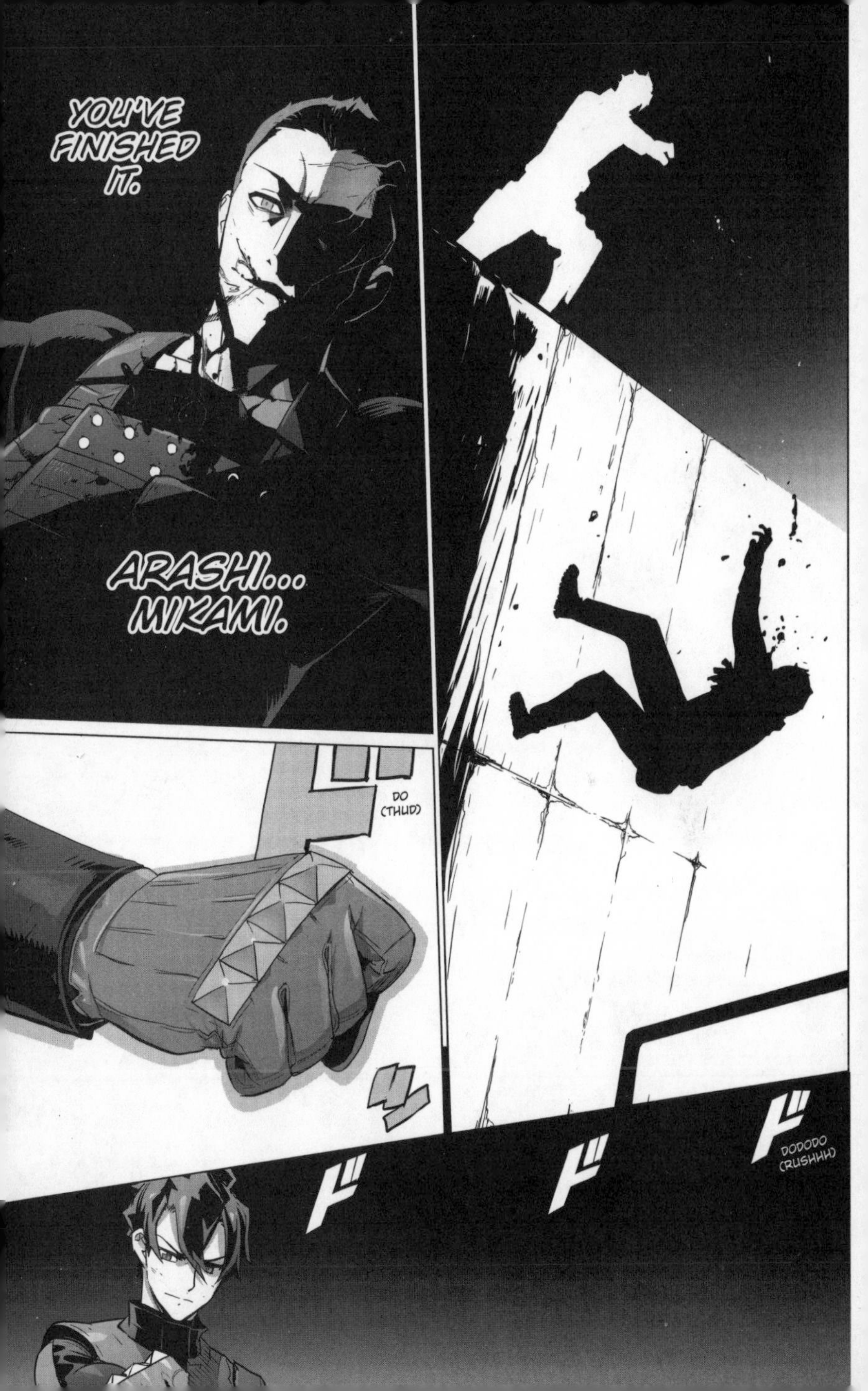
YOU'VE FINISHED IT.
ARASHI... MIKAMI.
DO (THUD)
ドドド
DODODO (RUSHHH)

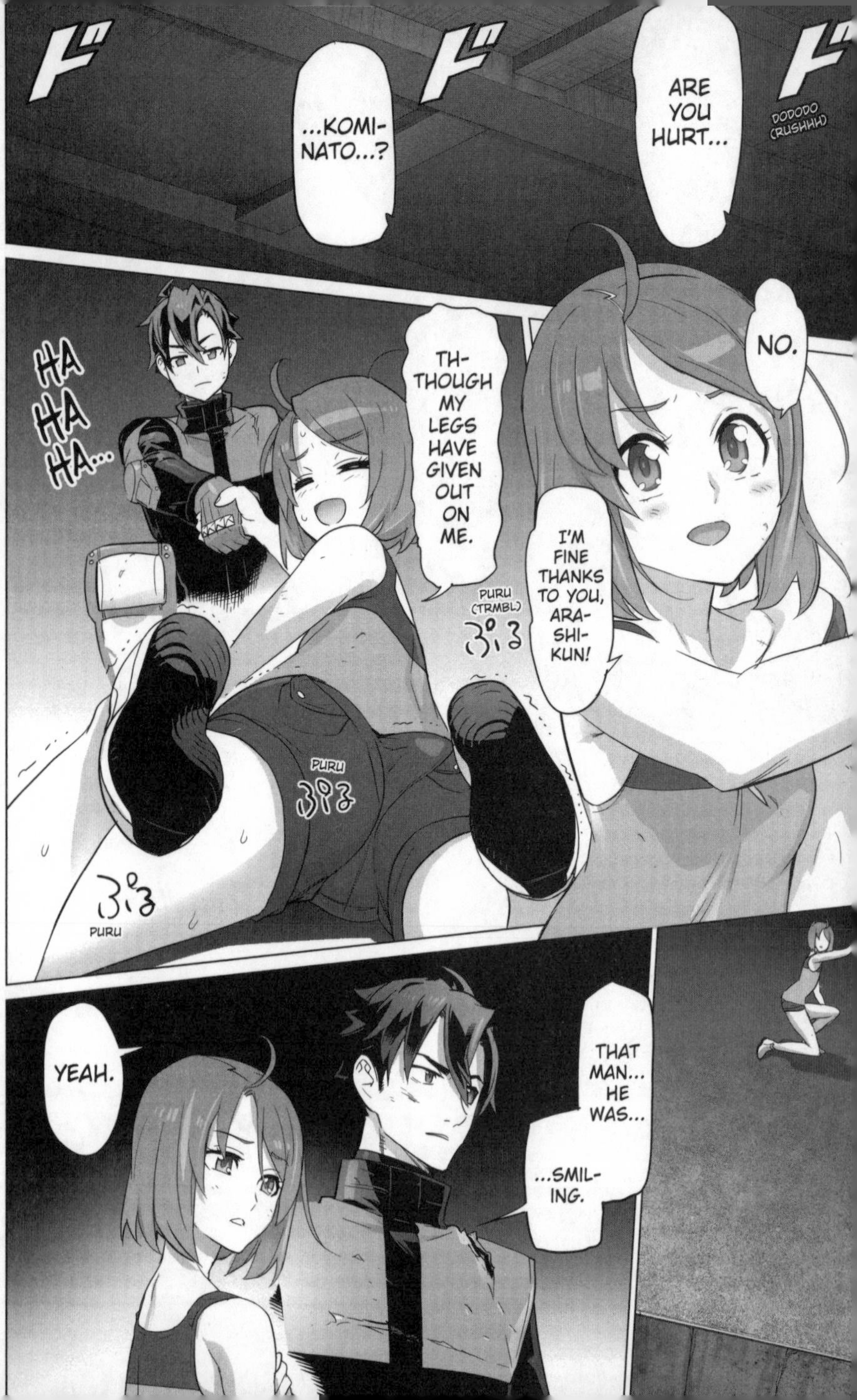
ド
ド
ド
DODODO (RUSHHH)
ARE YOU HURT...
...KOMI-NATO...?
NO.
I'M FINE THANKS TO YOU, ARA-SHI-KUN!
TH-THOUGH MY LEGS HAVE GIVEN OUT ON ME.
PURU (TRMBL) ぷる
HA HA HA...
PURU ぷる
ぷる PURU
THAT MAN... HE WAS...
...SMIL-ING.
YEAH.

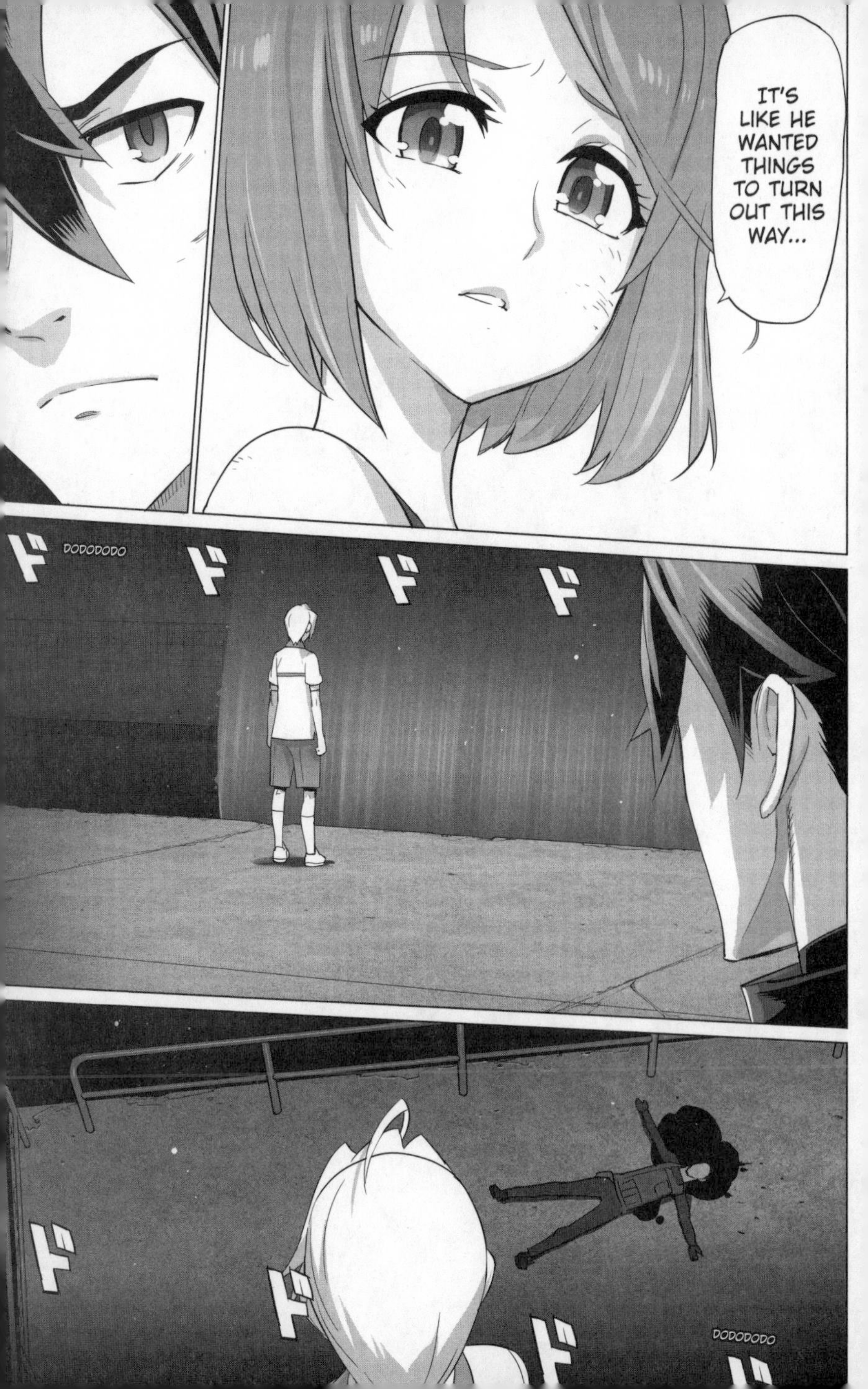
IT'S LIKE HE WANTED THINGS TO TURN OUT THIS WAY...
ドドドド
DODODODO
ドドドド
DODODODO

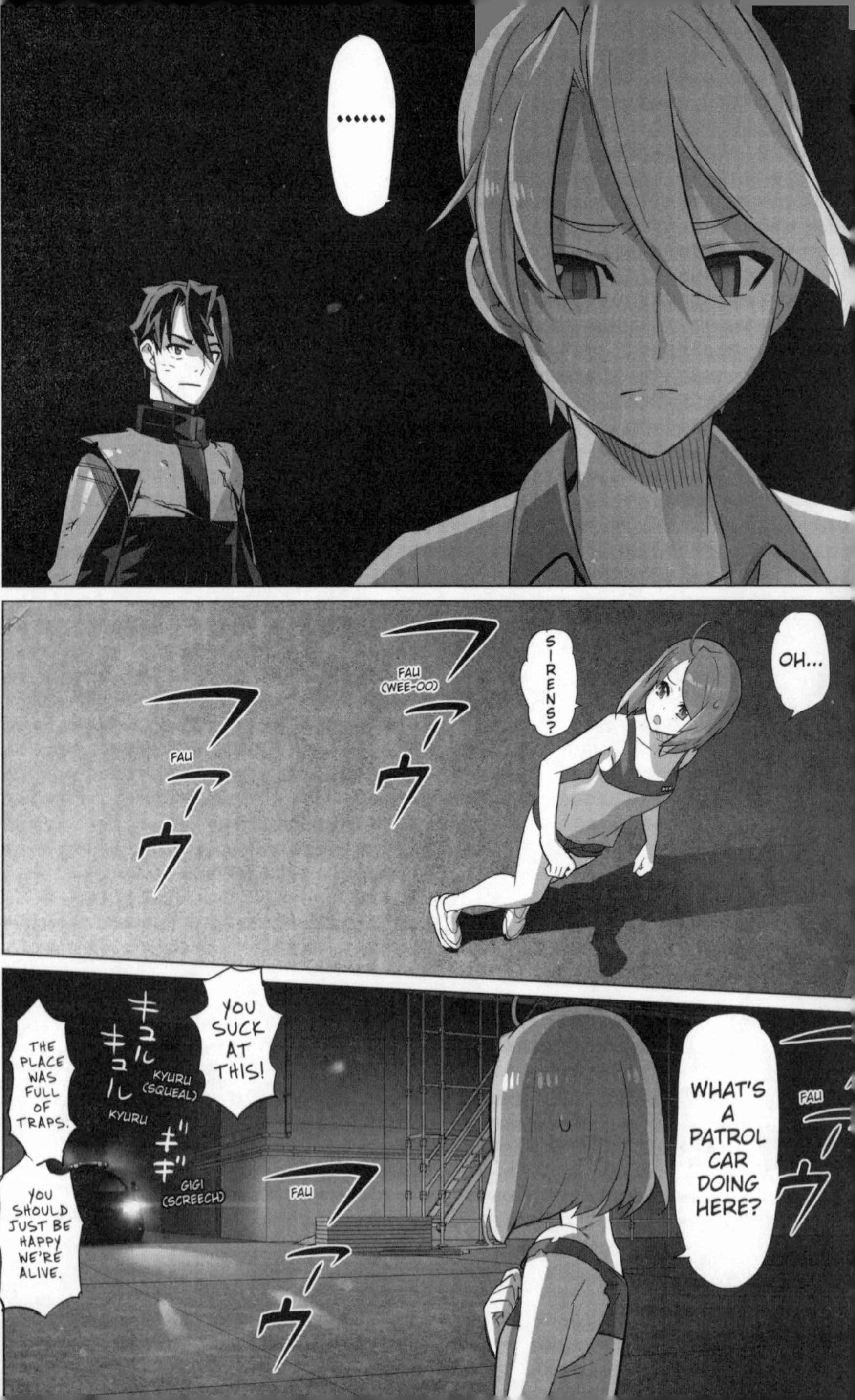
......
OH...
SIRENS?
ファウ
FAU (WEE-OO)
ファウ
FAU
WHAT'S A PATROL CAR DOING HERE?
ファウ
FAU
ファウ
FAU
YOU SUCK AT THIS!
キュルキュル
KYURU (SQUEAL) KYURU
THE PLACE WAS FULL OF TRAPS.
ギギ
GIGI (SCREECH)
YOU SHOULD JUST BE HAPPY WE'RE ALIVE.

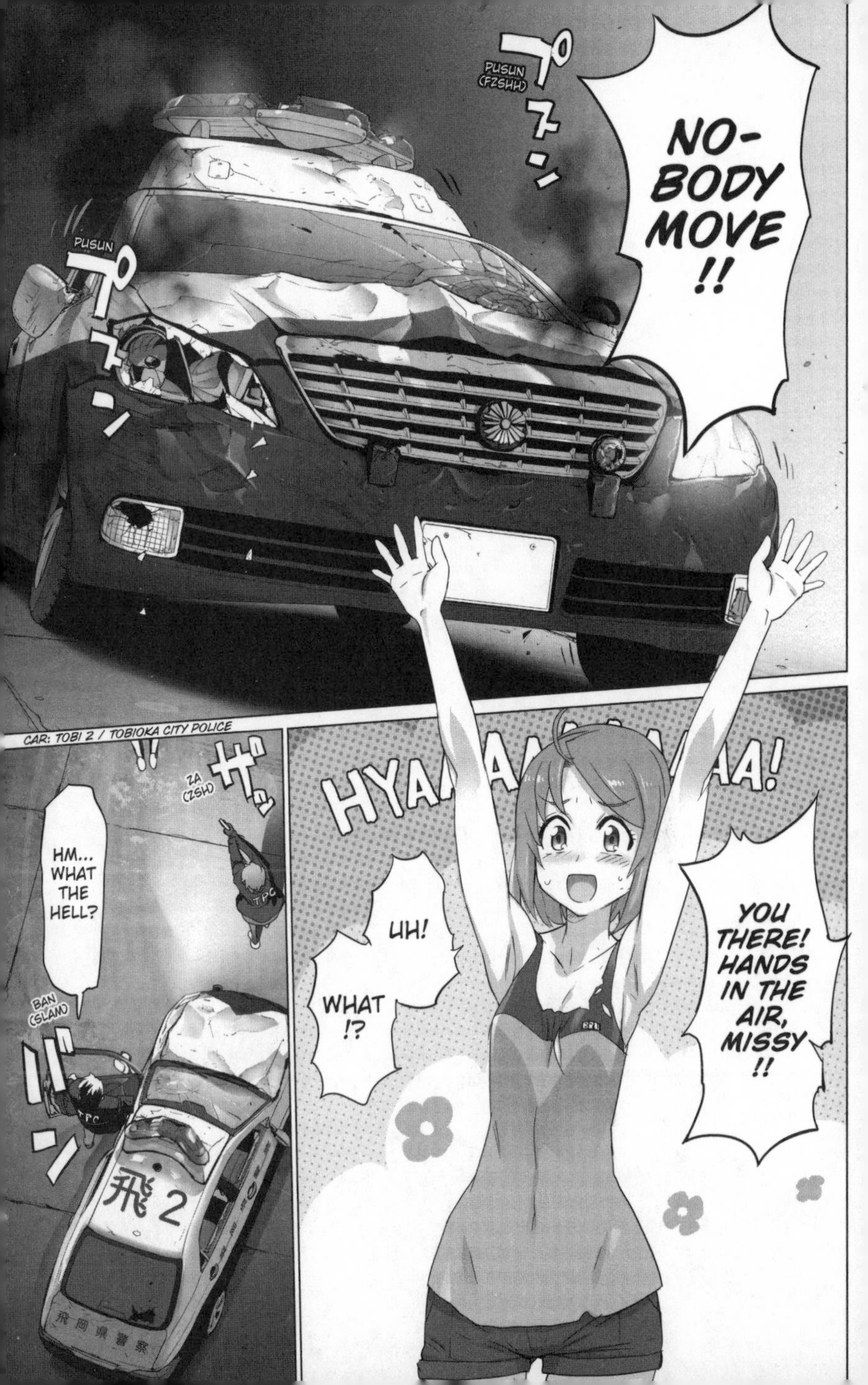
NO-BODY MOVE!!
PUSUN (FZSHH)
PUSUN
CAR: TOBI 2 / TOBIOKA CITY POLICE
YOU THERE! HANDS IN THE AIR, MISSY!!
UH!
WHAT!?
ZA (ZSH)
HM... WHAT THE HELL?
BAN (SLAM)
飛 2

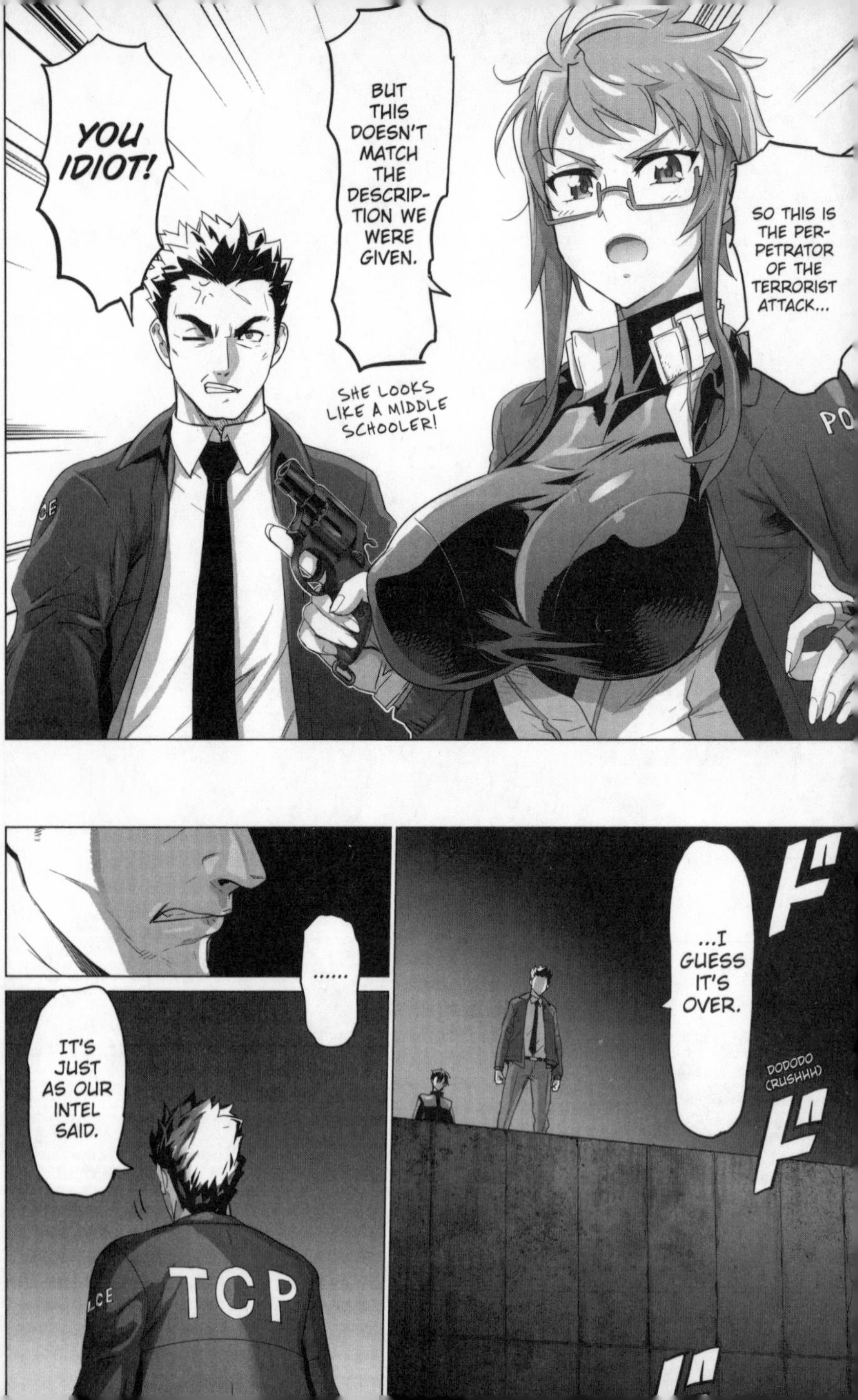
SO THIS IS THE PER-PETRATOR OF THE TERRORIST ATTACK...
BUT THIS DOESN'T MATCH THE DESCRIP-TION WE WERE GIVEN.
SHE LOOKS LIKE A MIDDLE SCHOOLER!
YOU IDIOT!
...I GUESS IT'S OVER.
DODODO (RUSHHH)
......
IT'S JUST AS OUR INTEL SAID.
TCP

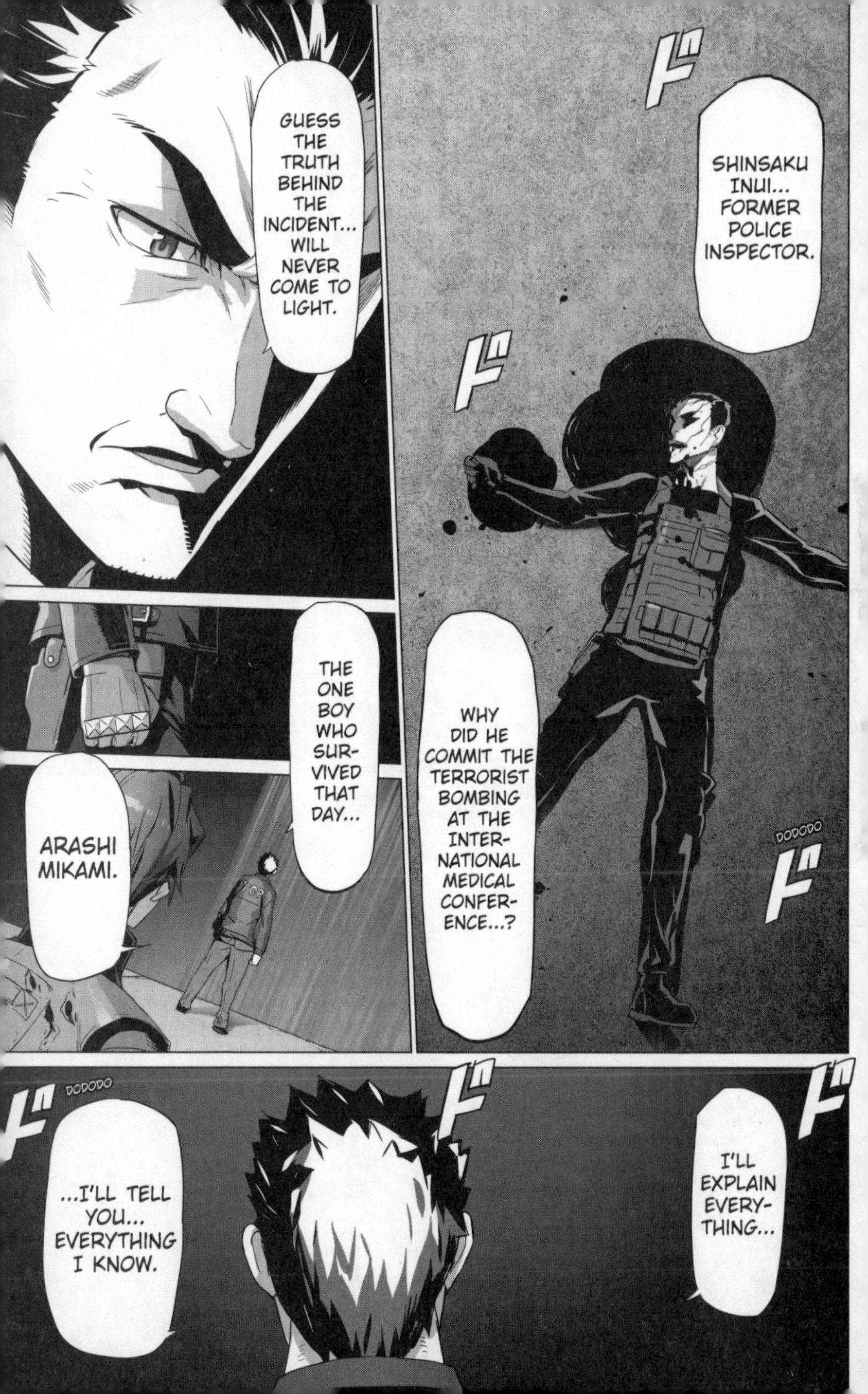
SHINSAKU INUI... FORMER POLICE INSPECTOR.
WHY DID HE COMMIT THE TERRORIST BOMBING AT THE INTERNATIONAL MEDICAL CONFERENCE...?
DODODO
GUESS THE TRUTH BEHIND THE INCIDENT... WILL NEVER COME TO LIGHT.
THE ONE BOY WHO SURVIVED THAT DAY...
ARASHI MIKAMI.
I'LL EXPLAIN EVERYTHING...
...I'LL TELL YOU... EVERYTHING I KNOW.
DODODO

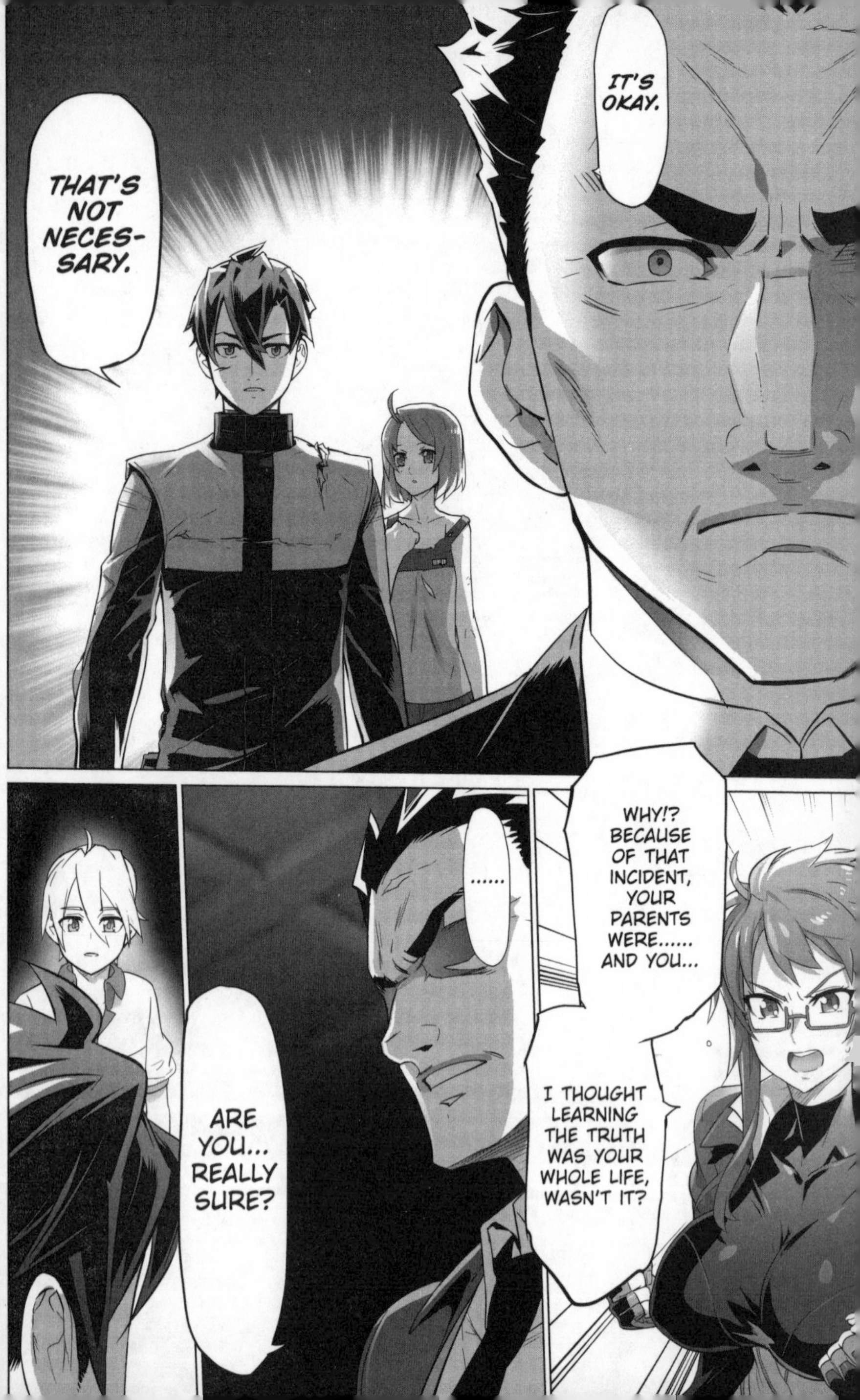
IT'S OKAY.
THAT'S NOT NECES-SARY.
WHY!? BECAUSE OF THAT INCIDENT, YOUR PARENTS WERE...... AND YOU...
I THOUGHT LEARNING THE TRUTH WAS YOUR WHOLE LIFE, WASN'T IT?
......
ARE YOU... REALLY SURE?

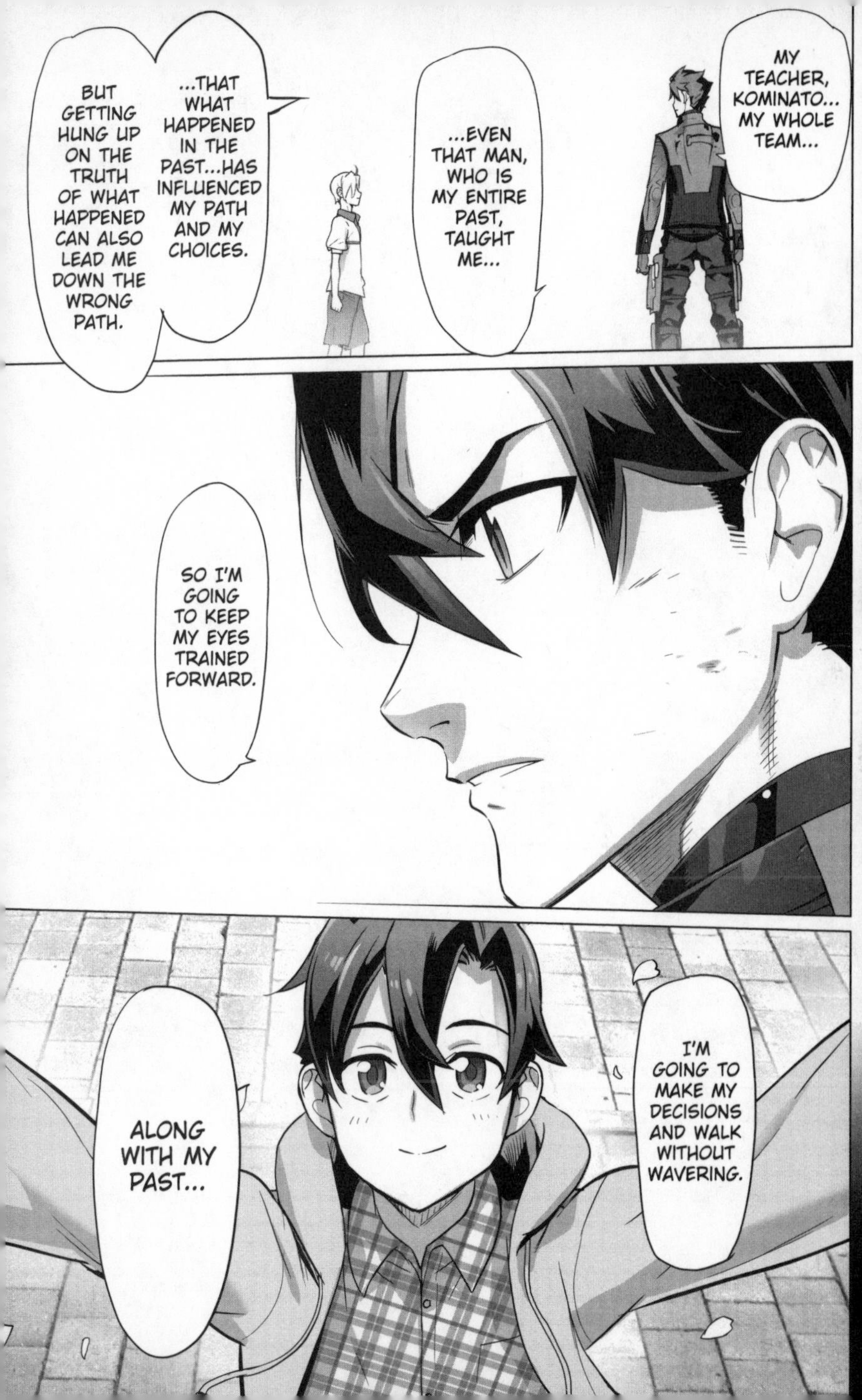
MY TEACHER, KOMINATO... MY WHOLE TEAM...
...EVEN THAT MAN, WHO IS MY ENTIRE PAST, TAUGHT ME...
...THAT WHAT HAPPENED IN THE PAST...HAS INFLUENCED MY PATH AND MY CHOICES.
BUT GETTING HUNG UP ON THE TRUTH OF WHAT HAPPENED CAN ALSO LEAD ME DOWN THE WRONG PATH.
SO I'M GOING TO KEEP MY EYES TRAINED FORWARD.
I'M GOING TO MAKE MY DECISIONS AND WALK WITHOUT WAVERING.
ALONG WITH MY PAST...

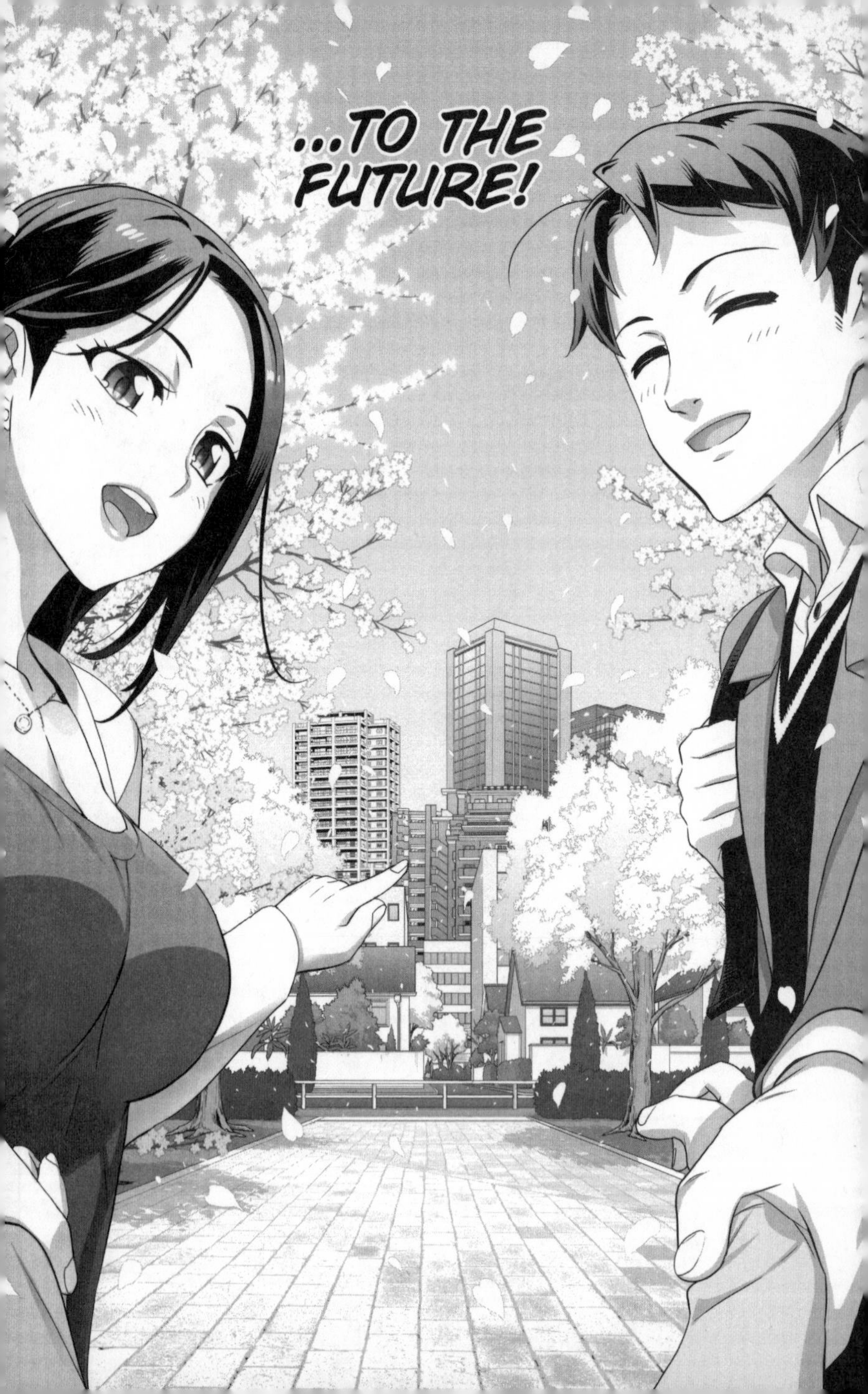
...TO THE FUTURE!

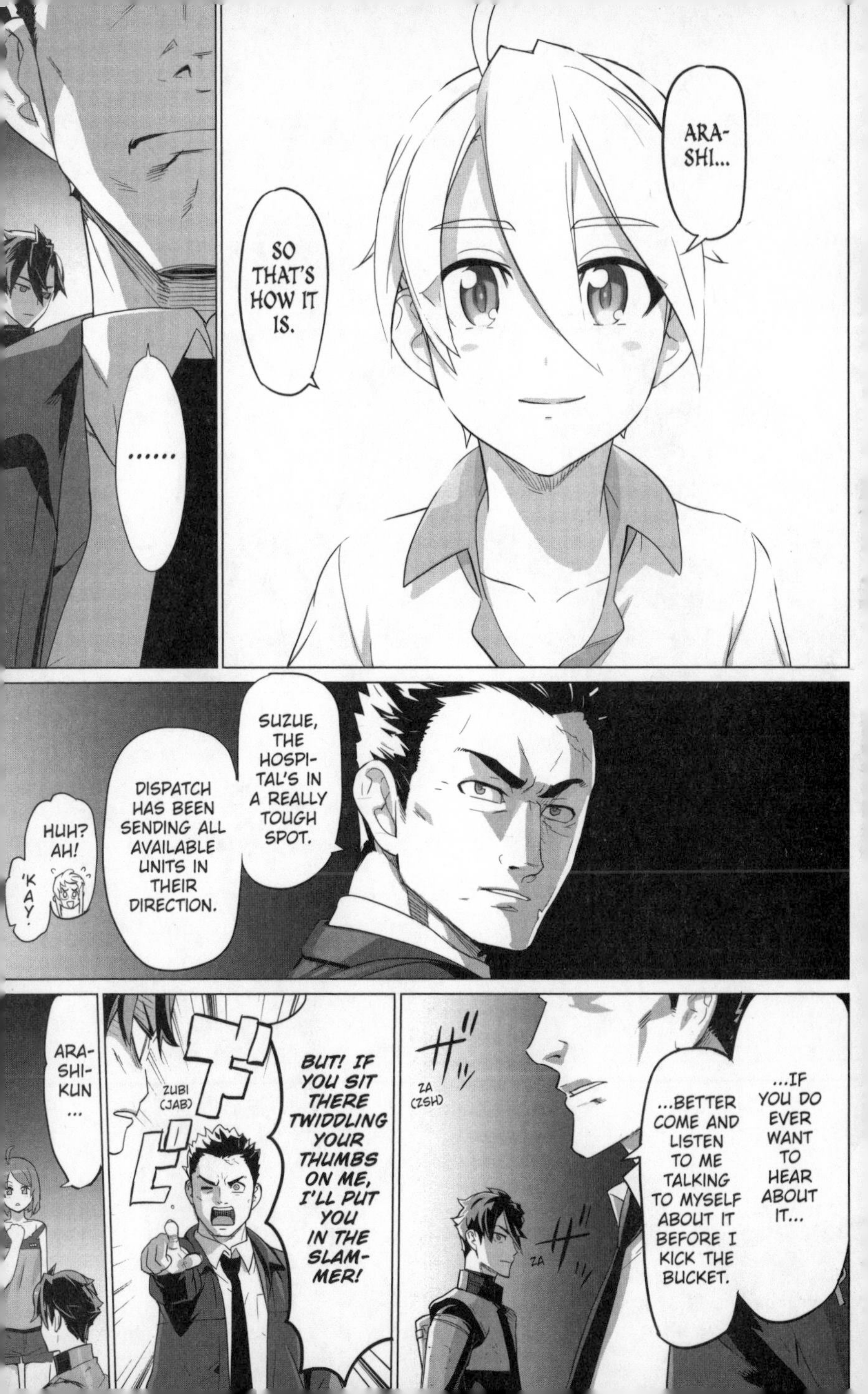
ARA-SHI...
SO THAT'S HOW IT IS.
......
SUZUE, THE HOSPITAL'S IN A REALLY TOUGH SPOT.
DISPATCH HAS BEEN SENDING ALL AVAILABLE UNITS IN THEIR DIRECTION.
HUH? AH!
'KAY.
...IF YOU DO EVER WANT TO HEAR ABOUT IT...
...BETTER COME AND LISTEN TO ME TALKING TO MYSELF ABOUT IT BEFORE I KICK THE BUCKET.
ZA (ZSH)
ZA
ZUBI (JAB)
BUT! IF YOU SIT THERE TWIDDLING YOUR THUMBS ON ME, I'LL PUT YOU IN THE SLAMMER!
ARA-SHI-KUN...

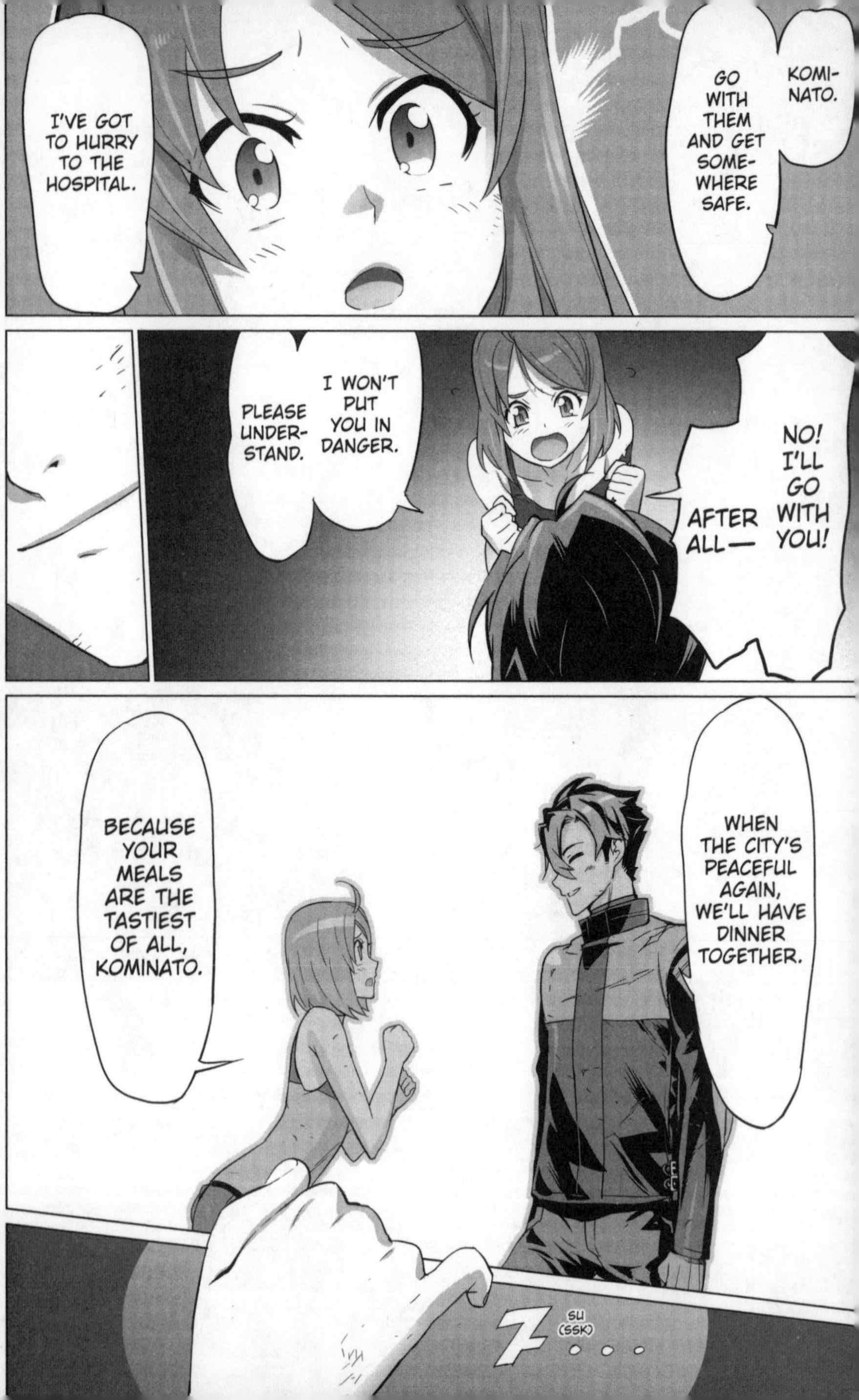
KOMINATO.
GO WITH THEM AND GET SOMEWHERE SAFE.
I'VE GOT TO HURRY TO THE HOSPITAL.
NO! I'LL GO WITH YOU!
AFTER ALL—
I WON'T PUT YOU IN DANGER.
PLEASE UNDERSTAND.
WHEN THE CITY'S PEACEFUL AGAIN, WE'LL HAVE DINNER TOGETHER.
BECAUSE YOUR MEALS ARE THE TASTIEST OF ALL, KOMINATO.
SU (SSK)

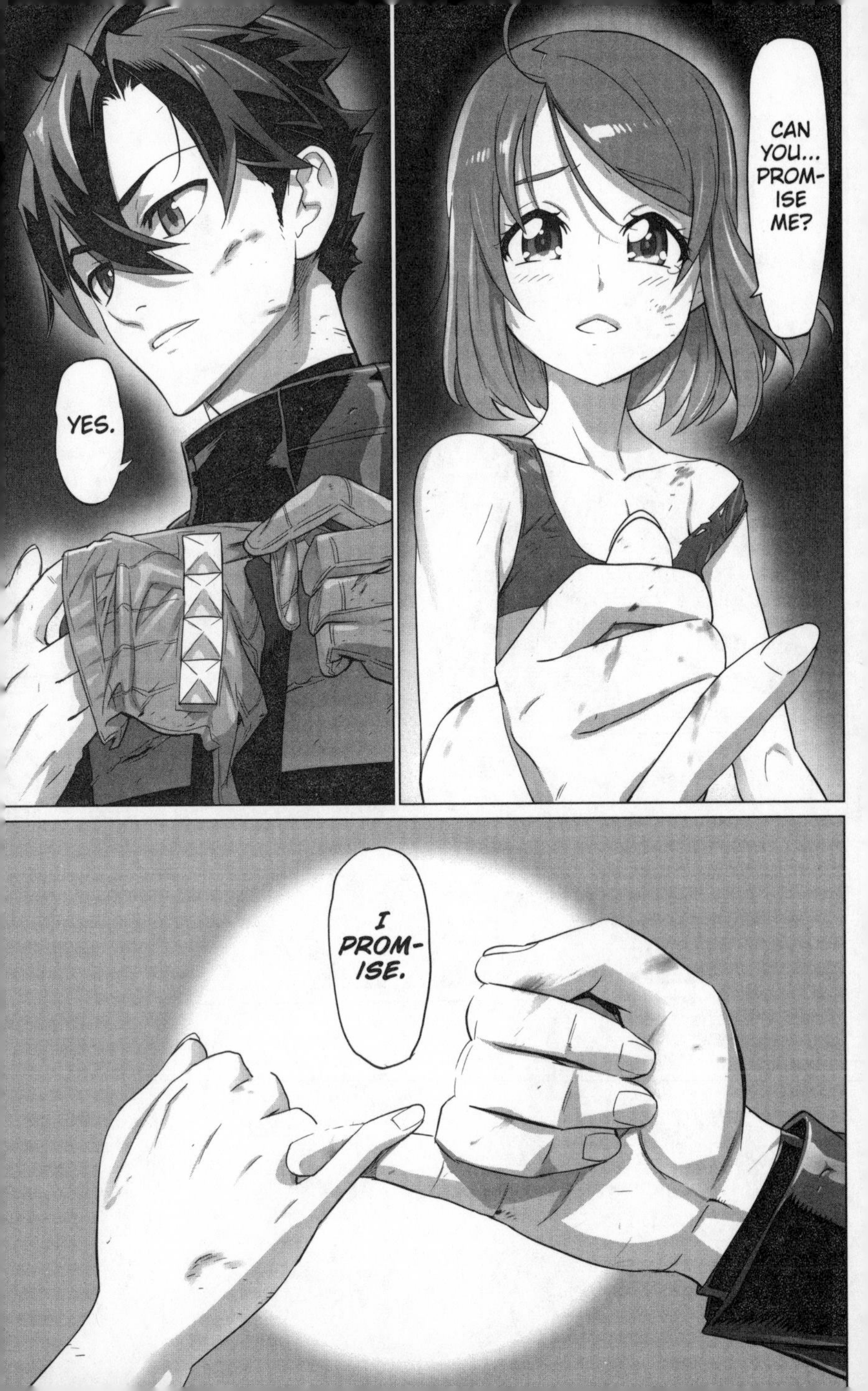
CAN YOU... PROMISE ME?
YES.
I PROMISE.

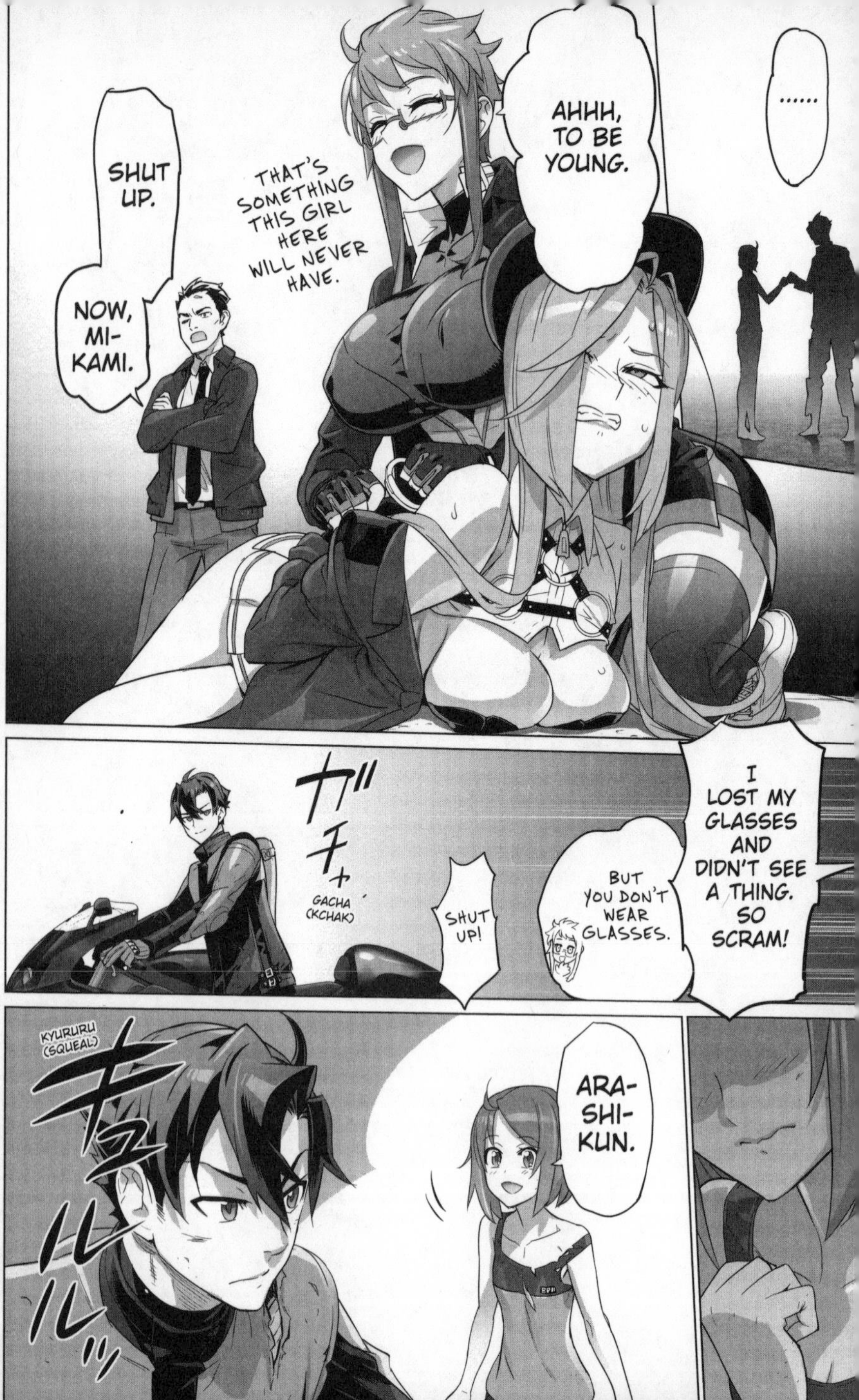
......
AHHH, TO BE YOUNG.
THAT'S SOMETHING THIS GIRL HERE WILL NEVER HAVE.
SHUT UP.
NOW, MI-KAMI.
I LOST MY GLASSES AND DIDN'T SEE A THING. SO SCRAM!
BUT YOU DON'T WEAR GLASSES.
SHUT UP!
ガチャ
GACHA (KCHAK)
ARA-SHI-KUN.
キュルルッ
KYURURU (SQUEAL)

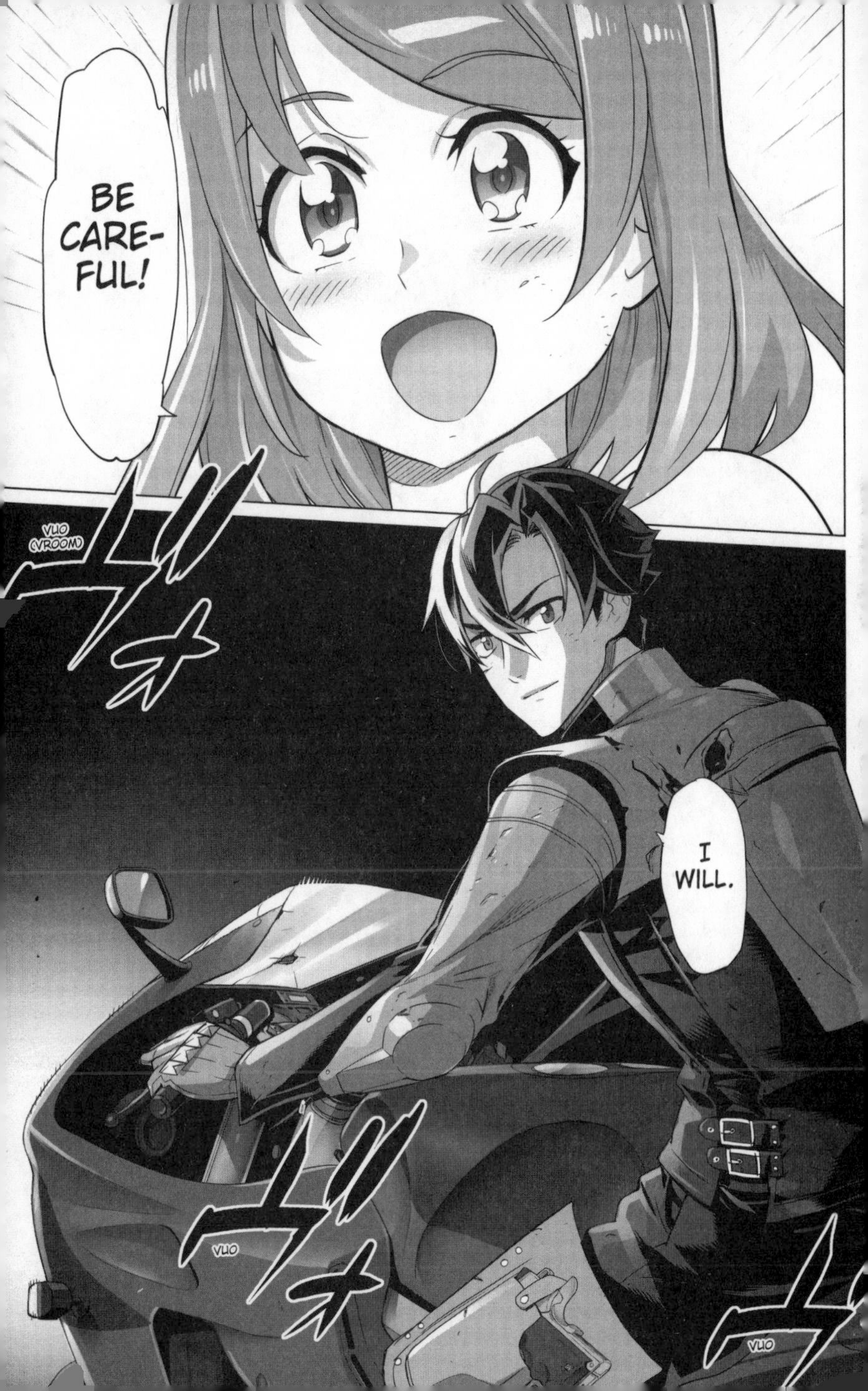
BE CARE-FUL!
VUO (VROOM)
I WILL.
VUO
VUO

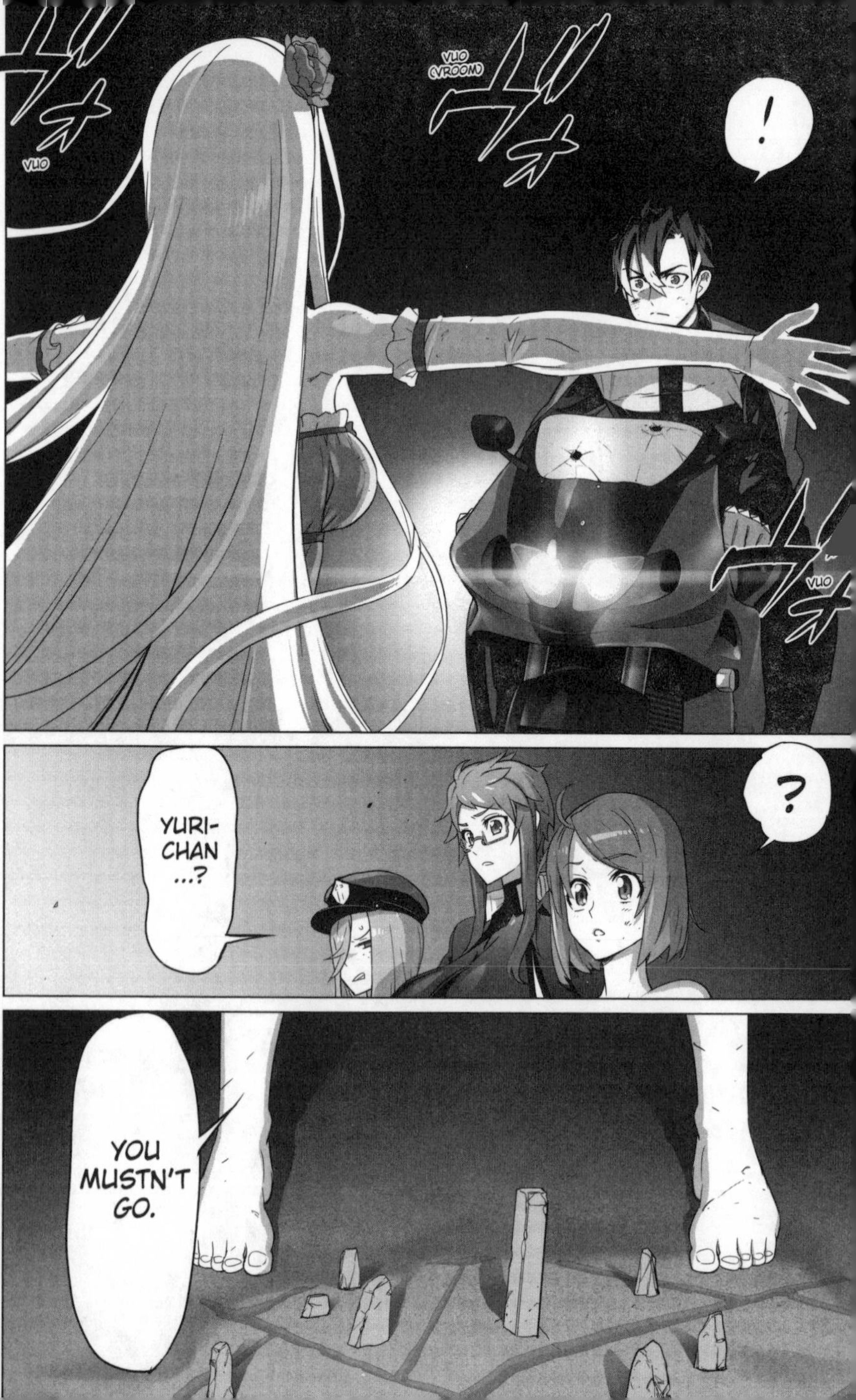
!
VUO (VROOM)
VUO
VUO
?
YURI-CHAN ...?
YOU MUSTN'T GO.

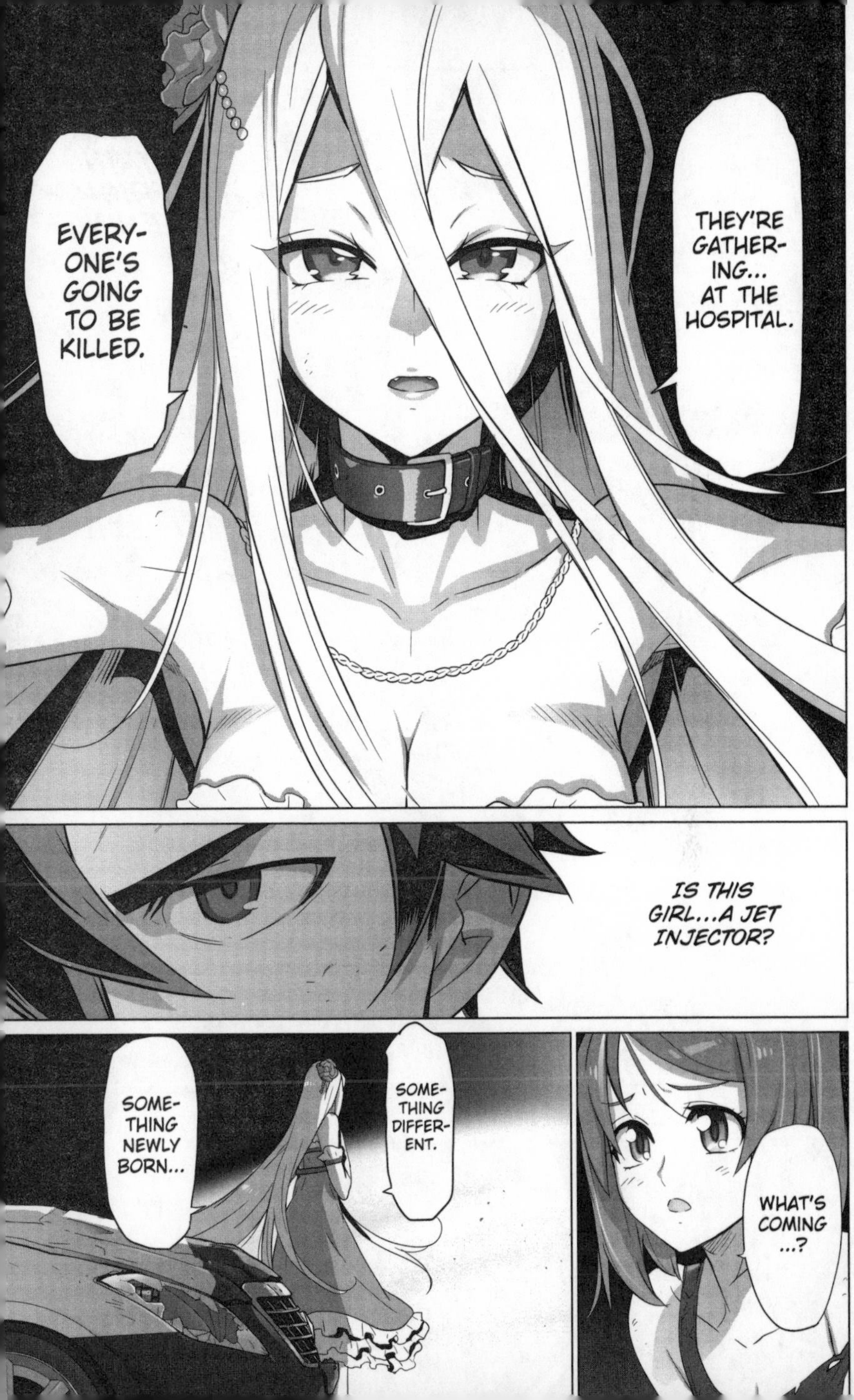
THEY'RE GATHERING... AT THE HOSPITAL.
EVERYONE'S GOING TO BE KILLED.
IS THIS GIRL...A JET INJECTOR?
WHAT'S COMING...?
SOMETHING DIFFERENT.
SOMETHING NEWLY BORN...

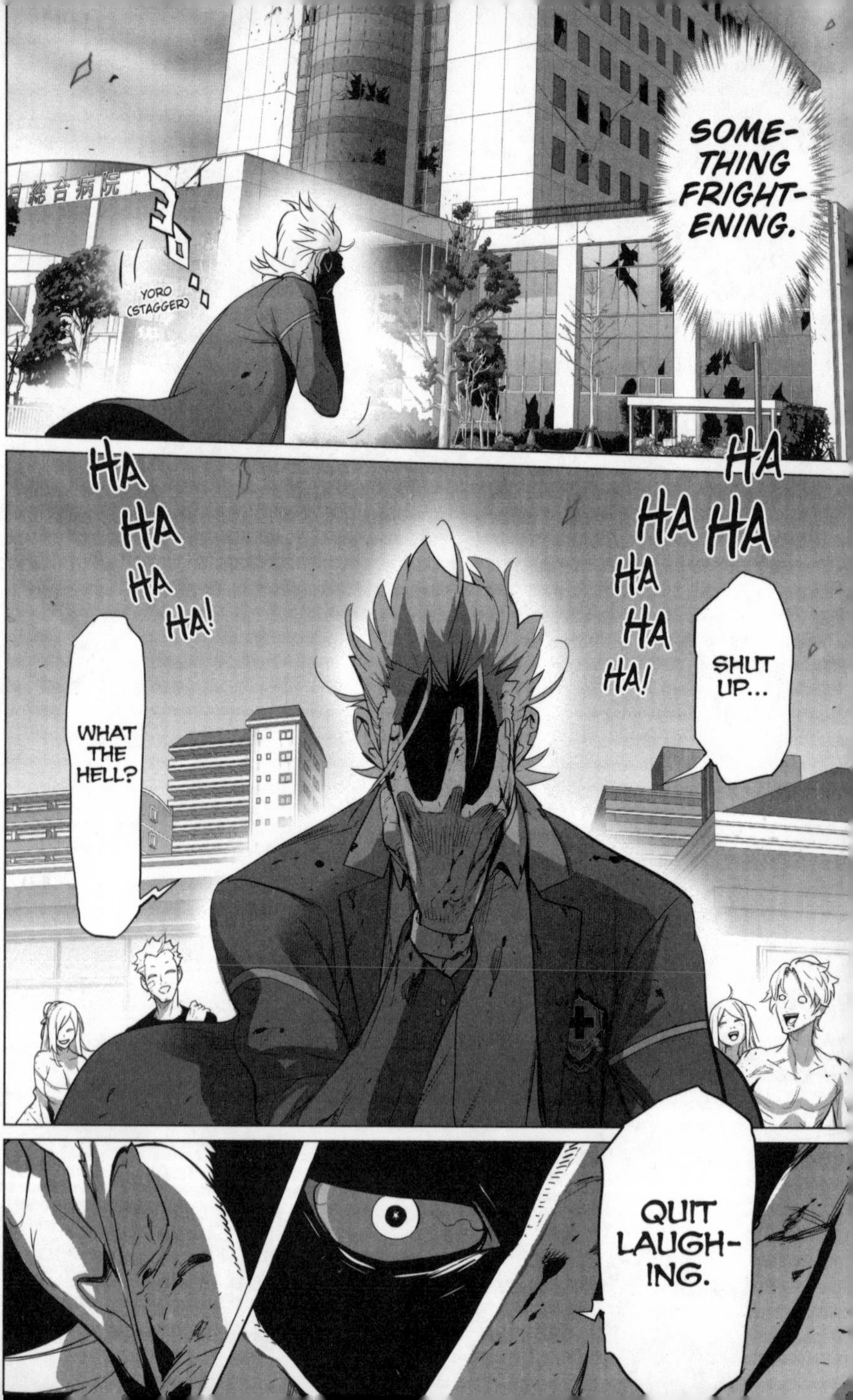
SOMETHING FRIGHTENING.
日総合病院
YORO (STAGGER)
HA HA HA HA HA HA!
SHUT UP...
HA HA HA HA!
WHAT THE HELL?
QUIT LAUGHING.

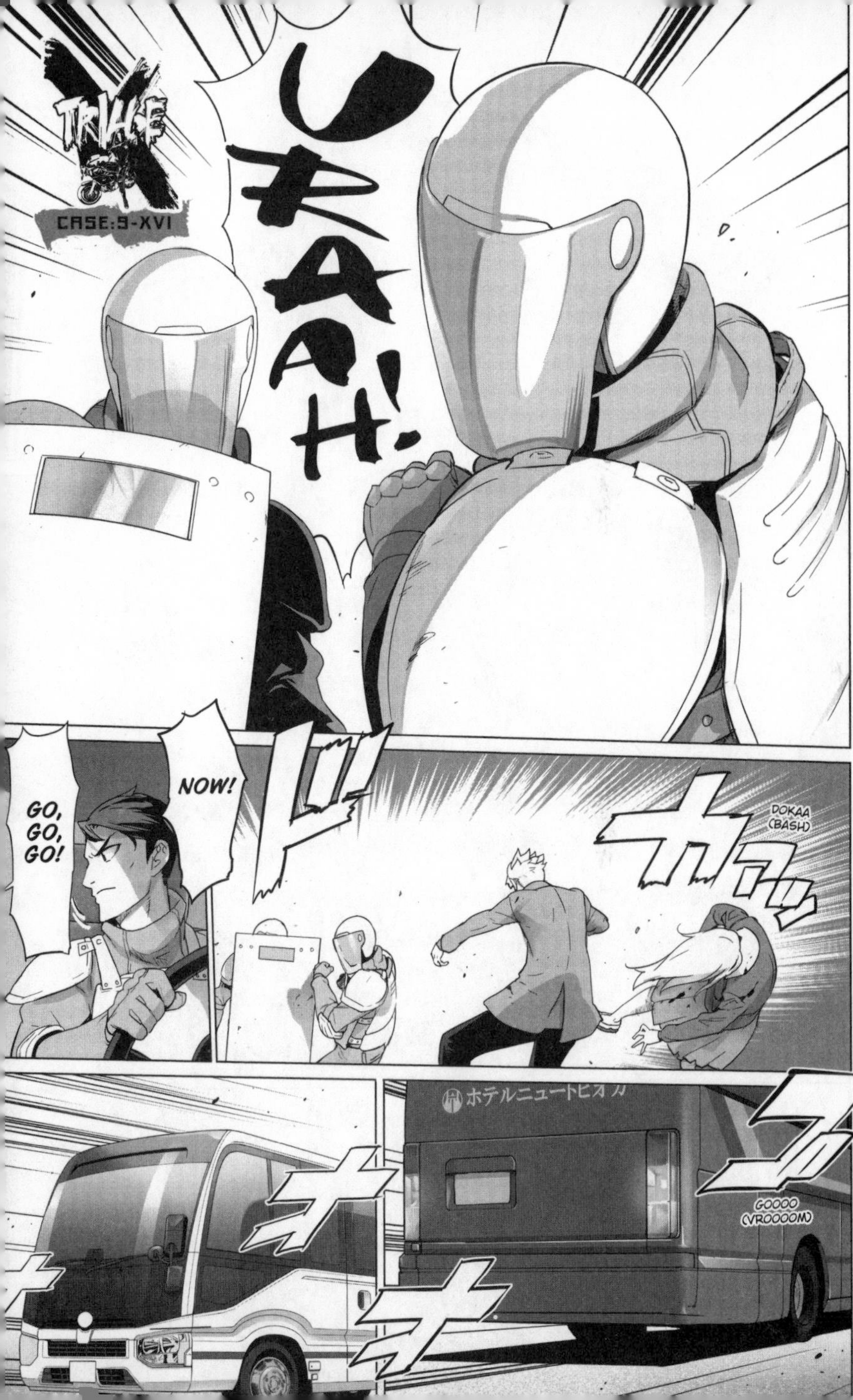
TRIAGE X
CASE:9-XVI
UOAAH!
DOKAA (BASH)
NOW!
GO, GO, GO!
GOOOO (VROOOOM)

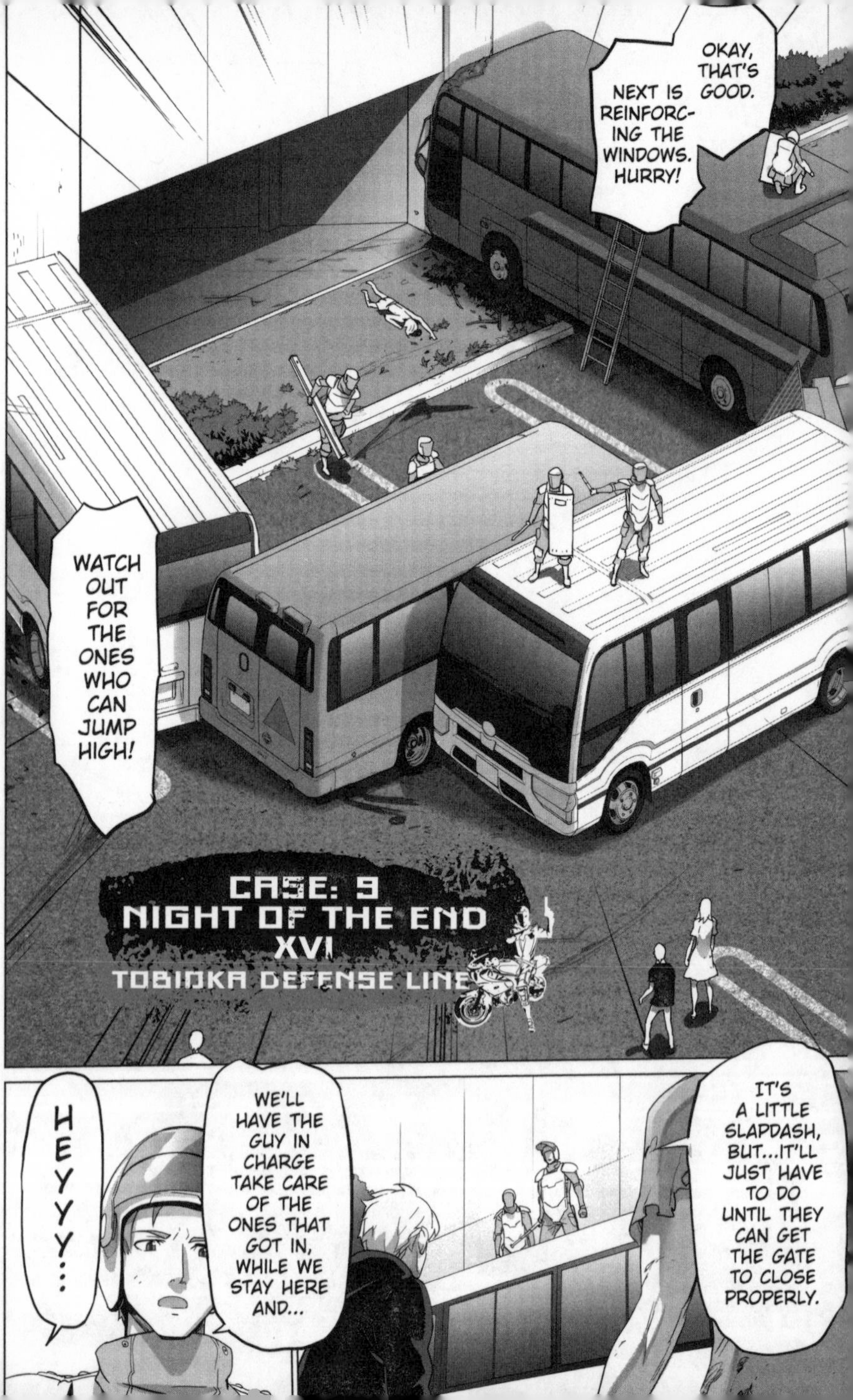
OKAY, THAT'S GOOD.
NEXT IS REINFORC-ING THE WINDOWS. HURRY!
WATCH OUT FOR THE ONES WHO CAN JUMP HIGH!
CASE: 9
NIGHT OF THE END
XVI
TOBINKA DEFENSE LINE
IT'S A LITTLE SLAPDASH, BUT...IT'LL JUST HAVE TO DO UNTIL THEY CAN GET THE GATE TO CLOSE PROPERLY.
WE'LL HAVE THE GUY IN CHARGE TAKE CARE OF THE ONES THAT GOT IN, WHILE WE STAY HERE AND...
HEYYY...

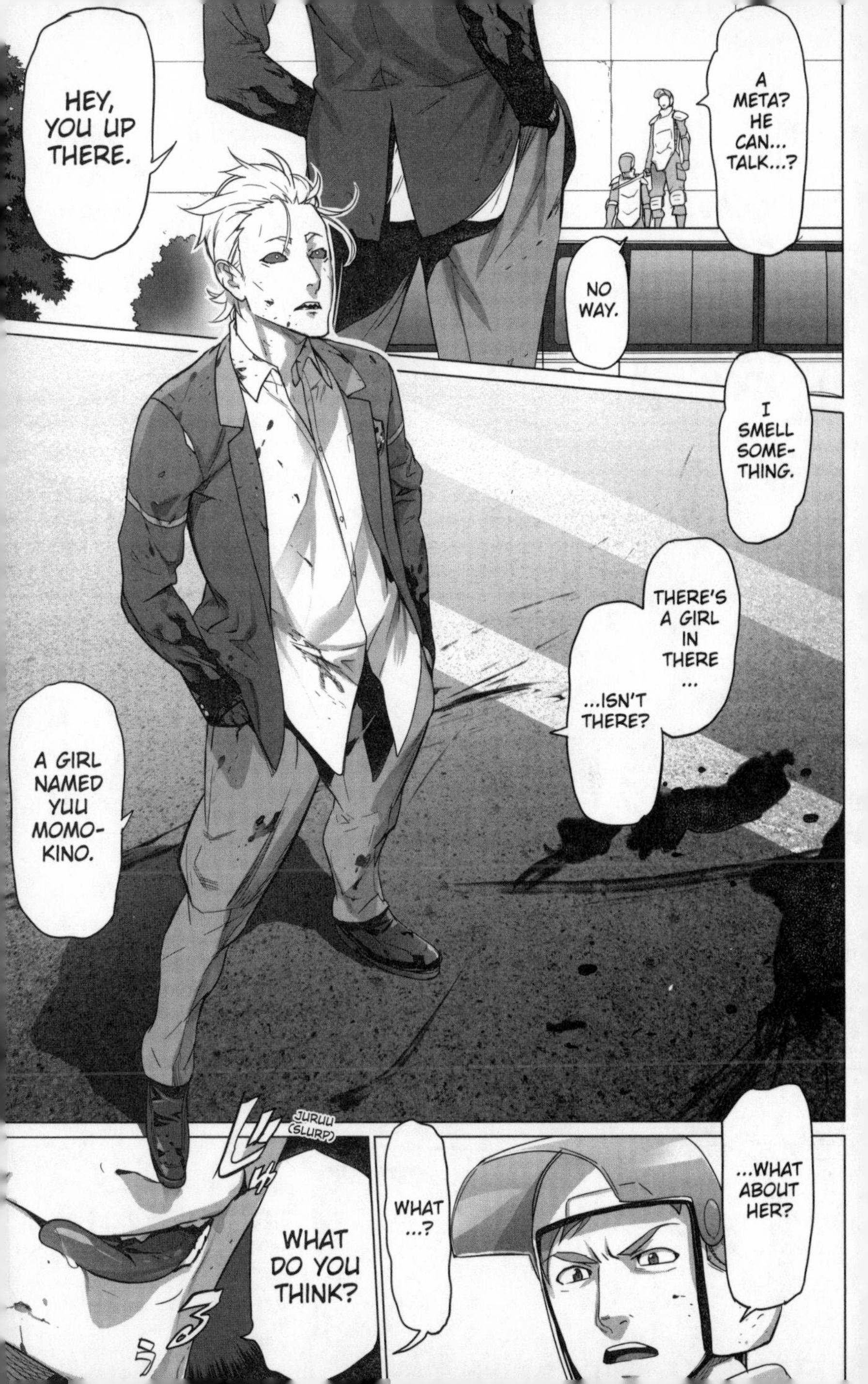
A META? HE CAN... TALK...?
HEY, YOU UP THERE.
NO WAY.
I SMELL SOME-THING.
THERE'S A GIRL IN THERE ...
...ISN'T THERE?
A GIRL NAMED YUU MOMO-KINO.
...WHAT ABOUT HER?
WHAT ...?
JURUU (SLURP)
WHAT DO YOU THINK?

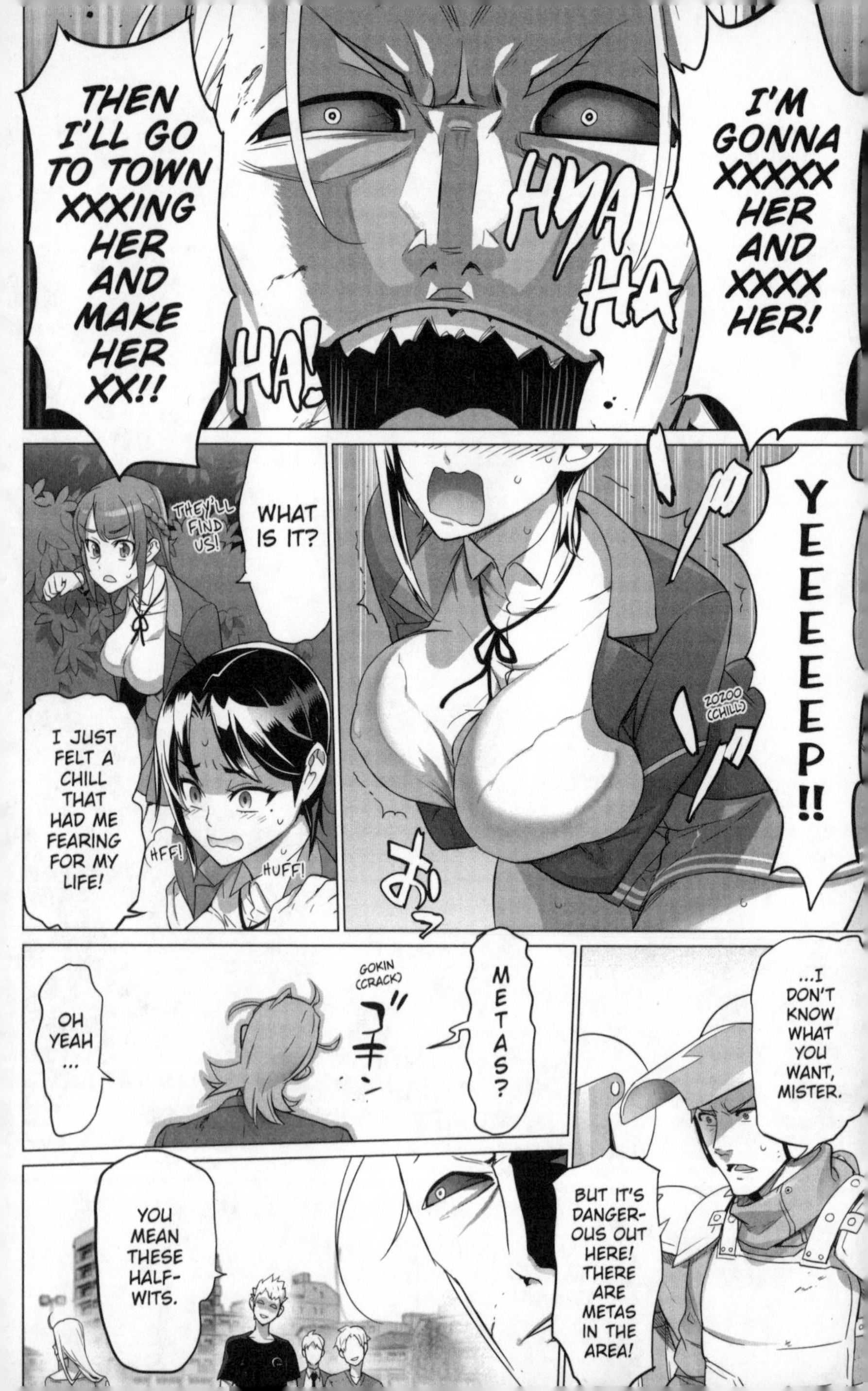
I'M GONNA XXXXX HER AND XXXX HER!
HYA HA HA!
THEN I'LL GO TO TOWN XXXING HER AND MAKE HER XX!!
YEEEEEEP!!
ZOZOO (CHILL)
WHAT IS IT?
THEY'LL FIND US!
I JUST FELT A CHILL THAT HAD ME FEARING FOR MY LIFE!
HFF!
HUFF!
...I DON'T KNOW WHAT YOU WANT, MISTER.
BUT IT'S DANGER-OUS OUT HERE! THERE ARE METAS IN THE AREA!
METAS?
GOKIN (CRACK)
OH YEAH ...
YOU MEAN THESE HALF-WITS.

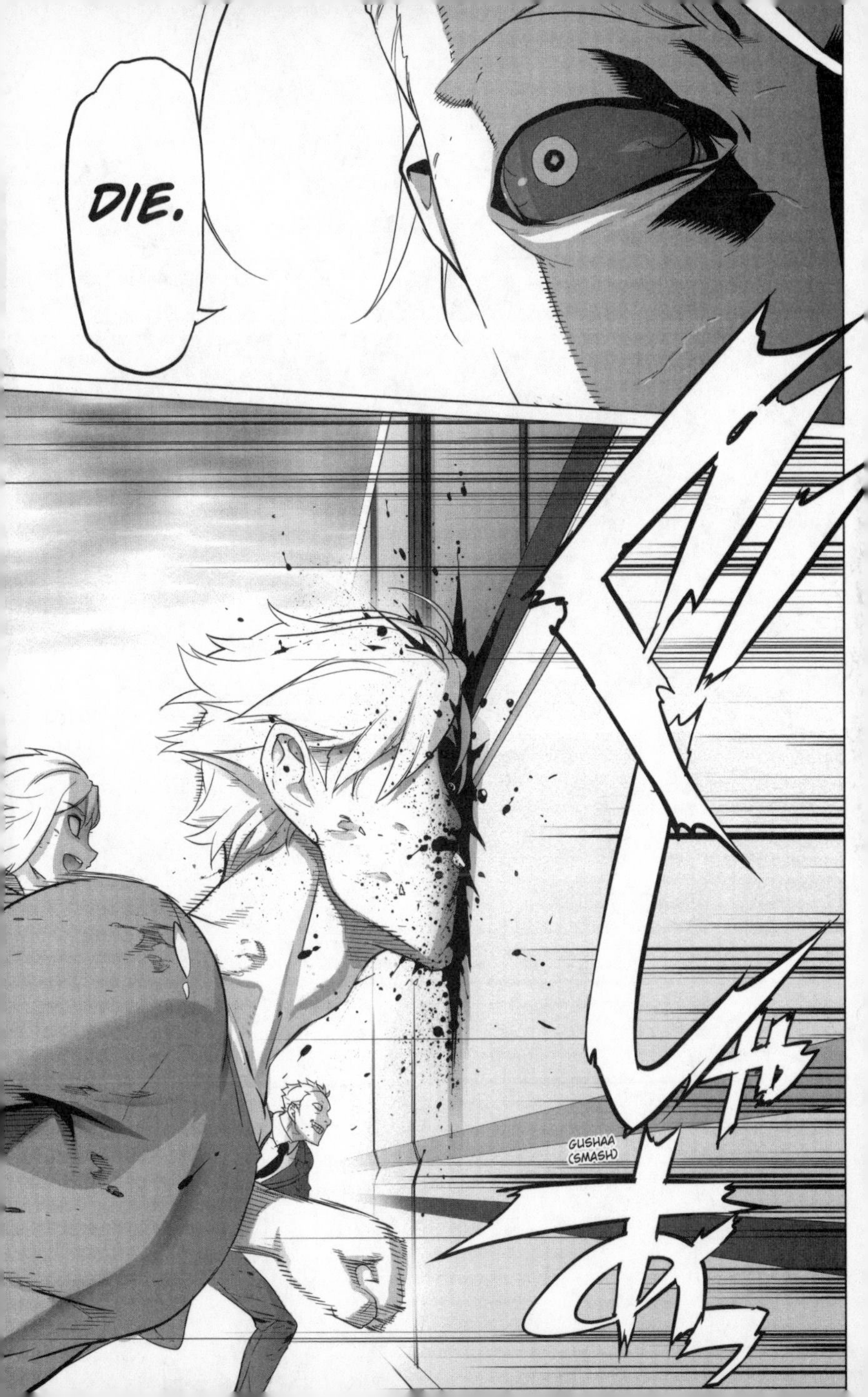
DIE.
GUSHAA (SMASH)

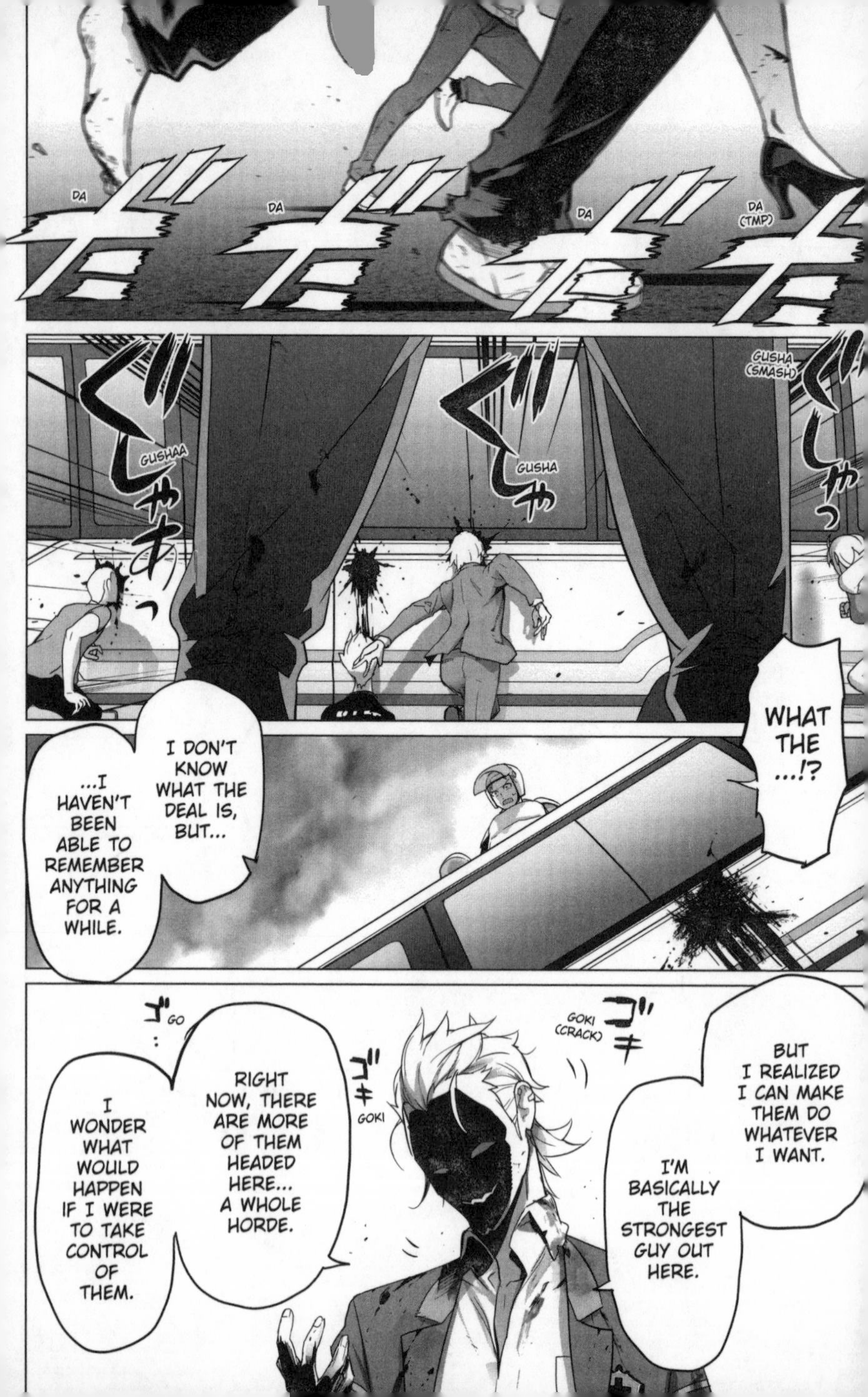
DA (TMP)
DA
DA
DA
GUSHA (SMASH)
GUSHA
GUSHAA
WHAT THE ...!?
I DON'T KNOW WHAT THE DEAL IS, BUT...
...I HAVEN'T BEEN ABLE TO REMEMBER ANYTHING FOR A WHILE.
BUT I REALIZED I CAN MAKE THEM DO WHATEVER I WANT.
I'M BASICALLY THE STRONGEST GUY OUT HERE.
GOKI (CRACK)
GOKI
RIGHT NOW, THERE ARE MORE OF THEM HEADED HERE... A WHOLE HORDE.
GO
I WONDER WHAT WOULD HAPPEN IF I WERE TO TAKE CONTROL OF THEM.

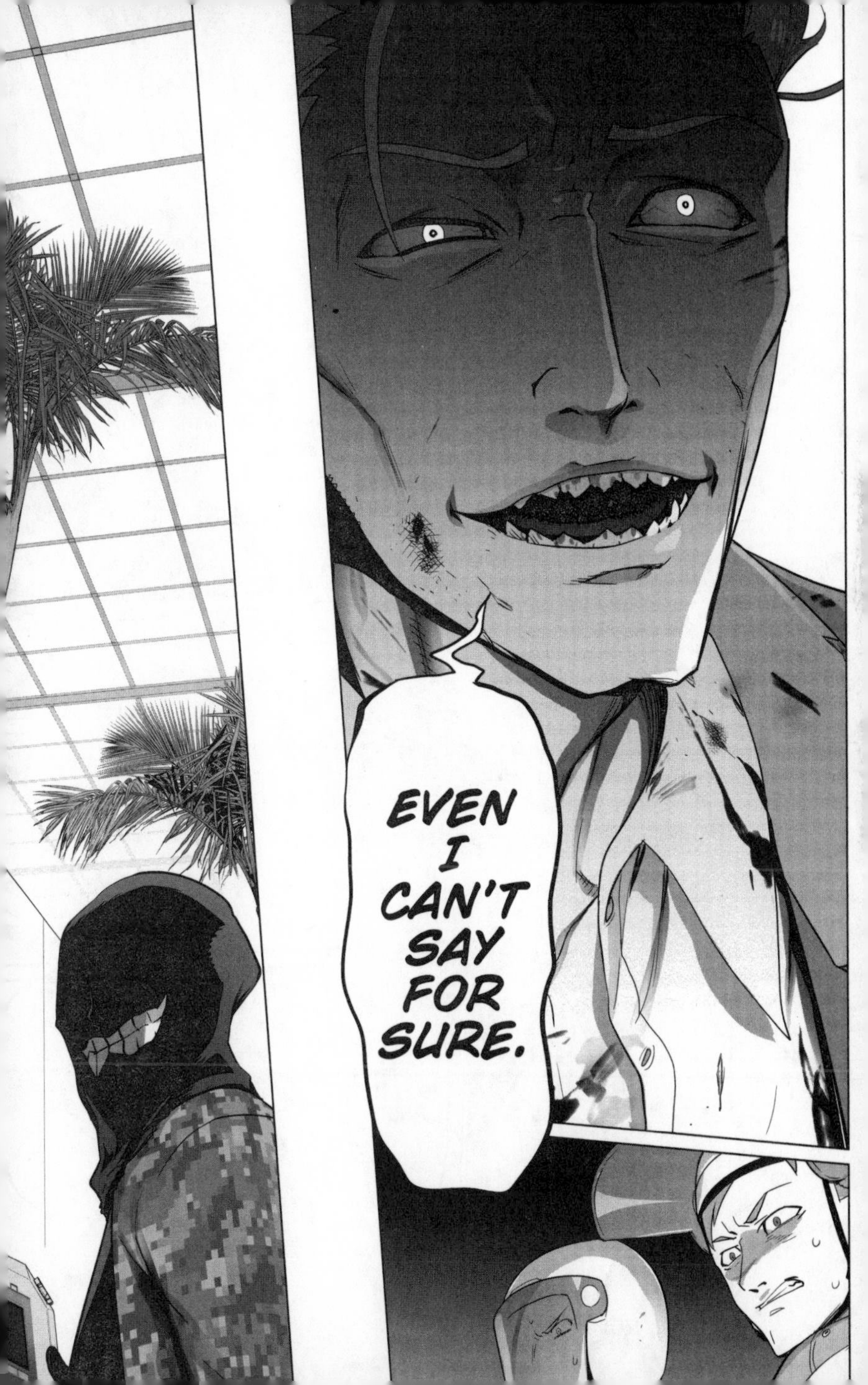
EVEN I CAN'T SAY FOR SURE.

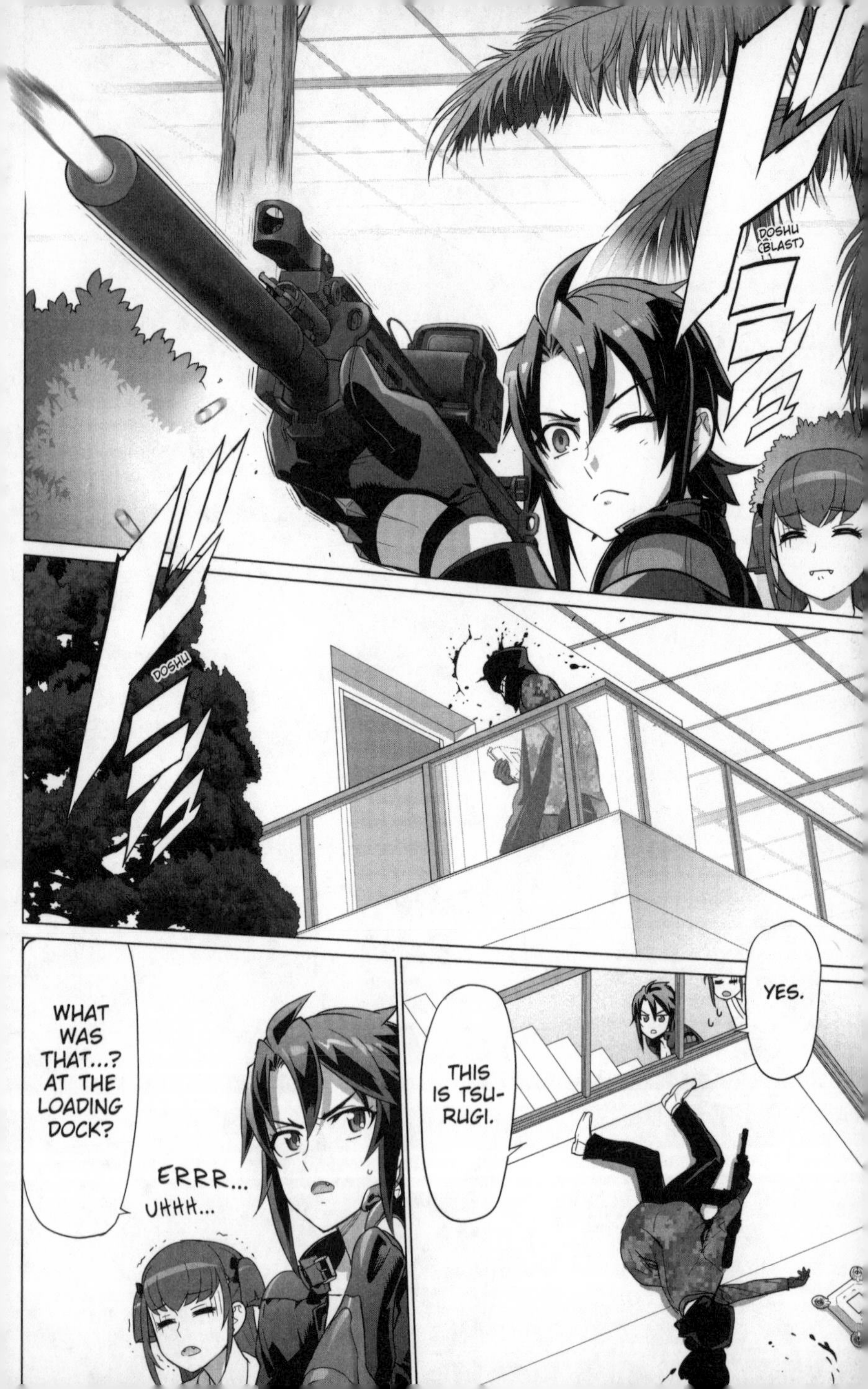
DOSHU (BLAST)
DOSHU
YES.
THIS IS TSU-RUGI.
WHAT WAS THAT...? AT THE LOADING DOCK?
ERRR... UHHH...

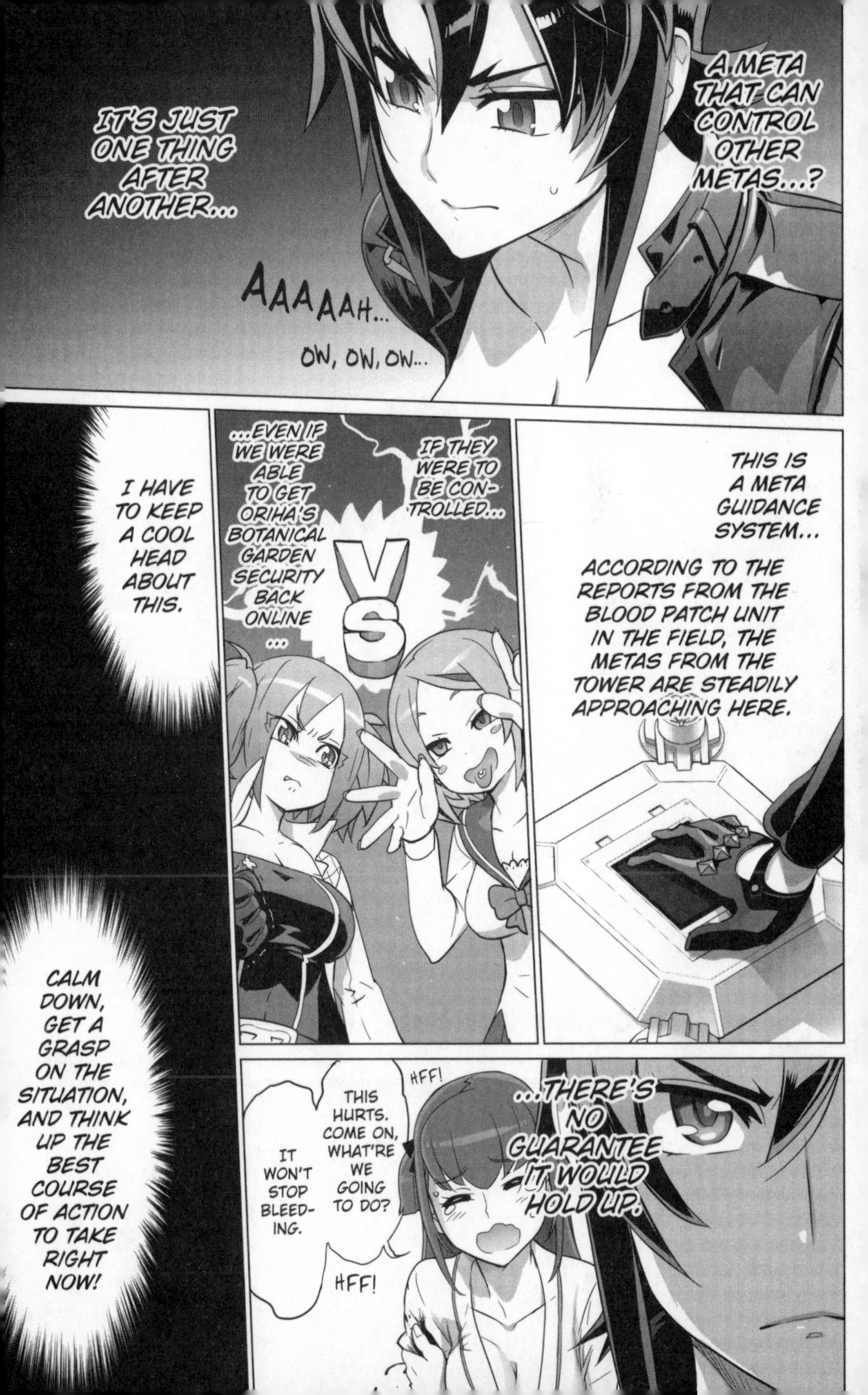
A META THAT CAN CONTROL OTHER METAS...?
IT'S JUST ONE THING AFTER ANOTHER...
AAAAAH...
OW, OW, OW...
THIS IS A META GUIDANCE SYSTEM...
ACCORDING TO THE REPORTS FROM THE BLOOD PATCH UNIT IN THE FIELD, THE METAS FROM THE TOWER ARE STEADILY APPROACHING HERE.
IF THEY WERE TO BE CON-TROLLED...
...EVEN IF WE WERE ABLE TO GET ORIHA'S BOTANICAL GARDEN SECURITY BACK ONLINE...
VS
I HAVE TO KEEP A COOL HEAD ABOUT THIS.
...THERE'S NO GUARANTEE IT WOULD HOLD UP.
HFF!
THIS HURTS. COME ON, WHAT'RE WE GOING TO DO?
IT WON'T STOP BLEED-ING.
HFF!
CALM DOWN, GET A GRASP ON THE SITUATION, AND THINK UP THE BEST COURSE OF ACTION TO TAKE RIGHT NOW!

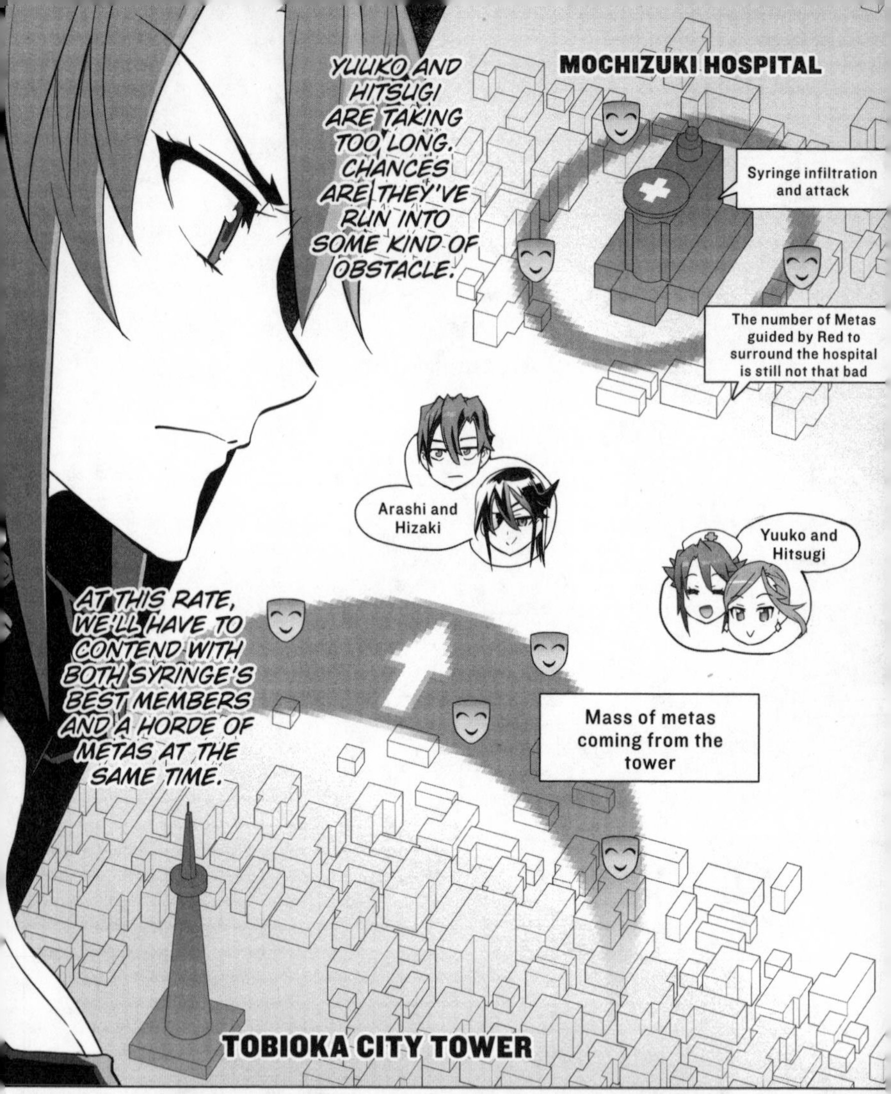
MOCHIZUKI HOSPITAL
YUUKO AND HITSUGI ARE TAKING TOO LONG. CHANCES ARE THEY'VE RUN INTO SOME KIND OF OBSTACLE.
Syringe infiltration and attack
The number of Metas guided by Red to surround the hospital is still not that bad
Arashi and Hizaki
Yuuko and Hitsugi
AT THIS RATE, WE'LL HAVE TO CONTEND WITH BOTH SYRINGE'S BEST MEMBERS AND A HORDE OF METAS AT THE SAME TIME.
Mass of metas coming from the tower
TOBIOKA CITY TOWER
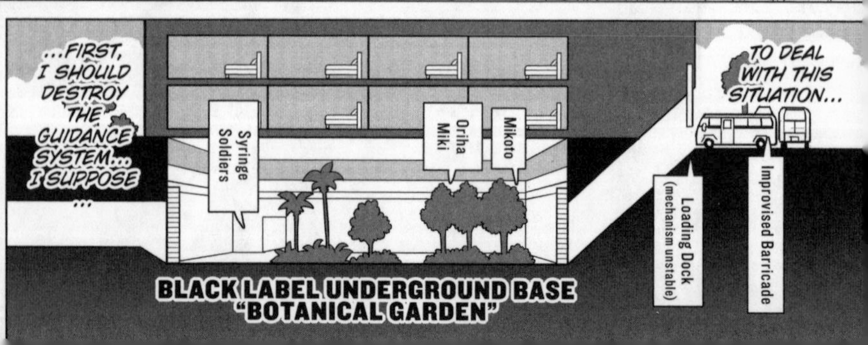
TO DEAL WITH THIS SITUATION...
Improvised Barricade
Loading Dock (mechanism unstable)
Mikoto
Oriha Miki
Syringe Soldiers
...FIRST, I SHOULD DESTROY THE GUIDANCE SYSTEM... I SUPPOSE...
BLACK LABEL UNDERGROUND BASE "BOTANICAL GARDEN"

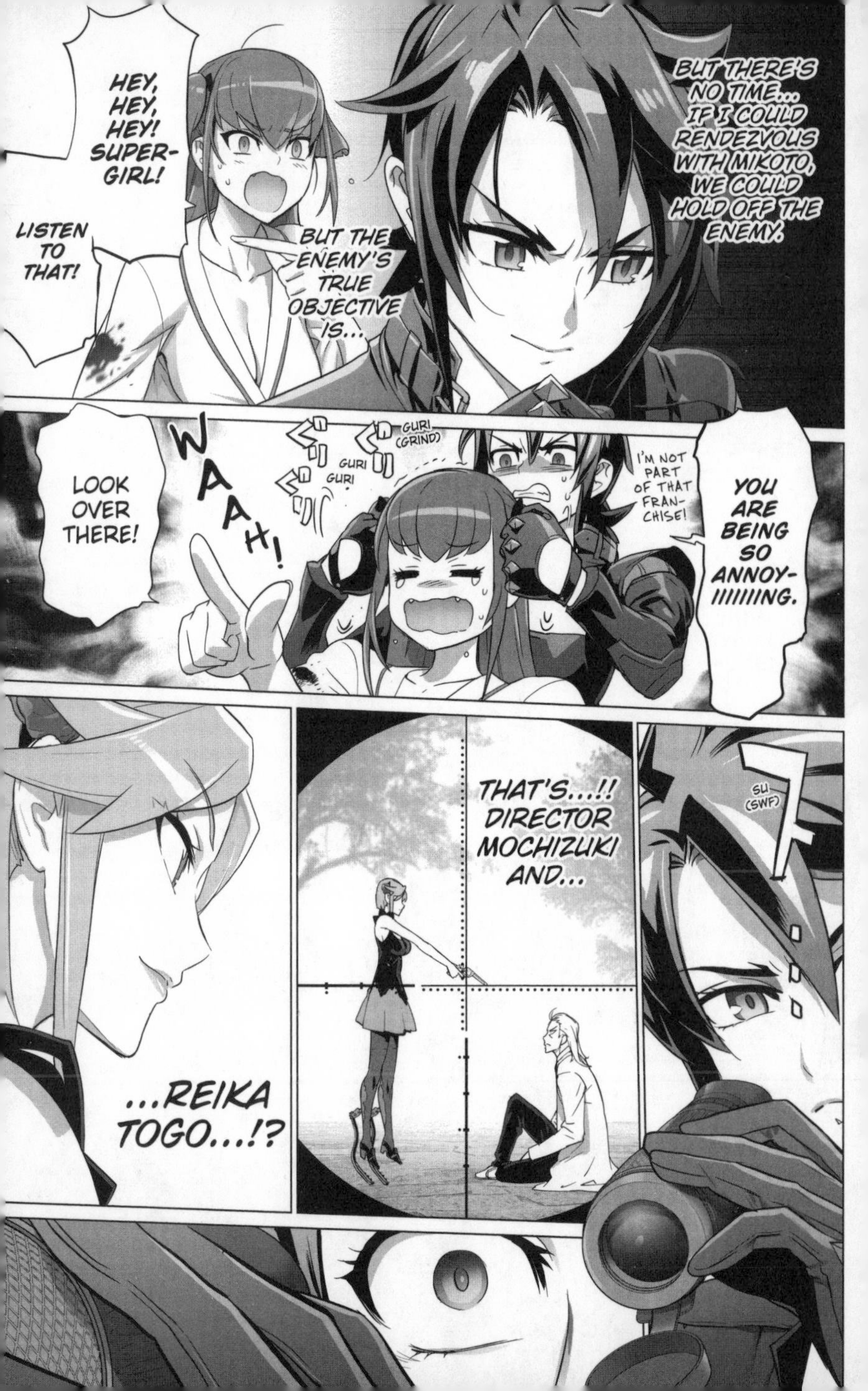
BUT THERE'S NO TIME... IF I COULD RENDEZVOUS WITH MIKOTO, WE COULD HOLD OFF THE ENEMY.
BUT THE ENEMY'S TRUE OBJECTIVE IS...
HEY, HEY, HEY! SUPER-GIRL!
LISTEN TO THAT!
YOU ARE BEING SO ANNOY-IIIIIIING.
I'M NOT PART OF THAT FRAN-CHISE!
GURI (GRIND)
GURI GURI
WAAH!
LOOK OVER THERE!
SU (SWF)
THAT'S...!! DIRECTOR MOCHIZUKI AND...
...REIKA TOGO...!?

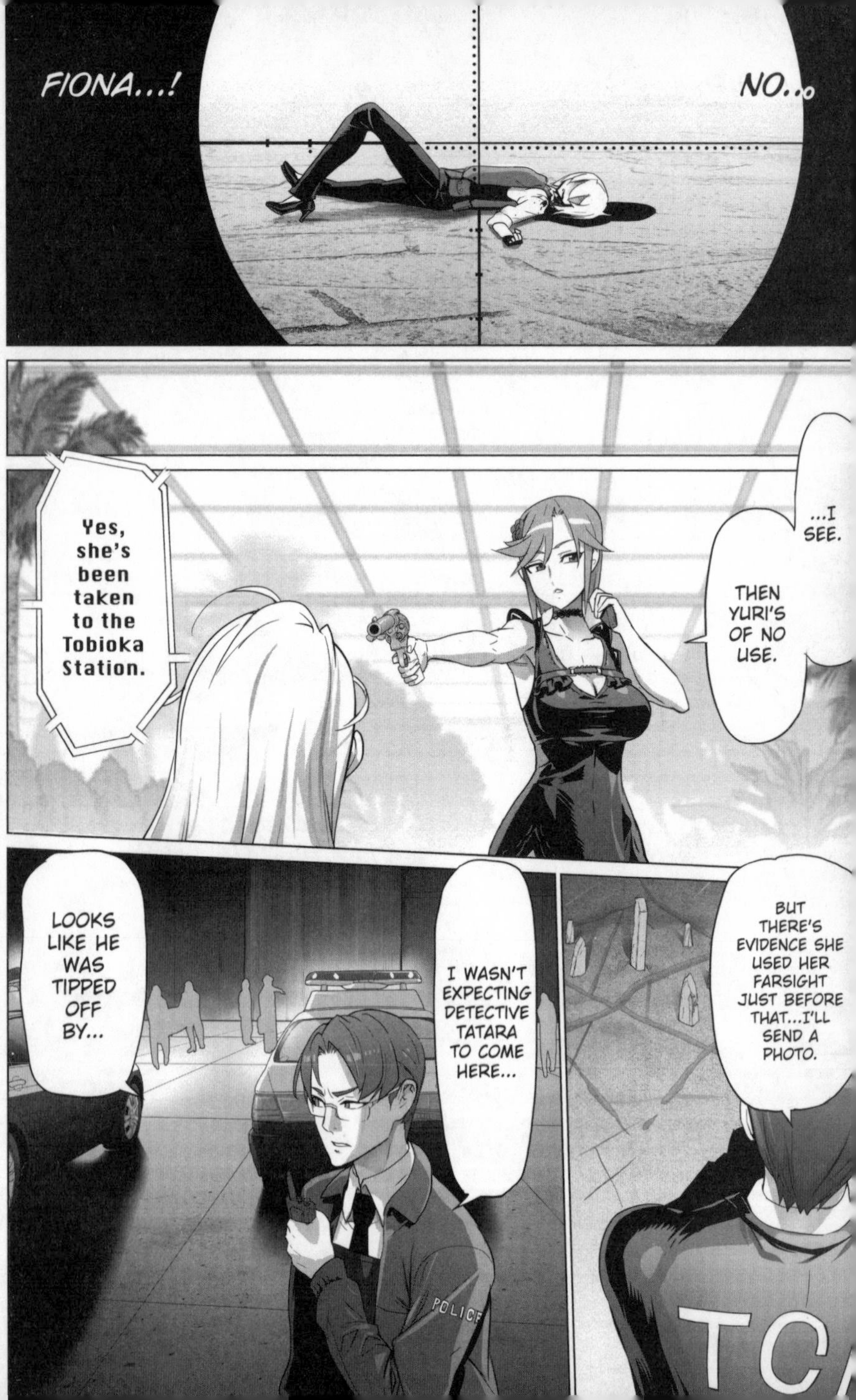
NO...
FIONA...!
...I SEE.
THEN YURI'S OF NO USE.
Yes, she's been taken to the Tobioka Station.
BUT THERE'S EVIDENCE SHE USED HER FARSIGHT JUST BEFORE THAT...I'LL SEND A PHOTO.
TCA
I WASN'T EXPECTING DETECTIVE TATARA TO COME HERE...
LOOKS LIKE HE WAS TIPPED OFF BY...
POLICE

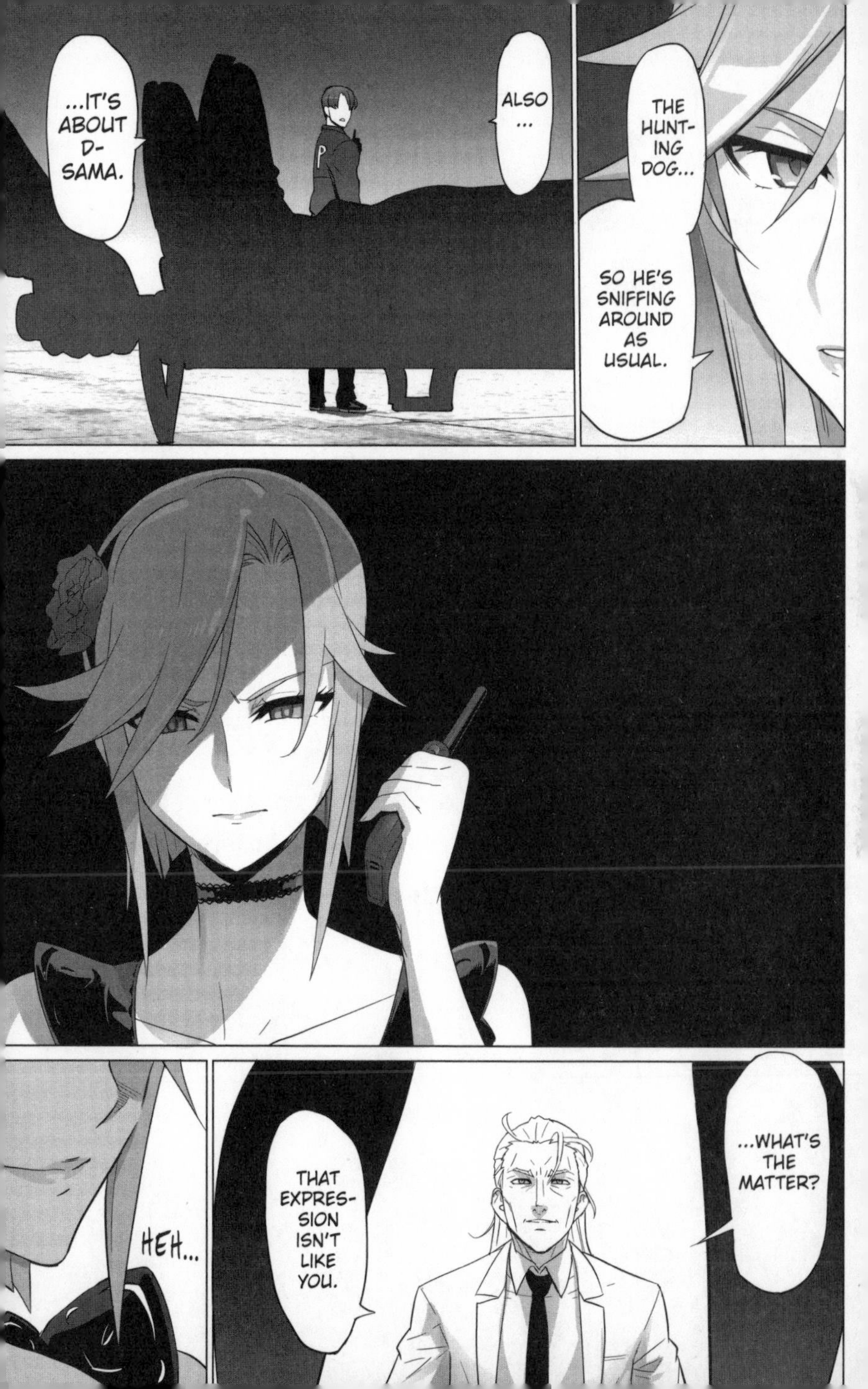
THE HUNTING DOG...
SO HE'S SNIFFING AROUND AS USUAL.
ALSO...
...IT'S ABOUT D-SAMA.
...WHAT'S THE MATTER?
THAT EXPRESSION ISN'T LIKE YOU.
HEH...

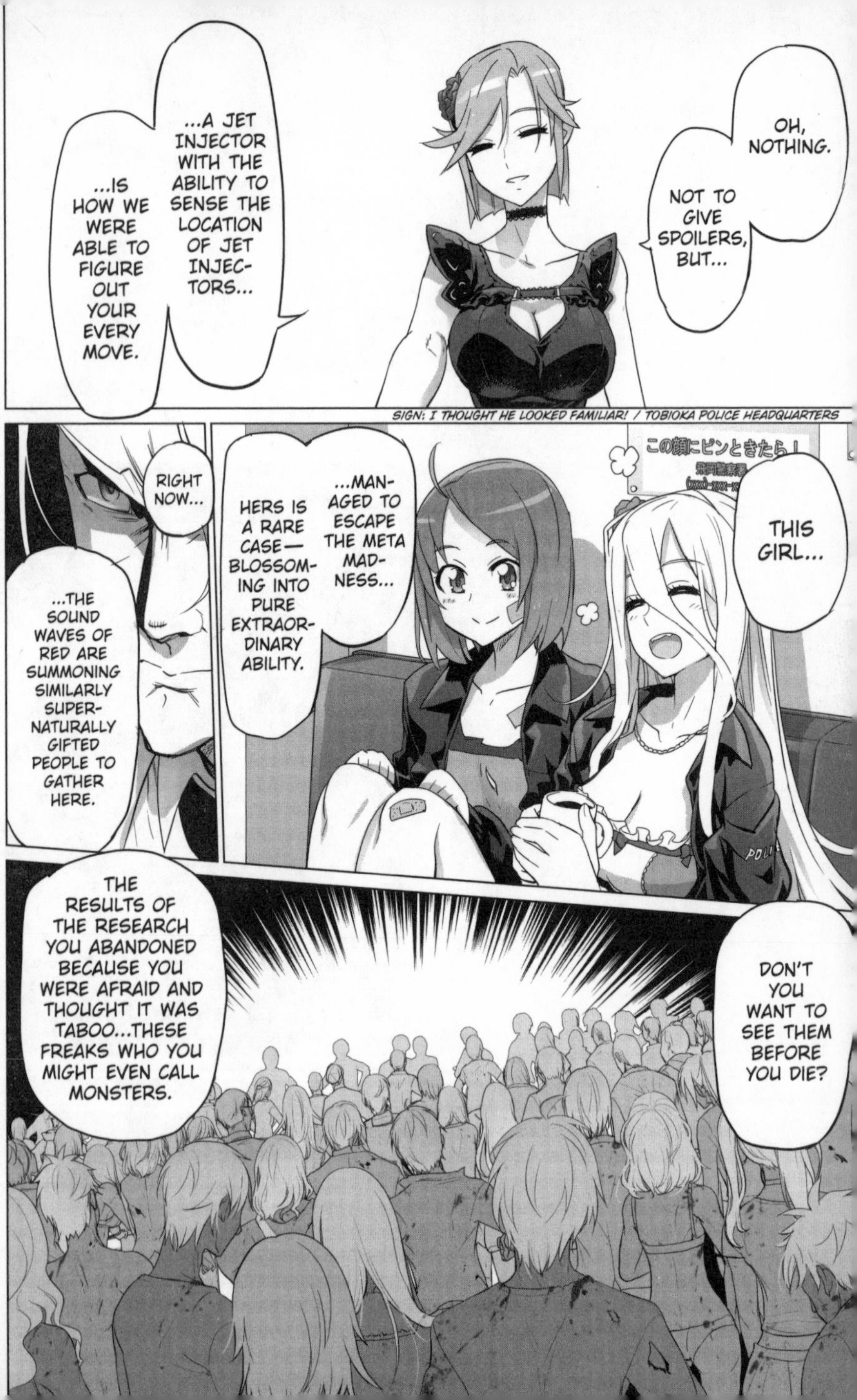
OH, NOTHING.
NOT TO GIVE SPOILERS, BUT...
...A JET INJECTOR WITH THE ABILITY TO SENSE THE LOCATION OF JET INJECTORS...
...IS HOW WE WERE ABLE TO FIGURE OUT YOUR EVERY MOVE.
SIGN: I THOUGHT HE LOOKED FAMILIAR! / TOBIOKA POLICE HEADQUARTERS
この顔にピンときたら！
THIS GIRL...
...MANAGED TO ESCAPE THE META MADNESS...
HERS IS A RARE CASE—BLOSSOMING INTO PURE EXTRAORDINARY ABILITY.
RIGHT NOW...
...THE SOUND WAVES OF RED ARE SUMMONING SIMILARLY SUPERNATURALLY GIFTED PEOPLE TO GATHER HERE.
THE RESULTS OF THE RESEARCH YOU ABANDONED BECAUSE YOU WERE AFRAID AND THOUGHT IT WAS TABOO...THESE FREAKS WHO YOU MIGHT EVEN CALL MONSTERS.
DON'T YOU WANT TO SEE THEM BEFORE YOU DIE?

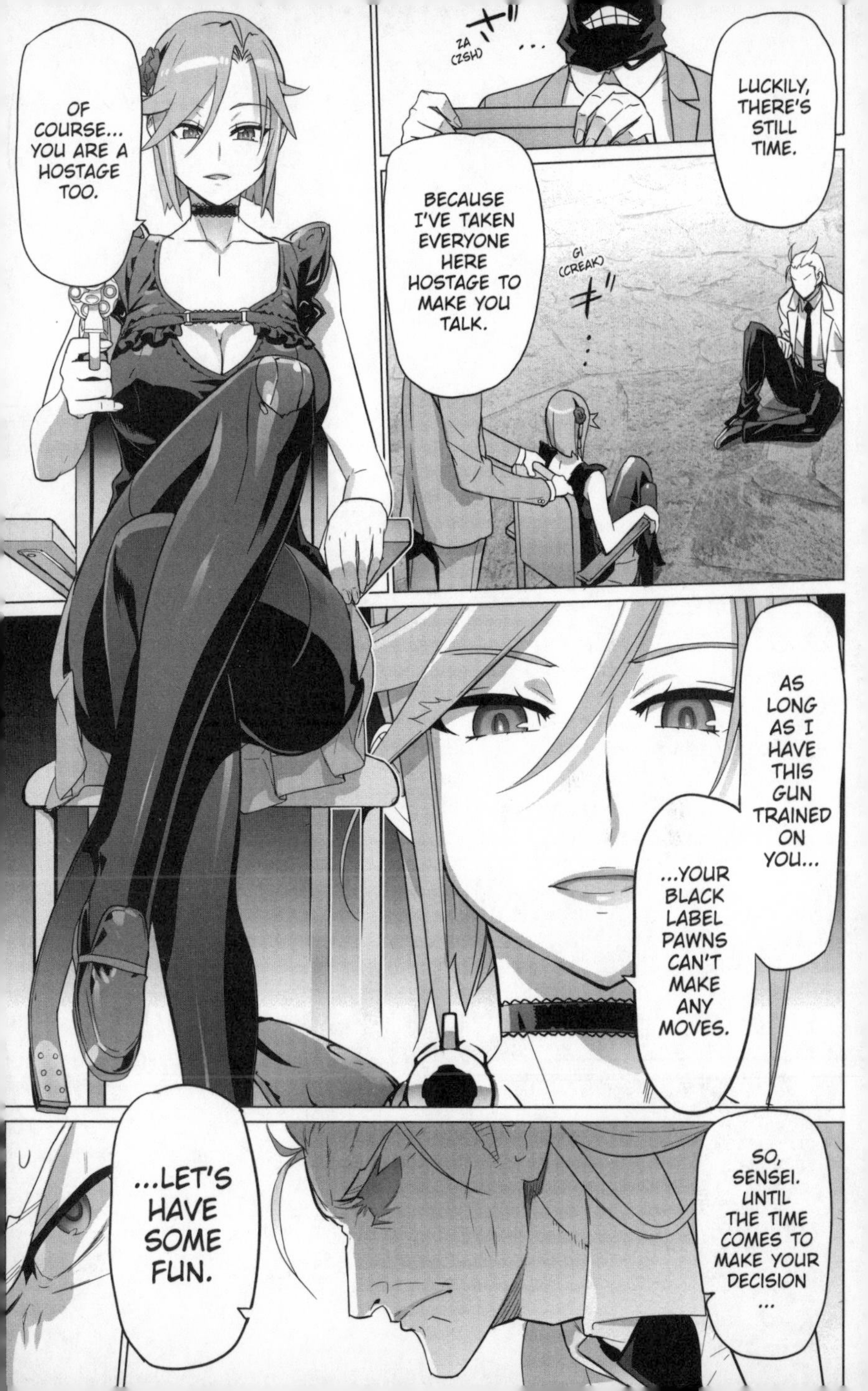
ZA (ZSH)
...
LUCKILY, THERE'S STILL TIME.
BECAUSE I'VE TAKEN EVERYONE HERE HOSTAGE TO MAKE YOU TALK.
GI (CREAK)
AS LONG AS I HAVE THIS GUN TRAINED ON YOU...
...YOUR BLACK LABEL PAWNS CAN'T MAKE ANY MOVES.
OF COURSE... YOU ARE A HOSTAGE TOO.
SO, SENSEI. UNTIL THE TIME COMES TO MAKE YOUR DECISION ...
...LET'S HAVE SOME FUN.

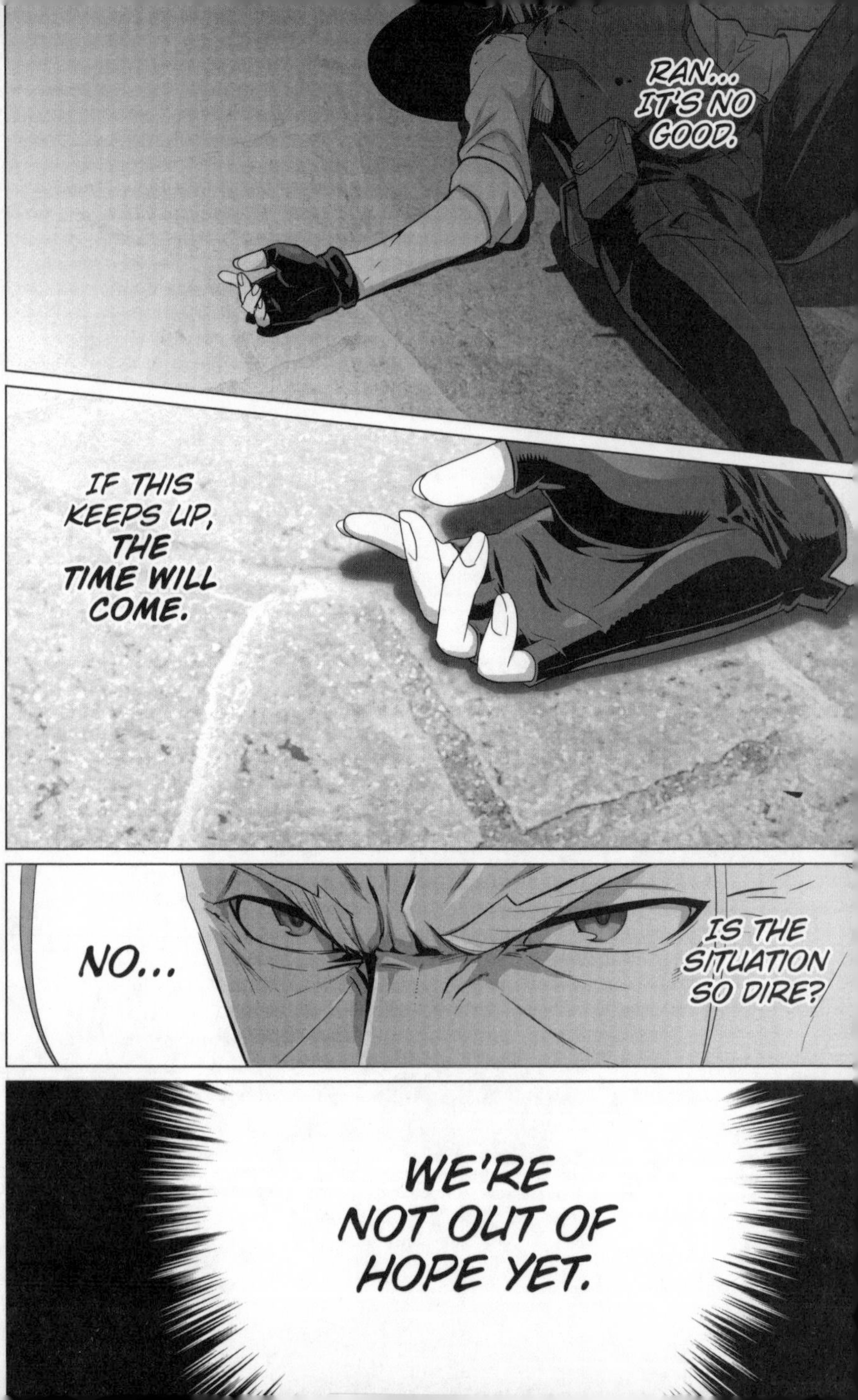
RAN... IT'S NO GOOD.
IF THIS KEEPS UP, THE TIME WILL COME.
IS THE SITUATION SO DIRE?
NO...
WE'RE NOT OUT OF HOPE YET.

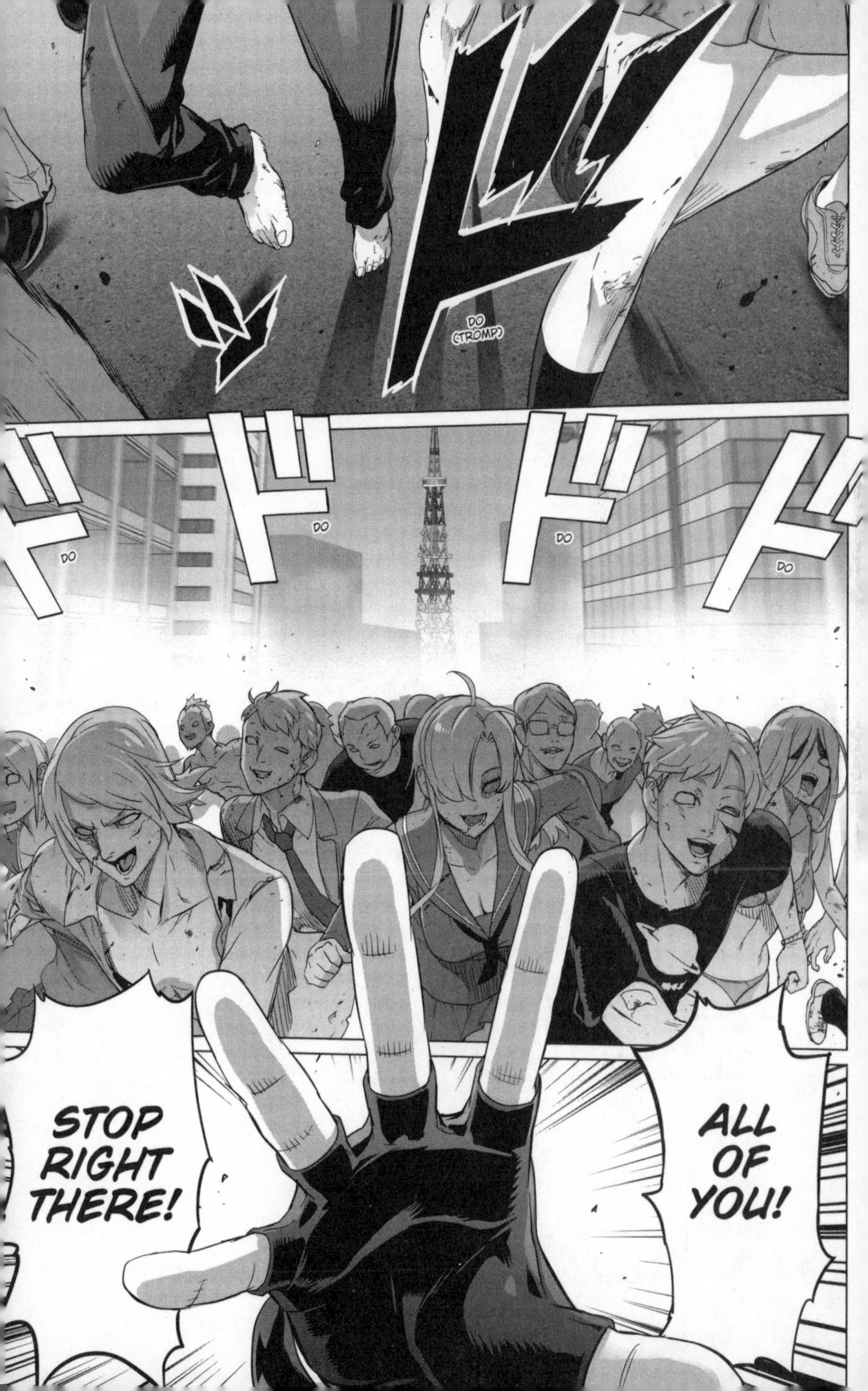
DO (TROMP)
DO
DO
DO
DO
ALL OF YOU!
STOP RIGHT THERE!

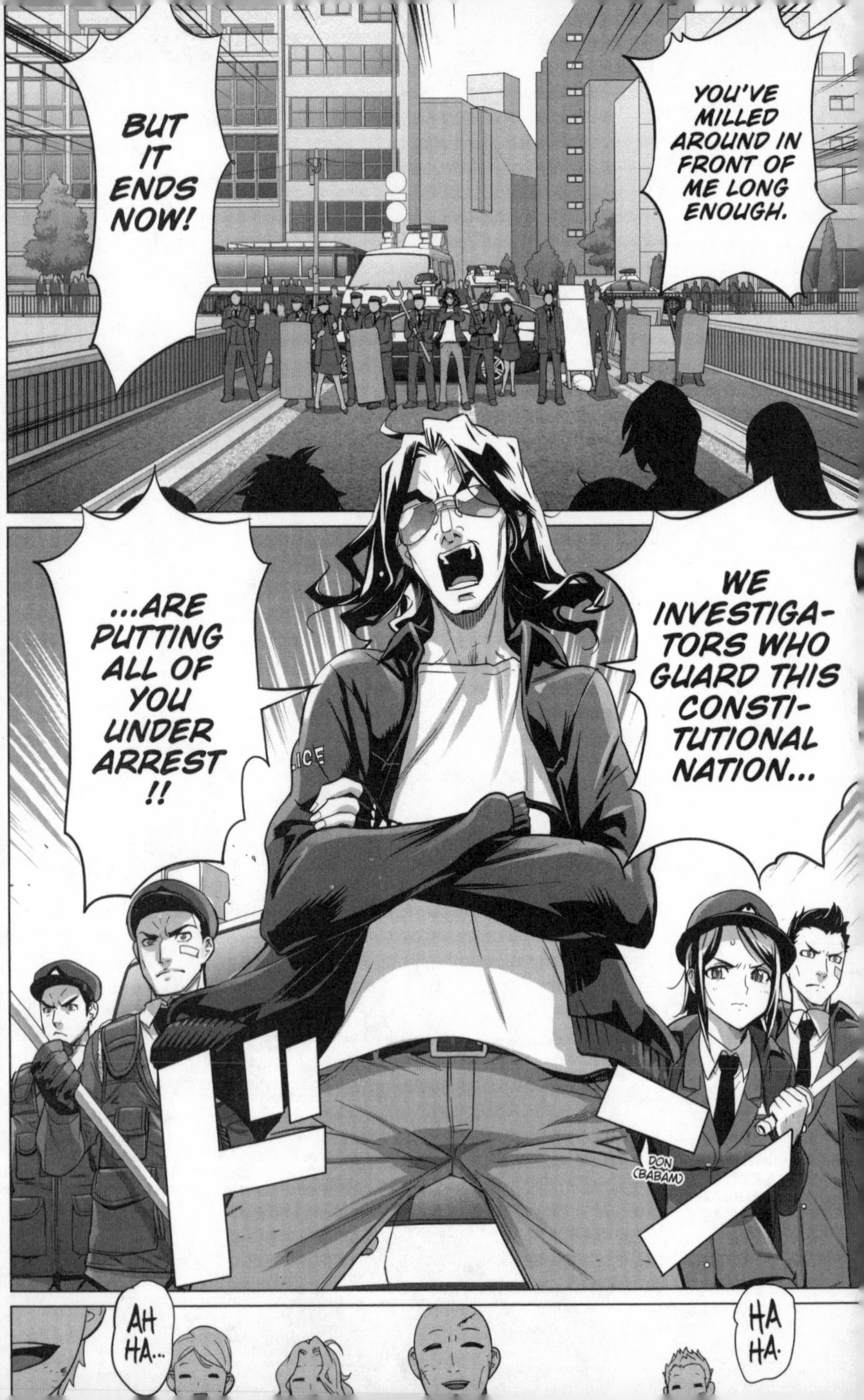
YOU'VE MILLED AROUND IN FRONT OF ME LONG ENOUGH.
BUT IT ENDS NOW!
WE INVESTIGATORS WHO GUARD THIS CONSTITUTIONAL NATION...
...ARE PUTTING ALL OF YOU UNDER ARREST!!
DON (BABAM)
HA HA.
AH HA...

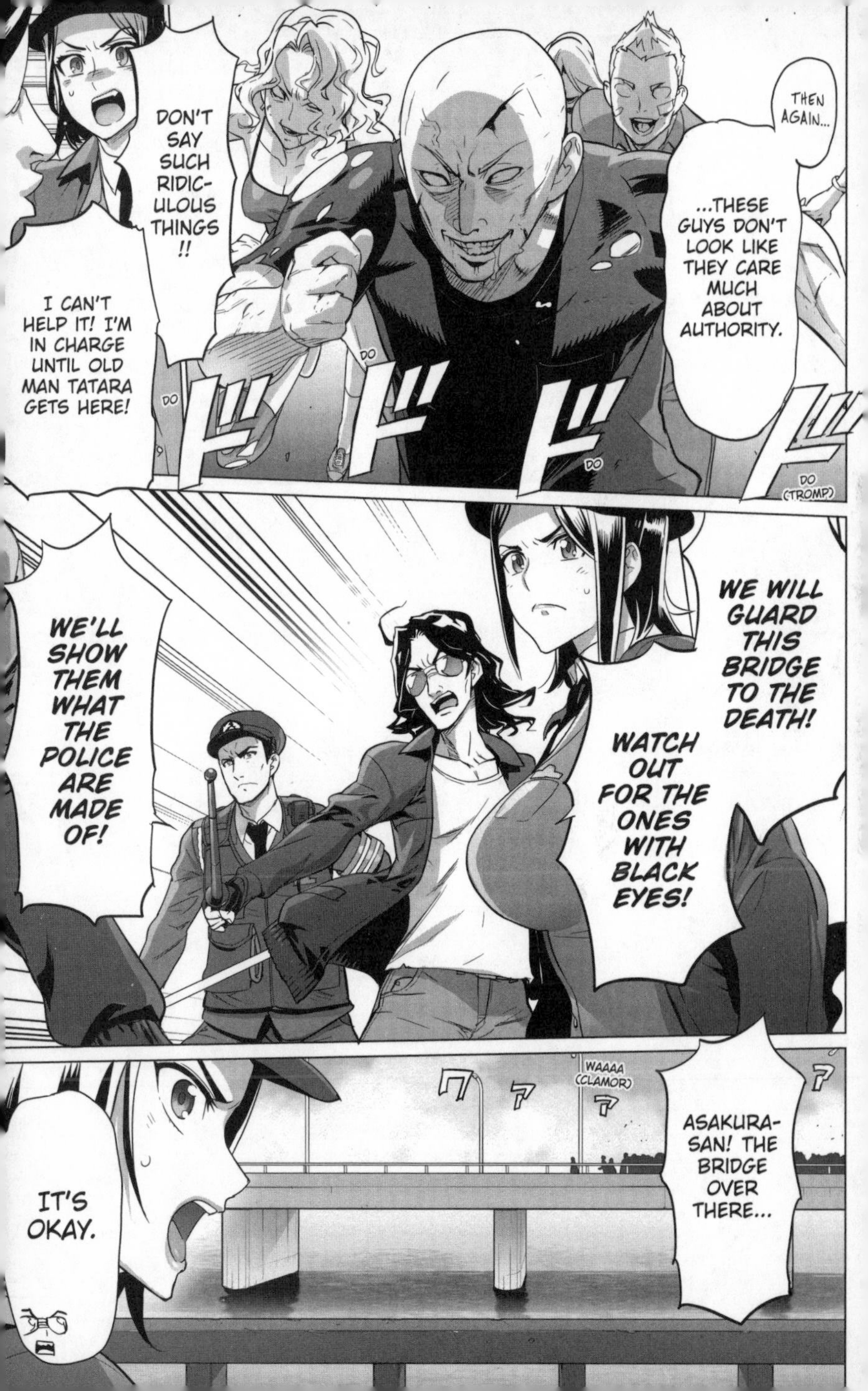

THEN AGAIN...
...THESE GUYS DON'T LOOK LIKE THEY CARE MUCH ABOUT AUTHORITY.
DO (TROMP)
DO
DO
DO
DON'T SAY SUCH RIDICULOUS THINGS!!
I CAN'T HELP IT! I'M IN CHARGE UNTIL OLD MAN TATARA GETS HERE!
WE WILL GUARD THIS BRIDGE TO THE DEATH!
WATCH OUT FOR THE ONES WITH BLACK EYES!
WE'LL SHOW THEM WHAT THE POLICE ARE MADE OF!
ASAKURA-SAN! THE BRIDGE OVER THERE...
WAAAA (CLAMOR)
IT'S OKAY.

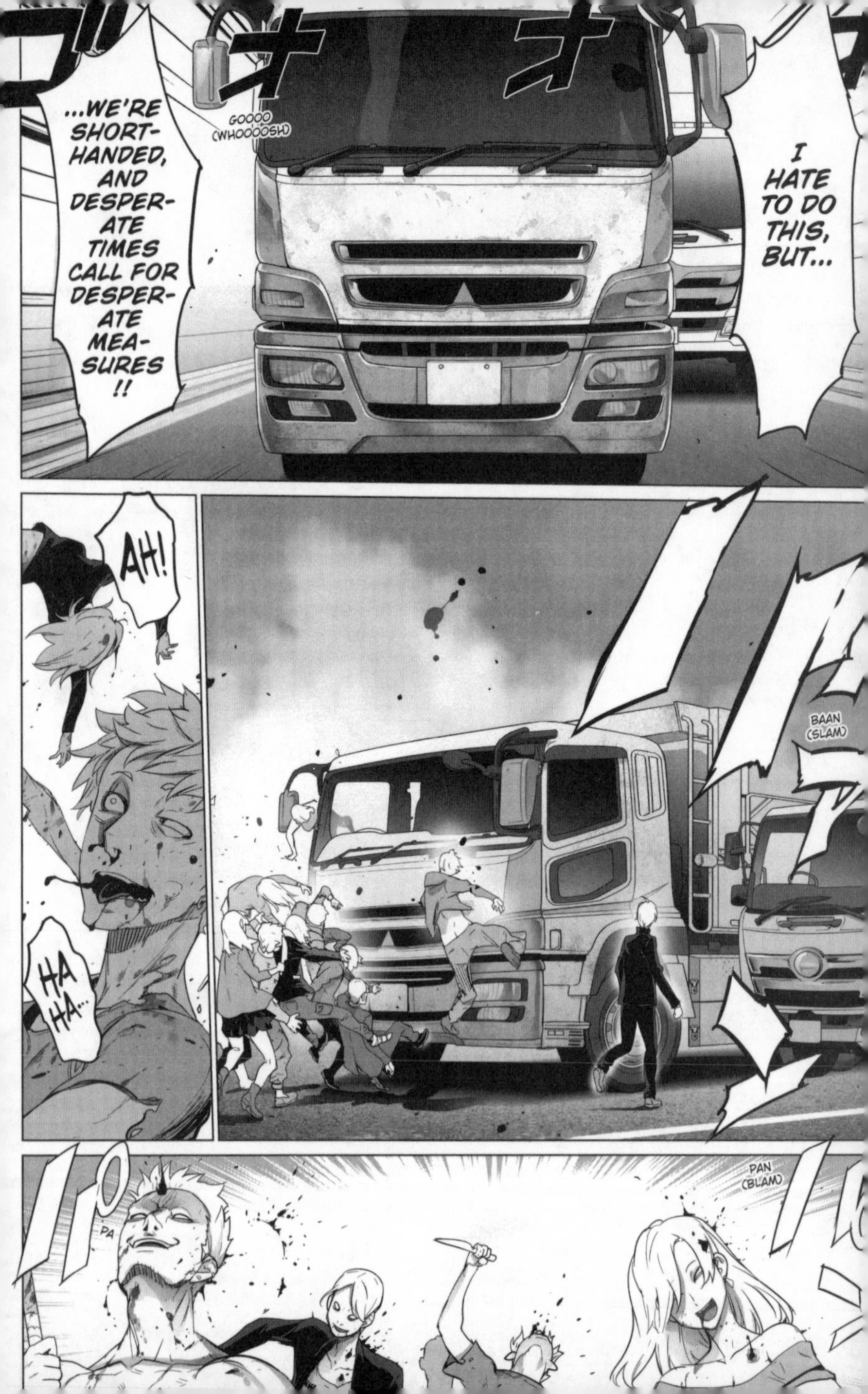
I HATE TO DO THIS, BUT...
...WE'RE SHORT-HANDED, AND DESPER-ATE TIMES CALL FOR DESPER-ATE MEA-SURES !!
GOOOO (WHOOOOSH)
BAAN (SLAM)
AH!
HA HA...
PAN (BLAM)
PA

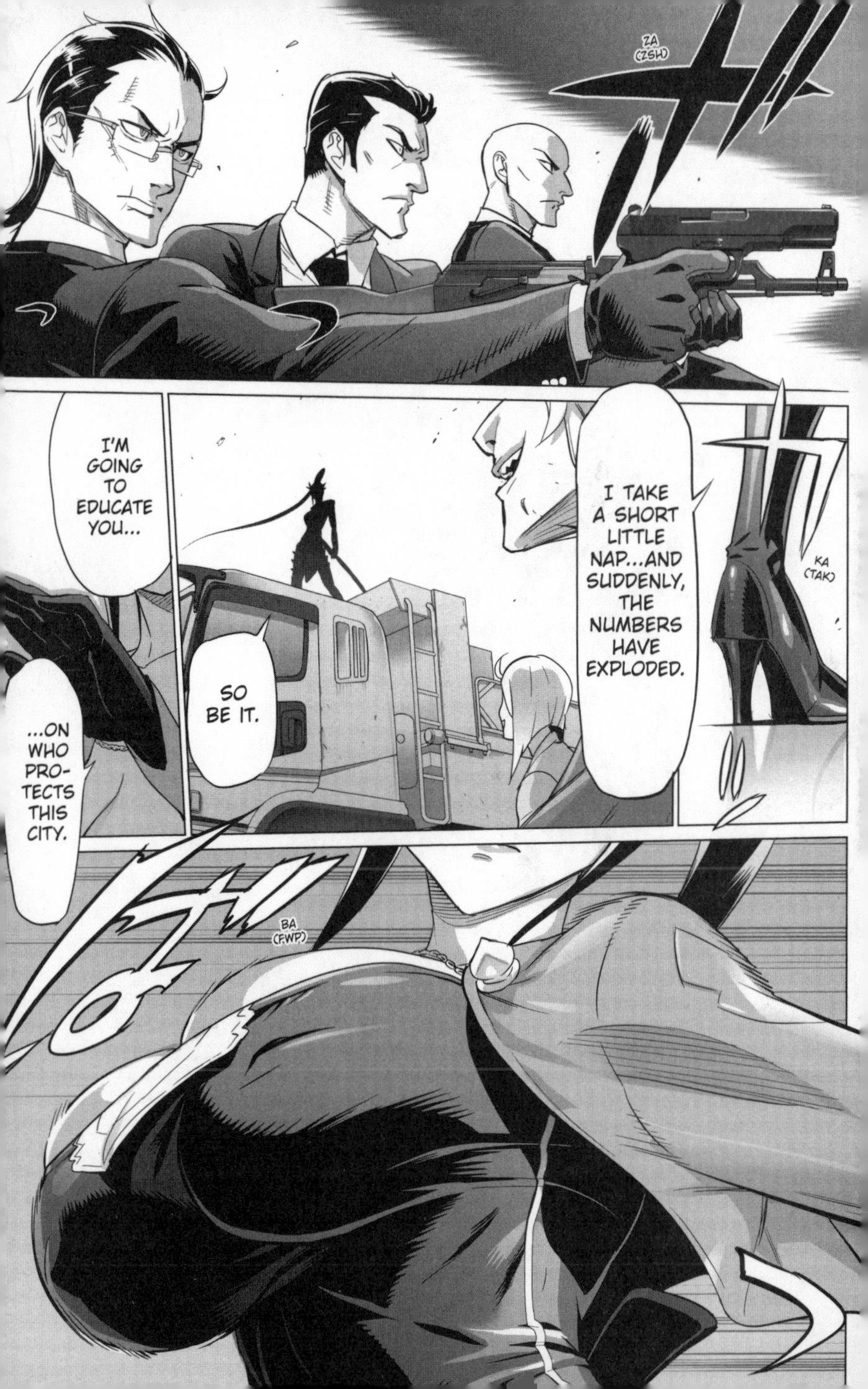
ZA (ZSH)
KA (TAK)
I TAKE A SHORT LITTLE NAP...AND SUDDENLY, THE NUMBERS HAVE EXPLODED.
SO BE IT.
I'M GOING TO EDUCATE YOU...
...ON WHO PROTECTS THIS CITY.
BA (FWP)

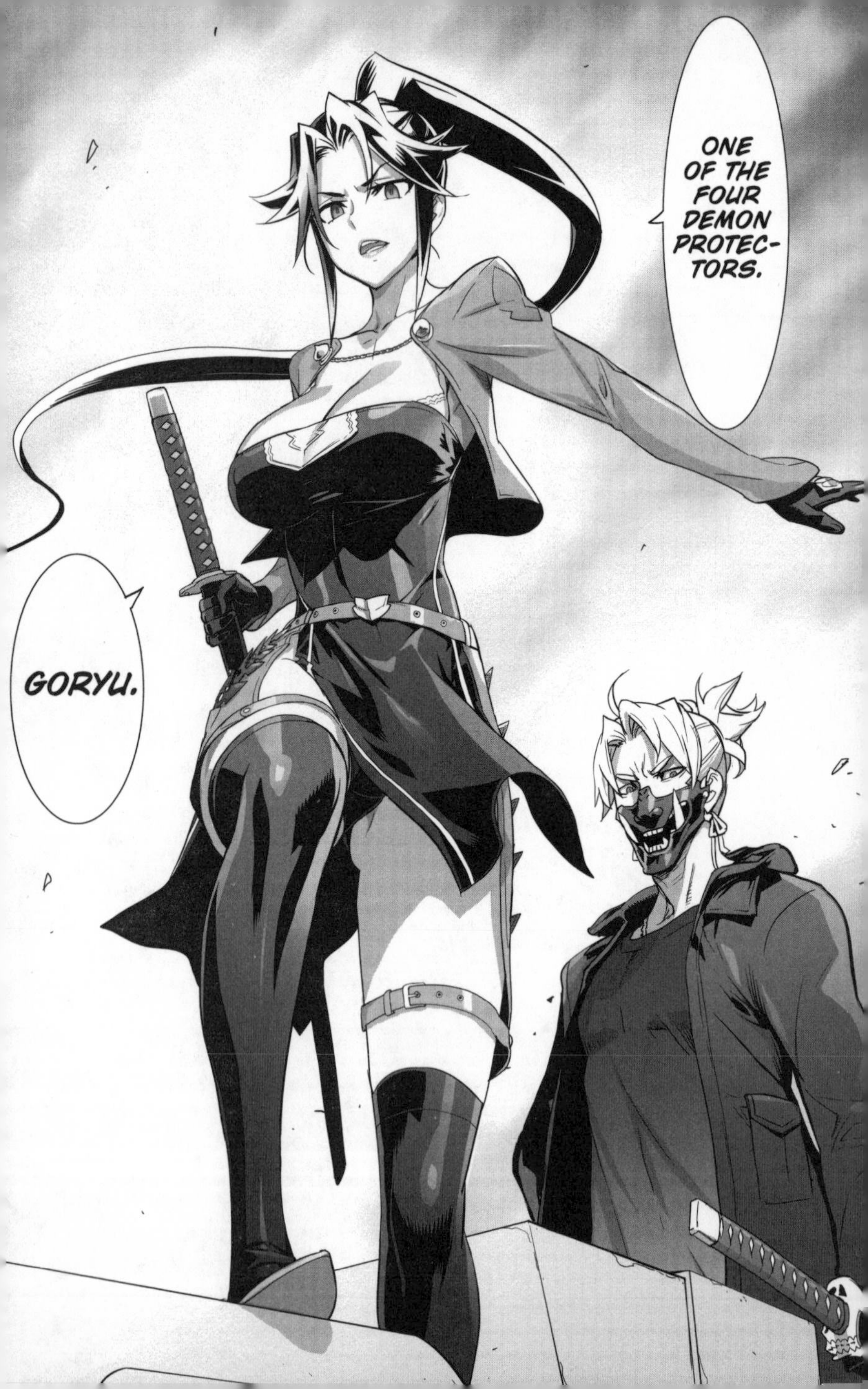
ONE OF THE FOUR DEMON PROTEC-TORS.
GORYU.

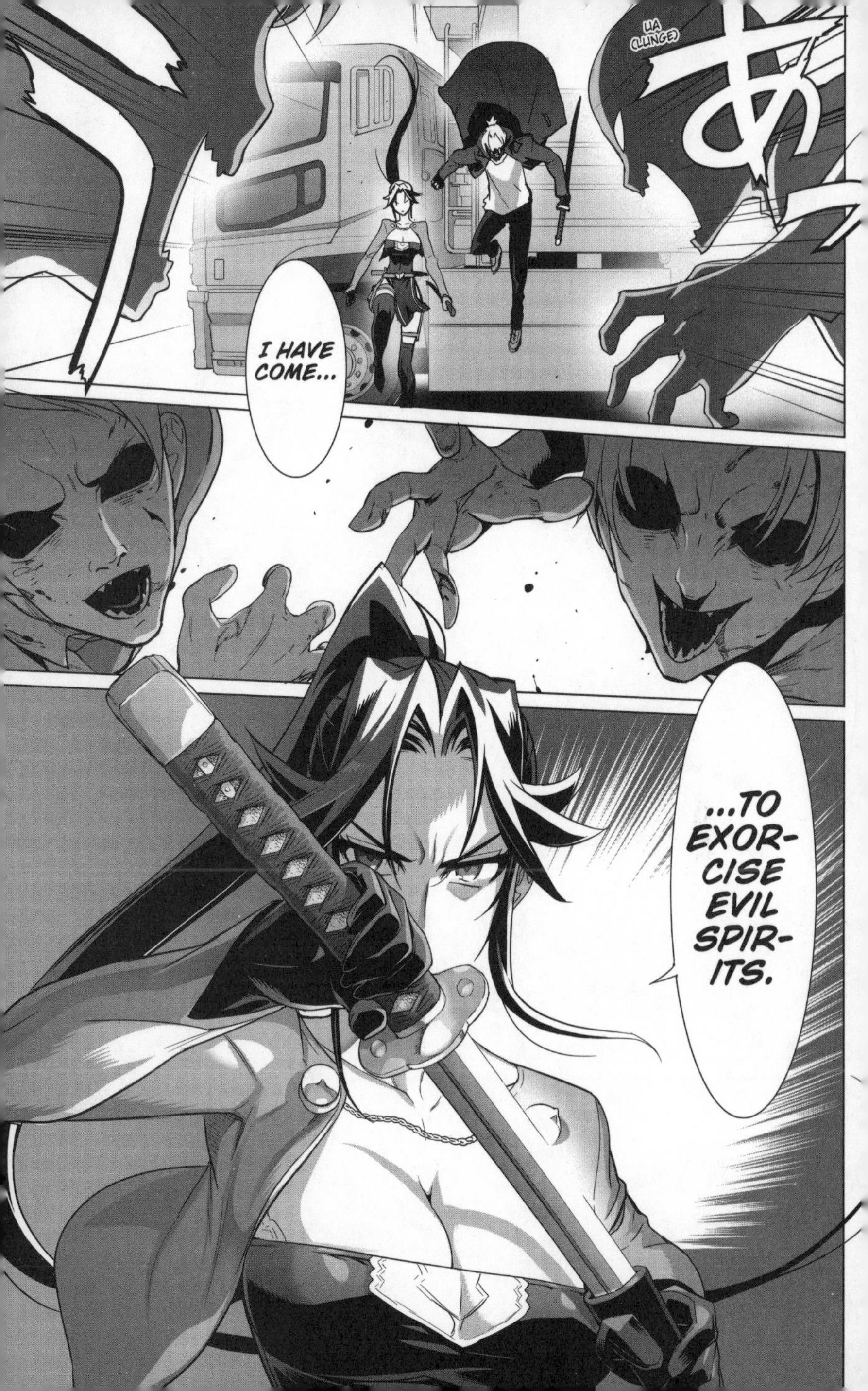
あ
UA (LUNGE)
I HAVE COME...
...TO EXORCISE EVIL SPIRITS.

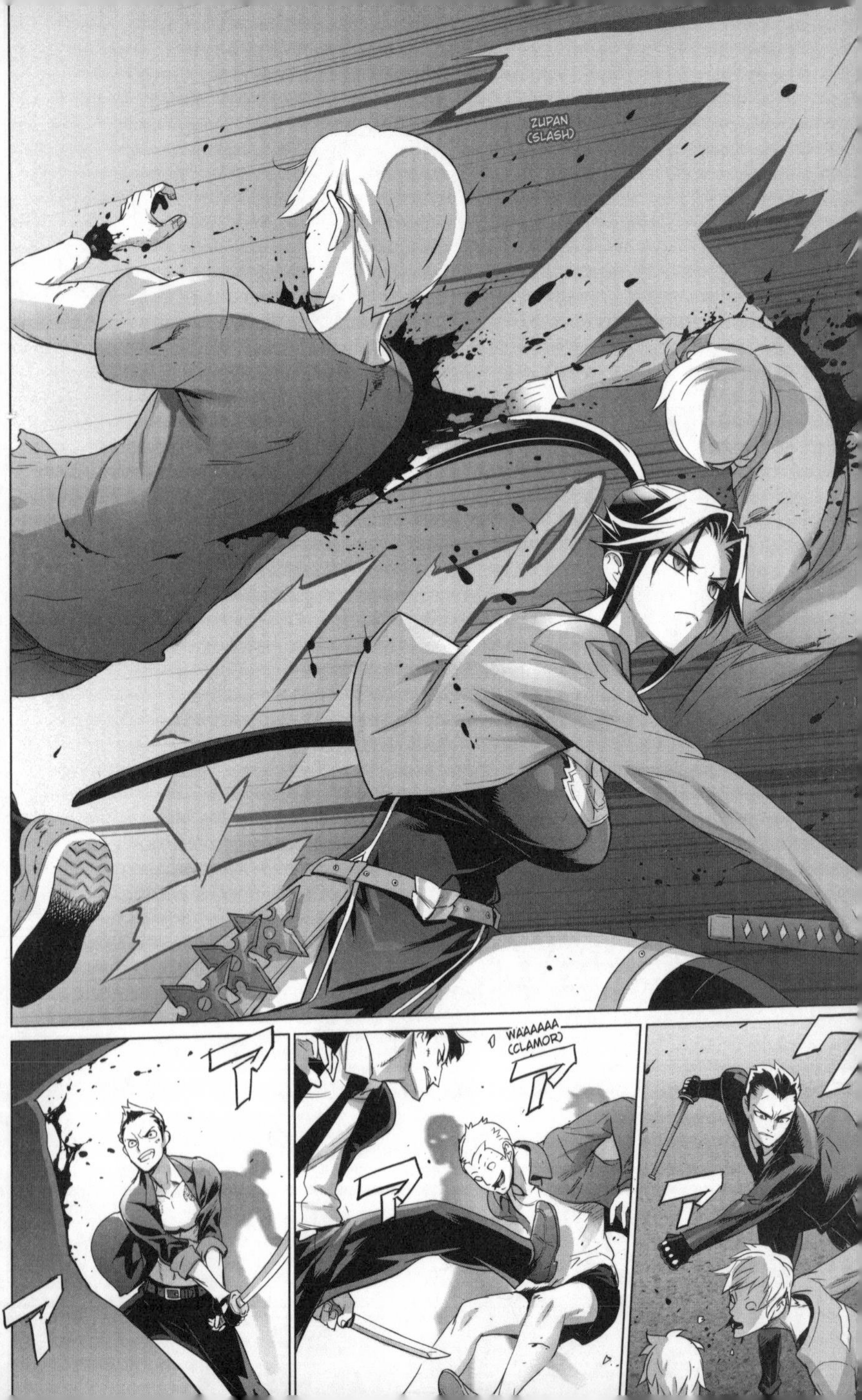
ZUPAN
(SLASH)
WAAAAAA
(CLAMOR)

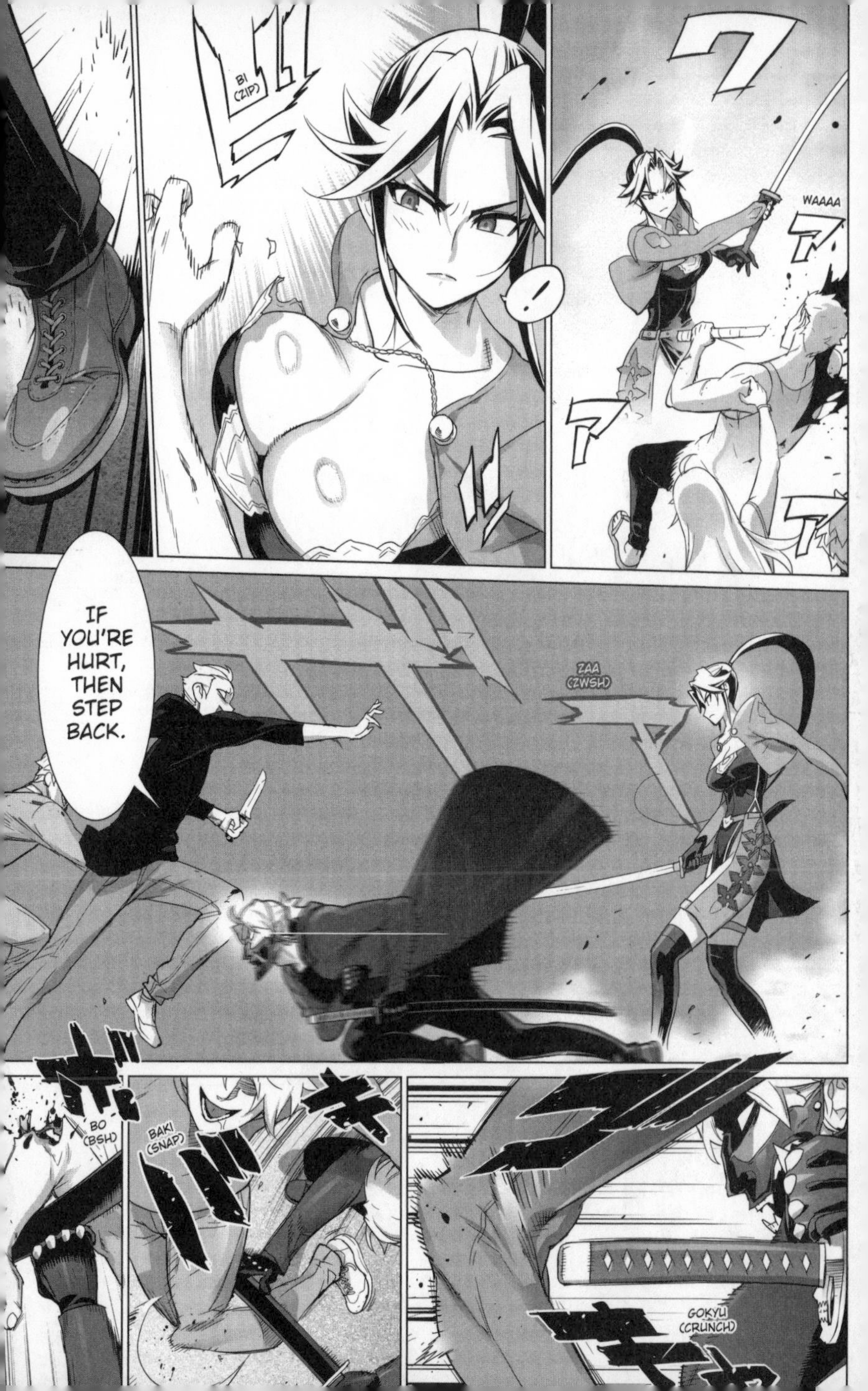
WAAAA
!
BI (ZIP)
ZAA (ZWSH)
IF YOU'RE HURT, THEN STEP BACK.
GOKYU (CRUNCH)
BAKI (SNAP)
BO (BSH)

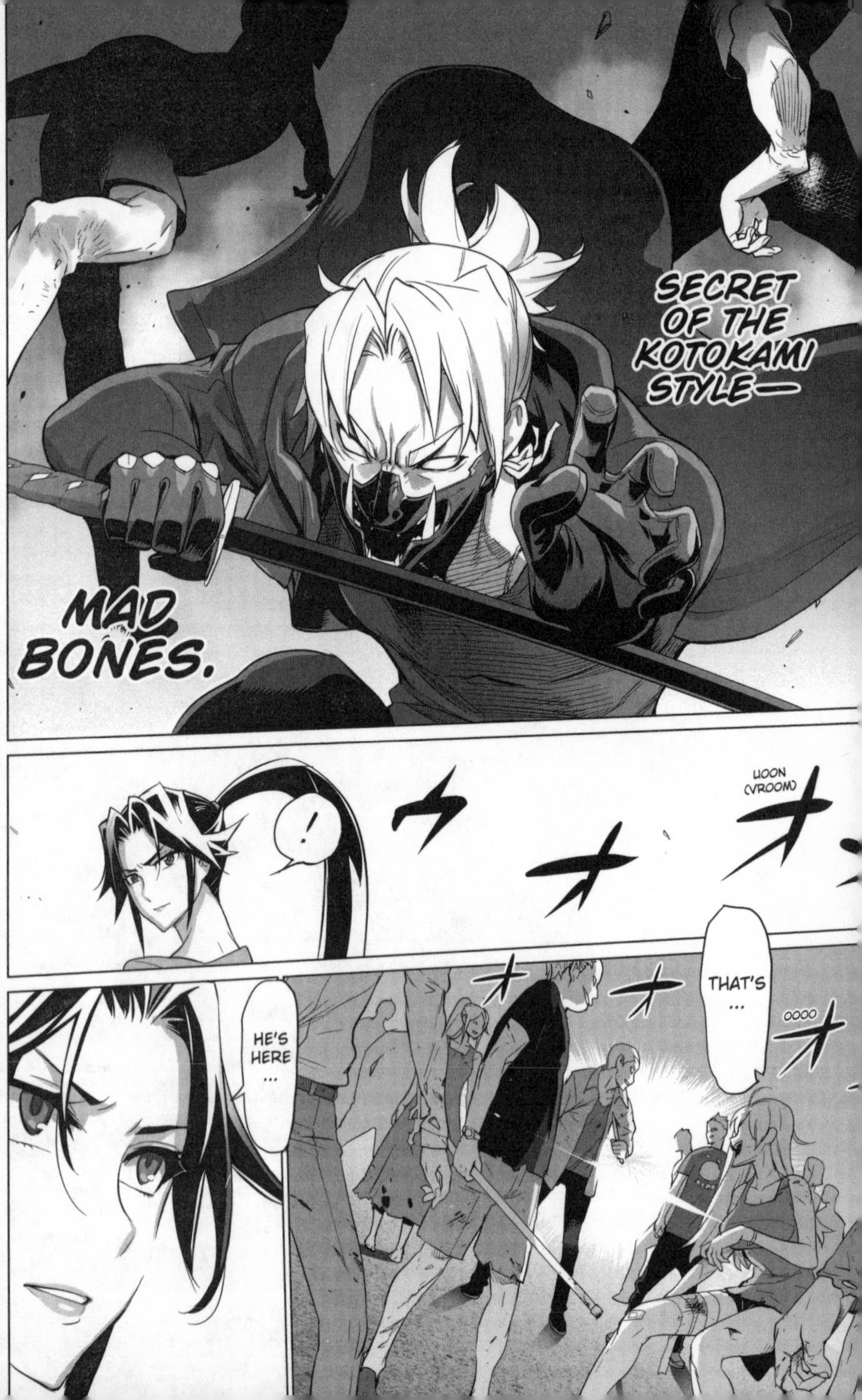
SECRET OF THE KOTOKAMI STYLE—
MAD BONES.
UOON (VROOM)
!
THAT'S ...
OOOO
HE'S HERE ...

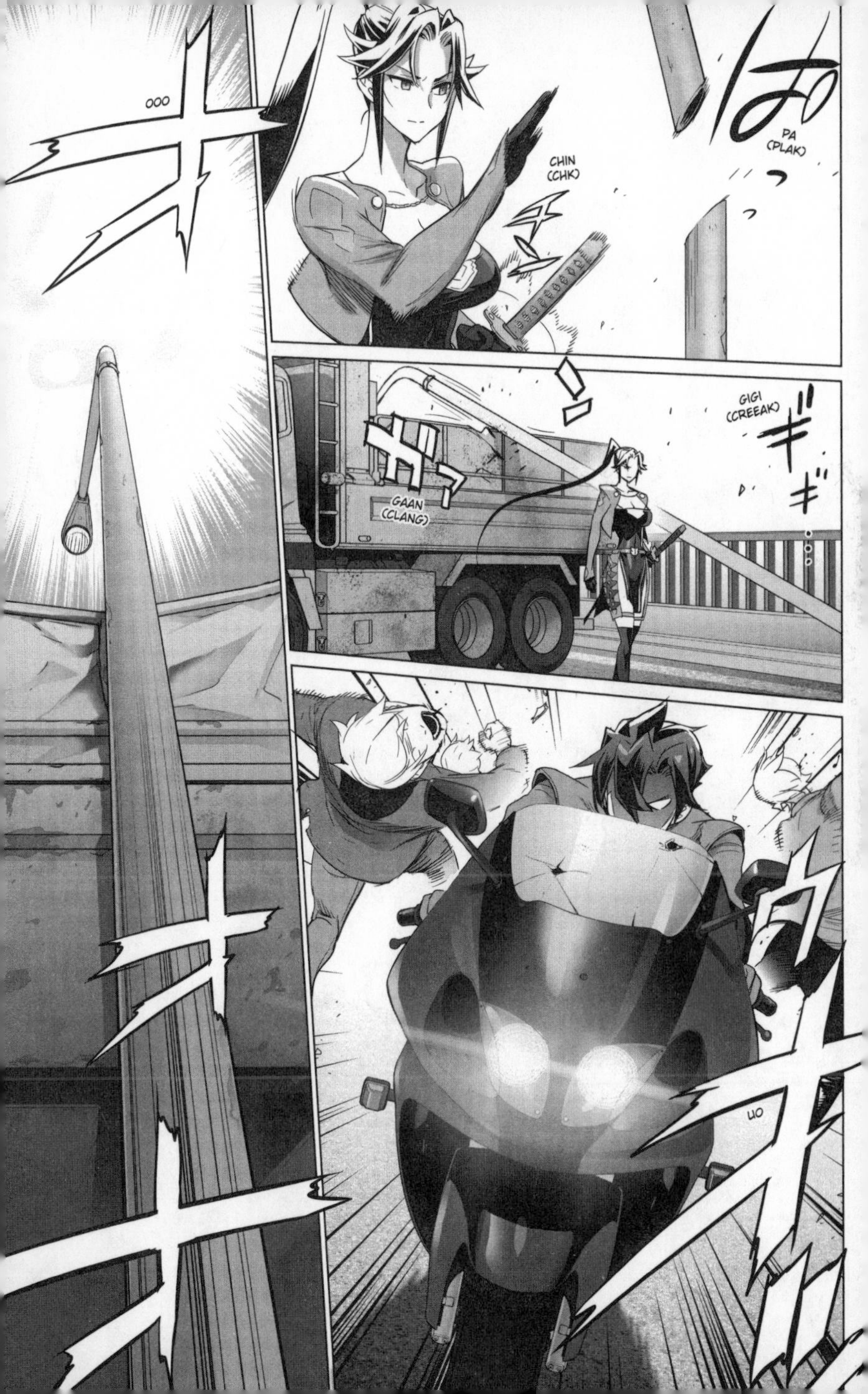
PA
(PLAK)
CHIN
(CHK)
GIGI
(CREEAK)
GAAN
(CLANG)
UO
OOO

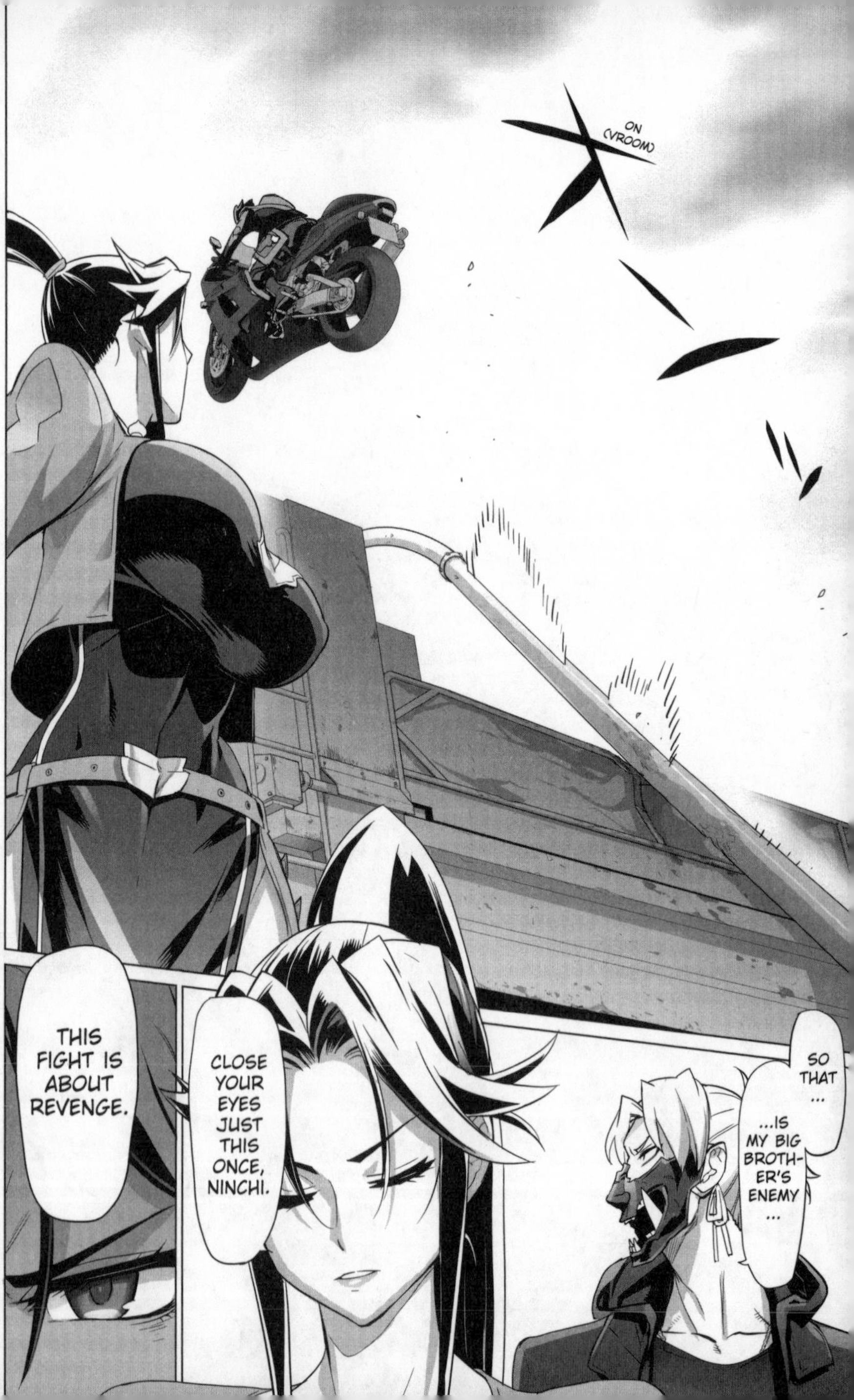
ON
(VROOM)
SO THAT...
...IS MY BIG BROTHER'S ENEMY...
CLOSE YOUR EYES JUST THIS ONCE, NINCHI.
THIS FIGHT IS ABOUT REVENGE.

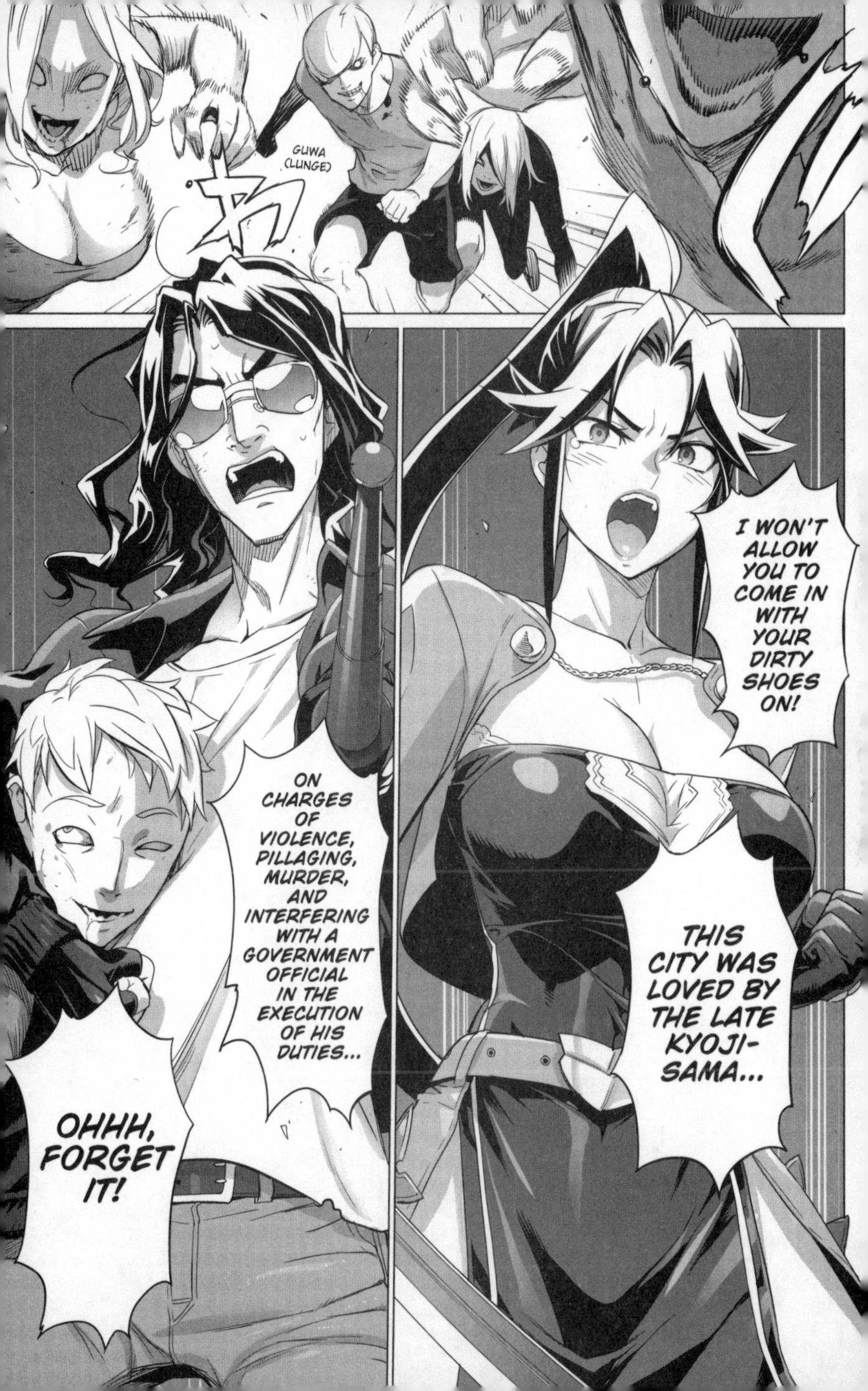
GUWA (LUNGE)
I WON'T ALLOW YOU TO COME IN WITH YOUR DIRTY SHOES ON!
THIS CITY WAS LOVED BY THE LATE KYOJI-SAMA...
ON CHARGES OF VIOLENCE, PILLAGING, MURDER, AND INTERFERING WITH A GOVERNMENT OFFICIAL IN THE EXECUTION OF HIS DUTIES...
OHHH, FORGET IT!

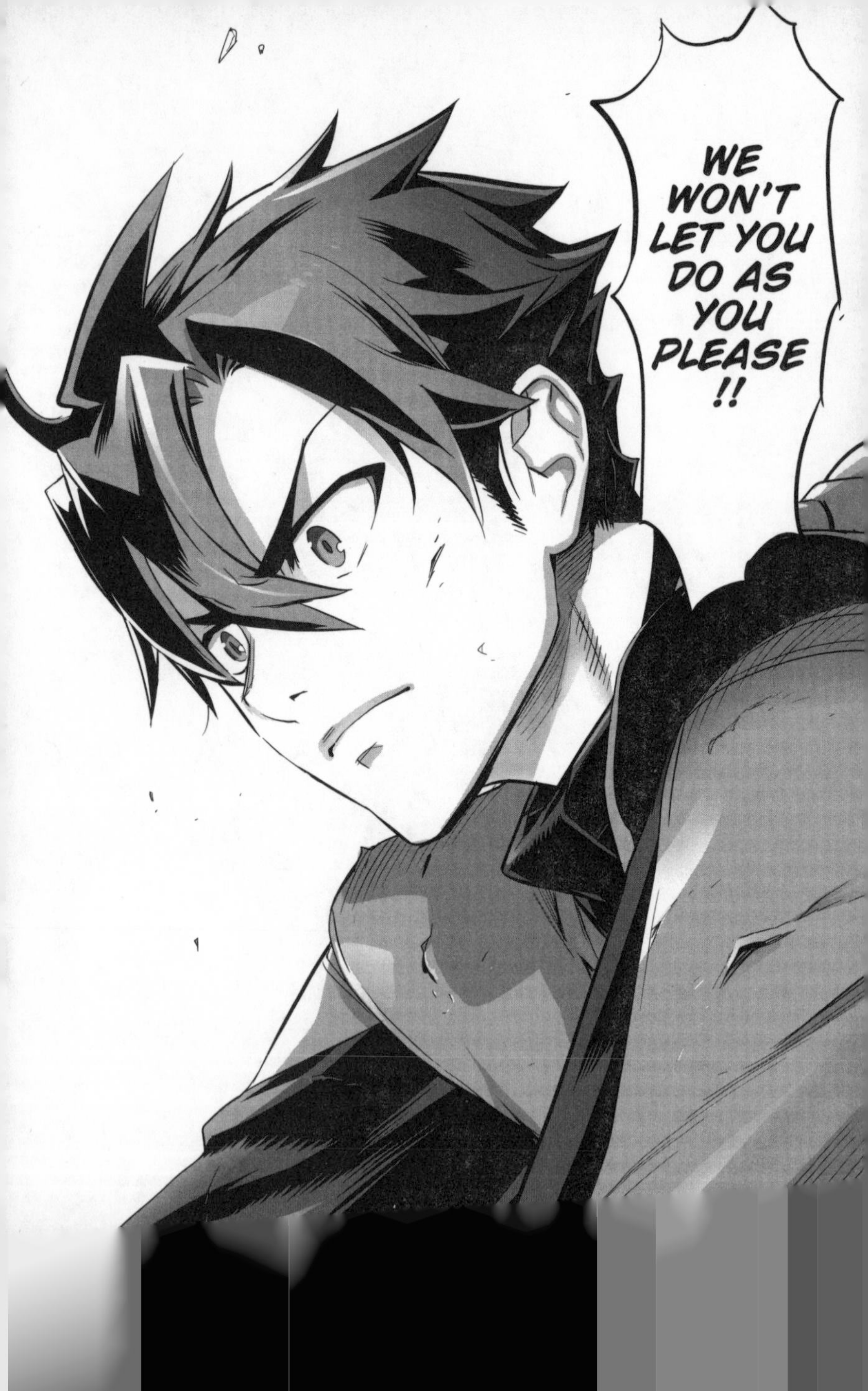
WE WON'T LET YOU DO AS YOU PLEASE!!

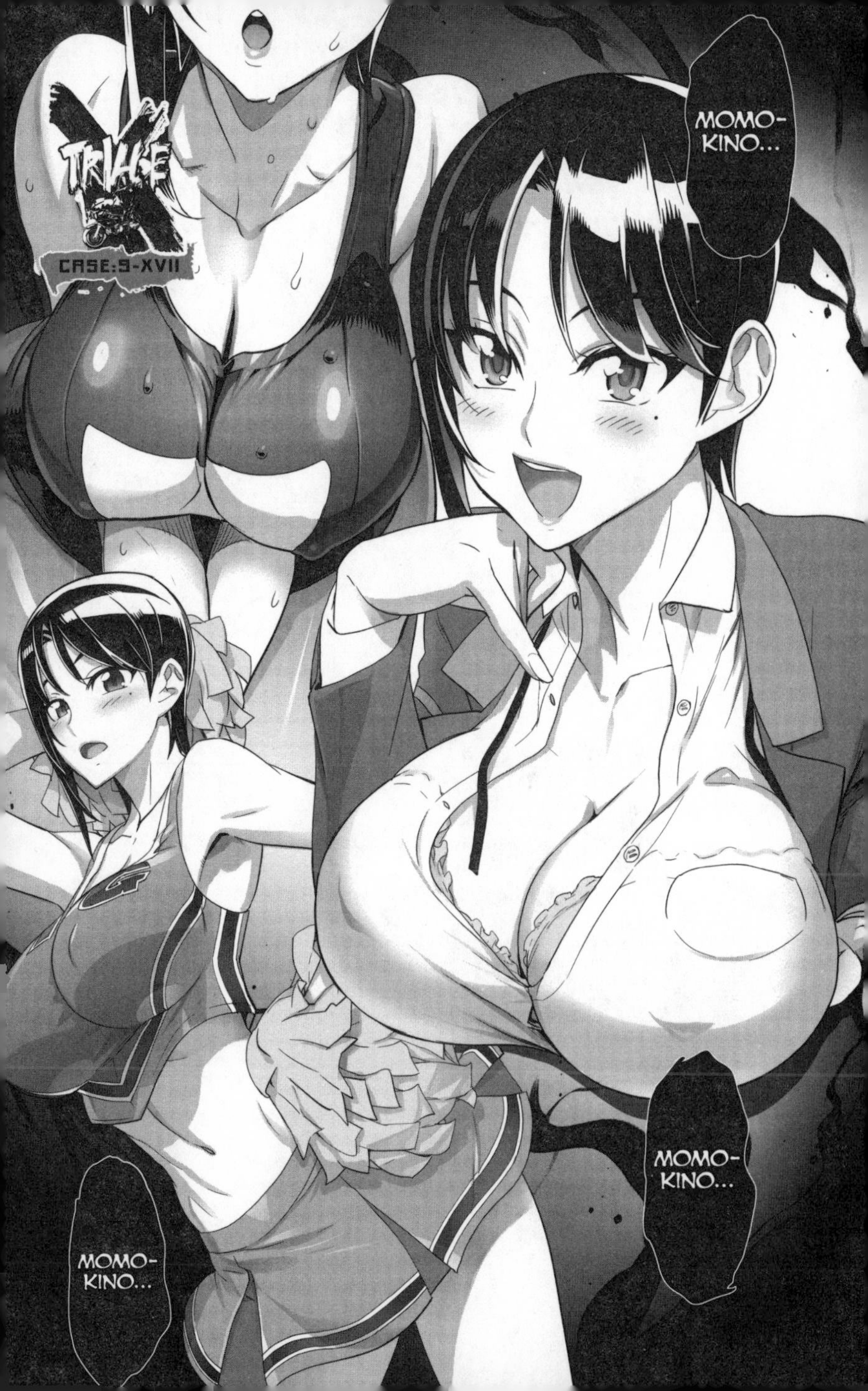
MOMO-KINO...
TRIAGE X
CASE:9-XVII
MOMO-KINO...
MOMO-KINO...

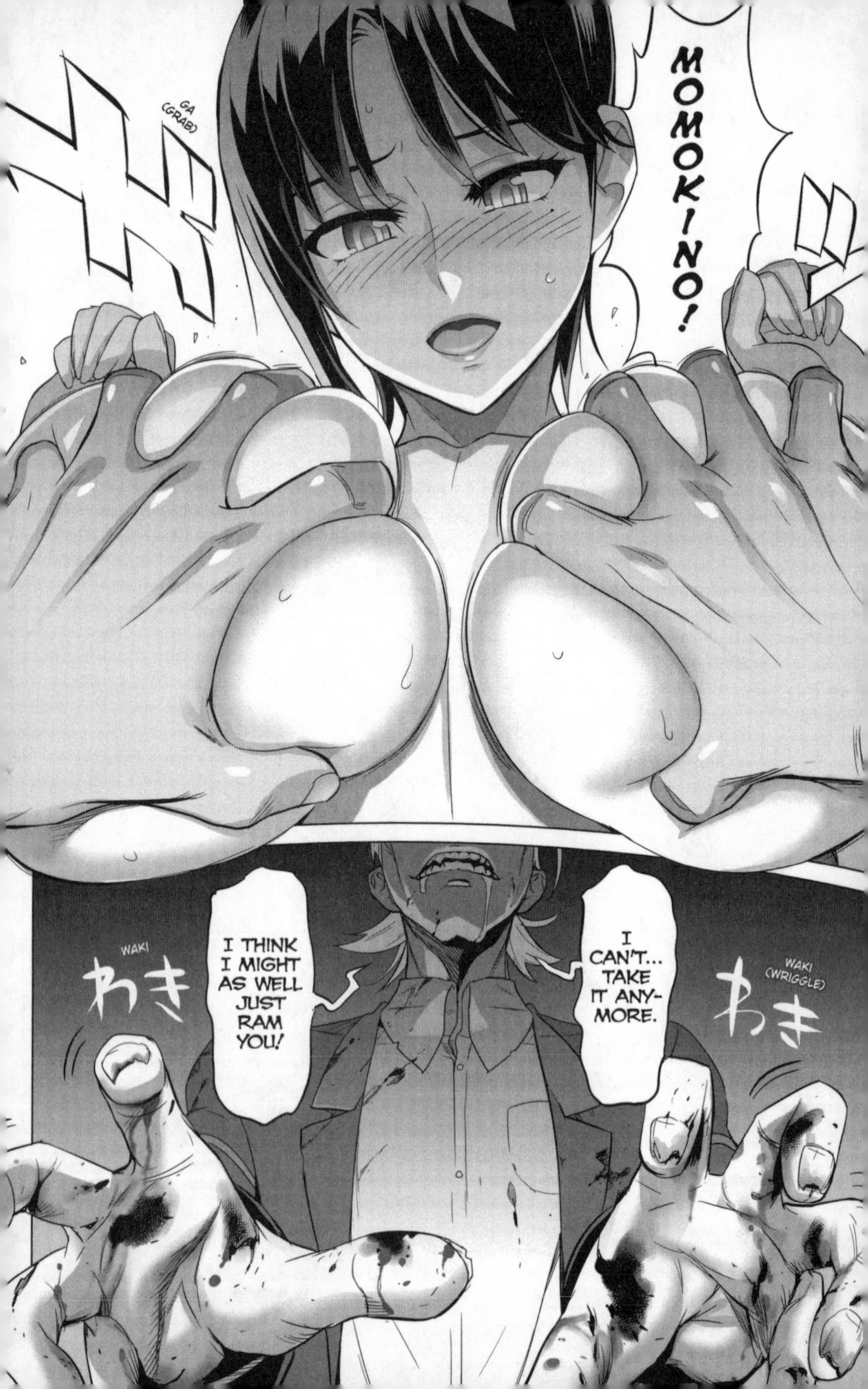
MOMOKINO!
GA (GRAB)
I CAN'T... TAKE IT ANY-MORE.
I THINK I MIGHT AS WELL JUST RAM YOU!
WAKI (WRIGGLE)
わき
WAKI
わき

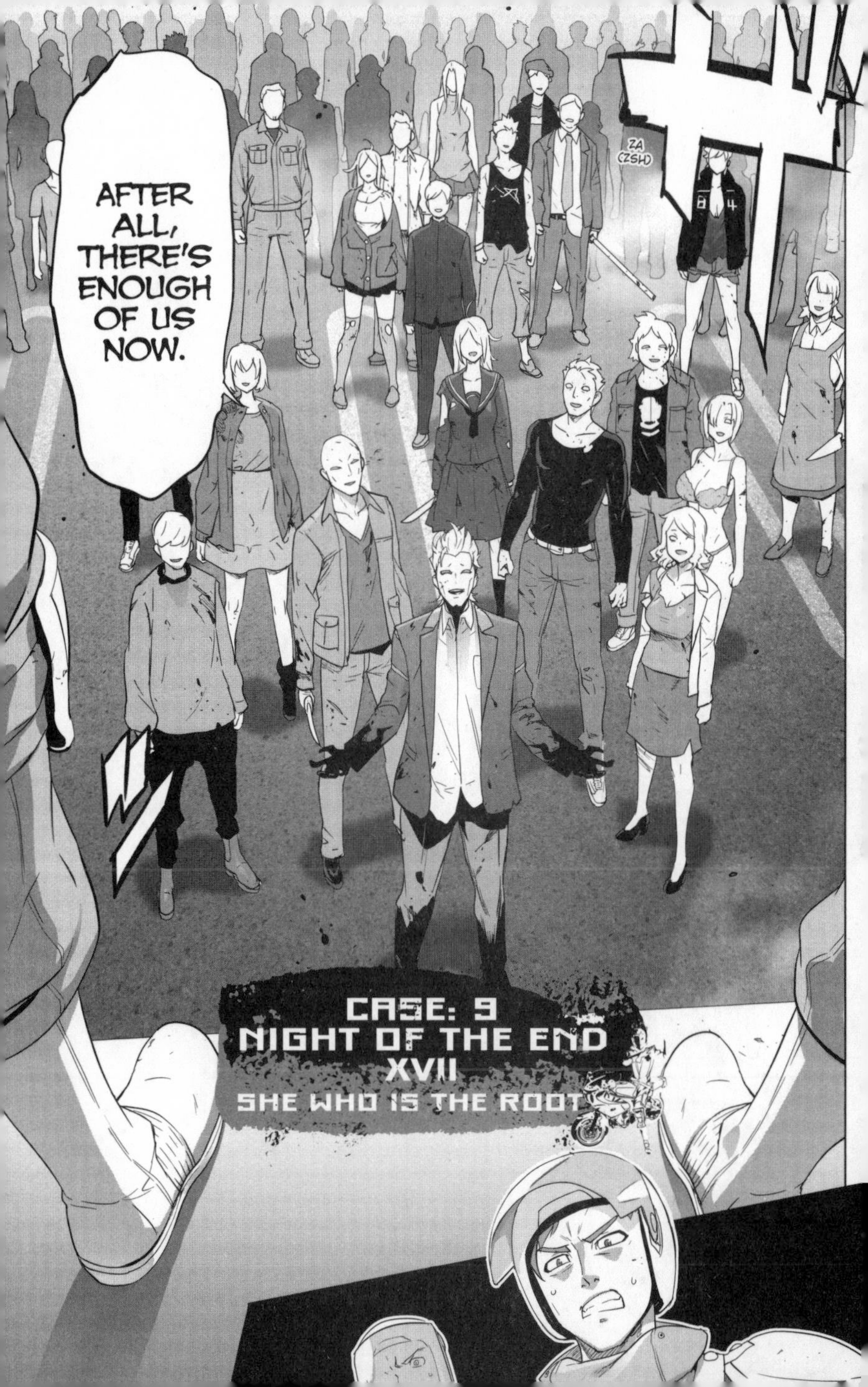
AFTER ALL, THERE'S ENOUGH OF US NOW.
ZA (ZSH)
CASE: 9
NIGHT OF THE END
XVII
SHE WHO IS THE ROOT

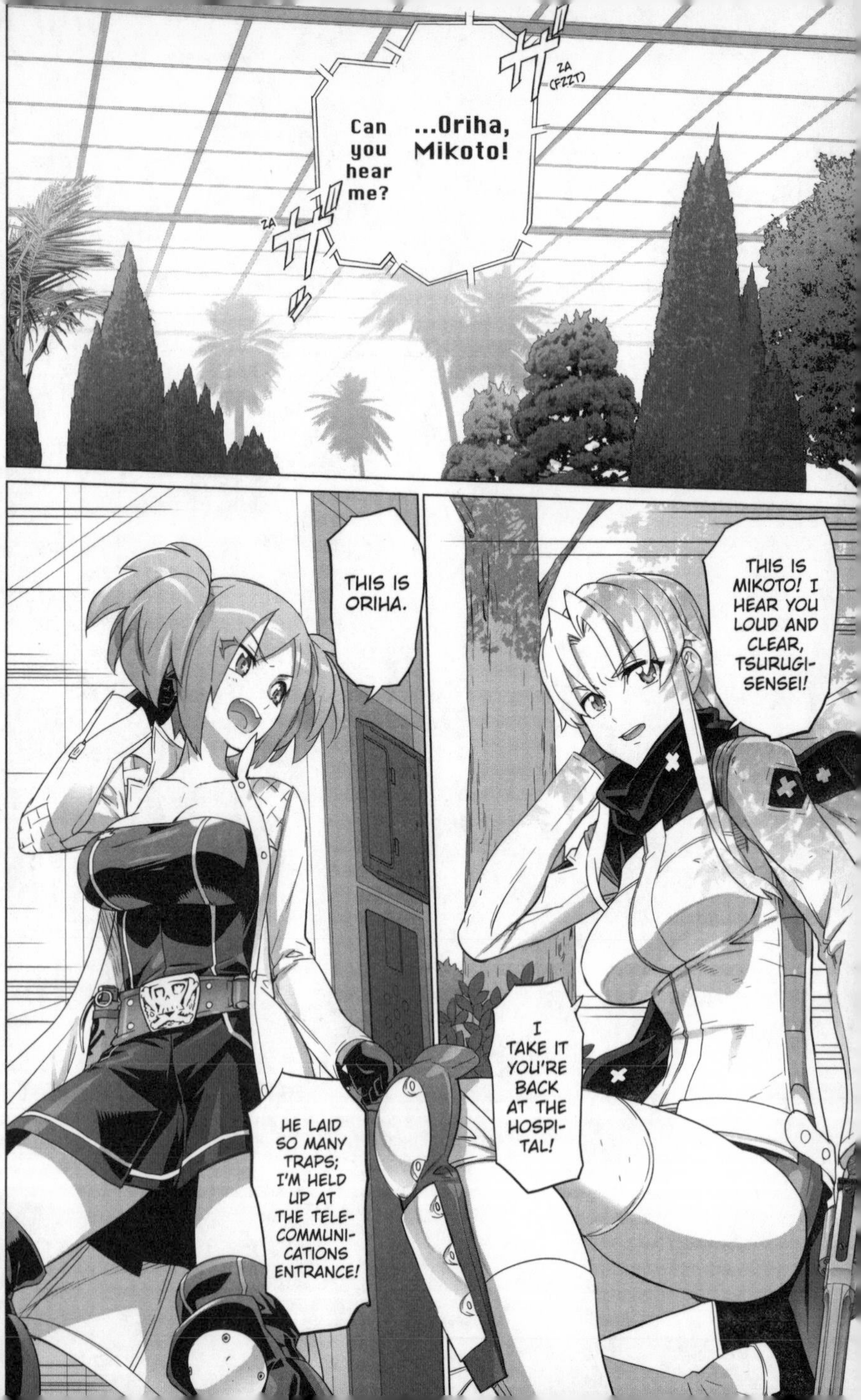
ZA (FZZT)
...Oriha, Mikoto! Can you hear me?
ZA
THIS IS MIKOTO! I HEAR YOU LOUD AND CLEAR, TSURUGI-SENSEI!
I TAKE IT YOU'RE BACK AT THE HOSPITAL!
THIS IS ORIHA.
HE LAID SO MANY TRAPS; I'M HELD UP AT THE TELE-COMMUNICATIONS ENTRANCE!

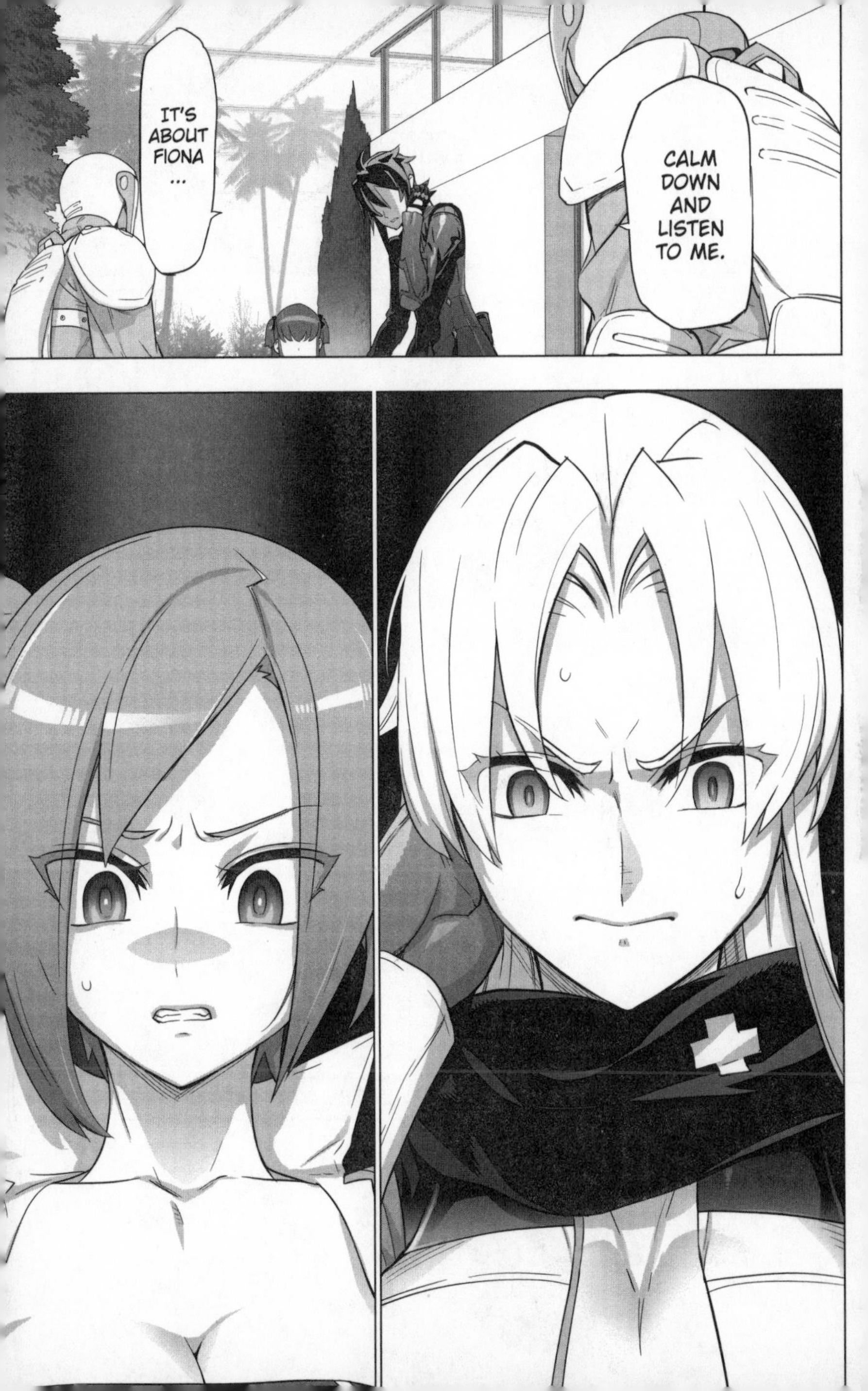
CALM DOWN AND LISTEN TO ME.
IT'S ABOUT FIONA ...

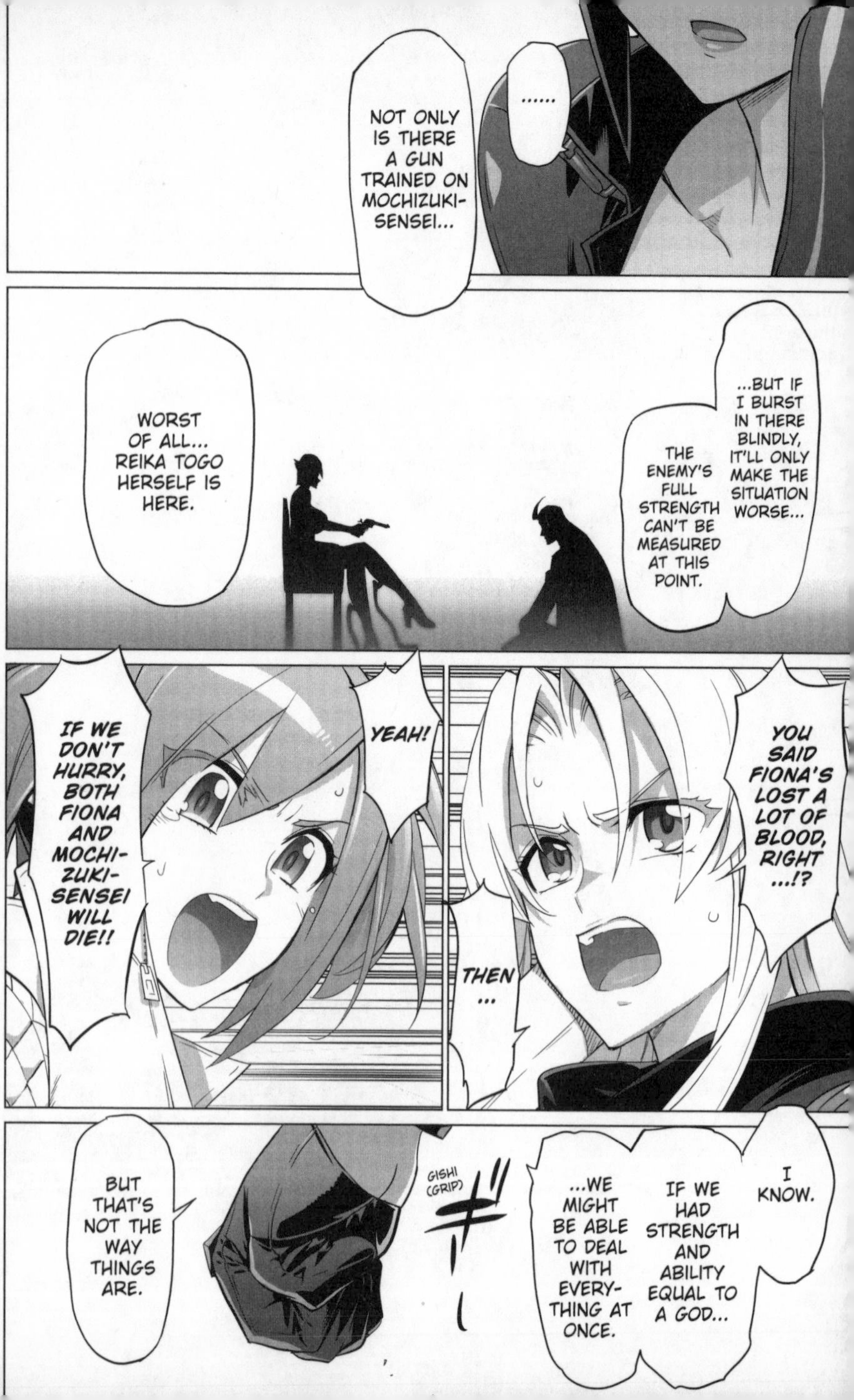
......
NOT ONLY IS THERE A GUN TRAINED ON MOCHIZUKI-SENSEI...
...BUT IF I BURST IN THERE BLINDLY, IT'LL ONLY MAKE THE SITUATION WORSE...
THE ENEMY'S FULL STRENGTH CAN'T BE MEASURED AT THIS POINT.
WORST OF ALL... REIKA TOGO HERSELF IS HERE.
YOU SAID FIONA'S LOST A LOT OF BLOOD, RIGHT ...!?
THEN ...
YEAH!
IF WE DON'T HURRY, BOTH FIONA AND MOCHIZUKI-SENSEI WILL DIE!!
I KNOW.
IF WE HAD STRENGTH AND ABILITY EQUAL TO A GOD...
...WE MIGHT BE ABLE TO DEAL WITH EVERYTHING AT ONCE.
GISHI (GRIP)
BUT THAT'S NOT THE WAY THINGS ARE.

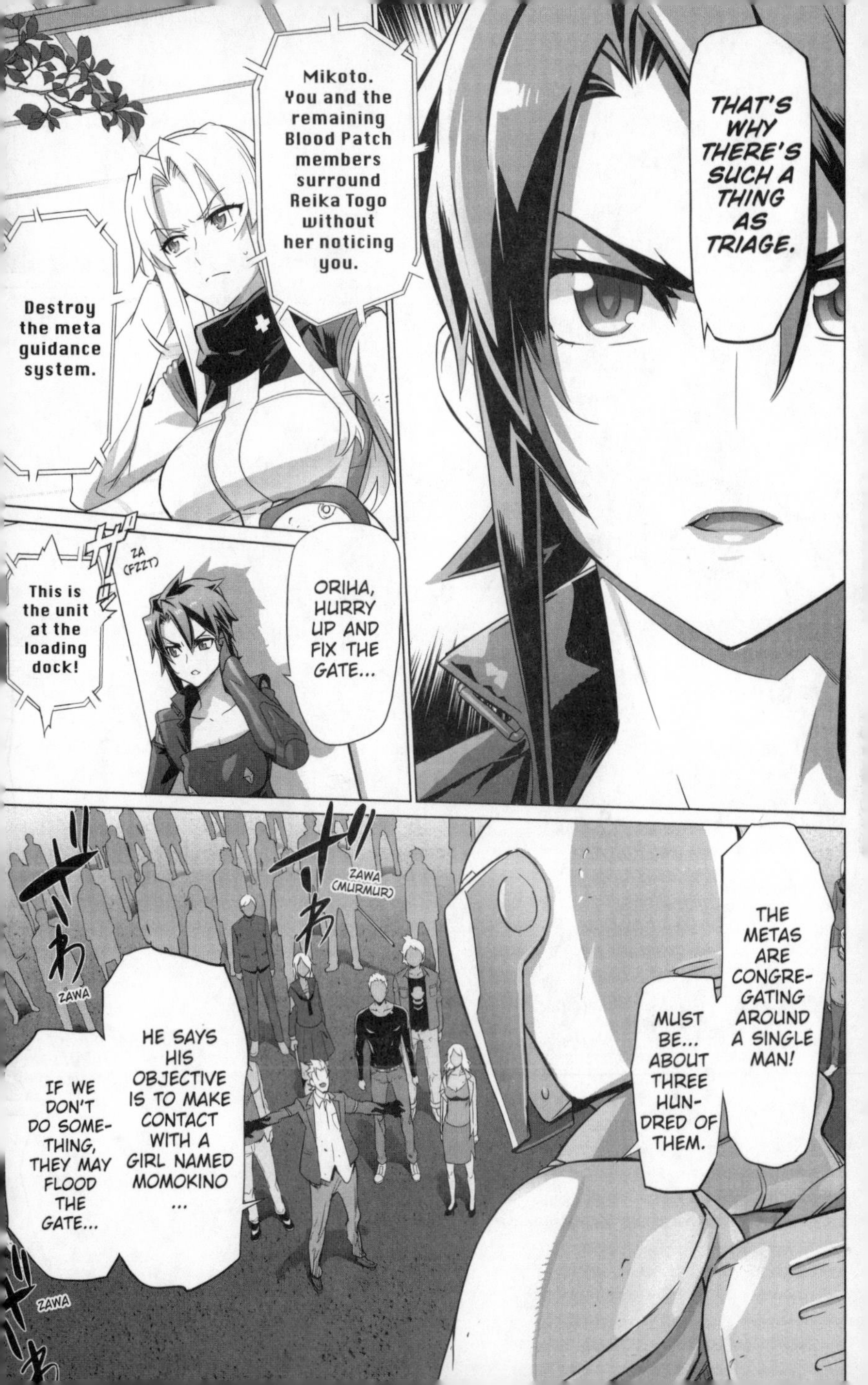
THAT'S WHY THERE'S SUCH A THING AS TRIAGE.
Mikoto. You and the remaining Blood Patch members surround Reika Togo without her noticing you.
Destroy the meta guidance system.
ORIHA, HURRY UP AND FIX THE GATE...
ZA (FZZT)
This is the unit at the loading dock!
THE METAS ARE CONGREGATING AROUND A SINGLE MAN!
MUST BE... ABOUT THREE HUNDRED OF THEM.
ZAWA (MURMUR)
HE SAYS HIS OBJECTIVE IS TO MAKE CONTACT WITH A GIRL NAMED MOMOKINO...
IF WE DON'T DO SOMETHING, THEY MAY FLOOD THE GATE...
ZAWA
ZAWA

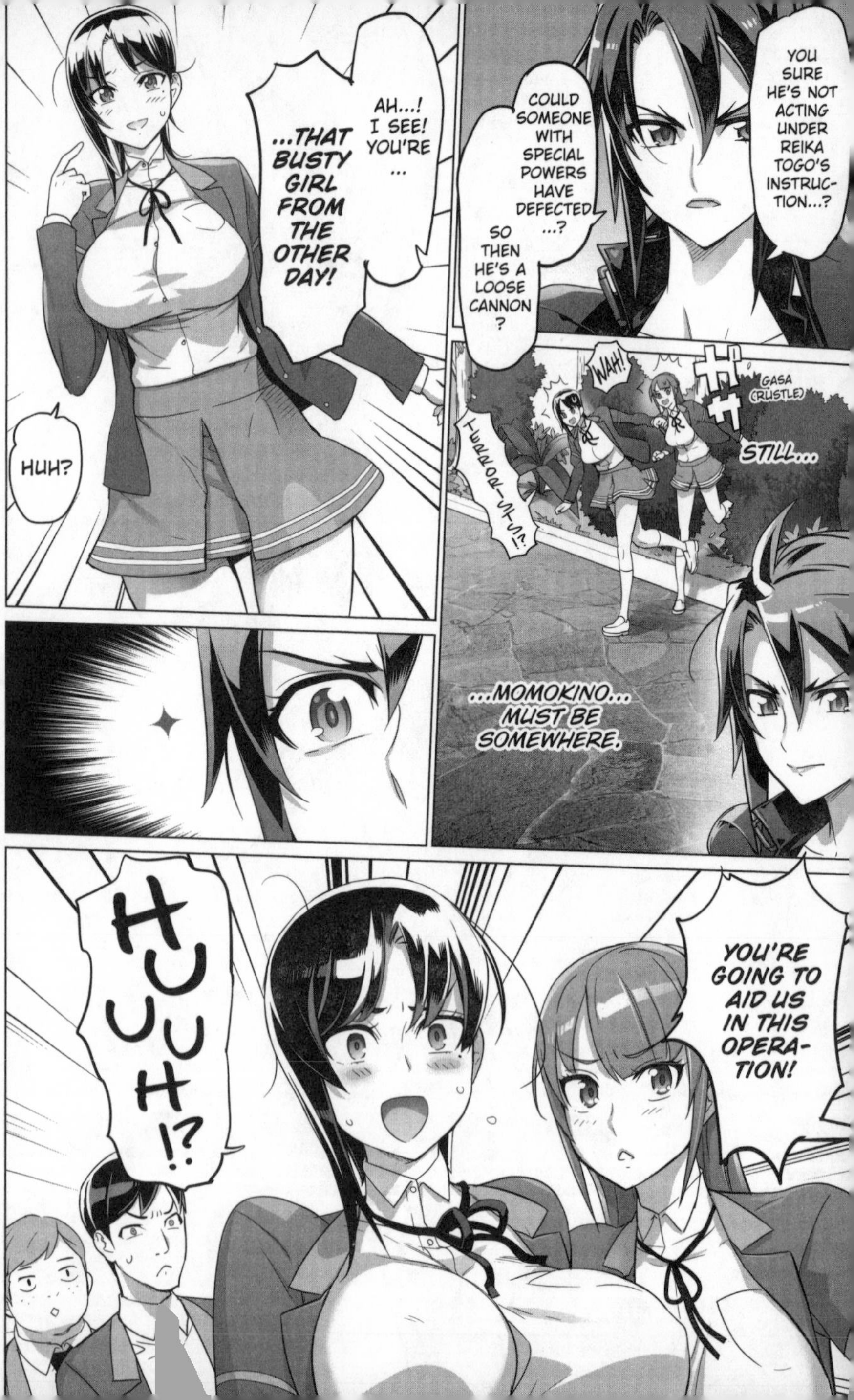
YOU SURE HE'S NOT ACTING UNDER REIKA TOGO'S INSTRUCTION...?
COULD SOMEONE WITH SPECIAL POWERS HAVE DEFECTED...?
SO THEN HE'S A LOOSE CANNON?
ガサ
GASA (RUSTLE)
WAH!
TERRORISTS!?
STILL...
...MOMOKINO... MUST BE SOMEWHERE.
AH...! I SEE! YOU'RE ...
...THAT BUSTY GIRL FROM THE OTHER DAY!
HUH?
YOU'RE GOING TO AID US IN THIS OPERATION!
HUUUH!?

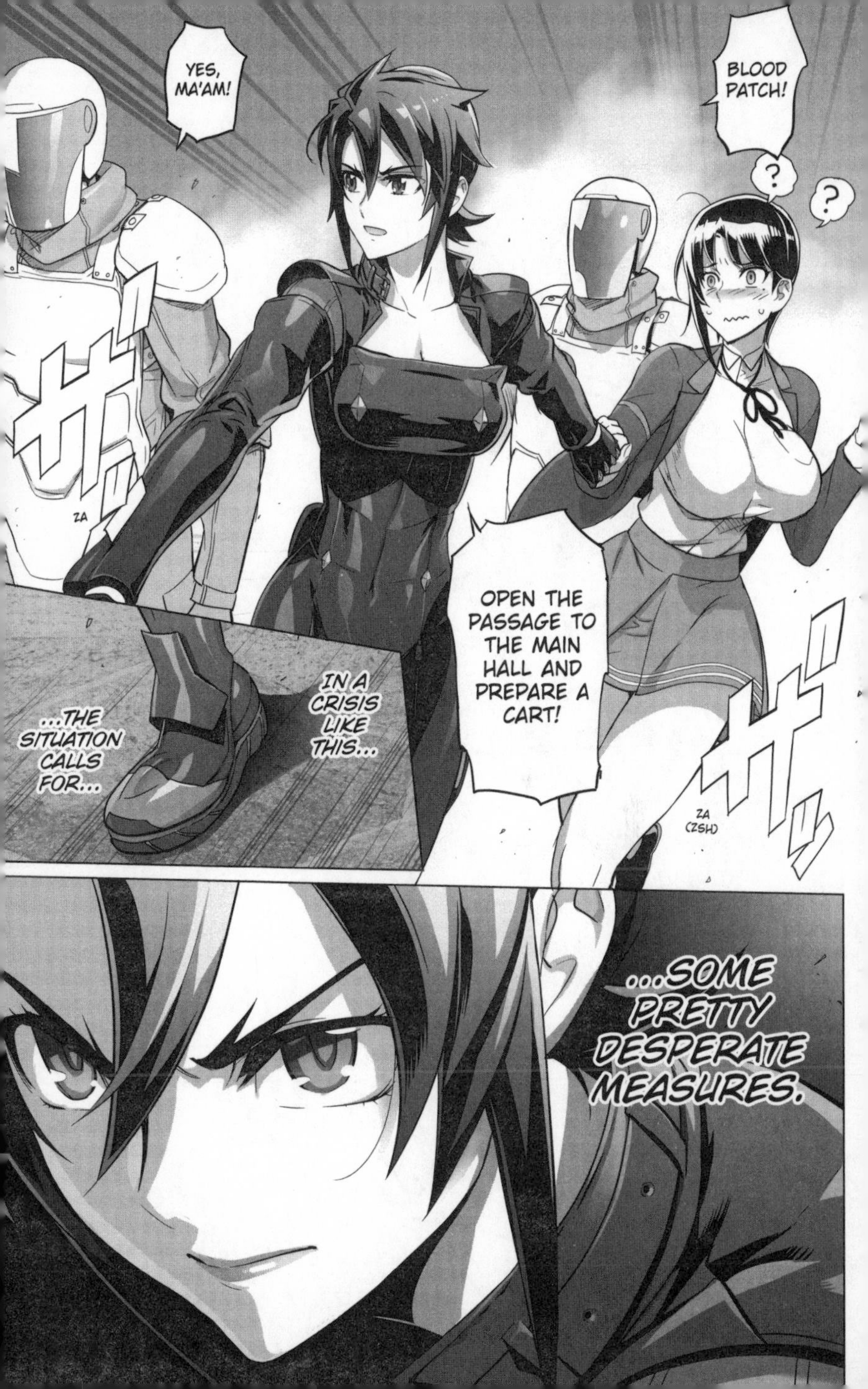
BLOOD PATCH!
?
?
YES, MA'AM!
OPEN THE PASSAGE TO THE MAIN HALL AND PREPARE A CART!
ZA (ZSH)
ZA
IN A CRISIS LIKE THIS...
...THE SITUATION CALLS FOR...
...SOME PRETTY DESPERATE MEASURES.

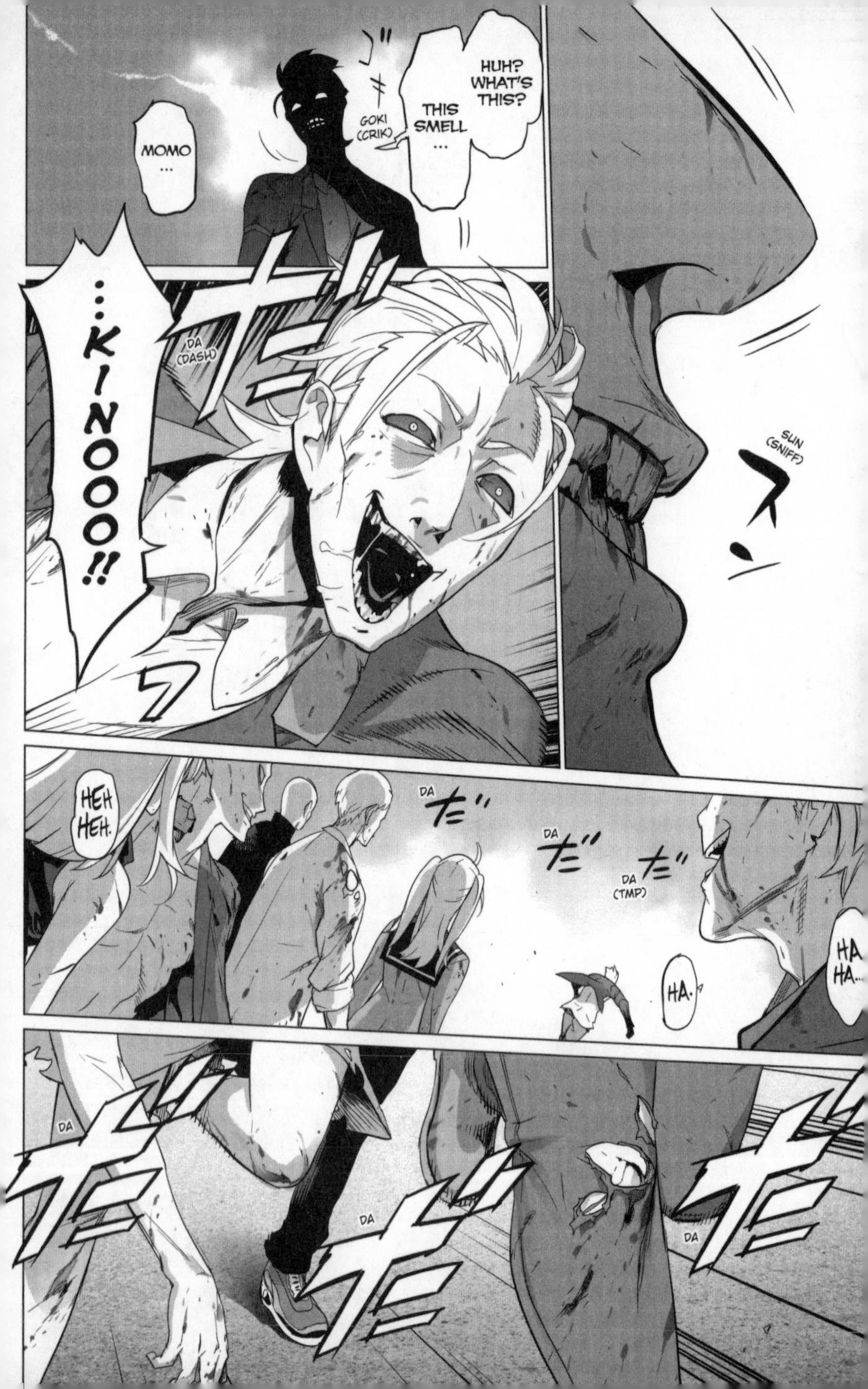
SUN (SNIFF)
HUH? WHAT'S THIS?
THIS SMELL ...
GOKI (CRIK)
MOMO ...
DA (DASH)
...KINOOOO!!
HA HA...
HA.
DA (TMP)
DA
DA
HEH HEH.
DA
DA
DA

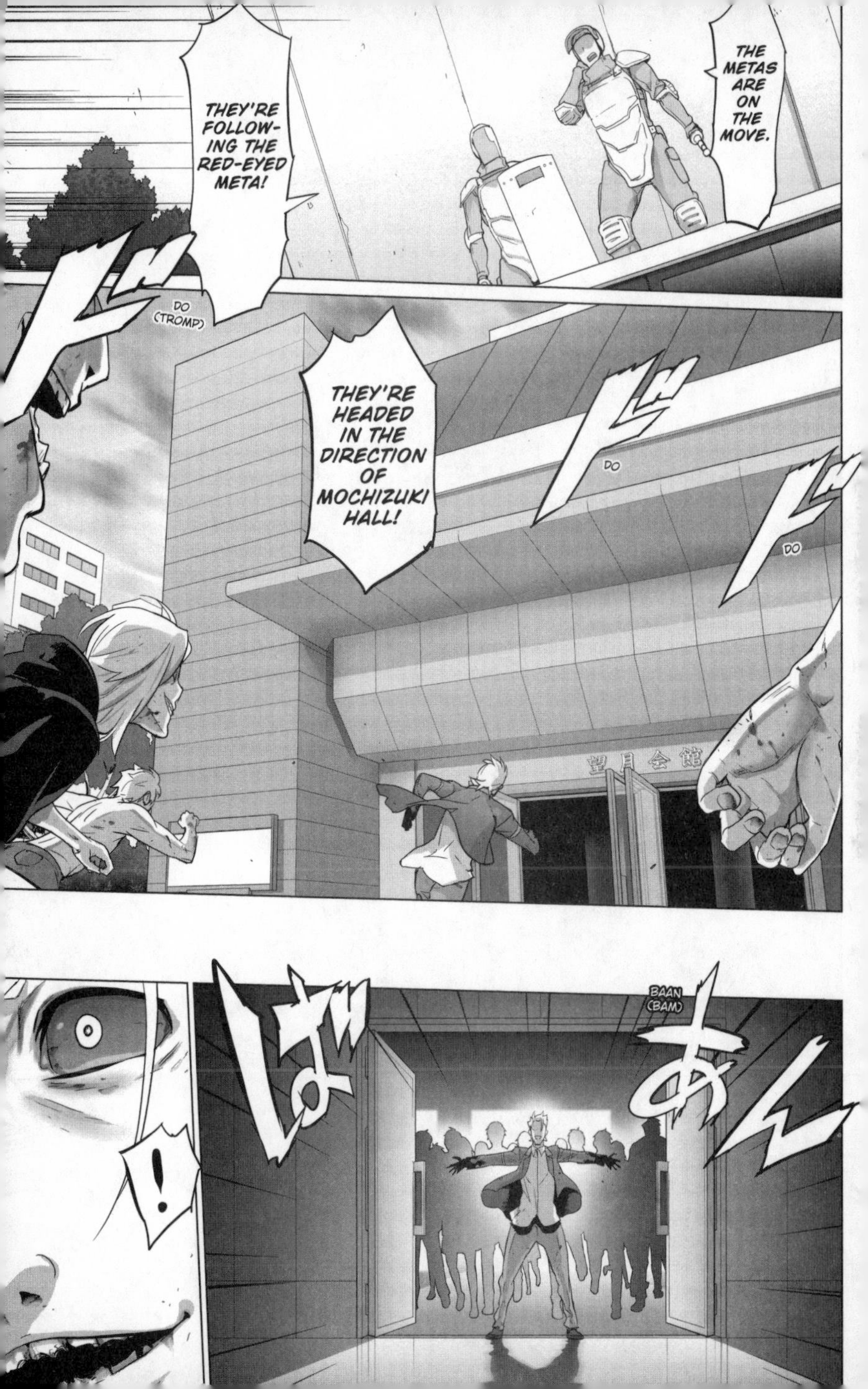
THE METAS ARE ON THE MOVE.
THEY'RE FOLLOWING THE RED-EYED META!
DO (TROMP)
THEY'RE HEADED IN THE DIRECTION OF MOCHIZUKI HALL!
DO
DO
望月会館
BAAN (BAM)
!

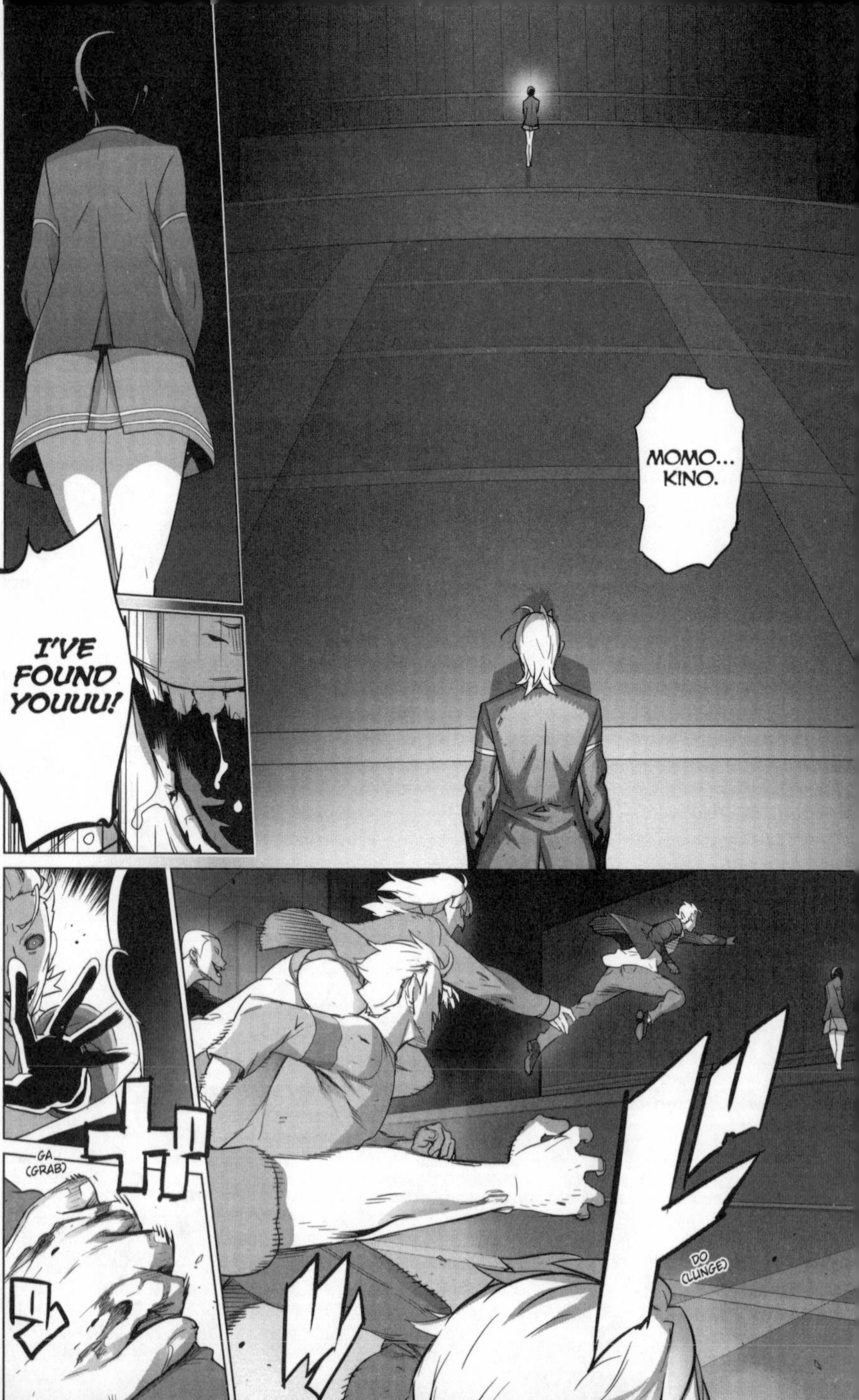
MOMO... KINO.
I'VE FOUND YOUUU!
DO (LUNGE)
GA (GRAB)

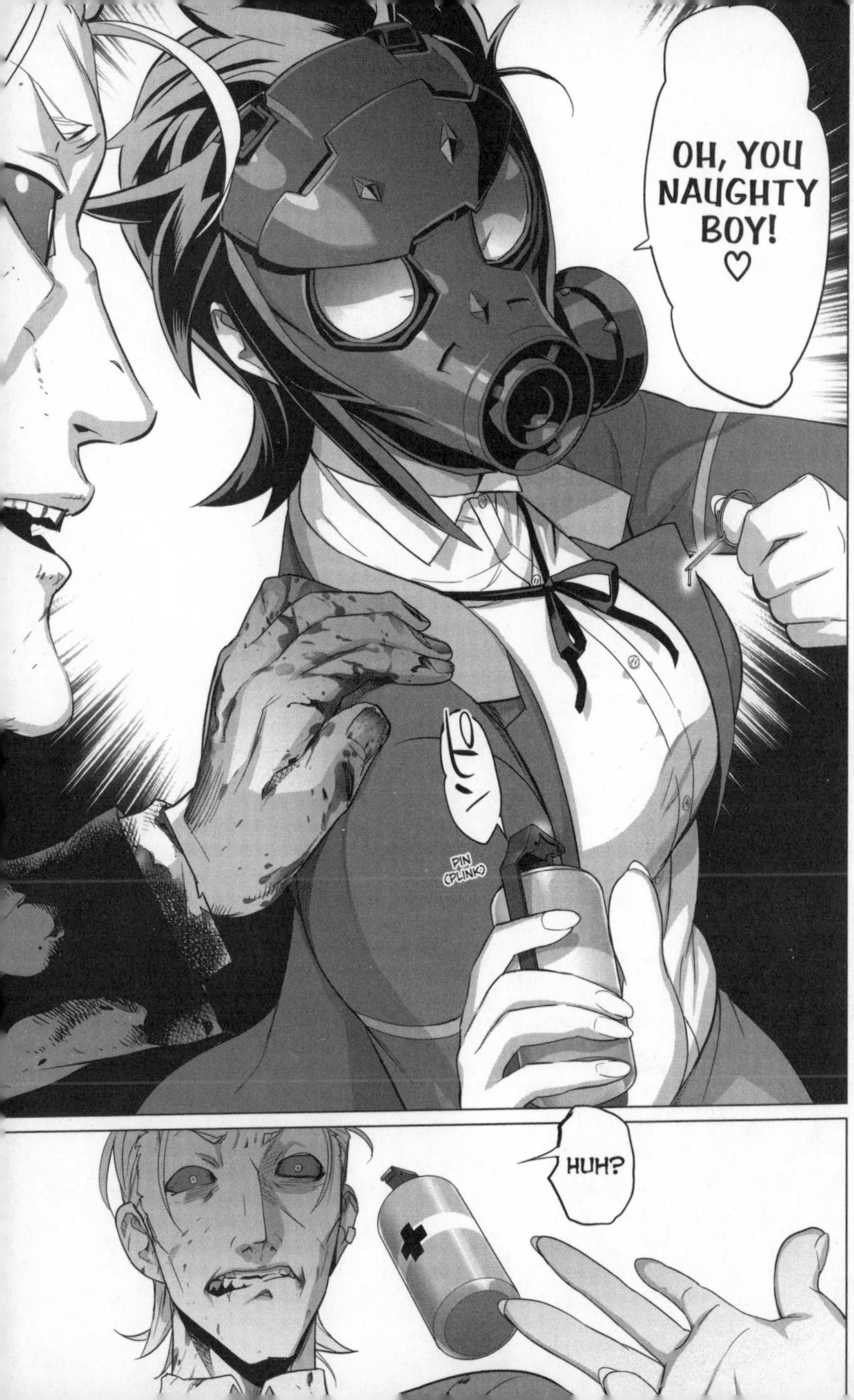
OH, YOU NAUGHTY BOY! ♡
PIN (PLINK)
HUH?

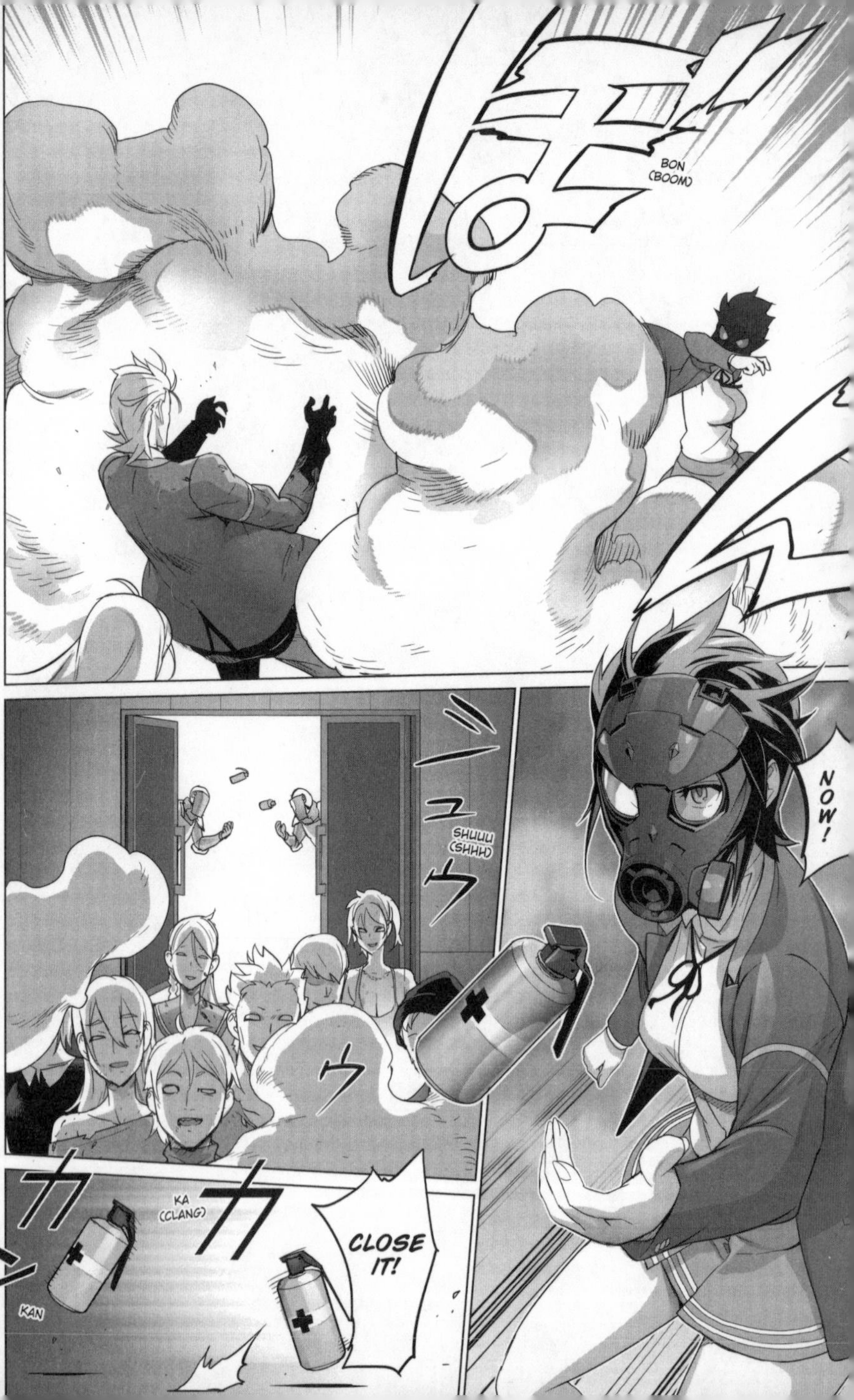
BON
(BOOM)
NOW!
SHUUU
(SHHH)
KA
(CLANG)
CLOSE IT!
KAN

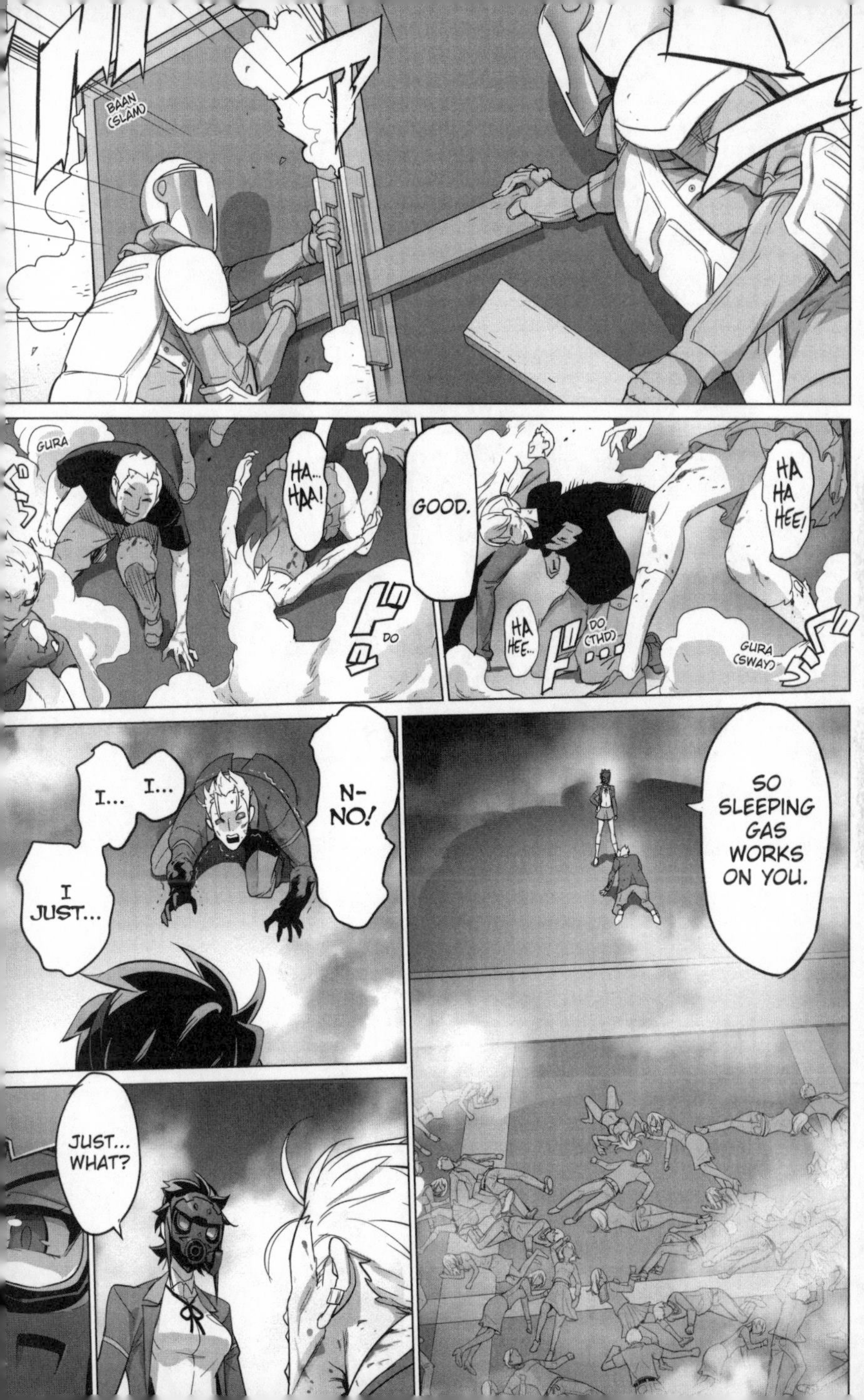
BAAN (SLAM)
HA HA HEE!
GOOD.
GURA (SWAY)
DO (THD)
HA HEE...
HA... HAA!
GURA
DO
SO SLEEPING GAS WORKS ON YOU.
N- NO!
I... I...
I JUST...
JUST... WHAT?

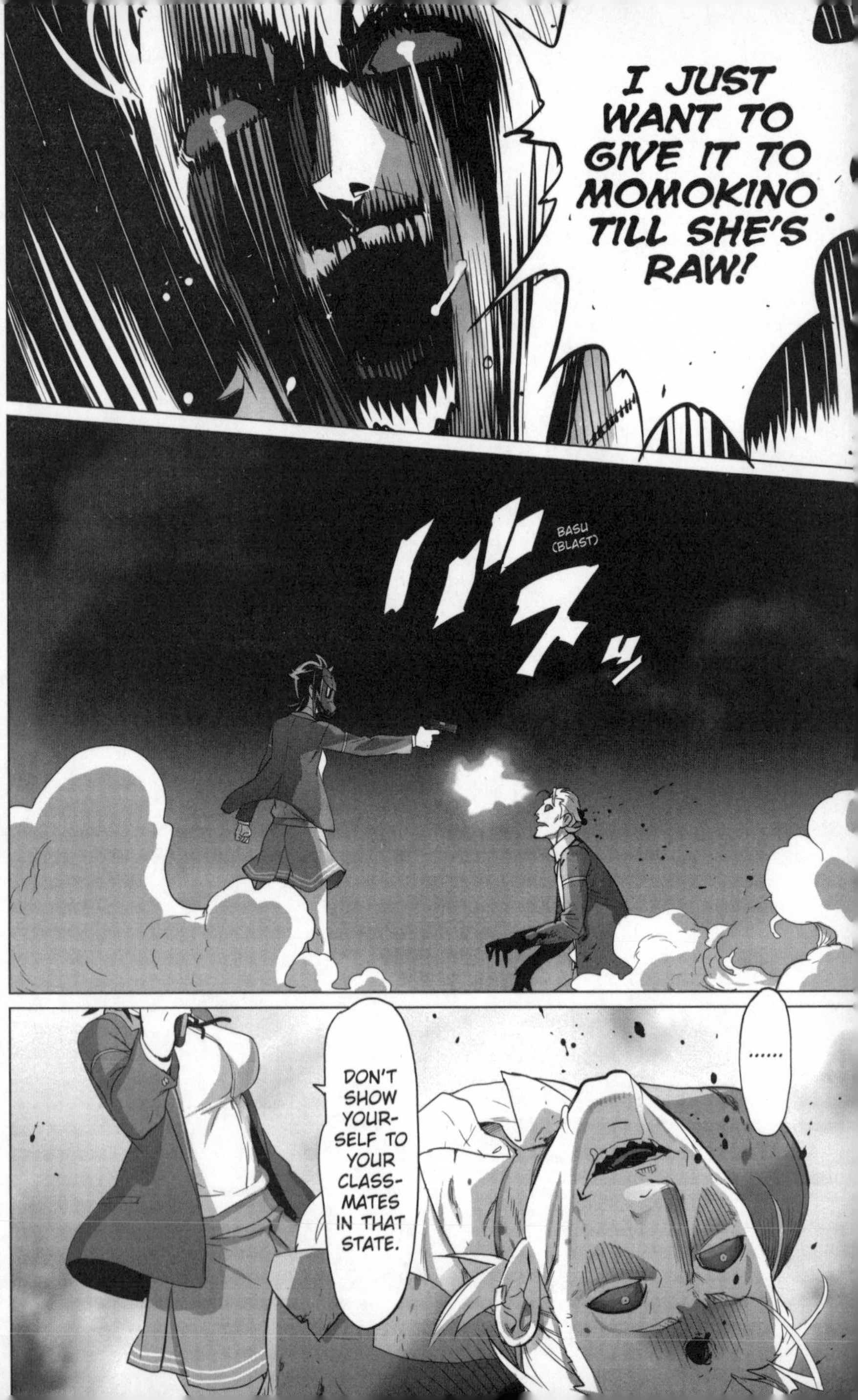
I JUST WANT TO GIVE IT TO MOMOKINO TILL SHE'S RAW!
BASU (BLAST)
......
DON'T SHOW YOURSELF TO YOUR CLASSMATES IN THAT STATE.

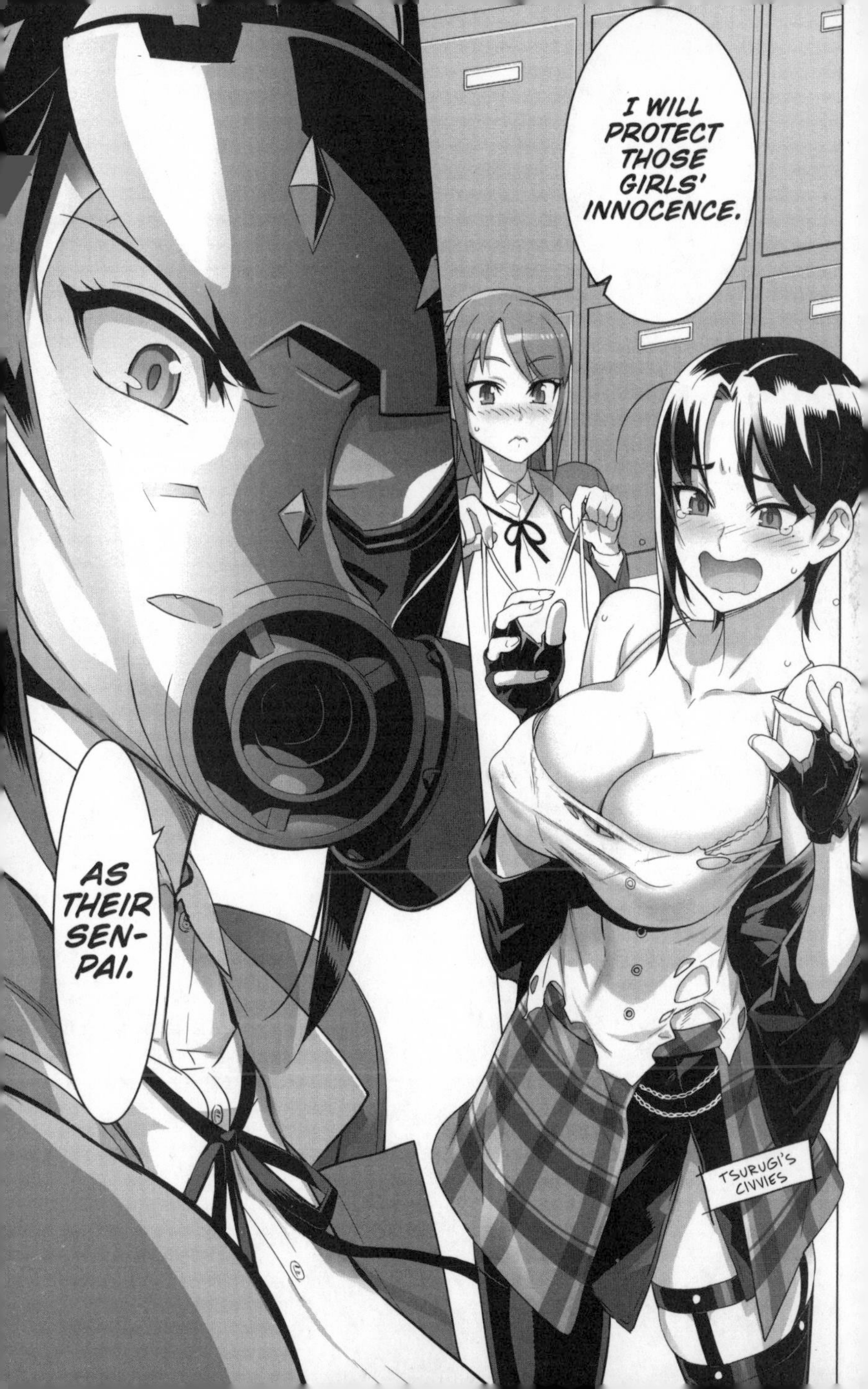
I WILL PROTECT THOSE GIRLS' INNOCENCE.
AS THEIR SEN-PAI.
TSURUGI'S CIVVIES

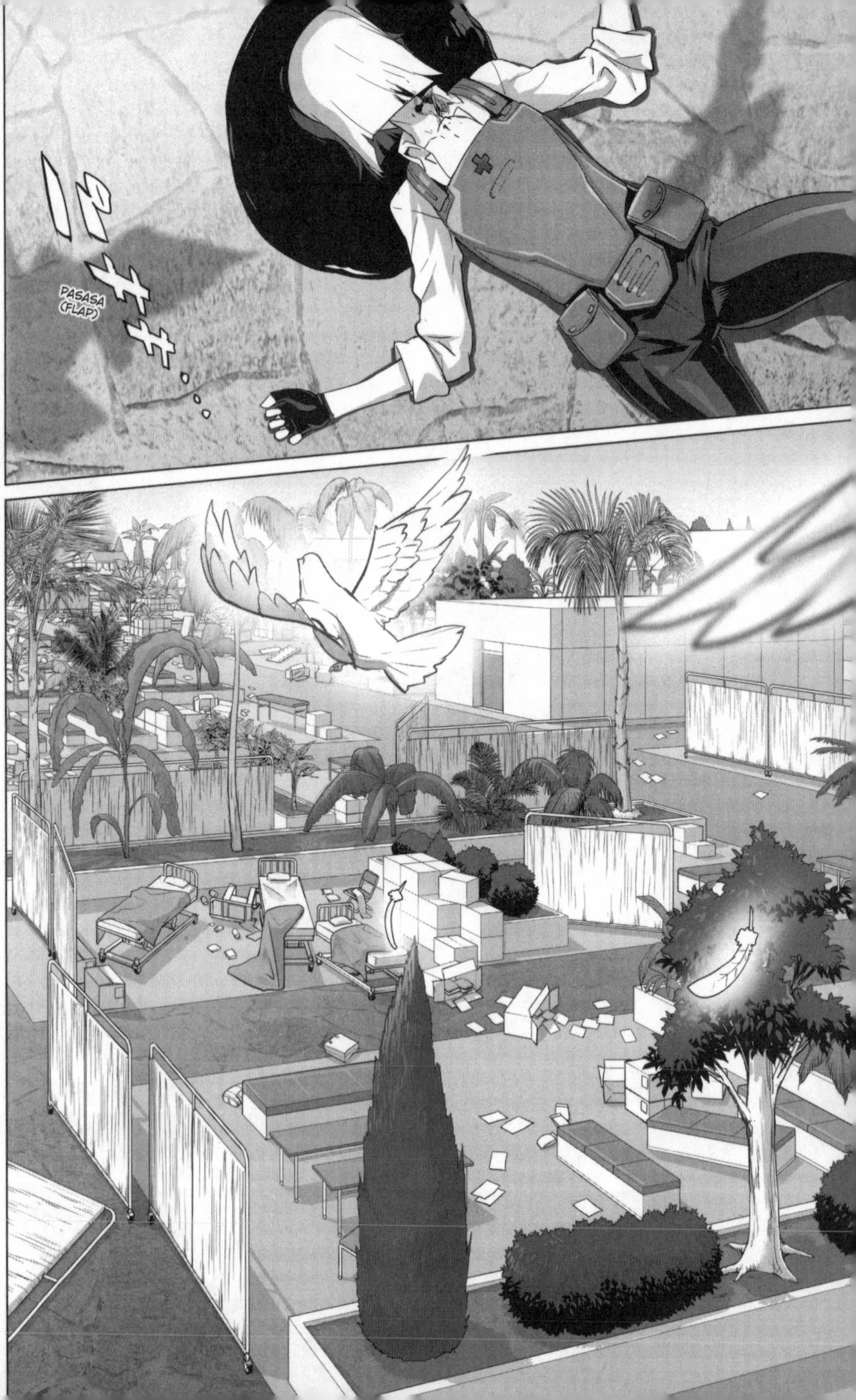
PASASA
(FLAP)

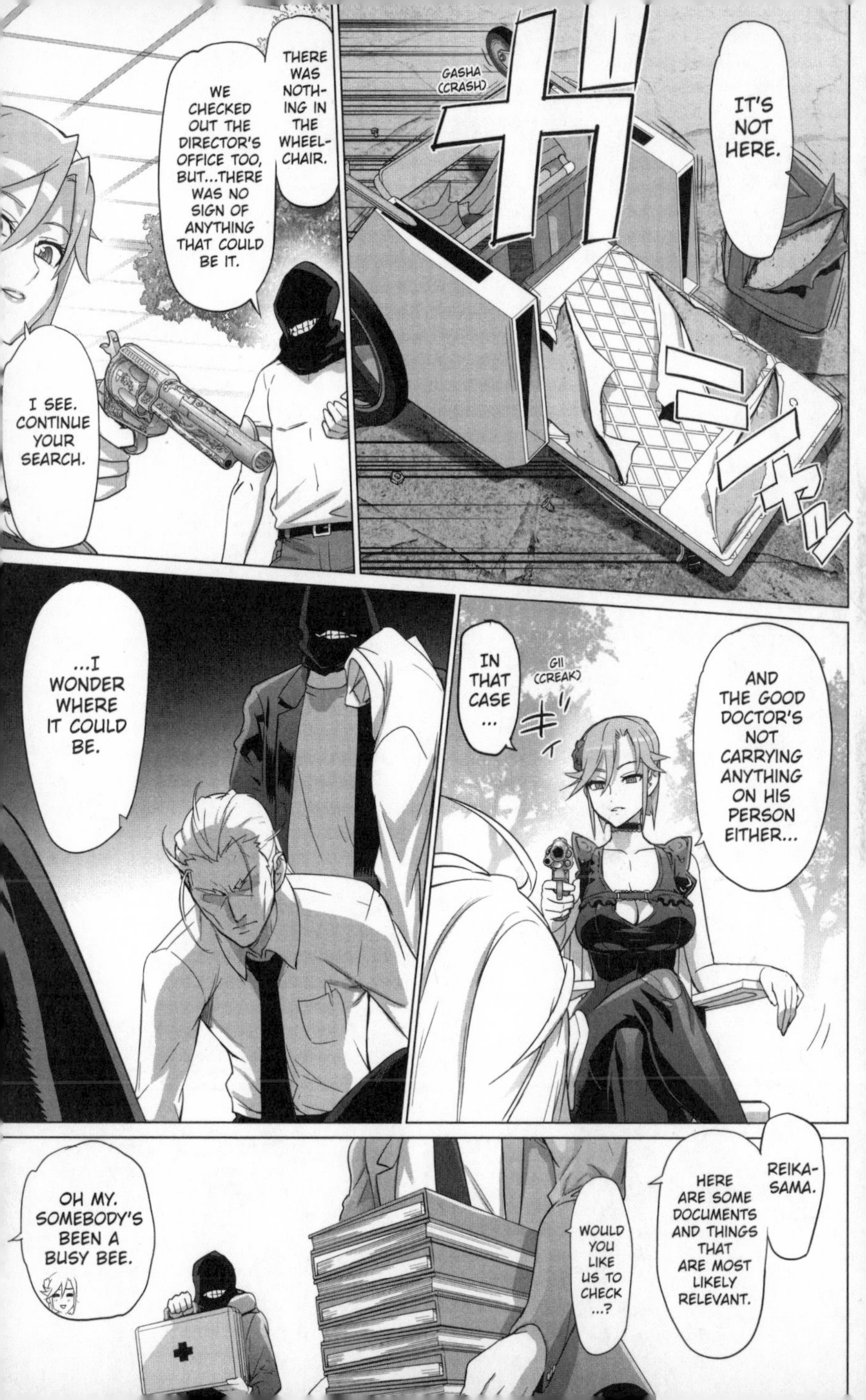
IT'S NOT HERE.
GASHA (CRASH)
THERE WAS NOTHING IN THE WHEELCHAIR.
WE CHECKED OUT THE DIRECTOR'S OFFICE TOO, BUT...THERE WAS NO SIGN OF ANYTHING THAT COULD BE IT.
I SEE. CONTINUE YOUR SEARCH.
AND THE GOOD DOCTOR'S NOT CARRYING ANYTHING ON HIS PERSON EITHER...
GII (CREAK)
IN THAT CASE ...
...I WONDER WHERE IT COULD BE.
REIKA-SAMA.
HERE ARE SOME DOCUMENTS AND THINGS THAT ARE MOST LIKELY RELEVANT.
WOULD YOU LIKE US TO CHECK ...?
OH MY. SOMEBODY'S BEEN A BUSY BEE.

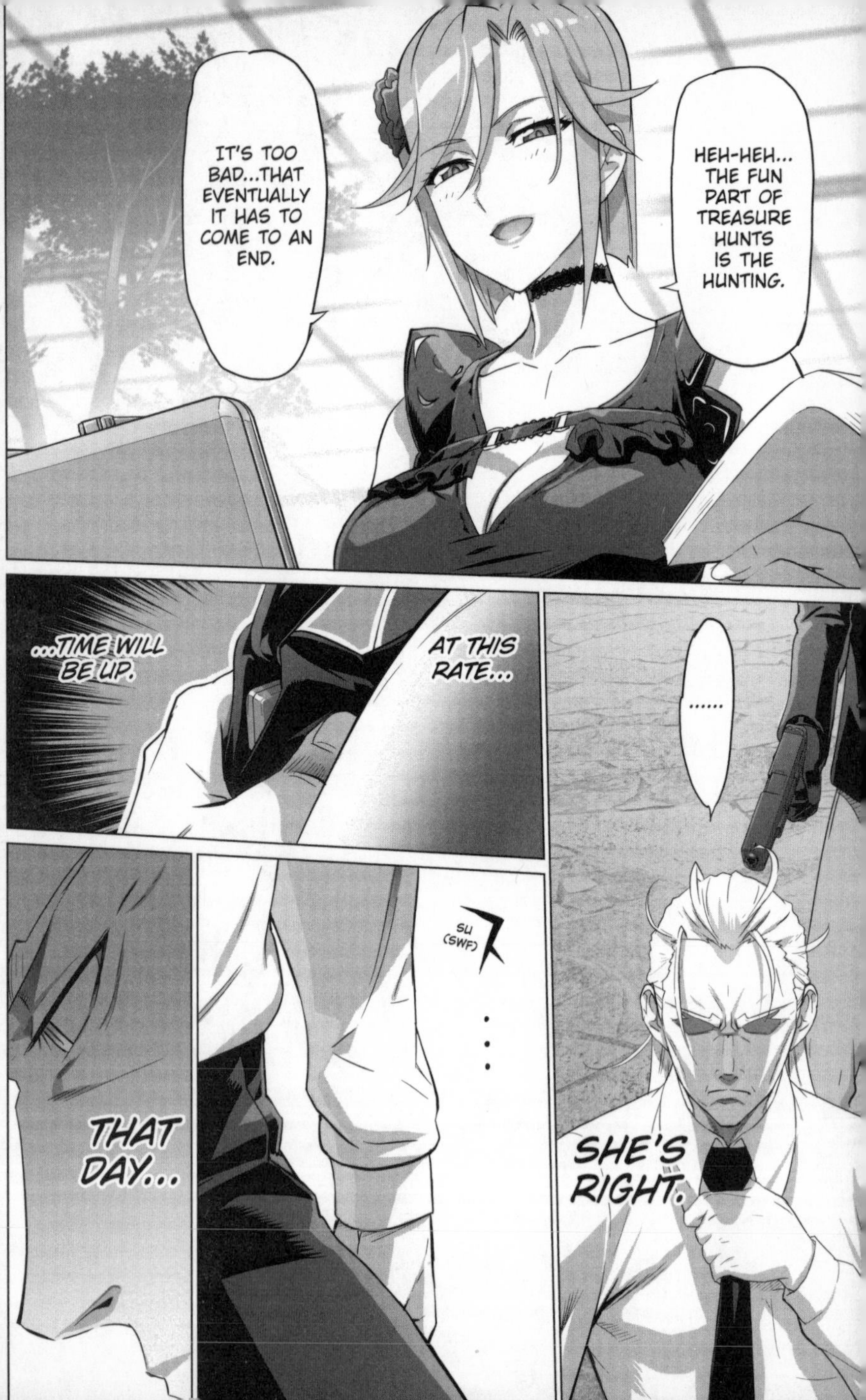
HEH-HEH... THE FUN PART OF TREASURE HUNTS IS THE HUNTING.
IT'S TOO BAD...THAT EVENTUALLY IT HAS TO COME TO AN END.
......
SHE'S RIGHT.
AT THIS RATE...
...TIME WILL BE UP.
SU (SWF)
...
THAT DAY...

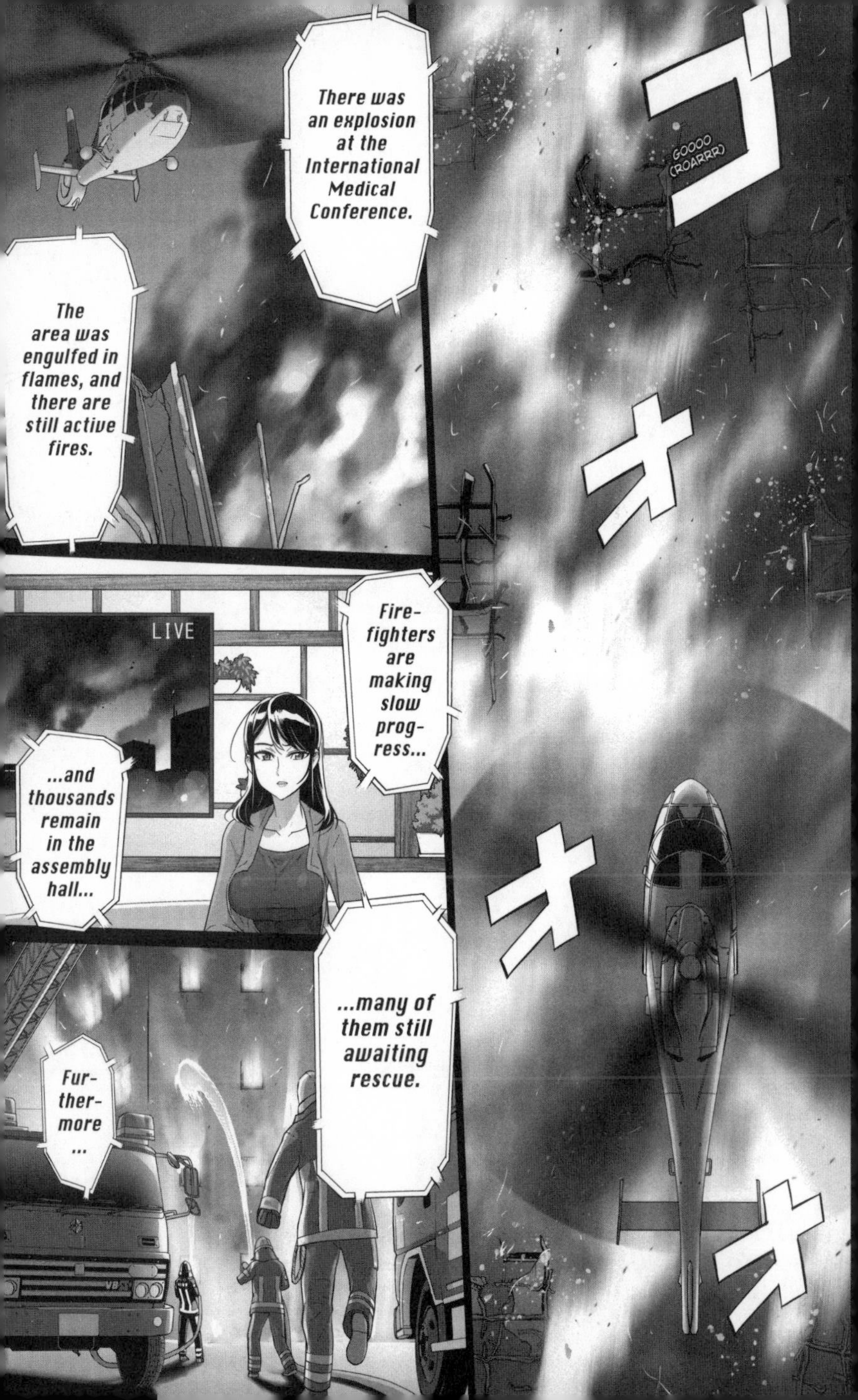

ゴオオオ
GOOOO (ROARRR)
There was an explosion at the International Medical Conference.
The area was engulfed in flames, and there are still active fires.
LIVE
Fire-fighters are making slow prog-ress...
...and thousands remain in the assembly hall...
...many of them still awaiting rescue.
Fur-ther-more ...

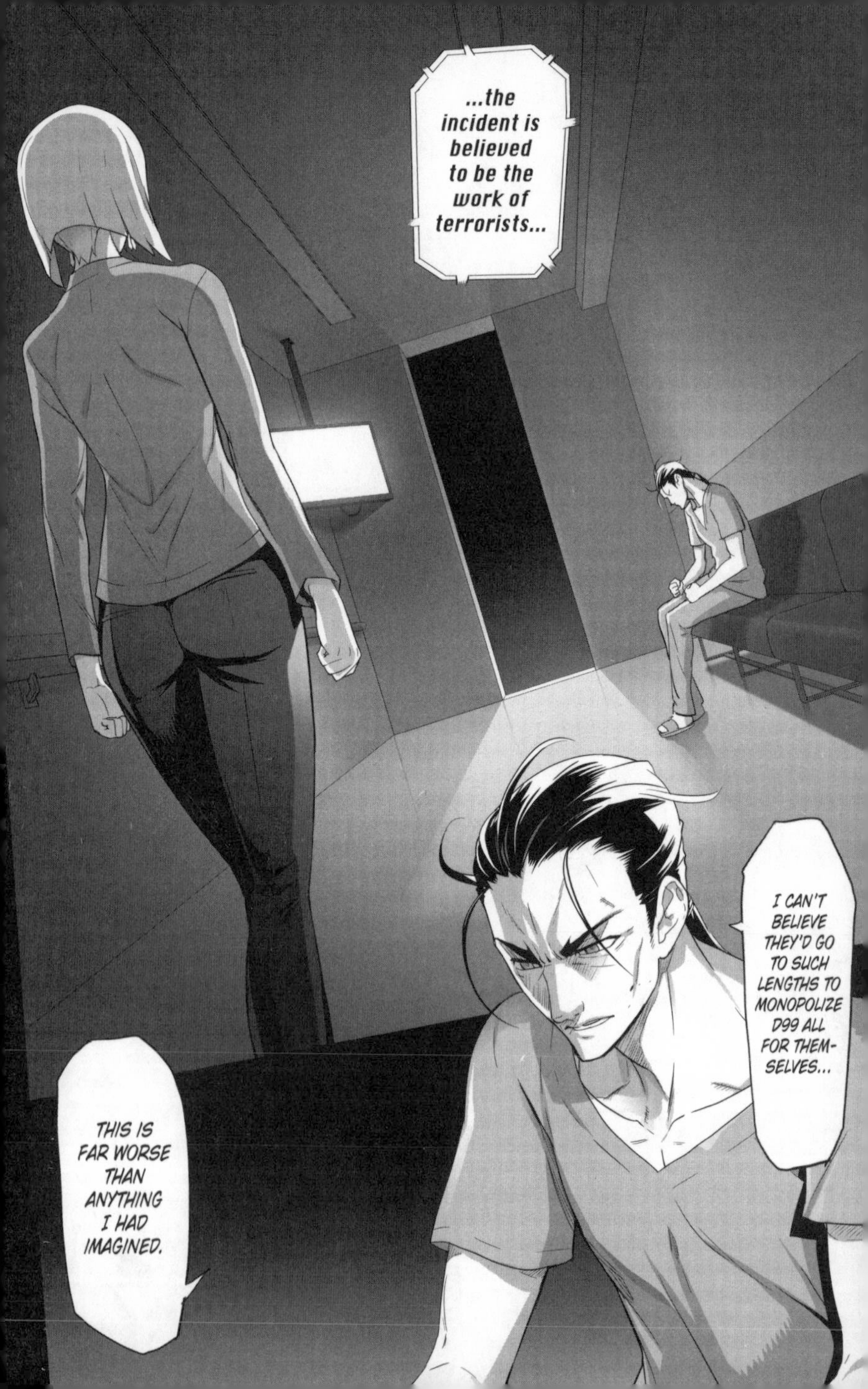
...the incident is believed to be the work of terrorists...
I CAN'T BELIEVE THEY'D GO TO SUCH LENGTHS TO MONOPOLIZE D99 ALL FOR THEM-SELVES...
THIS IS FAR WORSE THAN ANYTHING I HAD IMAGINED.

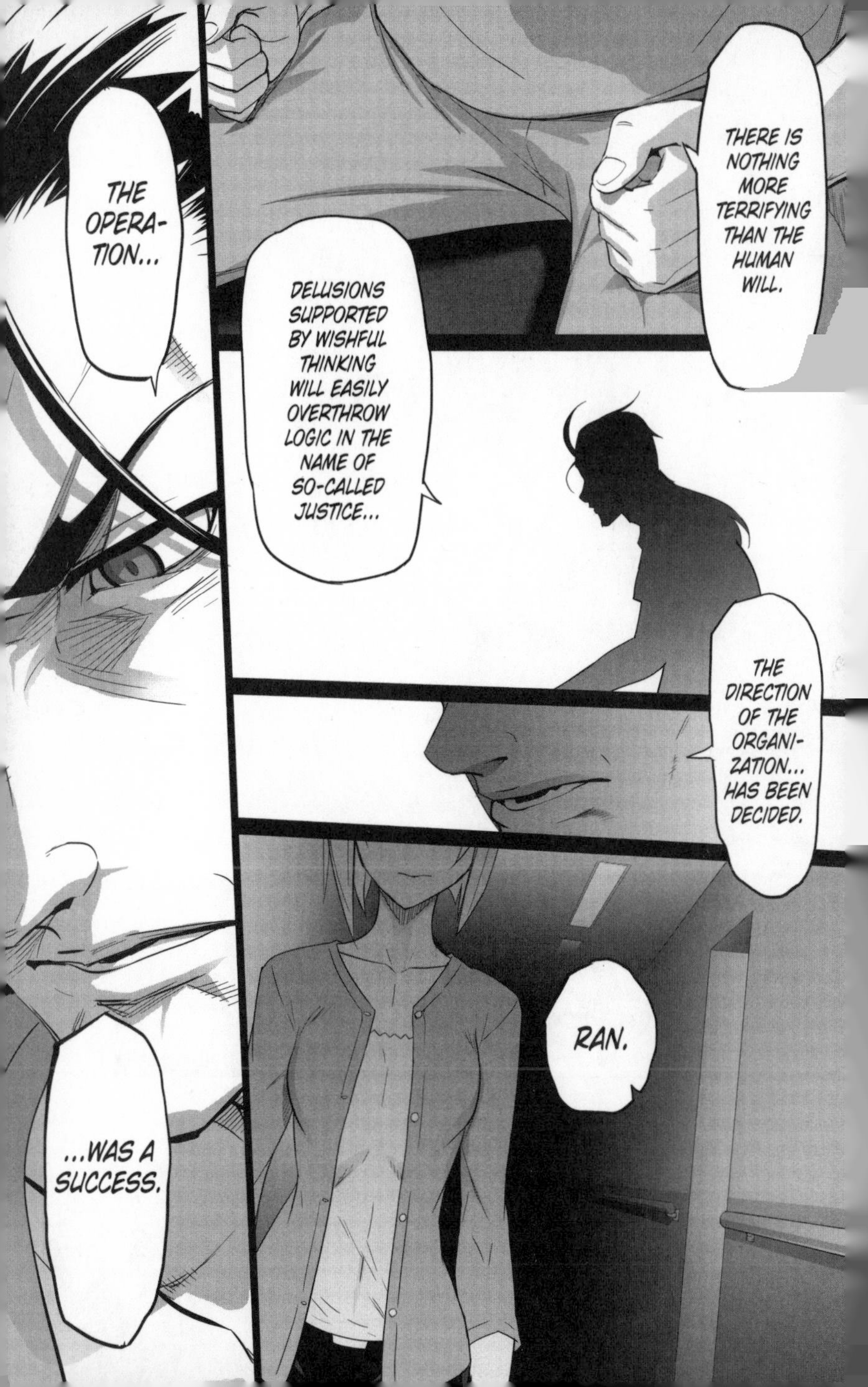
THERE IS NOTHING MORE TERRIFYING THAN THE HUMAN WILL.
DELUSIONS SUPPORTED BY WISHFUL THINKING WILL EASILY OVERTHROW LOGIC IN THE NAME OF SO-CALLED JUSTICE...
THE DIRECTION OF THE ORGANI-ZATION... HAS BEEN DECIDED.
RAN.
THE OPERA-TION...
...WAS A SUCCESS.

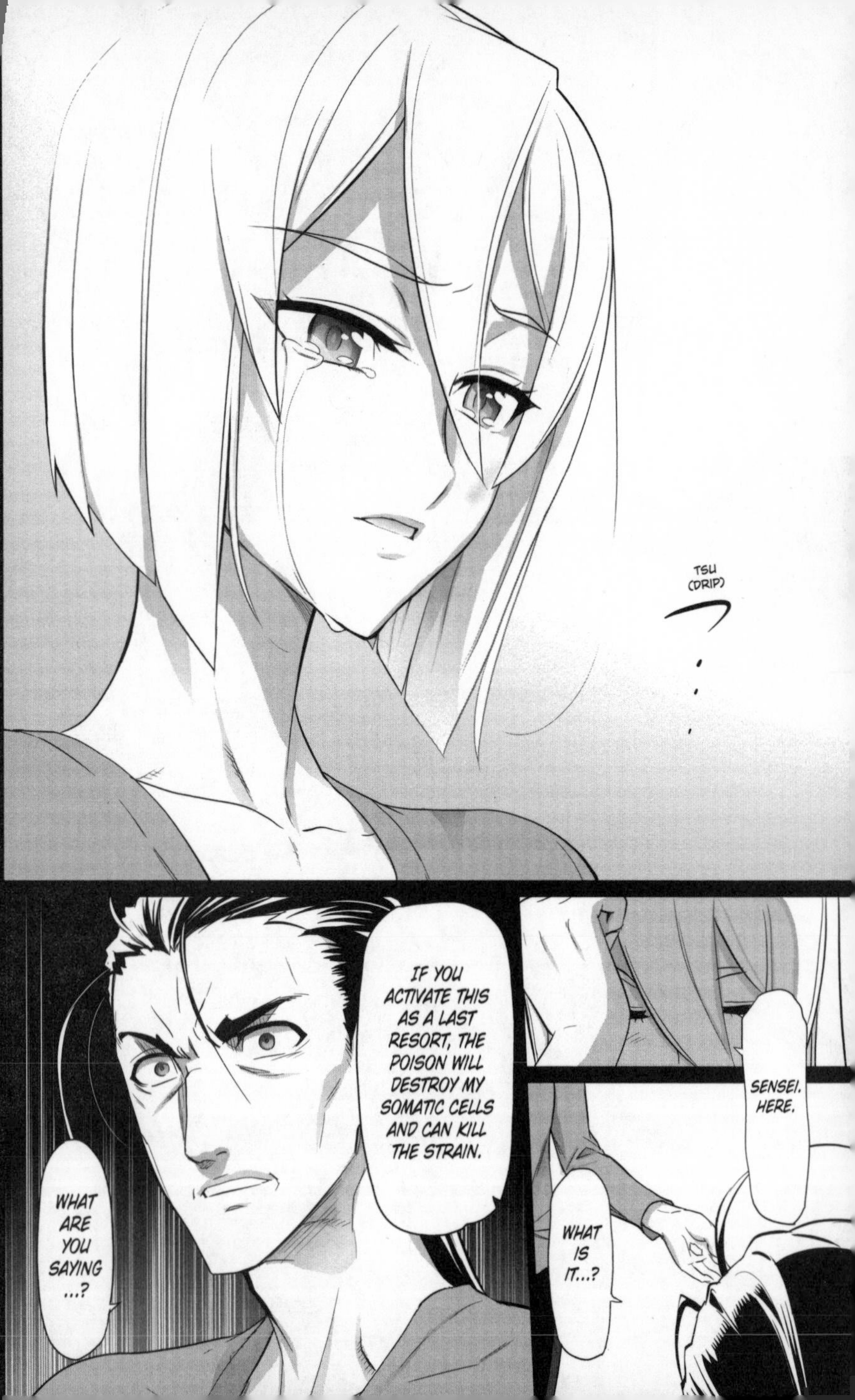
TSU (DRIP)
SENSEI. HERE.
WHAT IS IT...?
IF YOU ACTIVATE THIS AS A LAST RESORT, THE POISON WILL DESTROY MY SOMATIC CELLS AND CAN KILL THE STRAIN.
WHAT ARE YOU SAYING ...?

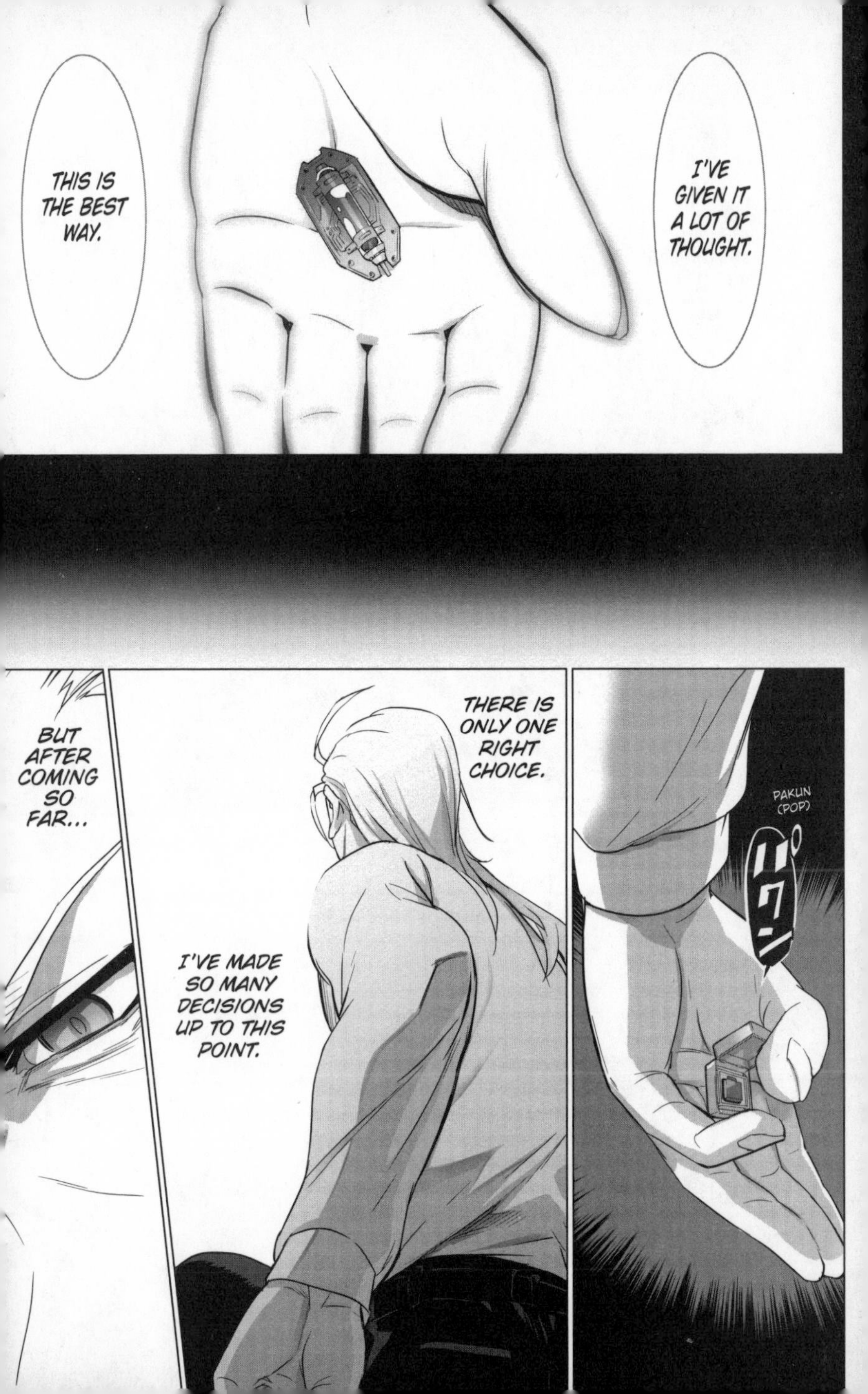
I'VE GIVEN IT A LOT OF THOUGHT.
THIS IS THE BEST WAY.
PAKUN (POP)
THERE IS ONLY ONE RIGHT CHOICE.
I'VE MADE SO MANY DECISIONS UP TO THIS POINT.
BUT AFTER COMING SO FAR...

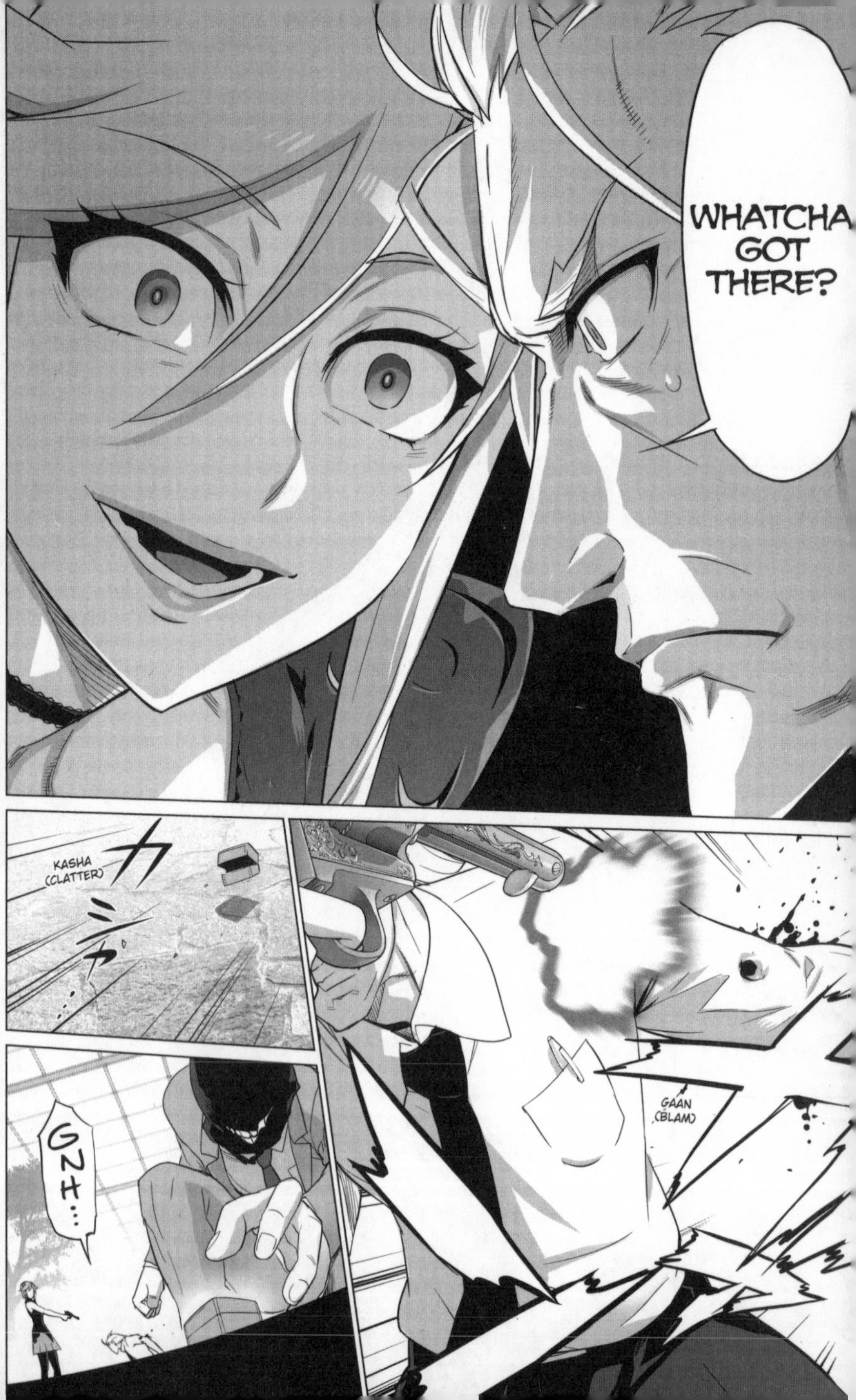
WHATCHA GOT THERE?
GAAN (BLAM)
KASHA (CLATTER)
GNH...

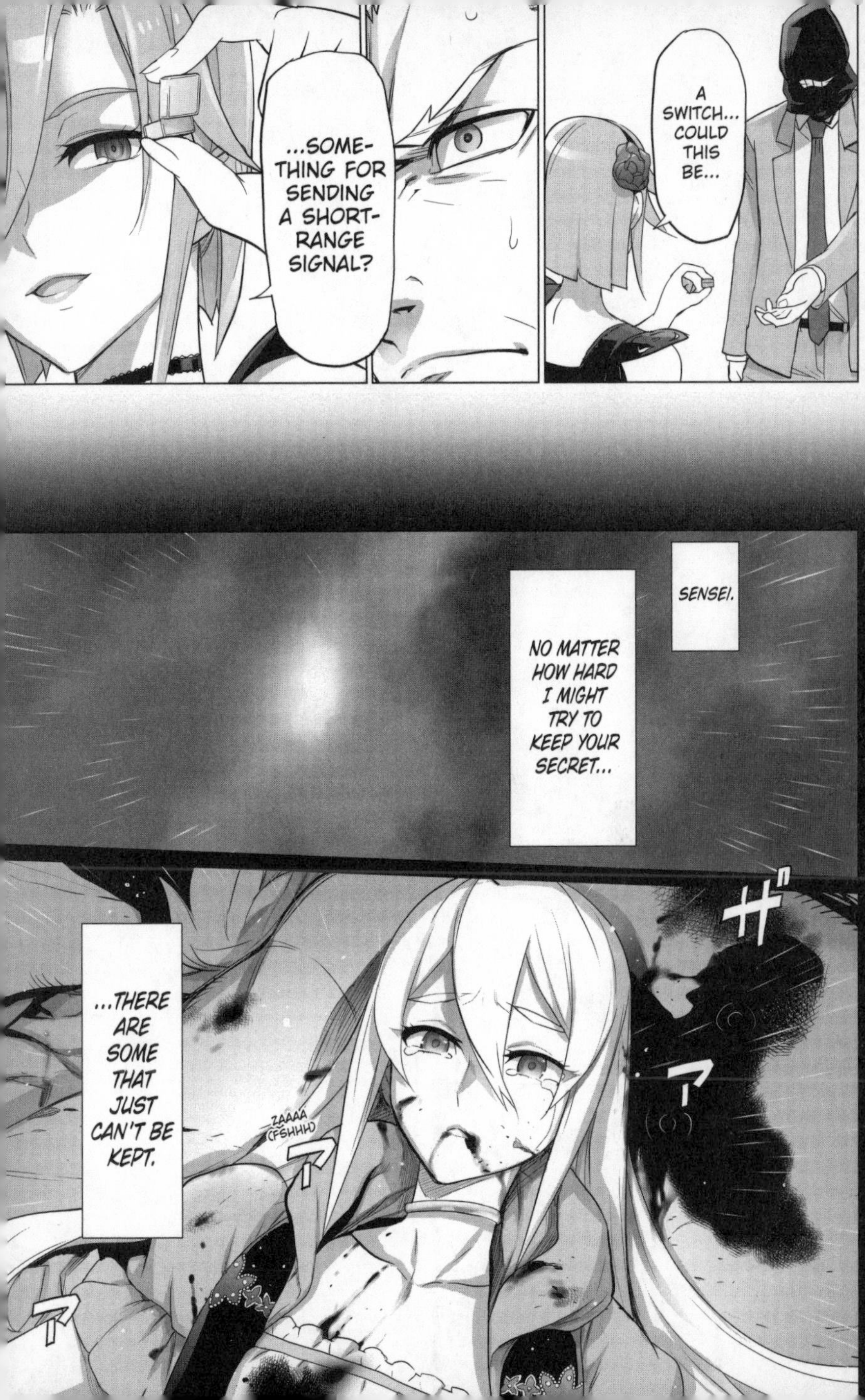
A SWITCH... COULD THIS BE...
...SOME-THING FOR SENDING A SHORT-RANGE SIGNAL?
SENSEI.
NO MATTER HOW HARD I MIGHT TRY TO KEEP YOUR SECRET...
...THERE ARE SOME THAT JUST CAN'T BE KEPT.
ZAAAA (FSHHH)

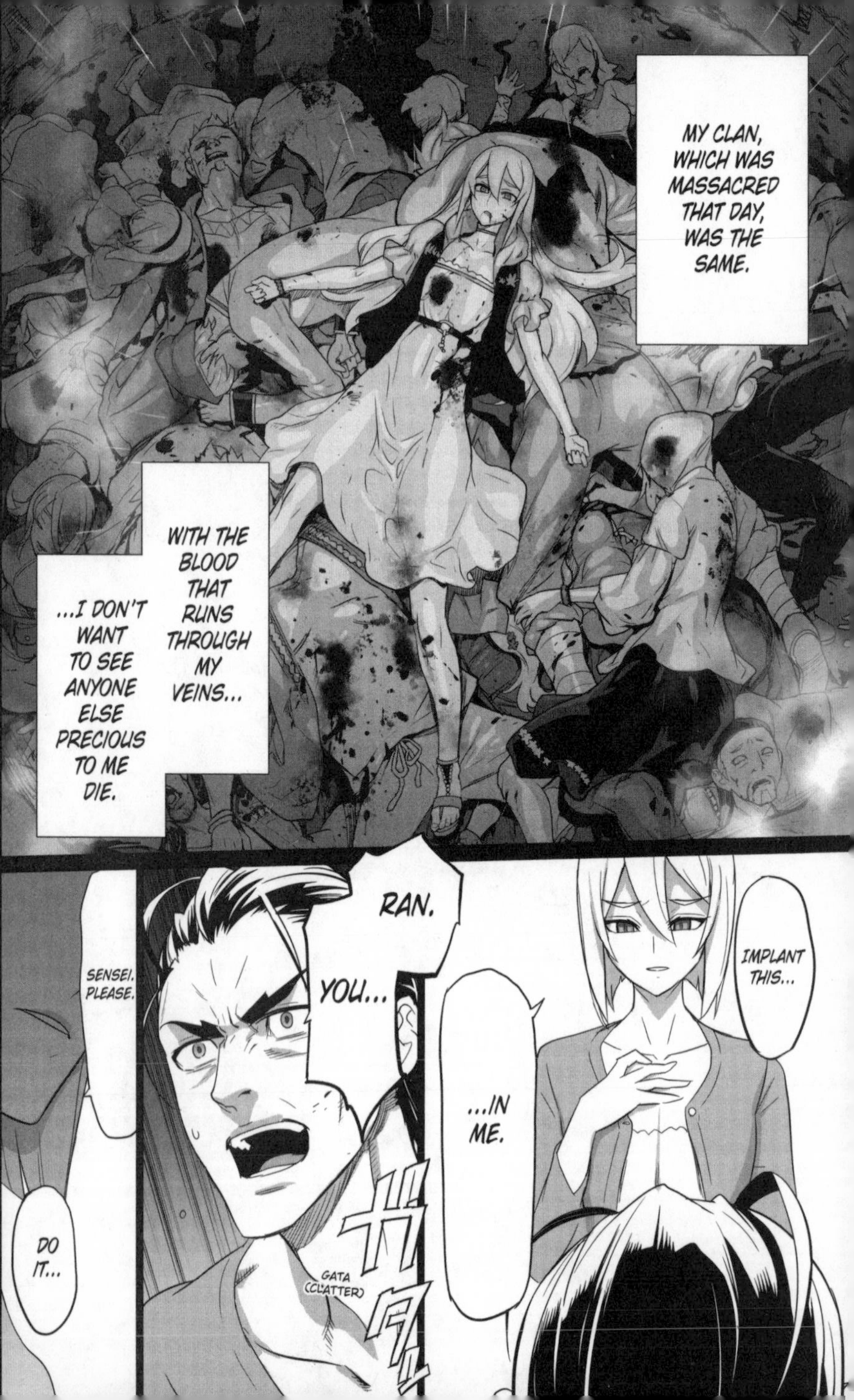
MY CLAN, WHICH WAS MASSACRED THAT DAY, WAS THE SAME.
WITH THE BLOOD THAT RUNS THROUGH MY VEINS...
...I DON'T WANT TO SEE ANYONE ELSE PRECIOUS TO ME DIE.
IMPLANT THIS...
...IN ME.
RAN.
YOU...
GATA (CLATTER)
SENSEI. PLEASE.
DO IT...

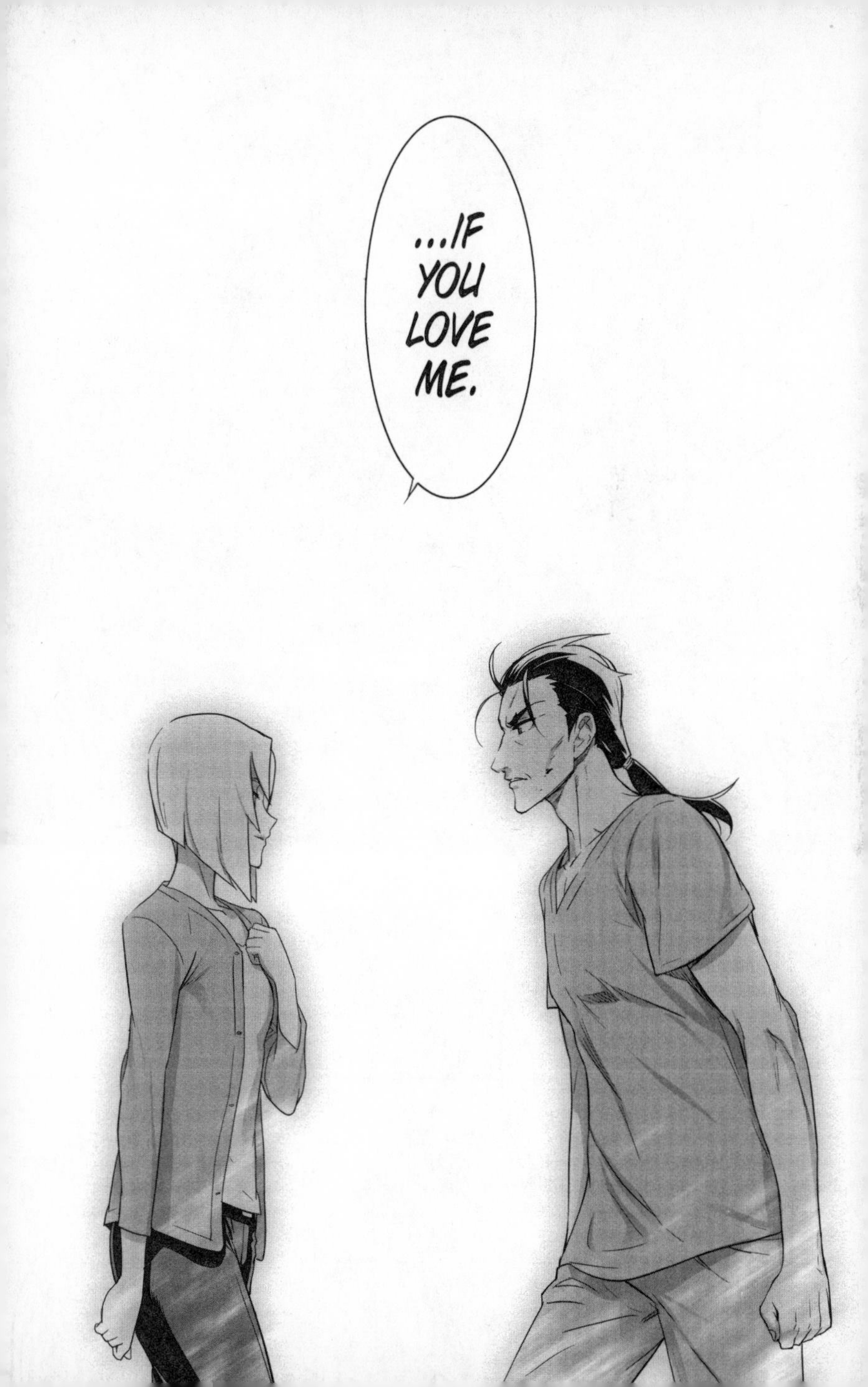
...IF YOU LOVE ME.

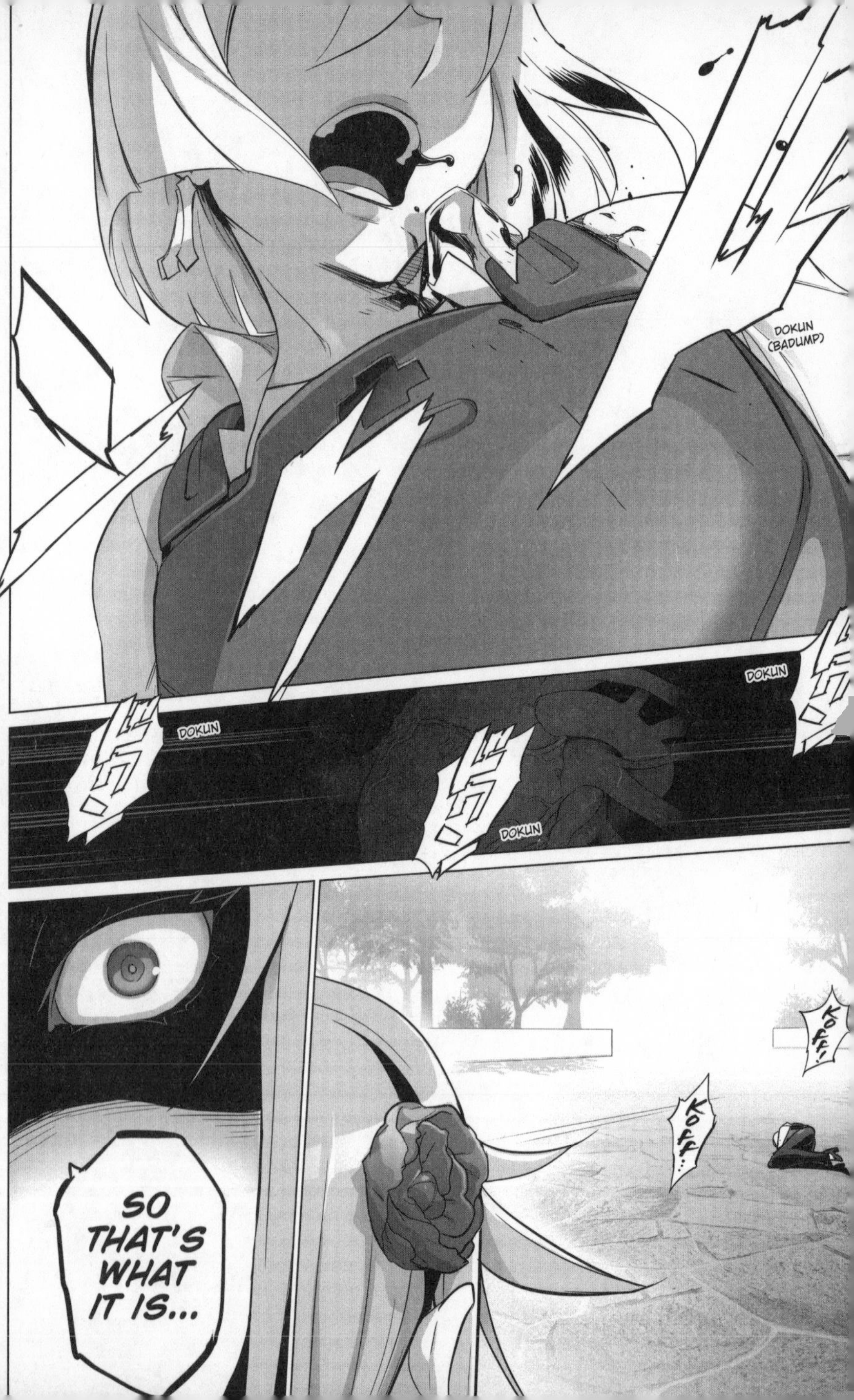
DOKUN (BADUMP)
DOKUN
DOKUN
DOKUN
KOFF!
KOFF...
SO THAT'S WHAT IT IS...

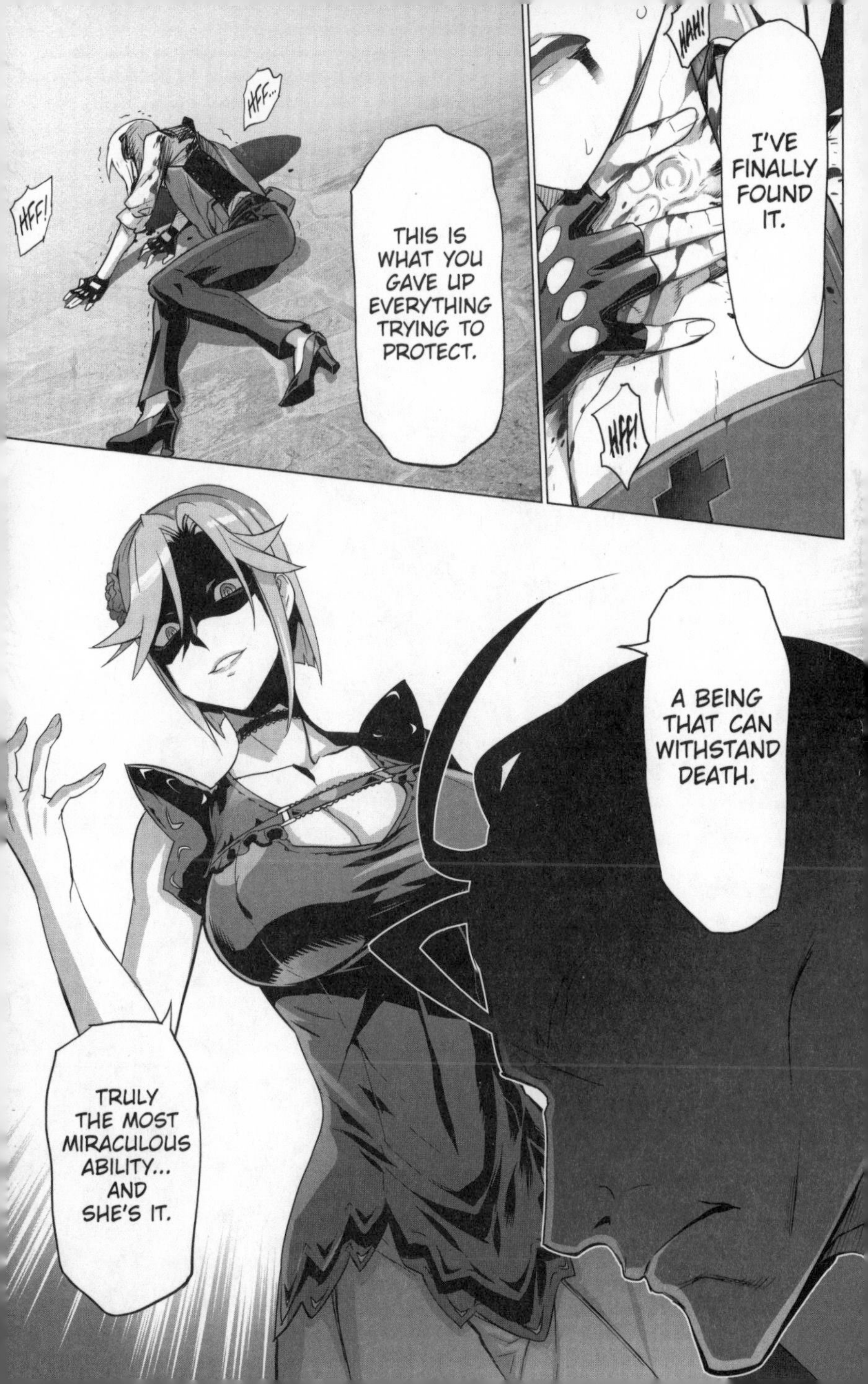
HAH!
I'VE FINALLY FOUND IT.
HFF!
HFF...
HFF!
THIS IS WHAT YOU GAVE UP EVERYTHING TRYING TO PROTECT.
A BEING THAT CAN WITHSTAND DEATH.
TRULY THE MOST MIRACULOUS ABILITY... AND SHE'S IT.

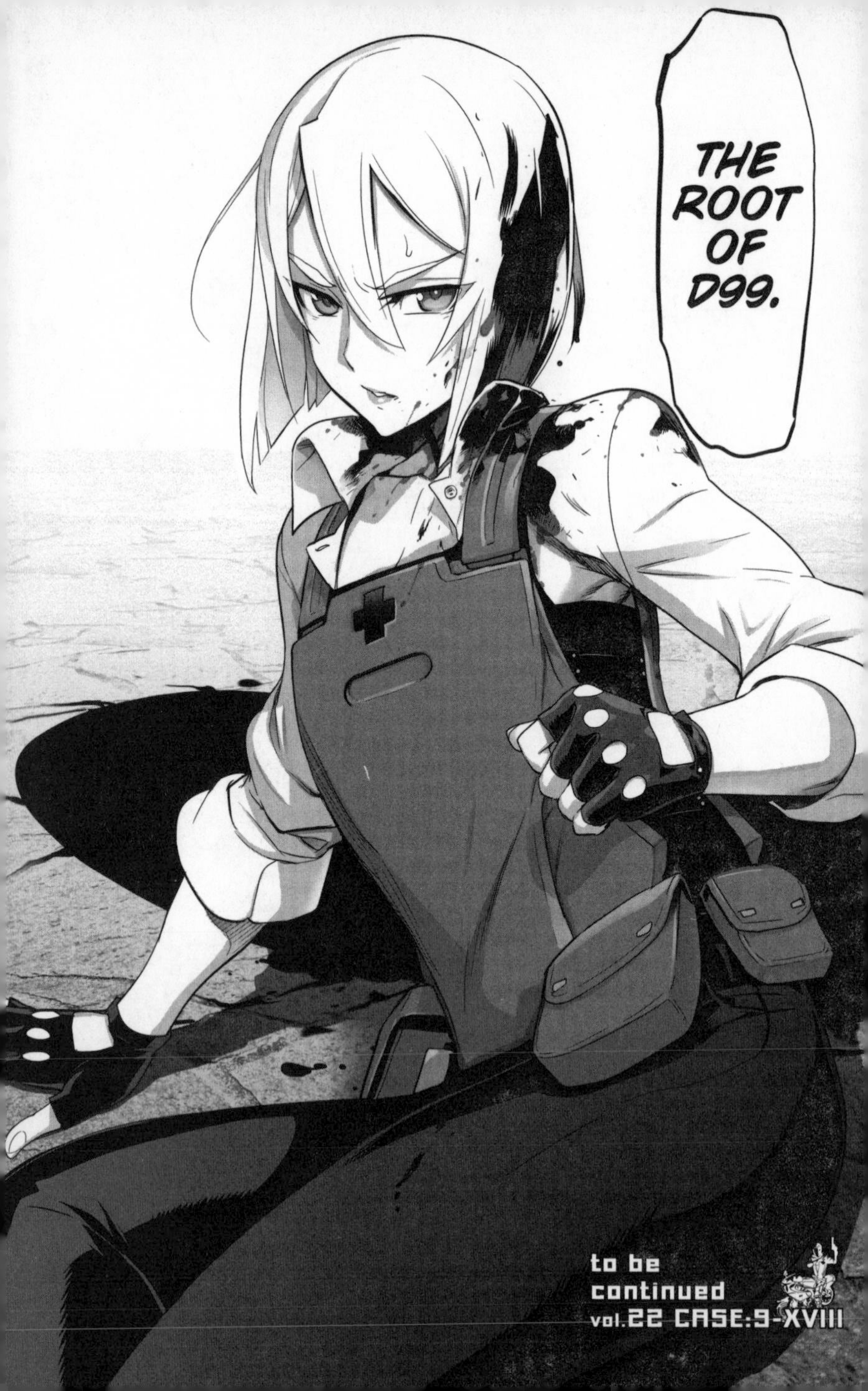
THE ROOT OF D99.
to be continued
vol.22 CASE:9-XVIII

TRIAGE X

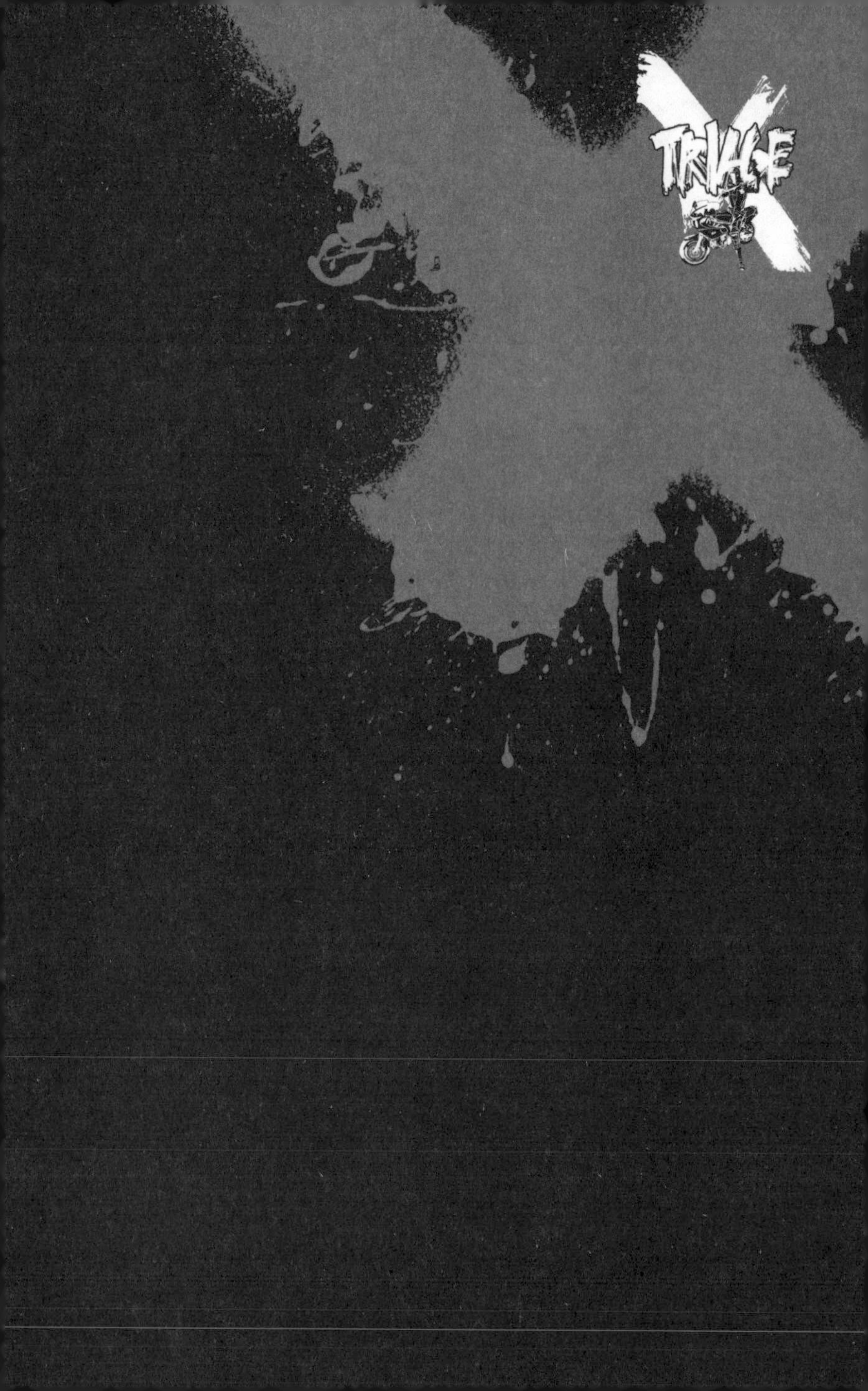
TRIAGE X

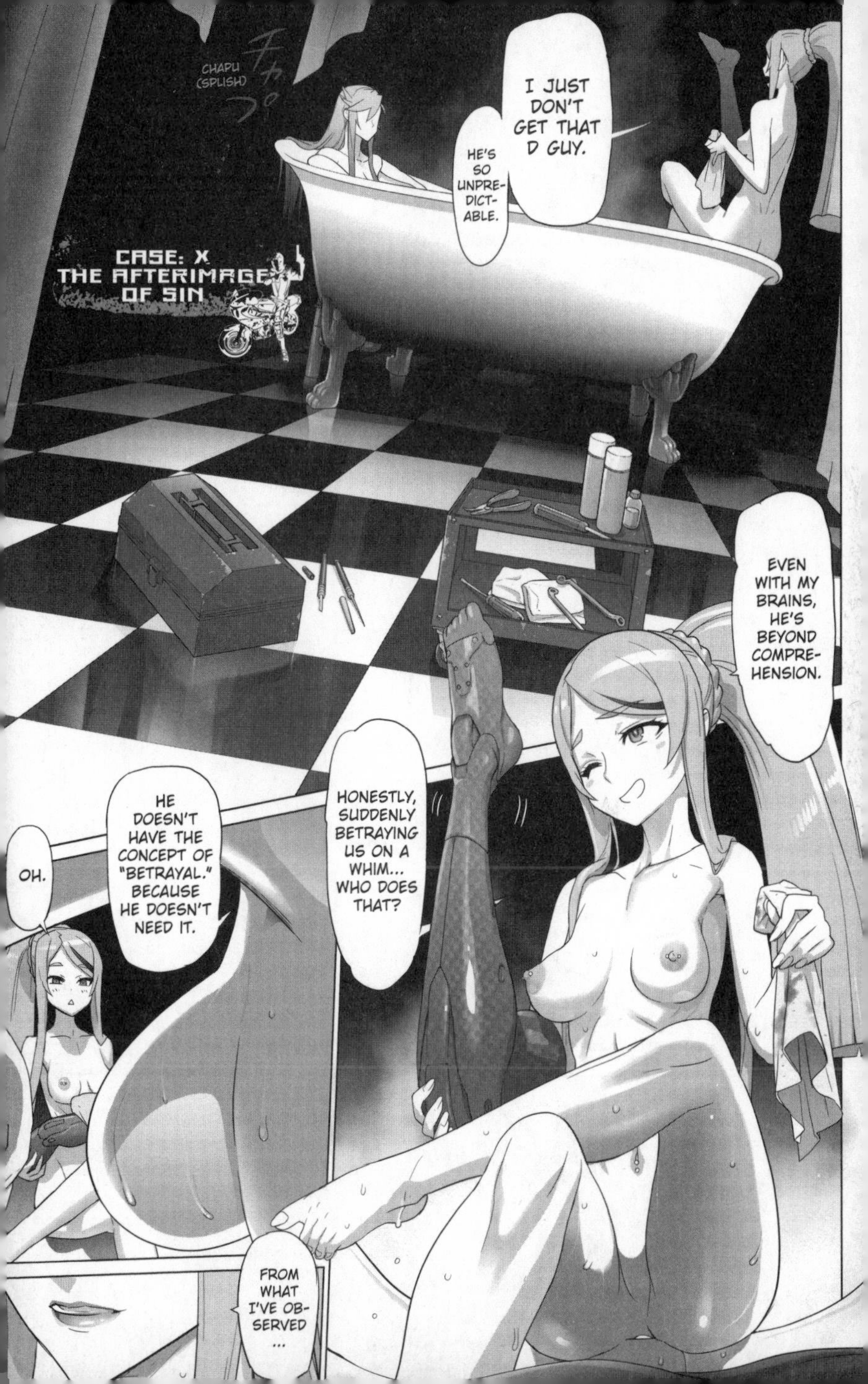
I JUST DON'T GET THAT D GUY.
HE'S SO UNPREDICTABLE.
CHAPU (SPLISH)
CASE: X THE AFTERIMAGE OF SIN
EVEN WITH MY BRAINS, HE'S BEYOND COMPREHENSION.
HONESTLY, SUDDENLY BETRAYING US ON A WHIM... WHO DOES THAT?
OH.
FROM WHAT I'VE OBSERVED...
HE DOESN'T HAVE THE CONCEPT OF "BETRAYAL." BECAUSE HE DOESN'T NEED IT.

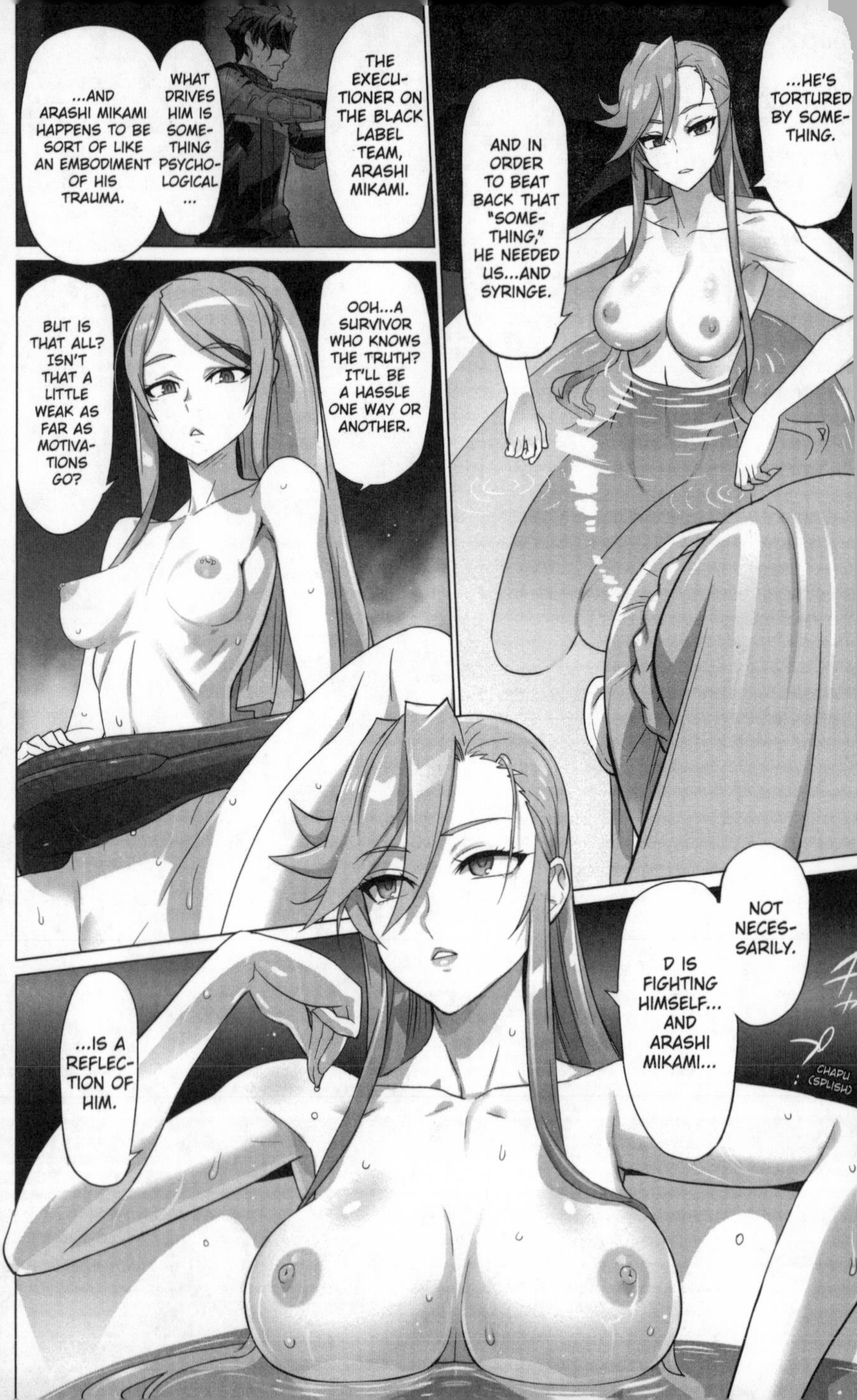
...HE'S TORTURED BY SOME-THING.
AND IN ORDER TO BEAT BACK THAT "SOME-THING," HE NEEDED US...AND SYRINGE.
THE EXECU-TIONER ON THE BLACK LABEL TEAM, ARASHI MIKAMI.
WHAT DRIVES HIM IS SOME-THING PSYCHO-LOGICAL ...
...AND ARASHI MIKAMI HAPPENS TO BE SORT OF LIKE AN EMBODIMENT OF HIS TRAUMA.
OOH...A SURVIVOR WHO KNOWS THE TRUTH? IT'LL BE A HASSLE ONE WAY OR ANOTHER.
BUT IS THAT ALL? ISN'T THAT A LITTLE WEAK AS FAR AS MOTIVA-TIONS GO?
NOT NECES-SARILY.
D IS FIGHTING HIMSELF... AND ARASHI MIKAMI...
CHAPU (SPLISH)
...IS A REFLEC-TION OF HIM.

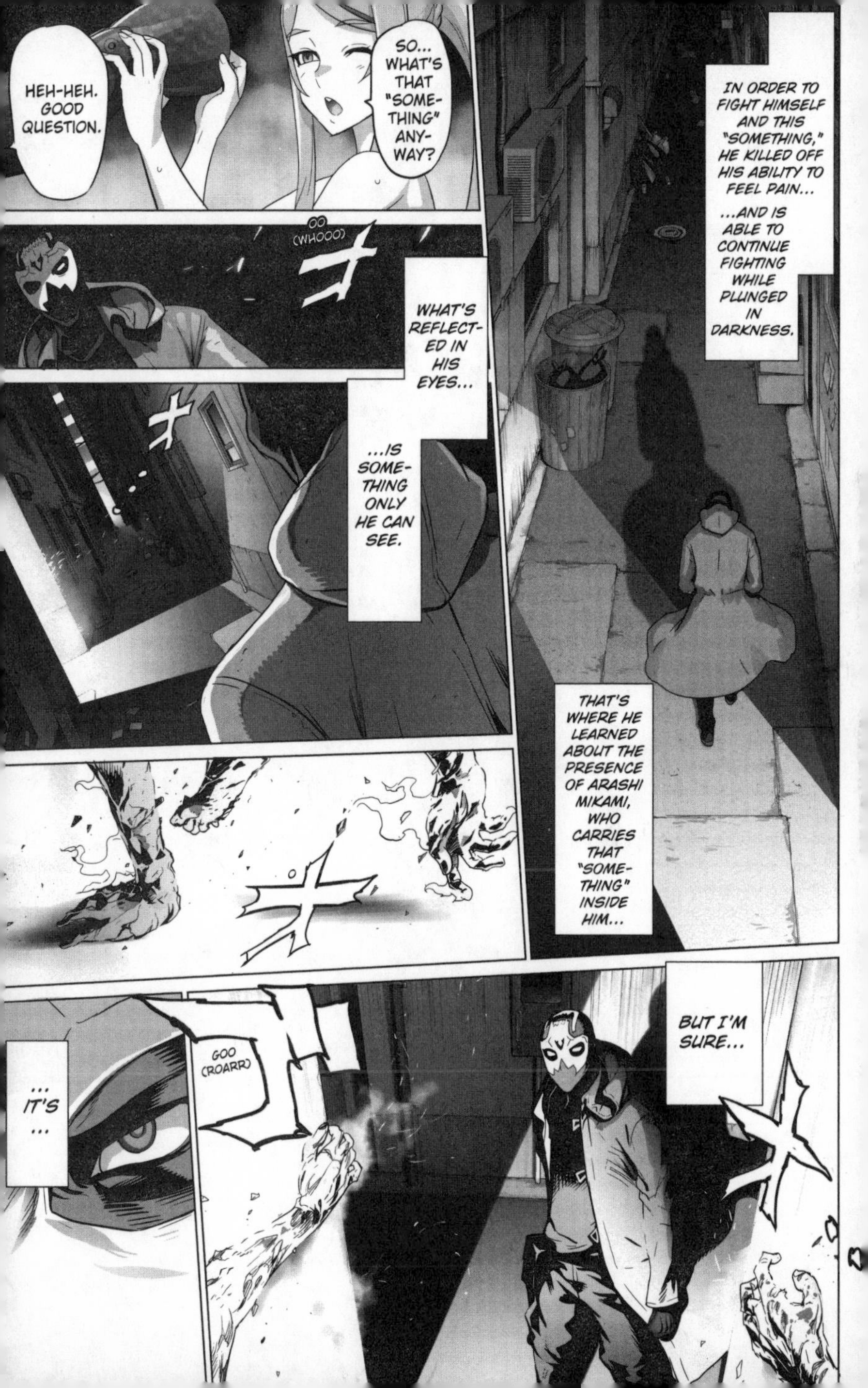
IN ORDER TO FIGHT HIMSELF AND THIS "SOMETHING," HE KILLED OFF HIS ABILITY TO FEEL PAIN...
...AND IS ABLE TO CONTINUE FIGHTING WHILE PLUNGED IN DARKNESS.
THAT'S WHERE HE LEARNED ABOUT THE PRESENCE OF ARASHI MIKAMI, WHO CARRIES THAT "SOME-THING" INSIDE HIM...
SO... WHAT'S THAT "SOME-THING" ANY-WAY?
HEH-HEH. GOOD QUESTION.
OO (WHOOO)
WHAT'S REFLECT-ED IN HIS EYES...
...IS SOME-THING ONLY HE CAN SEE.
BUT I'M SURE...
GOO (ROARR)
... IT'S ...

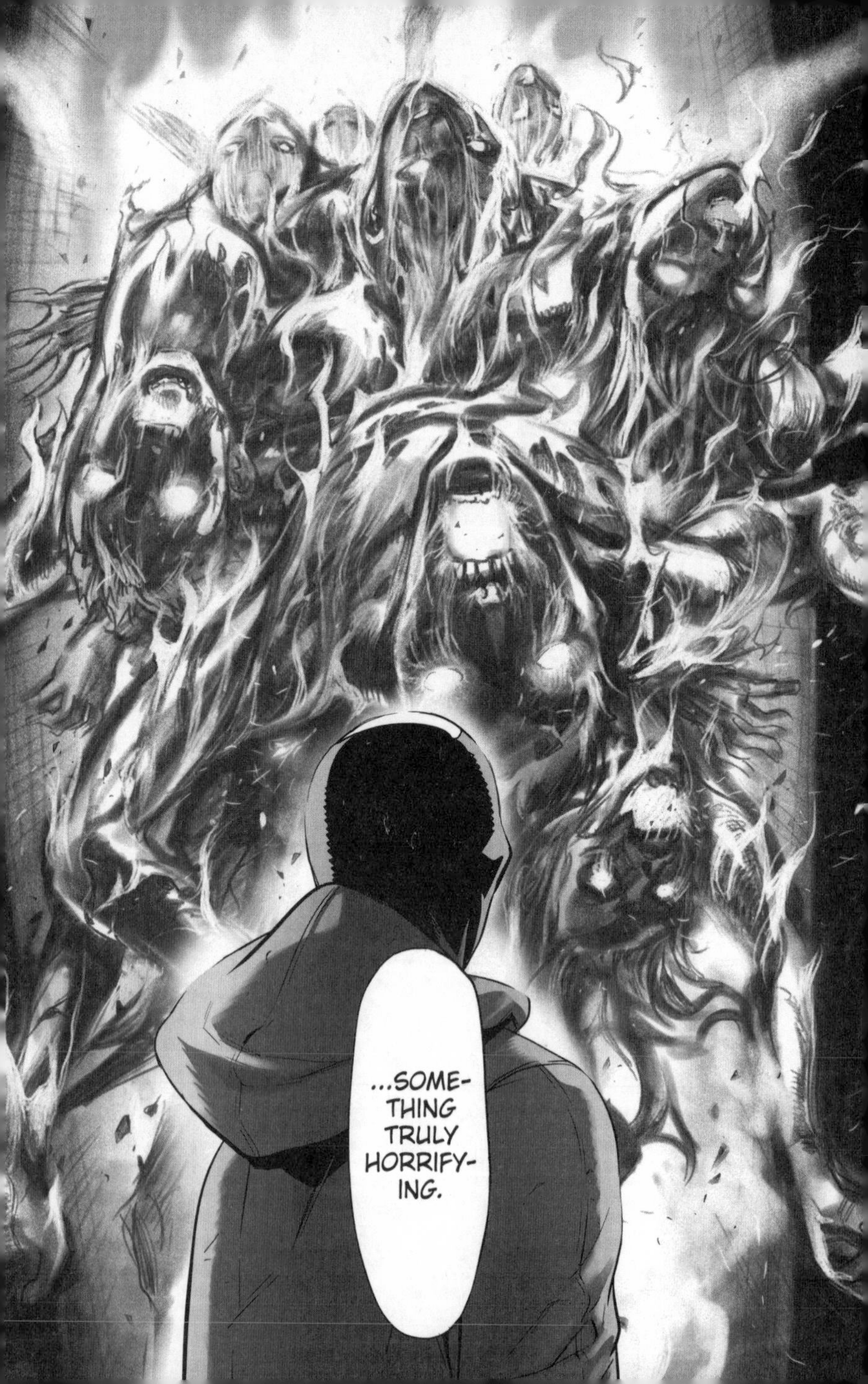
...SOME-THING TRULY HORRIFY-ING.

TRIAGE X

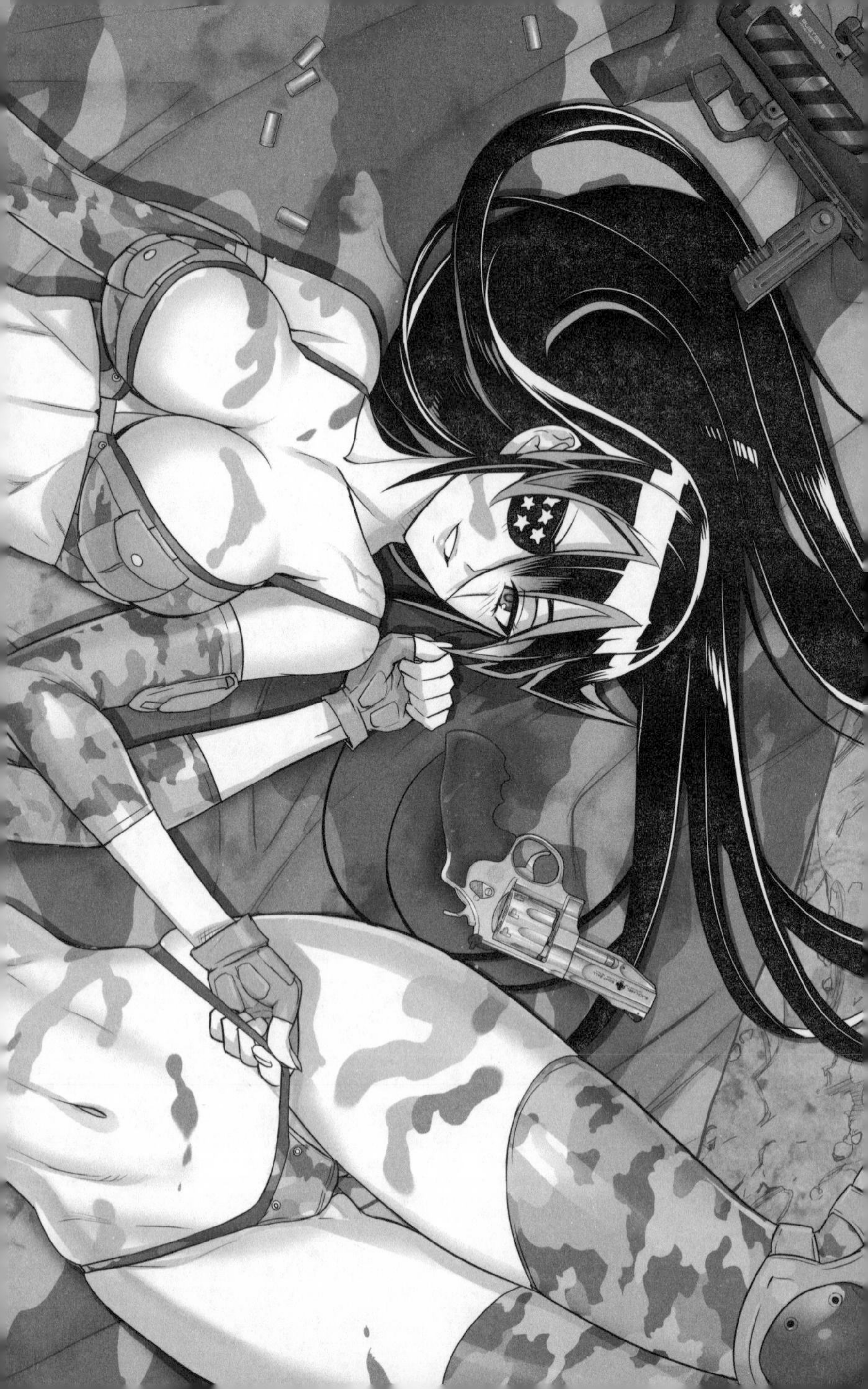

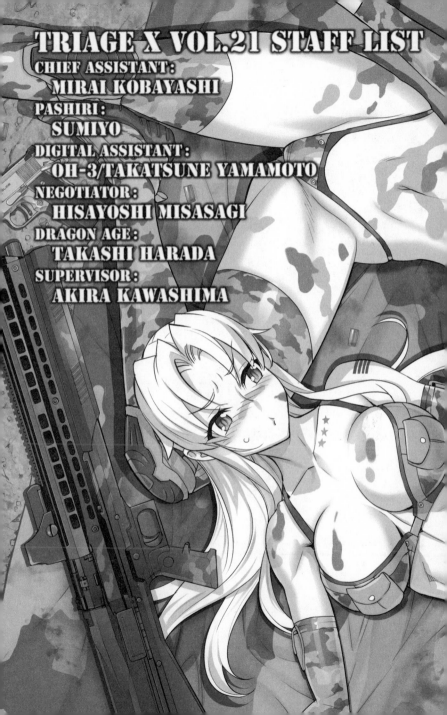

TRIAGE X VOL.21 STAFF LIST
CHIEF ASSISTANT:
MIRAI KOBAYASHI
PASHIRI:
SUMIYO
DIGITAL ASSISTANT:
OH-3/TAKATSUNE YAMAMOTO
NEGOTIATOR:
HISAYOSHI MISASAGI
DRAGON AGE:
TAKASHI HARADA
SUPERVISOR:
AKIRA KAWASHIMA

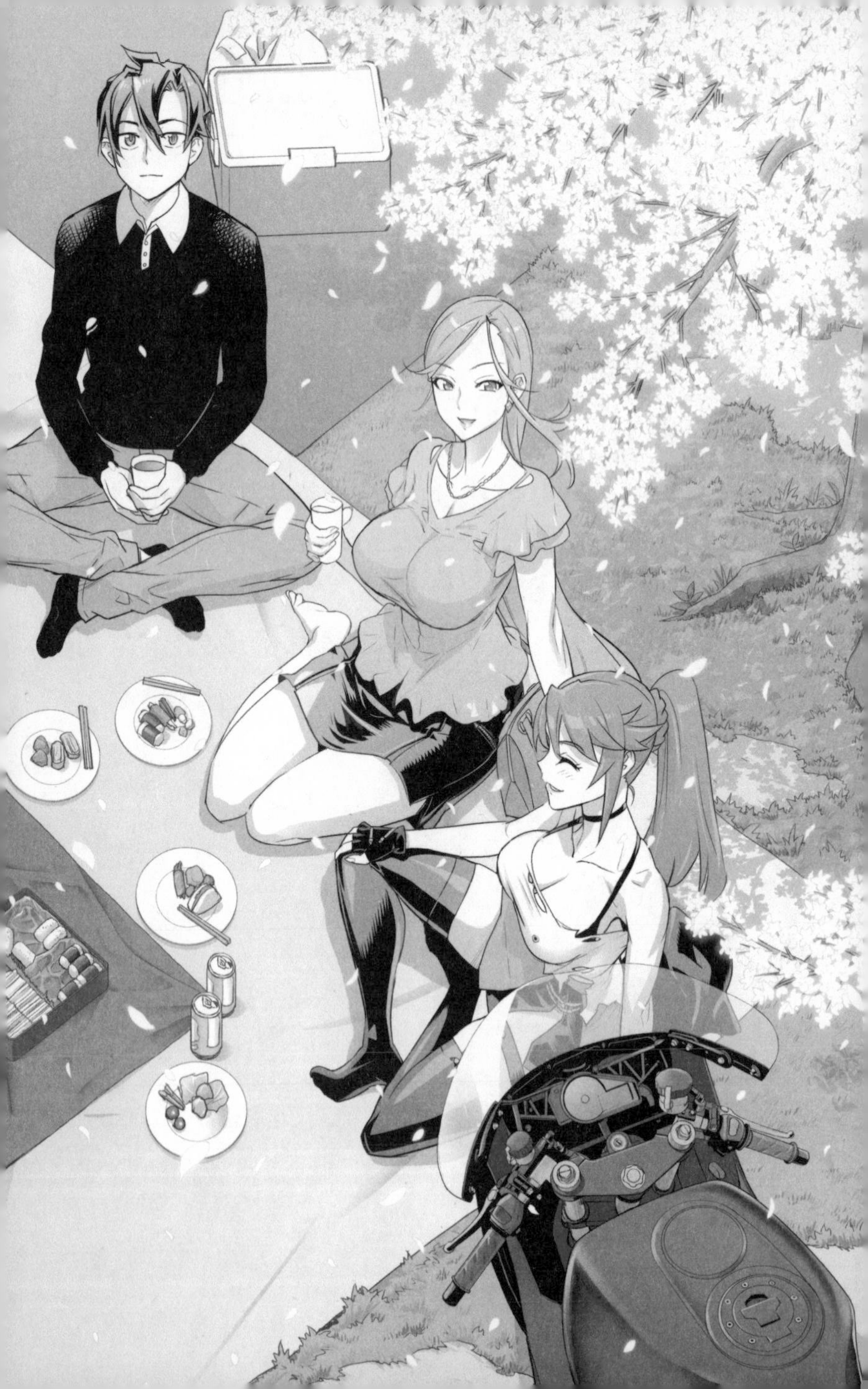

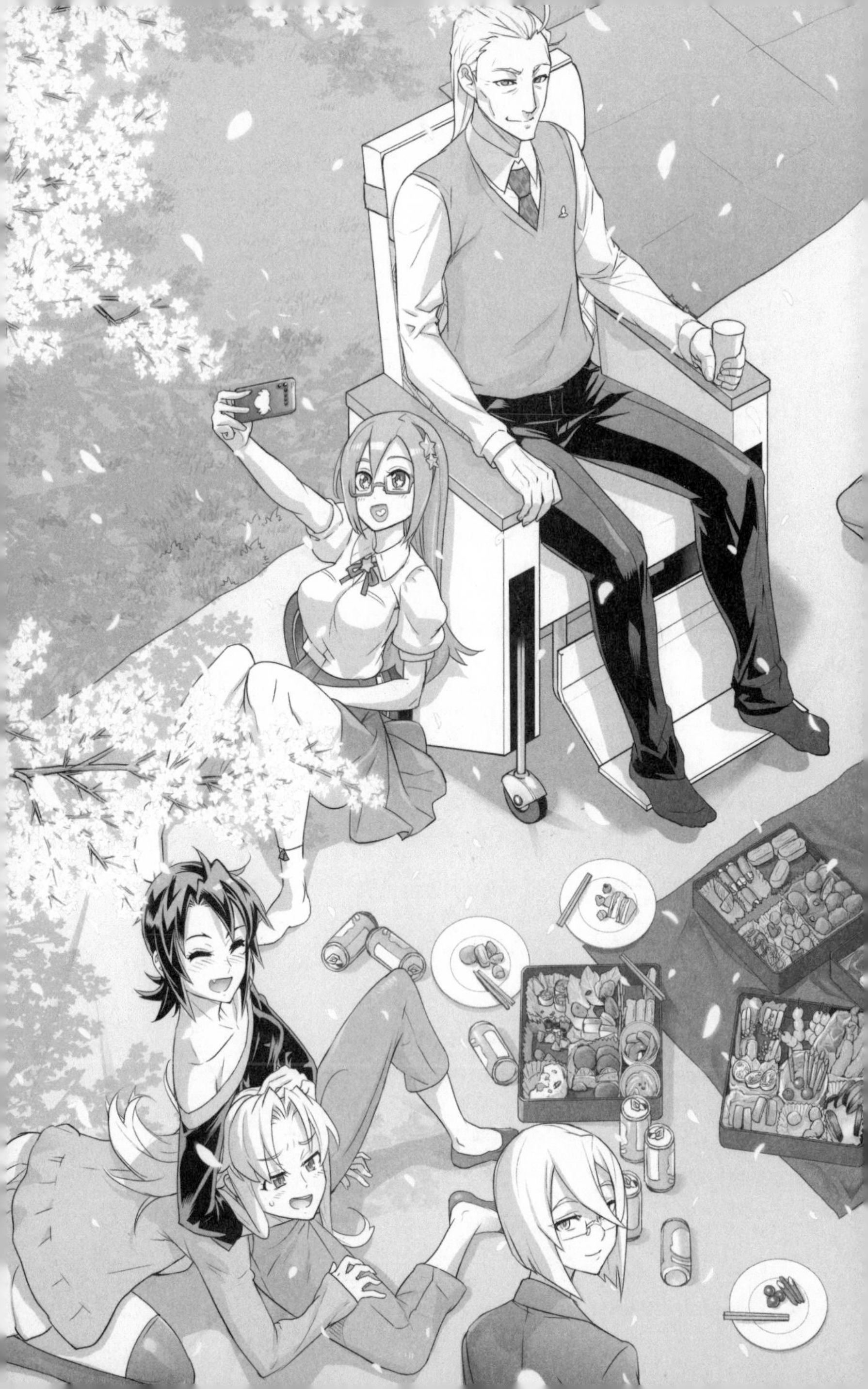

TRIAGE X ㉑

SHOUJI SATO

Translation: Christine Dashiell

Lettering: Abigail Blackman

TRIAGE X Volume 21 © Shouji Sato 2020. First published in Japan in 2020 by KADOKAWA CORPORATION, Tokyo. English translation rights arranged with KADOKAWA CORPORATION, Tokyo, through TUTTLE-MORI AGENCY, INC., Tokyo.

English translation © 2021 by Yen Press, LLC

Yen Press
150 West 30th Street, 19th Floor
New York, NY 10001

Visit us at yenpress.com
facebook.com/yenpress
twitter.com/yenpress
yenpress.tumblr.com
instagram.com/yenpress

First Yen Press Edition: May 2021

Yen Press is an imprint of Yen Press, LLC.
The Yen Press name and logo are trademarks of Yen Press, LLC.

Library of Congress Control Number: 2015952593

ISBNs: 978-1-9753-2402-5 (paperback)
       978-1-9753-2403-2 (ebook)

10 9 8 7 6 5 4 3 2 1

WOR

Printed in the United States of America